Asian
Cultural
Traditions

Asian Cultural Traditions

Carolyn Brown Heinz

California State University, Chico

WAVELAND
PRESS, INC.
Long Grove, Illinois

For information about this book, contact:
Waveland Press, Inc.
4180 IL Route 83, Suite 101
Long Grove, IL 60047-9580
(847) 634-0081 ˋ
info@waveland.com
www.waveland.com

Map and Photo Credits:
All text maps by Eric Allen, except those appearing on pages 14 and 234 by Lynsey Wickman.

Photographs appearing in the text that are not credited below are from the personal collection of Carolyn Heinz or her husband, Donald Heinz.

17. Source: Stein, 1912. *Ruins of Desert Cathay: Personal Narratives of Explorations in Central Asia and Westernmost China.* NY: Benjamin Blom. Plate 281. **64.** Stein, 1912. Plate 188. **66.** Stein, 1912. Plate 191. **177.** V & A Picture Library. **189.** Neg. No. 329047. Photo by Rota. Courtesy Department of Library Services, American Museum of Natural History. **197.** Corbis-Bettmann. **243.** Photo courtesy of Beijing Slides Publishing Company. **253.** The Nelson-Atkins Museum of Art, Kansas City, Missouri. (Purchase: Nelson Trust) **261 and cover.** "Interior of a Mandarin's House with a Woman and Child." Chinese School, mid-19th Century. Christie's Images. **281.** UPI/Corbis-Bettmann. **308.** "The Tale of Genji." Ink on paper. Anonymous, c. 1554. Christie's Images. **329.** "A Mandarin Receiving an Embassy of European Diplomats at His Court." Zhou Pei Chun, c. 1860. Christie's Images.

10-digit ISBN 1-57766-043-9
13-digit ISBN 978-1-57766-043-9

Printed in the United States of America

13   12   11   10   9   8   7

To my children,
Susan, Lise, and Rob,
who shared Asia with me,
and me with Asia

CONTENTS

ACKNOWLEDGMENTS

I was months into this writing project before I could bring myself to tell my friends its precise topic. A book about "all of Asia"? They would think I was mad. But if it seemed to some a dubious effort, I was convinced it could be done and that there was a need for such a work.

This book has emerged from dialog over many years with specialists in many fields. In a work as broad as this, I have had to lean heavily on the scholarship of a vast community of Asianists, indeed to cross intellectual boundaries we do not frequently or easily cross. Many of their names appear in the bibliography at the end of this book. Closer to home, I have benefited from conversations with and feedback from Barney Hope, David Hargreaves, Weikun Cheng, Henrietta Lo, Frank Li, Kimihiko Nomura, and above all my colleague and husband, Donald Heinz. My appreciation to those who read sections of the manuscript should include several semesters of students who encountered early versions of this book. Sandy Smith, formerly at Waveland Press, read every word with her keen editorial eye, saving me from numerous embarrassments, inconsistencies, and infelicities. Jan Weissman tracked down photos; Jeni Ogilvie pursued variant spellings through the text and helped pull its components into a harmonious whole. Adam Henderson and Lynsey Wickman put in long hours on the maps. Above all, I thank Tom Curtin, who believed in the project, took the risk of committing Waveland resources to it, and supervised the project from start to finish. Finally, of course, any errors of fact or interpretation which may lurk despite all this help from my friends can only be blamed on me. I pray they are few.

1
INTRODUCTION

I
f ever there was a time when Asia could be ignored, that time is not the present. At the end of the twentieth century—a century plagued by war, dominated in its first half by the great European colonial empires in their heyday and in the second half by the Cold War between the US and the USSR—most of the old certainties have slipped away. In the very last decade of the second millennium, the profiles of world power are looking unfamiliar. Economic and political weight is shifting eastward, to Asia.

An argument could be made that the last four hundred years, the centuries of European dominance, have been the aberrant ones. Prior to this period, the great civilizations of Eurasia—China, India, the Middle East, and Europe—had maintained a balance of power for many, many centuries. There were occasional interruptions of this balance by ambitious empires of conquest. The European one from 1700 to 1950 is only the most recent; before that, the Mongols in the eleventh through thirteenth centuries went thundering in every direction from their Central Asian homeland, conquering China, India, and invading Europe. But these civilizations absorbed the blows, civilized the invaders, and carried on, enriched by the new cultural strands contributed by the foreigners.

Asia is in such a period of recuperation now, in which great and ancient civilizations, after enduring humiliation and defeat at the hands of colonizing European powers, are absorbing the cultural contributions of the invaders and recasting their civilizations. Meanwhile, the old balance is being restored. Once again there are European, Middle Eastern, Indian, and Chinese cultural spheres.

By "Asia" I mean, in this book, only "monsoon Asia"—the geopolitical regions of South Asia, East Asia, and Southeast Asia. My focus is not nationalist, but cultural. I do not take as given or eternal the nation-states that have emerged in the postcolonial world, enduring as those may prove to be. Hard at work as they are at proving ancient natural rights to present borders, none of the current outlines of Asian nation-states, with the single and obvious exception of Japan, has a time depth of even a century.

My subject here is rather more amorphous; it is those old civilizations themselves. Not, of course, "Asian civilization," for there is not and never has been such a thing. Like "the Orient" and "the East," "Asia", has always been something of a fiction created by Europeans whose capacities to truly engage with a culture stopped at the eastern edges of the Greek world. Beyond lay "Asia," the "East." In fact, the word "Asia" appears to come from the Assyrian word for east, *asu*. In recent times the simple dichotomy between "the West" and "the East" has contrasted European civilization with all the rest of Eurasia, lumped together as "the East." However, we tend to think, more subtly, of the West as a plural place, but the Japanese playwright Masakazu Yamazaki (1996), looking at the history of European civilization, marveled at its early cultural—if not political—unity. Founded on ideas and institutions originating in Greece and Rome, the dominant unifying force of Western civilization from Constantine through the eighth century was Christianity, a fusion of Judaic and Hellenic traditions that gave a common cultural overlay to an ethnically diverse array of peoples in the far west of Eurasia. Even as this unity began to erode at the end of the eighth century, English, Germans, French, Italians, and others continued to think of themselves as sharing in Western civilization even though no single nation could claim to be the heartland to this pluralized civilization.

Nothing like this cultural unity ever existed in Asia. Despite the fact that nearly all of its rulers claimed to be emperors of the whole world, none ever conquered it all—though of all peoples, the Mongols came closest to doing so. Nor is there any one religion that provided a unifying creed for Asia as Christianity did for Europe. One might be tempted to speak of a "Buddhist civilization" in the same vein as one speaks of "Christian civilization" in the West, except for the fact that India, which gave birth to Buddhism, repudiated it after a dozen centuries, and even in China, to which it spread, it never successfully competed against Confucianism.

Far more, even, than Europe, the regions of Asia I focus on in this book are places of extraordinary and perplexing diversity. The peoples of this vast region have no common political system, no common language, no common history, religion, culture, geography, climate, or economy. To study Asia is to study its diversity. In fact, accounting for that diversity is part of the subject matter of this book. I will explore this diversity in several ways. First, I examine it as it exists *spatially*. The cultures of Asia are distributed across a geographically complex expanse whose features partially account for the extraordinary differences we find in human communities. The Himalayas present a barrier between South and East Asia, which ensured that they developed along different lines largely in isolation over four thousand years. Though they knew about each other in vague ways, there was never an Indian conquest of China or a Chinese conquest of India or any war between them of any significance. Yet there were periodic interconnections of profound importance. The Chinese sent emissaries to India to bring back knowledge of Buddhism. The Japanese sent shiploads of courtiers and students to bring civilization from China. Small rulers in Southeast Asia similarly sought civilization from India, and traders from India who settled in Southeast Asia brought along family priests who brought

Sanskrit culture, sacred texts, and the art of writing to emerging kingdoms in the valleys and islands of Southeast Asia.

The second way of exploring Asia's diversity is in terms of *cultural evolution*. Early states emerged by 2300 B.C. in the Indus valley and by 1700 B.C. in China, but pre-state cultures have persisted into the present throughout Asia, and today present problems of integration into modern nations that have, in a way, captured peoples who would prefer to remain independent. Before the period of nation-state definition by boundaries drawn on maps, there were extensive frontier regions between powerful states where small-scale (tribal) societies lived unnoticed or with only cursory acknowledgment of some distant centralized power. The luxury of independence is now lost to these peoples.

A third form of diversity in Asia is *linguistic*. When William Jones went to India in 1784 and began studying Sanskrit, he made a discovery that would change the way the world thinks about language. The Sanskrit language, he wrote, bore resemblances to both Greek and Latin more far-reaching than could have possibly occurred by chance; they must have all sprung from some common source. His discovery of a great family of languages that spread from England to North India enthralled Europe and was the late-eighteenth-century's moon walks; he lectured on the "Indo-European language family" to audiences of over a thousand on his return to England. Tracing out the complex family tree of this language family was one of the preoccupations and accomplishments of nineteenth-century linguistics. Only now are equivalent breakthroughs beginning to be made in another great language family, Sino-Tibetan.

The search for sacred texts that occupied Chinese, Japanese, and Southeast Asian intellectuals for better than half a millennium—India was the source for most of them—involved difficulties of translating mutually unknown languages and deciphering each other's exotic texts. India had one script, China another. Those who came in search of civilizing texts—Japan to China, Southeast Asia to India—had the problem of fitting scripts meant for one language to their own very different ones. Japan, with its polysyllabic language, could have had a better neighbor than China to borrow a script from; India's would have suited much better. Southeast Asia's Sino-Tibetan languages would have done well with China's logographic script, meant for monosyllabic languages, but the texts they were borrowing were Indian. Thus it went.

India and China are the two foundational civilizations of Asia. These two civilizations were creating their characteristic profiles during the pivotal first millennium B.C.; over a thousand-year period, both China and India were developing concepts of social order and institutions of civil society that have characterized them into the present. During this period, the Indian caste system was taking form. The Chinese centralized state had its earliest instance under the First Emperor,

Qin Shihuang, who became one model of the authoritarian emperor ruling under the Mandate of Heaven. In India, King Ashoka embodied the ideal ruler responsible for moral order in the state. The Upanishadic philosophers, Buddha, and Confucius lived and taught during the middle centuries of the first millennium B.C., and their philosophies became as foundational for their civilizations as the philosophies of Socrates, Plato, and Aristotle were for Europe. All these thinkers lived within a few centuries of each other during a period sometimes called the Axial Age because it was a kind of axis or pivotal point in history. Both civilizations were decisively configured during this epoch in ways that later centuries expanded, elaborated, and reformed.

Southeast Asia and Japan came under influence from India and China, respectively, in the following millennium (the first millennium A.D.) so that earliest forms of the state and court culture in those hinterlands resembled the more advanced cultures from which they borrowed. The early states of Southeast Asia borrowed, along with sacred texts and scripts from India, concepts of the sacred kingship, the *devaraja* or "god-king." They accepted first Hinduism, later Buddhism. Japan borrowed everything it possibly could from China: books, script, urban planning, Confucianism, Buddhism, and the imperial system—but without the undesirable feature of the Mandate of Heaven that could be withdrawn by Heaven in the case of a successful rebellion. The imperial dynasty founded during the period of borrowing from China, but subsequently projected backward in time to the Sun Goddess, has survived into the present; Emperor Akihito is the 126th emperor of Japan. Of course, both Southeast Asia and Japan made these cultural borrowings their own in unique ways, but their affinities to India and China remain clearly visible even in the present.

CULTURE AREAS OF ASIA

The terms I have been using—"South Asia," "East Asia," and "Southeast Asia"—are fairly recent geopolitical terms that have come into use in the postcolonial period as modern Asian nations have formed regional associations for trade and military security reasons (see map 1.1). Such maps represent current political alignments and desks at the US State Department more than long-term cultural affinities.

Anthropologists more typically use the concept of culture area. Behind the culture area concept is the assumption of a geographical region with some degree of environmental unity within which local societies have made similar cultural adaptations. For instance, humid lowland riverine regions of Southeast Asia have been cultivated by wet-

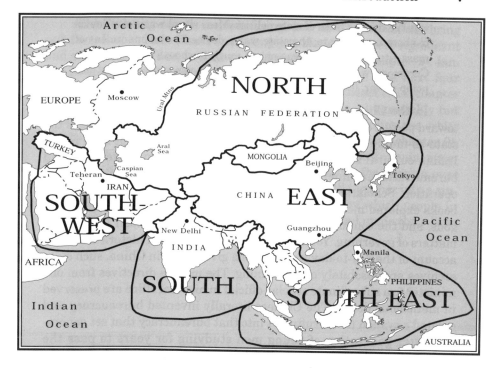

Map 1.1   Geopolitical Regions of Asia

rice methods that have supported a number of small states. By contrast, the cooler uplands support much smaller populations of slash-and-burn tribal cultivators.

Societies within a single culture area, it is assumed, will share similar political, economic, and religious institutions. Thus, in the Indian cultural sphere we find small, unstable kingdoms where the king models himself after Shiva or Vishnu, his capital is a replica of heaven, and Brahmans support the state with appropriate sacrifices and interpretation of sacred texts. Society is hierarchically organized in a moral order based on elaborate codes of rank and honor. The state in the Indian cultural sphere often looked like sacred theater, as Clifford Geertz describes in a famous study of one of the more byzantine Indic states, the Balinese:

> It was a theatre-state in which the kings and princes were impresarios, the priests, the directors, the peasantry, the supporting cast, stage crew, and audience. The stupendous cremations, teethfilings, temple dedications, the pilgrimages and blood sacrifices, mobilizing hundreds, even thousands of people and great quantities of wealth, were not means to political ends, they were ends themselves, they were what the state was for. Court ceremonialism

I n the fourteenth century, a Japanese scholar named Chikafusa summarized the knowledge of Asian landforms that had come to Japan
from ancient times: four great continents float in four great oceans.
The southern continent is Jambu, named for a tree twelve hundred
miles high that stands on the shore of a lake at the top of Mt. Anavatapta in the center of the continent. Just south of Mt. Anavatapta are
the Himalayas, and south of them lies India, in the true heart of Jambu.
To the northwest of India is Persia, and to the northeast is China.
Because this was not an age when the Japanese deferred to China,
Chikafusa added with a sniff: "China is thought to be a large country,
but compared to India it is a remote and small land on the periphery of
Jambu" (Varley 1980). Japan, on the other hand, was the "central land"
in the ocean between Jambu and the eastern continent, a land apart
ruled by a line of sovereigns descended from gods.

Asia's landscape has everywhere been overlaid with meanings, both
sacred and political. The Ganges River, sacred from source to mouth,
comes tumbling out of heaven and is caught in Shiva's matted locks to
release the waters slowly from his Himalayan abode on Mt. Kailash, thus
preventing destruction of the earth by floods. Asian rulers sought to build
their capitals at the central axis where heaven and earth connect, a fitting and authoritative location for a king. Throughout Southeast Asia,
the Himalayan "pillar of the universe," Mt. Meru (known to Chikafusa as
Mt. Anavatapta and to Hindus and Tibetan Buddhists as Mt. Kailash),
was reconstructed in capital after capital to assert the divinity of the god-
king who resided there.

As the above examples show, India plays a central role in most Asian
mytho-geographies. What is surprising is that India plays a central role
in modern geophysics as well.

THE "GREAT COLLISION" AND ASIAN LANDFORMS

In China, when the earth shook, it was taken as an ominous sign of
Heaven's displeasure with earthly regimes; when such regimes toppled,
such a heavenly sign was later interpreted as a forewarning. In 1556, an
earthquake near Xian (then the capital Chang-an) killed 830,000 people; seventy years later, when another earthquake shook the new
capital, Peking, the court astrologer said ominously: "The reason why
the earth growls is that throughout the empire troops arise to attack one
another, and palace women and eunuchs have brought about great dis-

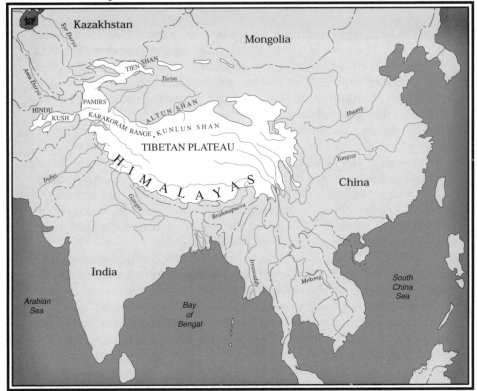

Map 2.1   Physical Map of Asia

order" (Lach 1965). The omen was fulfilled fifteen years later when China was conquered by the Manchus.

Modern science interprets those disasters differently. All the great earthquakes of India, China, Mongolia, and Tibet are caused by one colossal event: the slow-motion collision of India with the Eurasian continent that has been going on for 10 million years without interruption (Molnar & Tapponnier 1977). Riding on its own tectonic plate, India broke off from East Africa and drifted northeastward, traveling five thousand kilometers before beginning its collision with Eurasia. Isolated in the Indian Ocean during the emergence of mammals in the Eocene, it was only after the beginning of the collision 10 million years ago that mammals from Mongolia swarmed down into the subcontinent.

The collision radically altered Asia's landforms, compressing and distorting the earth's crust from the Himalayas to Siberia, and from Afghanistan to the China coast. Where Tibet and North India are now, there was once a low-lying coast and submerged continental shelf. Colliding with such force that India slid under the Eurasian crust and lifted up the Tibetan Plateau, the continent continued to shove northward another

The Highest Mountains in the World		
	Country	Elevation in feet
Everest	China-Nepal	29,029
K2	China-Pakistan	28,251
Kanchenjunga	India-Nepal	28,207
Dhaulagiri	Nepal	26,811
Annapurna	Nepal	26,503
Muztag	China	25,338
Tirich Mir	Pakistan	25,230
Pik Kommunizma	Tajikistan	24,590
Pobeda Peak	China-Kyrgyzstan	24,406

The highest mountains in the world are in the ranges created by the collision of India and Eurasia: the Himalayas, Hindu Kush, Pamir, Kunlun Shan, and Tien Shan.

two thousand kilometers, and continues its northward push at the same rate of five centimeters a year. It is unclear where exactly the suture of the two continents lies, but several features of the geology of the Tibetan Plateau are becoming clearer. Five major fault lines rim the plateau in an east-west direction. In the north, the Altyn Tagh and Kansu corridor is a strike-slip fault like the San Andreas Fault of California, clearly visible in satellite photographs and traceable for more than twenty-five hundred kilometers. The southern block is moving eastward and the northern block is moving westward. Portions of the former ocean floor have been lifted high and dry in central Tibet, a plateau four thousand meters in altitude known as Chang Tang, drained by no rivers and containing only brackish lakes that are the remnant of the ancient Tethys Sea. The mountains south of the Tibetan Plateau are the old northern portion of India, stacked up slice upon slice, the highest mountains in the world, the Himalayas. The Tibetan Plateau was squeezed like an accordian by the impact and at the same time stretched eastward, creating deep east-west gashes that became rivers draining the Himalayas across China and down into Southeast Asia. The plateau that was produced at the point of collision isolated India from Siberian winter winds, and isolated central Asia from the moderating influences of the southern oceans.

North of the Tibetan Plateau, stretching from the Karakorum Pass into India to the famous Kansu corridor into China proper, lies a desiccated region of arid grasslands, dry hills, and sheerest desert. If it were not for the barrier of the Himalayas, this region would be no more extreme than Nebraska, another continental heartland at the same lati-

myth encapsulates the expectation that rulers will be responsible for water control.

The river sometimes spills into the Bohai Sea but occasionally catastrophically changes its mind and drops south into the Yellow Sea. In the last millennium, spectacular course changes have come in 1194 (south into the Yellow Sea), 1855 (north into the Bohai Sea), 1938 (south), and 1946 (north)—where it flows today. At every course change, the human suffering has been immense. The 1938 change was deliberate. In an act counter to the historic role of rulers as protectors of the dikes, Chiang Kai-shek blew them up in order to halt the Japanese advance by flooding the North China Plain. It did slow them down, but it also caused half a million deaths and produced six million refugees.

By contrast, the Yangtze is "China's Main Street," sometimes compared to the Mississippi for commercially profitable navigability. It has ten times the volume of the Huanghe and is far more stable. Geologists suspect that in prehistoric times the Yangtze and the Red River, which flows out into the Gulf of Tonkin, were one and the same river. Somehow that course was interrupted and the Yangtze turned eastward, flowing across two thousand miles to the East China Sea and capturing dozens of rivers in its path.

The Italian merchant Marco Polo spent time in the lower Yangtze region in the early 1290s and was impressed by the commercial activity along the river. More than two hundred cities in sixteen provinces were involved in the river's great trade network. One of those cities may have been Shanghai, although until the mid-nineteenth century it was only a small coastal town. Only after it was acquired as a "Treaty Port" by the British, because of its strategic location for international shipping at the mouth of the Yangtze, did it grow into China's largest and richest city.

The great challenge for early rulers was to link the rich, rice-growing southern provinces with the north so that tribute- and tax-bearing barges could reach the northern capitals. The earliest piece of what became known as the Grand Canal may have been dug in the sixth century B.C., contemporary with early stretches of the Great Wall. Over the next centuries, work on the Grand Canal was undertaken during periods of strong regimes and allowed to fall into disrepair during periods of disorder. Between A.D. 600 and 610, two to three million laborers (including women when they ran short of men) constructed over fourteen hundred miles of canal. It began at Hangzhou on the coast, cut north to the Yangtze, curved around several large lakes and then northeast to meet the Yellow River, from where it was an upriver journey to the capital, Chang-an (Xian), with a five hundred-mile extension northeast toward a town near what later became Peking. This canal was in use for the next seven hundred years. When, after the Mongol conquest in A.D. 1280, they made their capital at Peking, much of the course of the Grand Canal that

At hundreds of sites all along the Ganges River, but especially at certain sacred sites like the upriver towns of Rishikesh and Haridwar, the Goddess Ganga—the river itself—is worshipped with fire (arati) at dawn and dust. Brahmans perform the worship, but are joined by hundreds of thousands of worshippers.

led to Chang-an was irrelevant. So between 1290 and 1300, they rerouted the canal, shortening it by four hundred miles to just over one thousand miles—about the distance from Miami to New York. Nothing comparable existed anywhere else in the world.

In the western Himalayan "pinch" are the headwaters of India's three great rivers, the Indus, Brahmaputra, and Ganges. Their sources— much sought by Hindu and Buddhist pilgrims—are within seventy-five miles of each other at the foot of Mt. Kailash near the northwestern corner of Nepal in Tibet.[1] Pilgrims circumambulate the mountain in arduous but holy three-day treks. From Mt. Kailash, the Brahmaputra flows eastward across Tibet almost to the Mekong-Salween-Yangtze group, then suddenly plunges south to mix its waters with the Ganges in the Bengal delta. Across the entire southern fringe of the Himalayas, more than a dozen rivers drain south to be caught like so many ribbons in the two great North Indian rivers, the Indus and the Ganges.

All Hindus long to die on the banks of the Ganges, and families will make great effort to take their dead to cremation sites along the river. The corpse must be burned within twelve hours of death. They are carried, wrapped in cloth, by stretcher to the cremation site where the expenses of wood and attendants may be high.

Every day several million Hindus bathe away not only their physical dirt but also their sins in the holy waters of the Ganges. No Asian river is more beloved, more revered, or more transformed by mythology than the Ganges. Called "Ganga Ma" (Mother Ganges) by Hindus, the Ganges is also a goddess, one of the wives of Shiva, who flows from his hair at his abode on Mt. Kailash down through the Himalayan foothills, spills out onto the plains of North India at the sacred town of Haridwar, and gathering river after river in her eastward flow, finally empties into the Bay of Bengal. In sacred towns up and down the river, Ganga Ma is worshipped daily at dawn and dusk by priests waving sacred flames while devout Hindus sing the great hymn, *"Om Jai Gange Mata"* ("Hail to Mother Ganga").

However, there is increasing worry about the health of the river. With millions washing and shampooing, "doing latrine," laundering clothes, dumping the remains of cremation and, often enough, uncremated bodies into the river, Mother Ganga does indeed carry away the pollution of humans. "Ganga coexists with this *gandagi* (pollution) and lovingly carries it out of sight," anthropologist Kelly Alley was told in Banaras. "Ganga is like a mother who cleans up the messes her child makes" (Alley 1994). And I was told, with pious certainty by a high school physics teacher in Banaras, that Ganga water is the purest water in the world, water that even after twelve years in a jar on a shelf would still be fresh and clean. Yet scientists report that levels of pseudomonas, Escherichia coli, enterobacteria, klebsiella, and Acinetobacter are alarmingly high, and epidemiologists since the nineteenth century have traced cholera outbreaks to major festival bathing such as happens every twelve years at Allahabad at the confluence of the Ganges and the Yamuna.

The Outer Ring of Islands

Where, exactly, is the eastern edge of Asia? Looking at a map of Southeast Asia as it is today, we see the familiar southwestward curve of Vietnam, ending just a little beyond the Mekong Delta. The shallow (thirty-six meters) South China Sea separates Mainland Southeast Asia from Island (Insular) Southeast Asia, the group of islands that make up Indonesia and the Philippines. A long peninsula of which Burma, Thailand, and Malaysia own pieces, drops almost to the equator and comes within a few miles of Sumatra.

If we were to look back a mere ten thousand years, however, we would see a far different coastline. Then, the eastern protrusion of Vietnam dropped straight down to Borneo. Sumatra, Java, and Borneo were the southern highlands of mainland Southeast Asia. A vast and fertile riverine basin was drained by Thailand's Chao Phrya River, then the largest river system in Southeast Asia (Higham 1989). The only islands in

Southeast Asia were the Philippines, Sulawesi, and the smaller islands east of Bali. The area that was raised from the sea is known as the Sunda Shelf, the true eastern limit of Asia. During glacial periods, it rises and dries; during warm interglacials such as the one we have been in for the last several thousand years, it sinks beneath the surface of the South China Sea. (Actually, waters melted from the glaciers rise and drown it.) The inundating of the coastline has been going on very recently, perhaps as recently as a thousand years ago, though the main inundation was between eight thousand and four thousand years ago. These are comparatively recent times; ancestors of present populations, including human ones, have lived through at least three of these cycles.

Beyond the true eastern edge of Asia—beyond Borneo and beyond what is called Wallace's Line—is a biogeographically distinct region. Placental mammals are found on the Asia side; marsupials are on the far side.[2] Since there was never a time when a land bridge connected New Guinea and Australia to Asia, human settlement there depended on seagoing skills, which must have developed early (see later in this chapter).

A spectacular arc of volcanic peaks follows the outer curve of Indonesia, north through Sulawesi and the Philippines, and on to Japan. The most famous of the volcanic eruptions in recent times occurred on August 27, 1883, when an island between Sumatra and Java called Krakatau began a series of paroxysmal explosions that ended up blowing away two thirds of the island (Francis & Self 1983). No witnesses survived. Its effects, however, were felt around the world. The explosion was heard fifteen hundred miles away in Australia and in South India, and the ash caused atmospheric effects and gorgeous sunsets around the world for months. Tsunamis moving as fast as air waves churned through the Sunda Straits and lashed the shores of Sumatra and Java, killing over thirty thousand people. Waves from Krakatau reached Honolulu in eleven hours. It is thought that the thick ash in the immediate aftermath of the eruption may have muffled the noise of the explosion for people nearby and so failed to warn them of the coming tidal waves.

But Krakatau was an exceptional event; most people in the island regions live near potentially dangerous active volcanoes and simply get used to the danger. To the east of Java is the small island of Bali (only 144 km by 80 km), which has its own chain of volcanic mountains. The highest of these peaks is Mt. Agung (3,142 feet), presided over by a male god who has power over fire. A lower but perhaps more sacred cone is Mt. Batur, a young volcano in the heart of an ancient crater. Part of this crater is Lake Batur, home of the Goddess of the Lake. Both of these deities, it is said, were given authority over Bali by the great god of Mt. Meru, Shiva, on the Indian continent. These deities preside over highly active volcanoes, which erupt with disastrous frequency, burying whole villages but often miraculously sparing temples (see box 2.2).

2.2   Eruption of Mount Batur, Bali

The village of Batur was situated before August 1926 at the foot of the volcano Batur. It was a neat, well-kept village, which could be seen clearly from the crater. Along the northwestern slope a long crevice appeared with a lot of noise and thunder, from which fires and many lava fountains spewed forth. I was informed of this and went to Kintamani, and descended to the village of Batur. It was impossible to get an overview of the situation: the inhabitants were not worried and trusted in the power and will of the gods and in the temple, which already once before had stopped the lava-stream. From above you could see that the lava-stream was not moving toward the village. However, it seemed to me that the eruptions would eventually fill the hollow in which the village was nestled. In the afternoon of the first day a new source of lava came into being at about 1,200 meters distance from the village. With the sound of a diesel engine, it regularly emitted large waves of blood-red glowing lava. A lava stream started to move towards the village.

Above all this, the sky was blood-red, dyed by twenty-one lava fountains, glowering and spouting lava. Very heavy explosions made the surroundings resound; the echo went on and on against the rim of the crater.

At 11:00 P.M. a huge mountain of cinders, under which the lava was hidden, reached the border of the village. At 1:00 A.M. the first house began to burn; trees were slowly pushed over, walls collapsed and everything within fifty meters of the lava stream was on fire. The lava stream was moving at about 200 meters per hour. But as yet the mountain of lava, which was about 8 meters tall, was not too hot on the outside. You could approach the edge of the lava to about 3 or 4 meters, while slowly being pushed back by the huge wall of moving cinderblocks.

In the meantime a number of people had cleared out their houses, and installed themselves on the path, in expectation of further events. I had ordered the military patrol to fetch 200 prisoners from the prisoner's camp in Bantang, and with the help of these troops the populations prepared their exodus.

At ten in the morning, after consultation with the anak agung (prince) of Bangli, the Temple of Batur was abandoned. All precious possessions were taken to safety after a brief ceremony by the Jeros and Mangkoes (temple priests). The market, the Baler banjar, and the big pavilion were on fire. Above the loud noise of the 50-meter-high flames, the sound of the twenty-one erupting craters could still be heard.

Memoir of Controleur J. C. C. Haar, quoted in Stephen Lansing, 1991.

These Asian volcanoes are part of the great "arc of fire" that rims the Pacific Ocean. Its American arm includes the Cascades, Sierras, and Andes. Another type of volcano in the mid-Pacific is of the basaltic type: great, fast-moving, fast-spreading, enormous volcanoes such as Mauna Loa and Kilauea in Hawaii, which build up from the ocean floor to the surface. But the volcanoes of the Pacific Rim are of a type known as andesitic; they erupt at lower temperatures, are stickier, and tend to pile up around the vent. They often throw large amounts of broken rock into the air, and build the pile of material around the rim higher and higher into pointy peaks, like Mt. Fuji in Japan, which we tend to admire as graceful and symmetrical. By contrast, Mauna Loa has about a hundred times more material in it than Mt. Fuji.

The reward for living with dangerous volcanoes is the most fertile soils in the world. In nonvolcanic regions of Indonesia, soils are often poor and the land sparsely populated, but volcanic areas have soil and climate conditions that allow for the highest population densities and some of the most successful agricultural systems ever devised. Before turning to those human adaptations, however, one more piece of the geographic picture must be put into place: the monsoons.

Monsoons

At midwinter in Asia, when the sun is far south over the Tropic of Capricorn, Central Asia and Siberia are intensely cold. The Tibetan Plateau prevents the warm southern oceans from moderating the frigidity, and (since cold air sinks) a vast region of high pressure pushes this cold air eastward into North China and southward over the edge of the Himalayas to spill onto the North Indian plains. But throughout the spring, as the sun begins moving northward, the situation reverses. Temperatures rise in North India and Southeast Asia and accumulated groundwater slowly evaporates. April and May are intensely hot and dry. The same thing is going on over the Indian Ocean and the seas of Southeast Asia, where ocean water is evaporating and rising into the atmosphere as moisture-laden clouds. These are the conditions that create the monsoons. Because the land heats faster than the ocean, the warmer air over the land rises. As it rises, denser, moisture-filled air from the ocean is pulled in to fill the vacuum. These are the monsoon winds. As the winds blow inland, this air, too, rises, releasing its heavy load of water vapor as monsoon rains (Webster 1981).

The coming of the monsoons is greeted with celebration throughout "monsoon Asia," even by the casual visitor who happens to experience the shift from the numbing heat of May to the dripping humidity—briefly relieved by daily deluges—of June and July. For farmers, it means their paddy fields, which they have plowed and weeded and repaired in preparation, will now fill with the water essential to the first growth of rice. If the monsoons come consistently over the next few months, they will have a good crop; if, as sometimes inexplicably happens, the rains begin and then stop, the young rice shoots will yellow in their dried-out fields, and then wither away. If the monsoons are overgenerous, the waters will rise until the ridges separating fields disappear and the rice drowns.

MONSOON ASIA AND RICE ADAPTATIONS

Monsoon Asia is the natural habitat for rice, although rice has been adapted by humans for cultivation outside this region. Monsoon Asia— the portions of Asia dominated by the wet-dry pattern described in the last section—is not the whole of Asia, by any means. In the equatorial islands of Indonesia, rain falls more or less evenly throughout the year, and little seasonal variation can be detected. And of course the mountainous regions of Tibet and the arid regions to the north are outside monsoon Asia. But India, mainland Southeast Asia, the lower, eastern regions of China, Korea, Manchuria, and southern Japan are all influenced by the monsoons. In monsoon Asia, rice is the single most important crop, covering one third of the total cultivated area. Parts of monsoon Asia have longer dry and weaker wet seasons, and so grains like wheat, millet, and sorghum are more reliable crops. You can draw an imaginary line north-south in India, leaving the southern tip of India and Sri Lanka on the eastern side; to the west is wheat, to the east is rice cultivation. You can draw another line east-west across China north of a rough line lying between the Yangtze and the Yellow Rivers. South is rice cultivation, north is millet and wheat.

Origins of Rice Cultivation

We know that rice originated someplace in monsoon Asia, but its prehistory is far less well documented than the prehistory of wheat in the Middle East. Rice still grows wild in the three valleys of the Red, Mekong, and Chao Phrya Rivers. All Asian rice belongs to a single species of annual grass: *Oryza sativa*. There the simplicity ends. There are over 120,000 varieties among the three subspecies: indica, japonica (also known as sinica), and javanica (Swaminathan 1984). The japonica variety, named by Japanese workers who made the discovery in 1928, evolved along a Chinese branch of the Brahmaputra (and so the Chinese call it sinica). And in the Indonesian islands, a third race of rice, javanica, evolved in adaptation to equatorial conditions. The huge number of varieties is a fabulous genetic resource that has made possible the hybridizing of a whole set of high yield varieties of rice (HYVs) since the Green

The International Rice Research Institute collects and stores thousands of samples of rice varieties that have emerged in the many microenvironments of southeast Asia. The rice is stored in labeled tin cans for preservation and later research.

Revolution. These thousands of strains are treated as national treasures in rice-growing nations, preserved in "germ plasm banks" where they are stored on shelves like so many tins of tuna.

Because of its efficient system for transporting oxygen from shoots to roots (ten times better than barley and four times better than maize), rice is highly adaptable to hot, wet, waterlogged environments such as are common throughout monsoon Asia, where rice is typically grown in several inches of water through most of its growing cycle. It was probably in such environments that rice as a cultivar first evolved, with later adaptations to dry, "hill rice" conditions. A second characteristic of rice is its extreme photosensitivity, requiring a precise number of minutes of sunlight per day at various stages of its growing season. It is for this reason that thousands of varieties have emerged in adaptation to microregions throughout monsoon Asia. It is this photosensitivity that required emergence of the javanica subspecies before rice could survive in the very different solar conditions of the equatorial region.

In the search for the origin of rice cultivation, however, the picture is not yet clear. Archaeology in Southeast Asia has documented a long period of successful foraging by peoples such as those who inhabited Spirit Cave in the northwestern hills of Thailand, and there is no easy explanation for why they gave up their adaptation for the hard work of rice cultivation (Higham 1984). We assume it took some kind of as-yet unidentified pressure to push them to it. The oldest phase of the Chinese Neolithic is about 6000 B.C., but that was based on millet, not rice, in the Huanghe basin. The oldest sites of rice cultivation now appear to be in southern Chinese coastal areas, running down as far south as the Red River basin in Vietnam. At the site of Hemudu in Zhejian Province, dated at 5000 B.C., is a whole Neolithic assemblage: pottery, carpentry, stone adzes, boats, paddles, spindle whorls for weaving, ropes and mats, evidence of domesticated pigs, dogs, chickens, possibly cattle and water buffalo—and lots of rice. There were layers of rice husks, grains, straw, and leaves twenty inches thick. Bellwood summarizes: "The main significance of southern China, and one which becomes ever firmer as the archaeological record unfolds, is that it was the zone where first developed the Neolithic technological and economic 'package' that fueled all later population expansions into mainland and island Southeast Asia" (Bellwood 1992: 91).

Two Rice Cultures

Since the earliest domestication of rice, its cultivation has diverged into two distinct patterns: swidden (known by a number of different terms, including "slash and burn," "shifting cultivation," "dry rice cultivation," and various indigenous terms such as *jhum*, and *taungya*) and paddy cultivation ("wet rice cultivation"). Clifford Geertz described the differences between the two types this way: "Any form of agriculture represents an effort to alter a given ecosystem in such a way as to increase the flow of energy to man: but a wet-rice terrace accomplishes this through a bold re-working of the natural landscape; a swidden through a canny imitation of it" (Geertz 1971).

Throughout much of rice-growing Asia, the two rice ecosystems correspond with two forms of societal complexity. Prestate peoples mostly inhabit upland environments where they practice swidden cultivation. State societies have emerged in the fertile riverine areas where they practice intensive wet-rice cultivation. We will return to these social concomitants in chapter 4, and for now keep our focus on the ecological dimensions of rice cultivation.

In the "generalized ecosystem" of the swidden plot, one will find a high diversity of species, as many as forty different crops reported on one three-acre field, thus retaining much of the species diversity of a natural

Wet rice cultivation is practiced in this terraced field. Rice must stand in water during the first phases of the growth cycle; as the plant matures, the water will be channeled out of this field for the final stages of growth. Paddy cultivators thus are skilled managers of water resources.

forest. There is a great deal of vegetation debris rapidly decaying in the humidity, but this does not produce the good soils that one might expect. In swidden areas one frequently sees a bright-red soil that looks rich to the untrained eye but is better used for making brick than growing rice. It is called ferralite. This porous, crumbly soil has been badly leached of nutrients by the process of relatively pure lukewarm monsoonal rainwater soaking downward, carrying away important silicates and bases and leaving behind an unhealthy mix of iron oxides and clay. Because so few nutrients remain in the upper levels of the soil where shallow plant roots can reach them, a significant proportion of the minerals available to crops comes from the ash produced in the burning phase of slash and burn. Between the first and second crop in a newly burned field, rice production drops as much as 80 percent because of the leaching process and because much of the value of the ash is used up by the first crop. The slashing part of slash and burn is to reduce the forest canopy somewhat in order to let in some — but not too much — light. The rice needs

This hill field has been slashed and burned prior to planting. Stumps of burned trees still stand in the field, but their removal allows essential sunlight to reach the young plants. These varieties of rice do not require to stand in water as does paddy rice. This field will only be cultivated for a year or two before it must be abandoned.

the light, but weeds like it, too. The combination of loss of soil fertility and weed growth will make swiddeners decide, after a few years, that it is easier to move than to keep working harder for less return in the same field.

Paddy (wet-rice) cultivation in China is known as the four stoops—stoop to plant, stoop to transplant, stoop to weed, and stoop to harvest. The phrase conveys something of the labor intensiveness of this system. It has been said about paddy cultivation that it has an endless capacity to respond to loving care. You can pregerminate seeds in the house; you can sow seeds in nurseries rather than broadcast them as in upland swidden practice; you can hand transplant in tight and even rows; you can weed three or more times during the growing season; you can double-crop and even triple-crop. You can dig irrigation channels, and you can go up mountainsides by carving terraces and channeling waters at enormous expenditures of labor. If you do these things, you can support population densities as high as thirty-two hundred persons per square mile in fields that never suffer a decline in productivity even after fourteen hundred years of continuous use.

Rice and the Green Revolution

In the past, little attention was paid to the sociology of this intensive agrarian pattern. Stover and Stover noted that paddy cultivation may not respond well to centralized state control as in China (Stover & Stover 1976). Rice is very sensitive to skill and additional effort, which it may not get with collectivized labor. Any delay in getting a labor brigade to repair embankments damaged by a rainstorm will leave the paddy fields to drain, causing ruin of the rice by drought and of the surrounding dry crops by flooding.

Similarly, Green Revolution scientists have tended to assume that correct technology is all that really counts. Farmers could get three crops a year on irrigated paddies with a new hybrid like IR36 (a high yield variety bred to resist four major rice diseases and four damaging rice insects, including the brown planthopper) along with appropriate fertilizers and pesticides. Premodern forms of agricultural activity—the ones that are responsible for the high population densities and longevity of paddies mentioned above—can then be modified or abandoned.

This is proving to be an inadequate view. In Bali, for instance, where some terraces have been in continuous use for more than a thousand years, Stephen Lansing has discovered a complex interrelation between the ritual system and the agricultural system (Lansing 1991). Individual family-owned paddies are the elementary unit, locked in a system of ever more inclusive temple congregations and irrigation management. To begin with the rice paddy, according to Stephen Lansing:

> In essence, the flow of water—the planned alternation of wet and dry phases—governs the basic biochemical processes of the terrace ecosystem. A general theory in ecology holds that ecosystems that are characterized by steady, unchanging nutrient flows tend to be less productive than systems with nutrient cycles or pulses. Rice paddies are an excellent example of this principle. Controlled changes in water levels create pulses in several important biochemical cycles. The cycle of wet and dry phases alters soil pH; induces a cycle of aerobic and anaerobic conditions in the soil that determines the activity of microorganisms; circulates mineral nutrients; fosters the growth of nitrogen fixing algae; excludes weeds; stabilizes soil temperature; and over the long term governs the formation of a plough pan that prevents nutrients from being leached into the subsoil. Potassium, for example, is needed for rice growth and depends largely on drainage. Phosphorus is also essential and may be increased more than tenfold by submergence.

The main crop produced is, of course, rice. But in addition, the paddy also produces important sources of animal protein, such as eels, frogs, and fish. . . . After each harvest, flocks of ducks are driven from field to field, gleaning leftover grain and eating some of the insects, like brown planthoppers, that would otherwise attack the next rice crop. Traditional harvesting techniques remove only the seed-bearing tassel, leaving the rest of the stalk to decompose in the water, returning most of its nutrients to the system. (Lansing 1991: 39)

From the Balinese point of view, all water has its source in a lake high in the crater of Mt. Batur presided over by the Goddess of the Lake, Dewi Danu. Her human representative is the High Priest, the Jero Gde, and together they reside in the Temple of the Crater Lake on the shores of Lake Batur. The life-giving waters of Lake Batur flow downhill via various rivers and streams, ultimately spilling out into the ocean, the end point of dissolution and regeneration. These streams are not broad meandering rivers that would be easy to dam and divert for agricultural use, but they flow through precipitous clefts where they may actually disappear underground for a length before reappearing. Nevertheless, over centuries an intricate web of thousands of diversionary weirs and channels have been built to bring this sacred water to irrigate the terraces of the Balinese.

Such a system needs carefully refined management, since many hundreds of farmers are upstream and downstream of each other, all dependent on a fair share of the available water in the right amounts at critical points in their growing season. Yet this management was never the responsibility of any state official or bureaucracy. There were kings of Bali, but they ruled by rituals focused on a different god, a different mountain, and a different chief temple.

Rather, it was the system of temple worship by farmers as worship-groups that managed not only the flow of water but also a number of collective cultivation issues, such as when to plant, when to burn to control pests across a whole hillside, when to harvest, and when to fallow. At every node of water diversion—i.e., at every weir across a stream or river—there is an altar or temple and a deity associated with it. Everyone downstream of that altar is part of its congregation. At the village level, water management associations composed of all farmers in the vicinity, known as *subaks*, were responsible both for worship and for collective agricultural and water use decisions. The temple festivals require obtaining holy water from upstream sources; the need to collect this holy water provides the means by which temple congregations are linked in ever more inclusive units. The intricate annual calendar for all those temple festivals is simultaneously the calendar for opening and closing the irrigation weirs. Ultimately, the high priest, the Jero Gde, has the right to make certain decisions with implications for the entire watershed, such as whether to open a new region to terracing and cultivation.

Although this system has tremendous practical results for life in Bali, its practical effects are not distinct from its ritual ones. For Balinese, the earth is a sacred place, the waters are sacred, life is sacred, and because the Goddess makes the waters flow, "those who do not follow her laws may not possess her rice terraces."

The lessons for the Green Revolution scientists were serious. As much good as rice research has done for rice-producing nations in Asia, there is also wisdom in patterns of rice cultivation honed over centuries of experimentation in Bali that technology alone could not improve upon. The Balinese have returned to the ancient system of management of irrigation by means of temple festivals and the ritual calendar.

EARLY ASIANS

In traditional Chinese pharmacology, one of the most potent substances is "dragon" bones. In powdered form stirred into tea, it is a remedy for a great number of ailments, from general weakness to specific illnesses such as dysentery and malaria. One might think dragon bones would be hard to come by, but an excellent source of them about thirty miles southwest of Beijing supplied the pharmacologists of the capital for many years. Around the turn of the century, a few scientists came to recognize that these dragon bones were actually fossils of ancient animals, some of them extinct, including saber-toothed tigers, rhinoceroses, horses, bears, hyenas, and buffaloes. Among these fossils were two teeth that ended up in the Swedish laboratory of paleontologist J. G. Andersson. In 1926 he made the astonishing announcement to the scientific world that they were human.

The scientific world responded cautiously. It was a fabulous find, if true. These teeth were found associated with extinct species like saber-toothed tigers in a bed assumed to be over a million years old. But it was, after all, only two teeth, a molar and a premolar. There was already controversy over a few specimens of an early man called Piltdown man, found in England, which was later proved to be an elaborate fake and exposed the scientific world to ridicule by the press. But the announcement of a hominid find at Dragon Bone Hill, now better known as Choukoutien (Zhoukoudian), led to a long but intermittent sequence of excavations and the discovery of a great many more remains of what is now called Peking man, or *Homo erectus pekinensis*.

There are now remains of forty individuals, males and females of various ages, plus tens of thousands of stone tools made by them (Wu & Lin 1983). They inhabited a large cave where they first took shelter about 460,000 years ago and continued to live until about 230,000 years ago. Something of the significance of that length of time can be grasped if we remember that only eight thousand years have passed since humans began cultivating grains in northern China. This earliest population is classified as *Homo* (man) *erectus* (upright), not *sapiens* (thinking); i.e., it is the same genus but not the same species as modern humans. The average cranial capacity of the *Homo sapiens'* braincase is 1,450 c.c.; Peking man's was 1,054 c.c. The skull was thicker and flatter, with protruding brows and a marked protrusion in the rear of the skull, very similar to *Homo erectus* specimens found widely throughout Eurasia and Africa. Over the long period of life in the cave, evolution of cranial capacity seems to have been occurring, since the most recent skull, dated at 200,000 B.P. was 1,140 c.c. During that time, their tools got nicer, too, beginning with awkward choppers (a few flakes knocked off a large pebble to produce a sharp ridge) and ending with delicate and well-made points that could be tied to sticks to make hunting spears.

These people lived during an interglacial much like the present one, so the climate was similar to now. The region was then covered with temperate deciduous forests. They were efficient hunters and gatherers, and may already have had a division of labor common among foraging communities in the present, in which men hunt and women gather. Whoever was gathering brought home hackberries, walnuts, hazelnuts, pinenuts, elmnuts, and rambler rose. They were also efficient deer hunters; over three thousand fossils of individual deer were found in the cave. One of the big surprises was evidence that they cooked their food and heated the cave with fire. What is not clear is whether they could start a fire on their own or had to capture it from natural fires and protect it as live coals in the cave.

Gradually the cave filled up with debris fallen from the roof, and it had to be abandoned. Between then and the emergence of clearly modern humans around forty thousand years ago lies a great deal of uncertainty among paleontologists, and a great deal more excavation and analysis waiting to be done.

Far to the south of Peking man in the easternmost extensions of Eurasia lived another *Homo erectus* population known as Java man. In over a dozen sites concentrated in central Java, with other sites in Borneo, Sulawesi, Timor, and in mainland Southeast Asia, there have been found human remains from as early as 1.3 million years ago.

What was the relationship between Peking man and Java man? What were the relationships between those ancient populations and modern Asians? This is currently a topic of hot debate, as paleontological debates go. The two principal theories can be summarized as the "direct descent" model and the "Noah's Ark" model (Bellwood 1992).

According to the direct descent model, the people who inhabited the Zhoukoudian Cave (and were of course more widely distributed in north China) stayed in the region for the next many millennia, slowly undergoing biological evolution into modern men. According to the "Noah's Ark" model, the earlier population died out and was replaced by a later migration of *Homo sapiens* who evolved in East Africa and spread throughout Eurasia. A compromise view holds that the second radiation from East Africa encountered and intermarried with the earlier *Homo erectus* peoples, although it is not known whether interbreeding between *erectus* and *sapiens* was possible. At present, the data that would settle the matter is lacking. Bellwood cautiously leans toward the "direct descent" view on the grounds that in both Java and China there is evidence of evolution between earlier and later *erectus* individuals, and all the similarities between *erectus* and modern forms seem hard to explain as identical results of natural selection on successive and unrelated species, which would be required by the "Noah's Ark" model. Finally, evidence from China of continuity between *erectus* and *sapiens* is becoming firmer. If true there, it would probably also be true in Southeast Asia.

By forty thousand years ago, then, Java man had evolved into a *sapiens* population known as Australo-Melanesian, widely distributed in Southeast Asia, both in the islands and perhaps as far north as Cambodia and Taiwan. Around that time, too, some of these people crossed into Australia and New Guinea, where they continued to evolve in isolation. Those who stayed behind also changed, in part because of gene flow from the north.

In China, modern humans evolved into a type known as Mongoloid, adapted to a northern climate that put far different selective pressures on them than was true in equatorial Asia. Beginning about 8,000 to 7,000 B.C., with the emergence of the Neolithic, these populations began to increase in number and move southward. (Any northward movement was blocked because their agricultural adaptation was impossible in arid central Asia.) Southern Mongoloids moved into Southeast Asia and intermarried with Australo-Melanesians, producing physical changes in those populations. A few of the original Australo-Melanesians survived in small and remote pockets as the Negritoes of the Philippines, central Malaysia, and the Andaman Islands, and continued to evolve as short-statured people. Only in the Andamans did they keep a pure foraging economy and their original languages, unrelated to any outside major grouping. This southward expansion of southern Mongoloids is continuing to this day, as even in the twentieth century, groups like the Akha, Lisu, Lahu, Hmong, and Mien have moved across the borders of China, Burma, Laos, and Thailand.

NOTES

[1] Since international borders are now guarded and unfriendly, pilgrimage to Kailash from India is rare, and Hindus have adapted by revering a source of the Ganges called Gaumukh, the "Mouth of the Cow," slightly to the southwest in the Indian Himalayas.

[2] The exception: a few species of bats and rodents (placental mammals) managed to swim or float to Australia and New Guinea in prehuman times.

3

TONGUES, TEXTS, AND SCRIPTS

I f any evidence were needed of Asia's tremendous diversity, you need look no further than language. There are over two thousand distinct languages spoken in East, South, and Southeast Asia. Language both creates communities through mutual intelligibility—a group in a room with a light on—and divides people, possibly even near neighbors, across language borders in the darkness of nonintelligibility. Language may, in fact, be the most severe of cultural boundaries, for when you cannot understand other people it is easy to suspect them of any number of other contrasts with yourself: *they* speak gibberish, *they* are barbarians (heathens, cannibals), *they* are uncivilized (uncultured, primitive, savage), *they* are irrational, *they* should learn from us. On the other hand, language creates communities of mutual comprehension, and becomes the base for other markers and reinforcers of community. We who speak a common language also share a common culture, have a sense of common identity, surely must have a common history and common ancestors, are a common "people," a nationality, an ethnicity. Many of these commonalities are actually fictions, but important fictions in the creation and maintenance of social unity (see chapter 4).

For instance, in the present age when so many national borders enclose people with no common language, there may be a desperate search for one. In India, where there are over 150 distinct languages, the effort to create a common one has been intense and controversial. The dominant language, Hindi (which is the fourth largest linguistic community in the world after Mandarin, English, and Spanish), has been hotly resisted in South India, where speakers of Dravidian languages resist imposition of a northern language. If there is a neutral common language, it is English, although the irony is that this is the language of the former colonial power. And of course a great number of Indians never learn this "common" language.

China, too, is a country of linguistic diversity, but it deals with the problem somewhat differently. It simply declares that all ethnic Han Chinese (93 percent of the population) speak dialects of Chinese, even though, since these dialects are mutually unintelligible, linguists consider them separate languages. The Chinese language is actually a language family equivalent to the Romance family of Italian, French, Spanish, and Portuguese. It helps, of course, that in written form, speakers of these separate languages of Chinese can actually read the same texts (see later in this chapter). It is as if all speakers of the various European languages had a single written language that everyone could understand.

On the other hand, Lao and Thai are mutually understandable and are therefore technically dialects, but since they are the national languages of Laos and Thailand, they are considered by their own national speakers to be two separate languages. This is one of those cases about which it has been said that a language is a dialect with its own army and navy.

There are many reasons for the study of language. You might want to study a particular language so you can speak it: that is, so you can go into the lighted room and converse with other speakers of that language. That may seem like the main point of language study. But that will not be the point of this chapter, nor could it be. Why else, then? In this book we are taking a view of Asia that seeks interconnections among people, which is not content with a "Holistic Asia" view, nor with the present nation-state configuration, nor with any simple view of the great traditions as bounded and eternal. We are attempting, rather, to order the diversity. The diversity of Asia's languages is not truly chaotic, though occasionally it might seem so. Although in one sense the languages appear as just so many separate lighted rooms, in another sense we are coming to know a great deal about the relationships between these languages and about the larger house, or family, of which each one is a part. The study of language families often uncovers startling connections—you might be surprised who your relatives are—but beyond this, historical linguistics is a key tool of prehistorical research, along with archaeology, paleontology, and biogenetic research.

VOICES FROM THE PAST

Making Family Connections: The Indo-Europeans

In 1784 a young Englishman named William Jones rented a thatched bungalow sixty miles upriver from Calcutta and began taking lessons in Sanskrit. The learned Brahmans at first refused to teach their sacred language to a foreigner, since not even their own women and lower castes were allowed to speak or hear it, but Jones managed to find a non-Brahman who would teach him. Only one other Englishman had learned the language before him. It proved to be an exceedingly difficult language even for a linguistic whiz kid like Jones. Before graduating from university he had already mastered French, Greek, Latin, Persian, and Arabic. Within a few months of beginning his lessons, he began to notice remarkable similarities between Sanskrit, which he was learning, and Greek and Latin, which he already knew. They even look suspiciously similar to English speakers. The Sanskrit word for mother is *matr*, for mouse is *mus*, for name is *nama*, for two is *dva*, for three is *tryas*, and so on. In grammar, too, the similarities are impossible to miss. Clearly he was on to something important. Two years later, he announced to the Asiatic Society:

> The Sanskrit language, whatever be its antiquity, is of a wonderful structure; more perfect than the Greek, more copious than the Latin, and more exquisitely refined than either; yet bearing to both of them a stronger affinity, both in the roots of verbs and the forms of grammar, than can possibly have been produced by accident; so strong, indeed, that no philologer could examine them all without believing them to have sprung from some common source, which perhaps no longer exists. There is similar reason, though not quite so forcible, for supposing that both the Gothick [i.e., Germanic] and Celtick, though blended with a different idiom, had the same origin with Sanskrit; and the old Persian might be added to the same family. (Keay 1988:30)

Prior to this time, European scholars who noticed similarities between, say, English and German or English and French assumed it was only because these languages had borrowed words and constructions from each other over the course of centuries. But with languages as far apart, geographically, as the Mediterranean and India, borrowing over centuries of close contact was ruled out as an explanation. The idea that languages could have similarities because they had "sprung from some common source" was novel. Jones' much-quoted statement is said to have begun the science of historical linguistics. These discoveries so enthralled Britain that at Jones' public lectures in later life, over a thousand people would show up. What was discovered, and over the next century more fully pieced together, was the prehistory of a set of languages now distributed from Europe to North India. The original language, which Jones speculated might once have existed and may no longer exist, is now called Proto-Indo-European.

The terms in the following table illustrate the kinds of similarities that needed to be accounted for. Two words with the same meaning in two different but related languages that are later forms of a common earlier form are called cognates. The word for "two" in Greek and Latin is the same: *duo*. The Sanskrit form is dva. Over time the /v/ of Sanskrit had become the /u/ of Greek and Latin. Aside from this somewhat minor, but recognizable, sound shift, the three words are clearly cognates. If English "two" is also a cognate, we have to account for two sound shifts: /v/ to /w/ and /d/ to /t/. Linguists know that these are easy shifts for languages to make. /V/ and /w/ are made in similar ways in the mouth, and easily shift from one to the other. (Try it and see.) In North Indian languages today, individual speakers vary in their pronunciation of /v/ on a range from a good hard /v/ to a soft and liquid /w/.

Similarly with /d/ and /t/, both are made with the tongue on the alveolar ridge (just behind the teeth) and by stopping, then freeing, the breath; the only difference between the two is a lack of voicing on the /t/.

English	Sanskrit	Greek	Latin	Old German	Japanese
one	ekas	heis	unus	ains	hitotsu
two	dva	duo	duo	twai	futatsu
three	tryas	treis	tres	thrija	mittsu
four	catvaras	tettares	quattuor	fidwor	yottsu
five	panca	pente	quinque	fimf	itsutsu
six	sat	heks	sex	saihs	muttsu
seven	sapta	hepta	septem	sibum	nanatsu
eight	asta	okto	octo	ahtau	yattsu
nine	nava	ennea	novem	niun	kokonotsu
ten	dasa	deka	decem	taihum	to

The numbers one through ten in five Indo-European languages and also, for contrast, in Japanese, which is not a member of the Indo-European family.

In the case of *dva/duo/twai* you can probably figure out which of these languages English is closest to. The spelling of the English word preserves a pronunciation now lost. If we were to spell English the way we pronounce it, we would spell it "tu." But once we pronounced it *two*, and in that pronunciation the similarity to Old German *twai* is apparent. The /d/ has already become /t/, and the /v/ has become /w/. The vowels, /u/ and /ai/ are different, but vowels are a lot more slippery than consonants.

If you were to work out the relationship of the five languages just on the basis of "two," you would probably come up with:

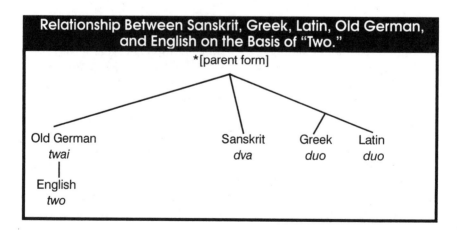

Relationship Between Sanskrit, Greek, Latin, Old German, and English on the Basis of "Two."

*[parent form]

Old German
twai
English
two

Sanskrit
dva

Greek
duo

Latin
duo

This tree diagram orders the similarities by degree of closeness and by generation. Greek and Latin are identical; between them and Sanskrit there has been one consonant change. Between those three and Old German, there have been two consonant changes. Of course, this is just one word. You would want to examine many words to discover repeating patterns or modify your diagram as more evidence seems to require it. Notice, for instance, the shift from /d/ to /t/ shows up again in "ten": *dasa / deka / decem* vs. *taihum / ten*. You would probably want to be selective about what words you chose for comparison. The word "motor," for instance, has passed into a large number of the world's languages along with the actual automobile. Languages do borrow words extravagantly (steal might be a better word; they rarely give them back), along with technological innovations, religious concepts, new foods, etc. Anything new can bring along its label from the original language. These words are called loanwords. When Christianity moved into Europe, hundreds of religious terms, most of them from Latin, came along with it. The French invaded England in 1066, and over the next three centuries more than ten thousand French words were added to English, often duplicating perfectly good Anglo-Saxon (Germanic) words. Similarly, when Hinduism and later Buddhism spread into Southeast Asia, thousands of Sanskrit words were added to local languages, and Japanese absorbed several thousand Chinese loanwords along with Confucian and Buddhist texts and the Chinese script. When tea was carried westward from China, its Chinese name went along with it. The English and French (*the*) forms are from a North China dialect, and the Russian (*cha*) and Hindi (*chai*) forms are from a South China dialect. Now, of course, new words are being created with new technology and being added not only to English but spread widely wherever the new technology travels; words like "internet," "software," "user-friendly," and "browser."

But some words change very rarely. Pronouns are among the stablest terms. So are kinship terms, body parts, and words like "sun," "moon," "sky," "path," "home," "name," "fire," "hot," and "cold." These are sometimes called core vocabulary, the oldest, most stable words in any language, and they are used by linguists in comparing languages and finding relationships. These words are most useful when the two daughter languages split off long ago. In linguistic terms, a split of one thousand years is so recent that even untrained observers would not deny that the languages have a common parent. But when the distance to the parent, or proto-language, is in the range of several thousand years, it may not be so readily apparent. Most linguists now agree that Proto-Indo-European was spoken some five thousand years ago. This is by far the best-documented language family in the world, partly because so many scholars have worked on it during the last two hundred years, and partly because there is documentation of old, intermediate forms in texts written in ancient Sanskrit, Greek, Latin, and Hittite.

In fact, much of the vocabulary of Proto-Indo-European (PIE) has been painstakingly reconstructed, and this reconstructed lexicon holds clues about where PIE was spoken. There were no words for elephant, tiger, banana, rice, or ocean; there *were* words for herd, cow, sheep, pig, goat, dog, house, wolf, bear, goose, duck, bee, salmon, beaver, squirrel, beech, willow, oak, grain, and wheel. It follows that the original Indo-Europeans must have been acquainted with these things, and an effort to map their distribution on a map of Eurasia has led to the hypothesis that the original homeland was the central grassland regions north of the Black and Caspian Seas. It is assumed they were a mounted warrior people who around 3000 B.C. began to move westward into Europe, south into Turkey, and southeast into Iran and India. The Indic, or Indo-Aryan, branch moved into North India around 1700 B.C., where they encountered a civilization in decline (the empty cities of Harappa and Mohenjo-Daro; see chapter 5) and speakers of a wholly different language family, Dravidian. Conquering and intermarrying, they spread across the northern half of the subcontinent, where their language, Sanskrit, began to undergo its inevitable regional transitions into such modern languages as Panjabi, Hindi, Bengali, Marathi, Gujarati, and Nepali.

The language that gave Sir William Jones his great insight, Sanskrit, provides the oldest known samples of an Indo-European language. It continues to be both written and spoken to this day but has not been a mother tongue—the first language learned by children in a language community—since some time in the first millennium B.C. It was already archaic by Buddha's time, the sixth century B.C., for Buddha insisted on preaching in the vernaculars, the languages actually spoken, and most of the Buddhist texts are written in such a language, Pali. But early Sanskrit and even earlier Vedic were preserved by the oral transmission of the most sacred compositions of the Hindus, the Vedas. These four works are regarded by all Hindus as the source of their religion, given directly to humans as revealed truth.

East Asian Homelands

The great success of reconstructing the Indo-European language family has naturally led linguists who work in East and Southeast Asia to attempt similar reconstructions there. But in this part of the world, the complexities are much greater and the time depth deeper. There have been far fewer linguists at work on far more languages, and the effort has really only begun in the last half-century. This means that at the present time, there is still much uncertainty and disagreement, though some general outlines are beginning to emerge. I intend to present a picture that

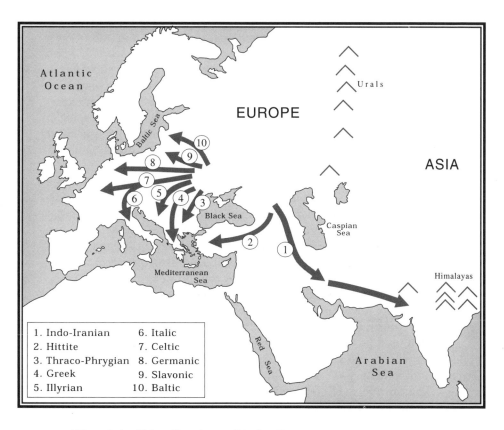

Map 3.1   Distribution of Indo-European Languages

is a good deal firmer and clearer than perhaps most experts would prefer. This emerging picture has come about as other kinds of scholars, particularly archaeologists, have brought their data to bear on questions also of interest to linguists.

As soon as a number of languages have been shown by linguists to be members of a language family, we want to know where the original mother tongue was spoken, when it was spoken, and why and how they began moving to where we now find them. With such questions, obviously, archaeology can be helpful. The archaeological record of excavated sites can be examined for important clues about the people. For instance, were they foragers or cultivators? What is the geographical range within which a typical assemblage of artifacts is found? What is the physical type of the human remains? What seems to have been the population density? How long were sites inhabited by the same people?

What, for instance, would cause a population to disperse? This is the first stage in the breakup of a language into a number of daughter languages. According to archaeologist Colin Renfrew (1989), there are four principal ways by which populations, together with their languages, spread. First, there were the earliest periods of human dispersal, when people settled in previously uninhabited territories, leaving the African homeland and moving throughout most of Eurasia, Australia, and New Guinea. In some parts of the world—the eastern Pacific islands, for example—this has happened recently enough that we have quite a lot of knowledge about the peoples and their languages. In Asia, those earliest *Homo sapiens*, we are certain, must have spoken some language; if only we could rediscover its traces in modern languages.

This initial migration was followed by the farming dispersal. The invention of farming in various places caused population growth, and as these agricultural populations expanded at the expense of earlier foragers, they took their languages with them. The full impact of these dispersals is only now coming to be recognized by historical linguists. For instance, Renfrew has argued that the Indo-European dispersal was not by mounted warriors of the steppes, but by the earlier agriculturists of the Middle East, very well documented archaeologically, who moved from the Mediterranean north into Europe, displacing earlier foragers (and leaving the Basques as a lonely remnant), and also eastward into the Iranian Plateau and India. (Indian historians are not yet accepting this hypothesis, however; if and when they do, it will require radical rethinking of early Indian history.)

The third form of dispersal came about during the global warming several thousand years ago when regions north of the 54th parallel became liveable, and pioneers settled in Siberia and crossed the Bering Straits into the circumpolar region where they became the Eskimo-Aleut.

Finally, the fourth form of migration, occurring in later historic times as societies became more complex, is elite dominance, which occurs when incoming groups, better organized and better armed, conquer indigenous groups and impose their languages on them. The Altaic languages (Mongolian, Manchurian, Turkish, Korean, and possibly Japanese) originated in Central Asia and were carried westward and eastward by well-documented conquests (though Khubilai Khan's invasion of China and the dynasty he established, the Yuan, left scarcely a trace on the Chinese language). Thai and Lao spread into Southeast Asia, shoving aside Khmer. The spread of English accompanying the era of colonialism would be a more recent example.

Just as archaeologists know that the Neolithic is invariably accompanied by population growth, linguists know that a region with the greatest diversity of languages is likely to be the oldest area of settlement and possibly the original home of the speakers of a language family. For an easy example that this might be so, think of the diversity of English dialects in the British Isles (in as small an area as London, "Queen's

English" and Cockney are extraordinarily different) or the dialect diversity of American English on the East Coast as opposed to the homogeneity of the more recently settled Midwest and West. The same process, allowed to develop over, say, seven thousand years, will turn dialects into languages and then into language families. If a region is an ancient center of agriculture, it is more likely to have resisted intrusion from people speaking other languages, and its own language(s) will go on modifying, diversifying, and transforming themselves into a family of related languages. Then, of course, if people begin to move around, at first because of the population explosion associated with agriculture, and later because of military adventuring by conquering peoples, the picture becomes quite complex.

Let me make a simple observation from a linguistic map of today: The greatest linguistic diversity in East and Southeast Asia can be found in a circle with a radius of a thousand miles, with its center on Canton. This circle will include the island of Taiwan, the whole eastern region south of the Yangtze, as far inland as Kunming, and the northern hills of Burma and Laos.

This is, first of all, the area where China's many dialects have their greatest diversity. Besides Chinese, Southern China also contains four additional language families: Austroasiatic, Tai-Kadai, Miao-Yao, and Tibeto-Burman. And just across the Formosa Straits on Taiwan is a member of the Austronesian family and the probable original homeland of a group of languages now spread from Madagascar to Hawaii.

The region thus demarcated is about halfway between the earlier Peking man and Java man. Remember that this vast area from Zhoukoudian to Java was inhabited by *Homo erectus* populations who gradually became *Homo sapiens*. Throughout millennia, these peoples, the initial settlers of this vast region, subsisted as foragers by hunting game and gathering roots, fruits, nuts, and berries. We are certain they had language, but it is impossible at present to know anything about that language. The southernmost of these people crossed Wallace's Line into Australia and New Guinea, remaining foragers in Australia but independently inventing agriculture in New Guinea. Then, quite recently in this grand view of things, some of those who remained in Asia began to cultivate grain. At about 6000 B.C. they were cultivating millet in North China, and at about 5000 B.C. they were cultivating rice over a region stretching from coastal South China through the hills of Burma and across into India as far as Bihar. We assume that these earliest cultivators were the first to experience the population growth that accompanies agriculture, and the first to disperse amongst foraging peoples, displacing and isolating them. We do not, of course, know anything about their languages. But based on the hard work of many linguists, we can perhaps piece together a picture as things stood between the end of the last glaciation, ten thousand years ago, and the period of the first written texts from China, about the fifteenth century B.C.

Several things seem certain during this long period. First, as the area being discussed is vast, it is unlikely that peoples living there ten thousand years ago would all have been speaking the same language. However paleolinguists eventually settle the great debate on the origin(s) of human language, by ten thousand years ago, there must have been several languages in existence in East and Southeast Asia. Second, no one could then have been living in the fully glaciated Himalayas; settlement of the Himalayas by Tibetans and others must have come later. Third, the Neolithic revolution must have spread slowly throughout the human communities in this vast area, but as a population acquired the new economy they would quickly have experienced population growth at the expense of others. These newly cultivating populations were Renfrew's farming dispersal at the expense of still-foraging populations.

Austroasiatic

There is a family of about 150 languages called Austroasiatic that we assume must be the languages of this first population explosion; it includes Vietnamese and Khmer in Southeast Asia. Over in India it survives among a few hill tribes such as the Munda. But once they must have been widespread throughout the region, including South China; the old name for the Yangtze, *jiang*, is believed to be Austroasiatic, and from their reconstructed vocabulary we find linguistic evidence attesting to their knowledge of rice agriculture. Some cognates of jiang, such as *song* (Vietnamese), *krung, kroung,* and *karung,* are now general-purpose words for river.

Austro-Tai

Somewhat later, around 4500 B.C., people who spoke another proto-language, called Austro-Tai, and also lived in South China began to migrate across the Formosa Strait to Taiwan. Their subsequent migrations are relatively well-documented archaeologically, and the linguistic evidence for much of what follows is also strong. Those who remained behind on the mainland of South China stayed put for millennia, and in historic times began moving into Southeast Asia as the Thai, the Shan of northern Burma, and the Lao of Laos. Those who went to Taiwan began their linguistic differentiation, and about a thousand years later, possibly around 3500 B.C., began moving southward into the Philippines. Here Malayo-Polynesian began to develop. Eventually a western branch moved into the Indonesian Islands of Borneo, Sulawesi, Sumatra, Java, and Bali, while an eastern branch headed out into the Pacific where they became the Polynesian peoples (Bellwood 1992).

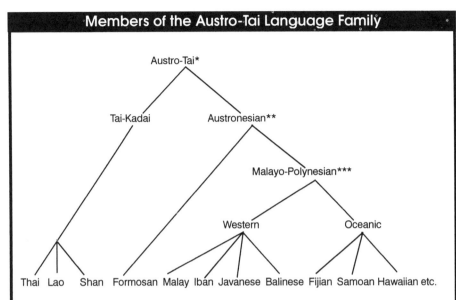

Members of the Austro-Tai Language Family

Austro-Tai*

Tai-Kadai   Austronesian**

Malayo-Polynesian***

Western   Oceanic

Thai Lao   Shan Formosan Malay Iban Javanese Balinese Fijian Samoan Hawaiian etc.

* *The Austro-Tai lived in South China prior to 4500 B.C., where they developed an economy based on rice cultivation. Their reconstructed lexicon contains words indicating a wet-rice adaptation: "field," "wet field," "garden," "plow," "rice," "sugarcane," the "betelnut complex," "cattle," "water buffalo," "axe," and "canoe." As populations grew, a group of these Austro-Tai speakers migrated across the Formosa Strait to Taiwan. Others stayed behind, and their languages became the Tai group, now reduced to areas of Southern China near the Laos and Vietnamese border. In historic times, some of these Tai began moving into Laos, Burma, and Thailand.*

** *On Taiwan, over the next thousand years new variants of the language emerged. This became the parent language known as Proto-Austronesian.*

*** *Around 3500 B.C. some of these Taiwanese set out for Luzon and settled the other Philippine Islands. The Malayo-Polynesian family began to emerge. As they then spread westward into the Indonesian Islands of Borneo, Sulawesi, Sumatra, Java, and Bali, and eastward into the Pacific, the economy of many of the groups again changed to suit equatorial conditions, and this is reflected in a new vocabulary: "taro," "breadfruit," "banana," "yam," "sago," "coconut." When they entered the Pacific, rice disappeared from their economy and from their language.*

The reconstructed proto-languages of Austro-Tai and Maiayo-Polynesian provide interesting evidence for the changes in the economies of peoples adapting to an equatorial environment. In the Proto-Austro-Tai lexicon are words for a wet-rice adaptation: "field," "wet field," "garden," "plow," "rice," "sugarcane," the "betelnut complex," "cattle," "water buffalo," "ax," and "canoe." A new set of terms appears in Proto-Malayo-Polynesian, indicating their new adaptation in the equatorial islands:

"taro," "breadfruit," "banana," "yam," "sago," "coconut." Rice disappears from the economy of the Malayo-Polynesians when they enter the Pacific.

Sino-Tibetan

This brings us to Sino-Tibetan. Surprisingly, Sino-Tibetan may be the least understood of all these language families. Though there have been scholars aplenty—for centuries—devoted to the study of Chinese, its vast written traditions have absorbed most of their energies. There has been far less interest in spoken forms of the language, and still less interest in establishing links between the elevated language of the Middle Kingdom and the most certainly lower forms of speech of western and southern Barbarians. As a result, as recently as a few decades ago, many scholars were still uncertain whether Chinese belonged with the Tibeto-Burman group at all. Tibeto-Burman consists of over a hundred poorly documented languages spoken mostly by small tribal groups, although a few of these, notably Tibetan and Burmese, have very important literary traditions. In fact, a seventh-century Tibetan text and a twelfth century Burmese text have been useful in reconstructing Proto-Tibeto-Burman.

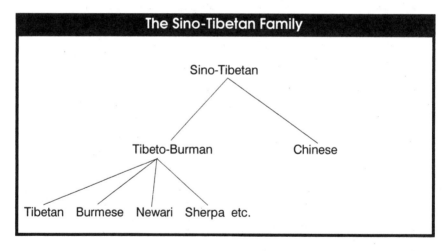

All the Sino-Tibetan languages are tonal, but so are a number of other nearby language families, like Tai-Kadai and Miao-Yao. Further, Chinese is one of the most purely isolating languages in the world; that is, its words, mostly monosyllabic, are very rarely modified with prefixes and suffixes (unlike English, Sanskrit, and Japanese, which are highly inflected languages). This, too, is a Sino-Tibetan characteristic, but Chinese is a more extreme form. However, the word order of the Chinese sentence is unlike the Tibeto-Burman languages: subject-verb-object (SVO) rather than subject-object-verb (SOV). (English also happens to be

SVO, a meaningless similarity since there are only six possible variations for all world languages to choose from, and only three are widespread.) That made Chinese the odd one out, and led some to doubt the existence of a Sino-Tibetan Family. However, when linguists got down to the exhausting job of comparing the core vocabulary of Chinese with the Tibeto-Burman languages, all doubts about their relationship vanished. Here is a sample:

	Chinese	Tibeto-Burman
sun, day	niet	*niy
name	mieng	*r-miŋ
neck, collar	lieng	*liŋ
tree, wood	sien	*siŋ
year	nien	*s-niŋ
fish	ngio	*ŋya
hair	sam	*tsam

Speakers of nontonal languages are usually intimidated by languages with tones, and don't quite understand how they work. In Chinese the issue is not really as terrifying as it seems. All languages need many thousands of words in order to talk about the wide ranges of topics humans want to discuss, and these words have to be constructed out of the limited number of sounds in their sound system (i.e., the phonemes). In order to construct enough words, most languages put together multisyllable words. With prefixes and suffixes, these can go to extremes, such as the infamous "antidisestablishmentarianism." Chinese, however, has opted for a lexicon of single-syllable words but gets quadruple duty out of them with their four-tone system. Take a simple word like *ba*. English only makes use of this as a quaint Dickensian expletive, as in "Bah humbug!" But in Chinese, meaning differences are conveyed by tones as well as by phonemes. If *ba* is spoken at a high-level pitch, it means "eight." If it is spoken at a high and rising pitch, it means "pull out." If it is spoken at a low falling-then-rising pitch, it means "grasp." If it is spoken with a high pitch that abruptly falls and stops, it means "dam." All of this requires that as a Chinese child learns her language, each new word has to be learned with its correct tone, not really such a difficult process. Even so, Chinese appears to have run short on words, as evidenced by the fact that there are a great number of homophones—words with identical pronunciations and tones but different meanings, like the English "to," "two," and "too." This has come about because of the simplification of Chinese morphemes over time. Once they had consonant-cluster beginnings (/ts/, /dj/, etc.) and final consonants, but most of these have disappeared, collapsing a set of words into a single consonant-vowel syllable such as those below.

Chinese Words Indicating the Four Tones							
bā	"eight"	bá	"pull out"	bǎ	"grasp"	bà	"dam"
xī	"tin"	xí	"mat"	xǐ	"wash"	xì	"opera"
līu	"slide"	liú	"flow"	liǔ	"willow"	liù	"six"

Column one is high level; column two is high and rising; column three is low-falling, then rising; column four is high pitch that falls abruptly and stops.

China's four-tone system is actually a bit on the simple side as tonal languages go in Asia. James Matisoff writes:

> It is Miao-Yao which is the tonal champion among the tone-prone languages of East Asia. Most dialects of Miao have more than 5 tones, and most dialects of Yao Mien have 6–8, though some have more than 10. The Pu-nu dialect of Yao provides a good example of the tonal virtuosity and "tone-consciousness" of the people of this linguistic area. Pu-nu already has 8 tones of its own in native syllables; but for words which it has borrowed from Chuang and (recently) from Chinese, it has gone to the trouble of introducing three new "foreign" tones, which it keeps distinct from the 8 others! Much can be crammed into the monosyllables of these languages, but there are limits! (Matisoff 1983:84)

The above shows how easily languages can borrow tones. It is believed that some Asian languages, such as Vietnamese, that were originally nontonal became tonal by borrowing tone systems from their neighbors. Matisoff thinks that Sino-Tibetan was the original "stronghold of tonality," and that the originally atonal Miao-Yao, Tai-Kadai, and Vietnamese acquired their tone systems from the culturally dominant influence of Chinese. The ancestors of the Miao (who call themselves Hmong) may once have been widely distributed throughout North China, and perhaps were the original millet cultivators in the Wei Valley.

Let us turn to the question of a Sino-Tibetan homeland. We have seen evidence of a Proto-Austro-Tai-speaking people inhabiting southeast China who must have been at the coast in order for some of them to spread to Taiwan. Others (the Tai, some of whom later became the Thai, Lao, and Shan) stayed on in southern China, while some spread to the south and west. It seems likely, then, that a different language group, the Proto-Sino-Tibetan speakers, were settled west of the Proto-Austro-Tai in the foothills of the eastern Himalayas, in the Sichuan and Yunnan provinces. When the last glaciation receded, some of them must have moved

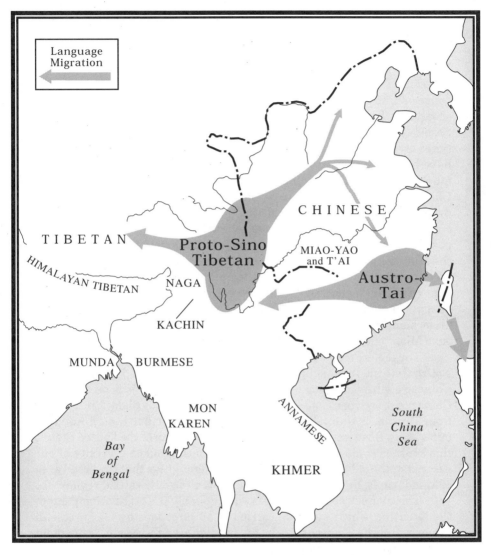

Map 3.2   Hypothetical Distribution of Proto-Sino-Tibetan

up into the headwaters of the Yangtze, Brahmaputra, Irrawadi, and Mekong around 4000 B.C. (Matisoff 1991). From there, one subgroup, the Tibeto-Burmans, followed the Brahmaputra into the Tibetan Plateau, or followed the Irrawadi and Salween south into Burma, where their languages continued to diverge. But another subgroup moved northeast, into the valleys of the Huanghe and Wei Rivers. These were the Chinese speakers.

These proto-Chinese speakers were surely not the original inhabitants of this central Huanghe region. Remember Choukoutien—there is record of continuous human habitation throughout these long millennia. The Chinese have no tradition of a migration from elsewhere, but their consciousness of an ethnic difference from other peoples in early texts suggests a multilinguistic situation from early on. The earliest records · speak of a Ti people to the north (possibly Altaic speakers) and a Jung people to the west (possibly Miao) with whom the ruling families sometimes arranged marriages. The original inhabitants of North China may have been the mysterious Miao; "mysterious" because there has been much speculation regarding this last language family from southern China, Laos, and Thailand to be accounted for. During the first Chinese dynasties, Shang and Zhou, a distinction was made between the aristocrats, designated by the phrase "the hundred surnames," and the peasants, the *min* (people). The people who came to know themselves as the Han (93 percent of modern China) have probably descended from a mix of early Chinese-speaking elites and the indigenous people with whom they intermarried. In the process they affected each other's languages. The SVO word order of Chinese may have been borrowed from Miao, along with some vocabulary, such as the word for dog. And Chinese gave Miao tones.

The dialect map for Chinese (see map 3.3) presents us with a puzzle. Notice that the region of greatest diversity is not the old center of early Chinese civilization on the Wei and Huanghe Rivers. It is on the south China coast between Canton and Shanghai. The Amoy dialect, just across from Taiwan, is unintelligible to anyone much further than a hundred miles away. If we were to compare it to a dialect map of the United States, this southeast coast would be equivalent to the dialect diversity of our east coast, the oldest settled area, and we might guess that the broad area of Mandarin is, like the Midwest and West, a recently settled region.

The complex south coast area was probably the originating point of the Neolithic, which was then carried in all directions by the successful farmers. But the Chinese state began to emerge on the North China plain in the second millennium B.C. Since then, according to Jerry Norman (1988), Chinese has evolved under the influence of two competing forces: first, the spread of Chinese to ever more marginal areas, and second, the conscious imposition of a standard dialect—Mandarin—throughout the empire to achieve greater uniformity. Interesting comparisons can be made between Chinese and Roman imperial expansion in the last few centuries B.C. and first few centuries A.D. The language of Rome, Latin, was carried to France and Spain through imperial conquest and colonization. Similarly, early Chinese was carried south and east by the Qin and Han dynasties. For instance, in 221 B.C. the First Emperor ordered half a million military families to settle in the newly conquered lands of the "Yue

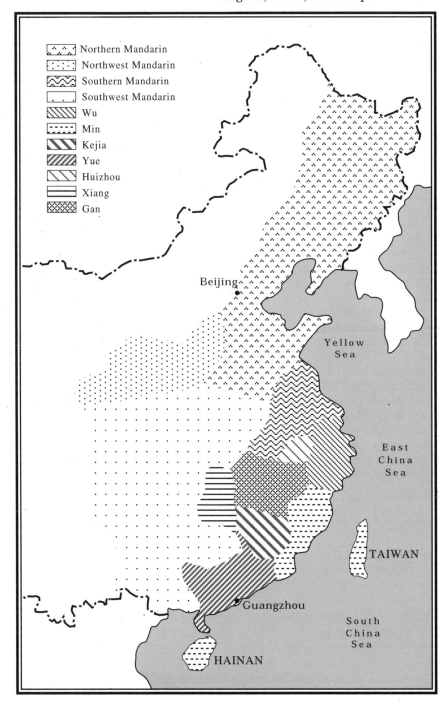

Map 3.3   Dialect Map of China

3.1 "Written Symbol" Is Its Name

Greatly may I be forgiven for my intention to call forth a story.
And where dwells the story?
There is a god unsupported by the divine mother earth,
Unsheltered by the sky,
Unilluminated by the sun, moon, stars, or constellations.
Yes, Lord, you dwell in the void, and are situated thus:
You reside in a golden jewel,
Regaled on a golden palanquin,
Umbrellaed by a floating lotus.
There approached in audience by all the gods of the cardinal directions. . . .
There, there are the young palm leaves, the one *lontar,*
Which, when taken and split apart, carefully measured are the lengths and
  widths.
It is this which is brought to life with *hasta, gangga, uwira, taru.*
And what are the things so named?
Hasta means "hand"
Gangga means "water"
Uwira means "writing instrument"
Taru means "ink."
What is that which is called "ink"?
That is the name for
And none other than
The smoke of the oil lamp,
Collected on the bark of the kepuh-tree,
On a base of copper leaf.
It is these things which are gathered together
And given shape on leaf.
"Written symbol" is its name,
Of one substance and different soundings.

Translation from a Balinese text by Mary Zurbuchen, quoted in A. L. Becker, 1995.

people." In the process of colonization in Europe, Latin diverged into Italian, French, Spanish, Rumanian, and Portuguese; while in China, Chinese diverged into Mandarin, Gan, Xiang, Hakka, Wu, Min, and Cantonese. These two families are roughly comparable in age and degree of difference between the daughter languages. However, there the similarity ends. For the Roman Empire never again rose to claim its old territories and assert the unity of its diversifying language(s), to claim them all as mere dialects of Latin; whereas that is exactly what China did. There is one language, Chinese, and its dialects are called *fangyan*, "regional speech." Chinese speak of "picking up" one of the other regional speeches but do not think of themselves as "learning another language" as an Italian learning French would say. Nor has there been a time in Chinese history, even during periods of disunity, when a region asserted its independence by the sort of linguistic nationalism that divides India, another place where the Latin model, not the Chinese model, has been followed.

The diversity we see in South China on the dialect map has therefore been growing for the last two thousand years. At the same time, the dialect of the Beijing area, Mandarin, has dominated since the fifteenth century. Called *guanhua*, the "language of the officials," it is spoken everywhere north of the Yangtze. It even has its own dialects. Thus, it is repeating the early history of Chinese, moving southward, diversifying, and absorbing earlier dialects in its wake (Norman 1988).

TEXTS

"You Are Hurting My Language"

The linguist A. L. Becker describes his first lesson in writing Burmese at the beginning of three years of study with a kindly old teacher, U San Htwe:

> As I had been taught to do, I would ask him words for things and then write them down. He watched me writing for a while and then said, "That's not how you write it," and he wrote the word in Burmese script. For the word evoked by English "speak," I wrote
>
> / ပယ၁ / and he wrote ၆ ၆ၥ. I insisted it made no difference. He insisted it did and told me I was hurting his language. And so I began, somewhat reluctantly, to learn to write Burmese: /p—/ was a central ပ , and /-y-/ wrapped around the ပ to make ၍ and the vowel /၆ —၁ / fit before and after it: ၆၍၁.

> This difference in medial representation made a great difference . . . I could not segment the Burmese syllable into a linear sequence. . . . But segmentation into linear sequence is a prerequisite for doing linguistics as most of us have been taught it. . . . To write my kind of grammar I had to violate his writing.

> At first it seemed to me a small price to pay, to phonemicize his language. But over the years—particularly twenty years later, in Java and Bali—I learned how that kind of written figure (a center and marks above, below, before, and after it; the figure of the Burmese and Javanese and Balinese syllable) was for many Southeast Asians a mnemonic frame: everything in the encyclopedic repertoire of terms was ordered that way: directions (the compass rose), diseases, gods, colors, social roles, foods—everything. It was the natural shape of remembered knowledge, a basic icon. (Becker 1995: 195)

This respect for writing, even to the single syllable, is pervasive throughout Asia. The mystery of capturing a sound in an inscribed symbol is thought to be divine. The name for the script of Sanskrit and the North Indian vernaculars, *devanagari*, suggests the writing of the gods (Horton 1992), and the earliest form, *brahmi*, meant "of Brahma," God. In early Japan, when writing was first borrowed from China, "its very words were pregnant with spiritual power, called 'word-mana' [*kotodama*]" (Horton 1992). When early writers began writing Japanese rather than just reading and copying Chinese, it was to write Japanese poetry once chanted orally and infused with kotodama. And about China, Chiang Yee writes:

> In every district of a Chinese city, and even in the smallest village, there is a little pagoda built for the burning of waste paper bearing writing. This we call *Hsi-Tzu-T'a*—Pagoda of Compassionating the Characters. For we respect characters so highly that we cannot bear them to be trampled under foot or thrown away into some distasteful place. (Yee 1973)

The sacredness of the captured word probably follows from the nature of what was written down in the earliest texts. Although some have argued that writing began in the Middle East as a way for merchants to keep track of their stock and sales, there is no evidence for a similar mundane origin of writing in Asia. Rather, writing began in China three thousand years ago to communicate with the ancestors; in India it was first used to declare the Buddhist message throughout King Ashoka's realm, and then to write down the sacred Sanskrit hymns of the Vedas that had been passed on orally for a millennium. When writing came to Southeast Asia, it came embodying Hindu and Buddhist teachings. How could the written word not be sacred, when all that was captured in it was?

The Search for Sacred Texts

The scripts with which to record sacred words were invented only twice in the whole of Asia, and all other scripts are adaptations of those originals. But before I turn to that story, there is the story of the texts to be told. Sacred texts spread through Asia in many directions and by many means. Priests carried them to serve kings and religious communities far from home. Pilgrims set out on long journeys seeking authoritative texts from their source. Adventurers sought hidden libraries and plundered them. Poor or unscrupulous dealers trafficked in stolen texts and occasionally created ingenious forgeries. Texts were translated from one language to the next, and the next.

In China, the process of getting Sanskrit texts translated into Chinese was tedious. Few Chinese ever learned Sanskrit, and finding ways to convey multisyllabic Sanskrit words into monosyllabic Chinese was not easy. For instance, the Sanskrit word, *nirvana*, was translated *niepan*, meaning "opaque place of retirement." And in the early years the "texts" were often oral and required translation teams of four persons: one to recite the oral Sanskrit, one to write the Sanskrit down (usually two monks from India), one to orally translate the Sanskrit into spoken Chinese, and one to record the oral Chinese into written Chinese (Tanabe 1988). You can imagine how cumbersome this process was. It also shows how closely linked were orality, text reading, and text writing. Recent studies of the performance of texts and the ethnography of reading show that the silent, lonely room in the mind where a reader is alone with his private decoding of the text and his private thoughts is a rarer and more recent phenomenon than we have supposed.

One of the most important of the early text gatherers was a Chinese pilgrim named Xuanzang, who grew up in the chaos following the fall of the Sui dynasty in A.D. 618, when the only books being studied, he complained, were military texts. He studied under two great Buddhist monks at Chang-an, but finding the Buddhist texts few, incomplete, and conflicting (probably because of the translation method described above), he resolved to go to India to acquire the originals. He was only twenty-eight years old when he left, in A.D. 630, and his lengthy record of his journey is one of the most important sources we have on early seventh-century India. (Xuanzang was not the first Chinese pilgrim to go to India in search of texts; two hundred years earlier, Faxian had made a similar journey, also to collect texts and visit the sites associated with the Buddha, and he, also, left an important record of his journey.) Crossing through the thirsty wastes of the great central deserts, endangered by bandits but also aided by devout rulers, Xuanzang finally reached India. There he visited all the major Buddhist sites and spent five years at Nalanda, learning Sanskrit and studying the Buddhist texts.

In India, Xuanzang found the Indian method of book making remarkable. Indians wrote on palm leaves and strung the leaves together on a string. Two types of palms, talipat and palmyra, were suitable (in Southeast Asia, the lontar palm is also used). Each leaf had to be cut from its central spine, trimmed to size, boiled in milk or water several times, and finally rubbed smooth with a cowry shell or stone. They could be written on with ink or incised with a stylus, and the type of writing implement affected the emergence of scripts, as we shall see. The disadvantage of palm leaves is their vulnerability to humidity and insects, which is why very few palm-leaf manuscripts older than the sixteenth century exist. They require tremendous care; they are kept wrapped in cloth when not in use, and have to be recopied frequently. They have survived better in dry climates outside India and Southeast Asia. In 608, twenty-two years before Xuanzang left for India, a Japanese envoy brought an Indian palmyra-leaf text that he had acquired from Sui dynasty China to Japan,

This book of genealogies is still in use today, though its style is ancient. Leaves are made of paper rather than palm leaf, but they are cut to the shape of the old palm leaves and are joined together by a string running through each page. Such books are stored wrapped in cloth to protect them from insects.

and it is still there, the oldest in existence (Tanabe 1988)! The fragility of texts probably contributed to the Buddhist notion of the fragility of *Dharma*, in continuous decay since the time of Buddha's existence on earth and constantly requiring protection and renewal.

Xuanzang was used to texts written on silk that could be hung or rolled up in a scroll to be stored compactly, although by his time paper was already in frequent use. Because silk was costly, the Chinese invented paper as an alternative as early as A.D. 105, at first by recycling old silk rags and later cheaper linen. The rags were first allowed to rot, then they were cleaned, bleached, pulped, mixed with wheat flour, and finally spread on a frame to dry in sheets. These sheets were then glued together in great lengths, typically twenty feet long, which could be rolled up like silk scrolls for storage (Tanabe 1988).

Xuanzang was a member of the intellectual elite of his time, in search of philosophical-religious texts, but these texts and the arguments they contained were embedded in a worldview where everything associated with the Buddha—himself no longer in existence—radiated power or spiritual merit. As a devotee, Xuanzang describes being overcome with emotion at sites where Buddha once taught or where relics of the Buddha's body were enshrined in a *stupa*. He later recalled the power of these places: "A mysterious sense of awe surrounds the spot; many miracles occur. Sometimes heavenly odors are perceived" (Hopkirk 1980). Fifteen years later, in 645, when he finally returned to the Monastery of Extensive Happiness in Chang-an, he deposited six statues of Buddha in various acts, 657 texts carried on twenty horses, and 150 particles of the Buddha's flesh. We should think of these not as eccentric or grisly souvenirs but as Dharma itself transported to China. The objects were at once symbols, carriers, and extensions of Dharma. The texts, the Buddha relics, and the images shared in the power of Buddha himself.

This began a whole new era of translating and then of "sutra copying," both in China and in Japan. There was first of all the task of translating the new works brought back by Xuanzang. In catalogs of Buddhist texts made two centuries later, the Chinese Buddhist canon had grown to 1,076 and then to 1,258 works. At first the concern was just to get good Chinese translations in an efficient manner, but later it became an act of religious merit making to have them copied. The wealthy employed monk-scribes, or if they were talented, copied the sutras themselves. Emperors commissioned copies of the entire canon, and for this, large official bureaus were set up and permanently staffed. Finally, attention turned to making them beautiful. The first sheets of scrolls were often decorated with scenes from the sutra that followed, and sometimes the paper was dyed a deep indigo and the sutra written in gold characters. Many of these have survived in Japan, with a postscript noting that the sutra had been commissioned by Empress Shotoku or Lady Fujiwara or Emperor Shomu to transfer merit to specific ancestors.

One of the places Xuanzang stopped for a little while on the outward and return trips was Dunhuang, at that time China's western outpost, the "Jade Gate" through which caravans left for the perils of the Taklamakan and the western world. Here there was a great Buddhist monastery carved into a mile of stony cliffs known as the "Caves of the Thousand Buddhas." Of more than a thousand caves, 469 still exist. For fifteen hundred years monks and devout laymen filled these grottoes with paintings and sculptures and earned merit by commissioning copies of sacred texts.

Dunhuang continued in use, though much reduced in importance, into the twentieth century, unlike many similar sites more in the reach of the desert. In one of the first years of the twentieth century, a Taoist priest named Wang Yuan-lu made a stupendous discovery. While carrying out an ambitious but underfunded and poorly conceptualized revamping of some of the caves, he discovered a concealed room that had been bricked

In this photo, taken at Dunhuang in 1907 by Aurel Stein, the secret door to the hidden chamber can be seen on the right. Found a short while earlier by a Taoist priest, the chamber, containing thousands of manuscripts, had been walled up 900 years earlier. Some of them are piled outside the door for inspection by Stein. Stein talked the old caretaker out of 13,000 of the manuscripts.

over around A.D. 1000. Yanking out some of the bricks, he was astonished to find thousands upon thousands of manuscripts, a whole library, in a dozen languages or more. Wang was no scholar, and actually reading these scrolls was not high priority for him. But he reverenced them because they contained the teachings of Lord Buddha and the labor of unknown thousands of monks who had lived and studied at Dunhuang since the fourth century, and he was willing to part with a few of them—there were so many!—in order to fund the repaintings of frescoes and other repairs he was trying to carry out. He notified the local authorities of his find, but they did not seem to have any clear idea about what should be done next—notifying scholars in Beijing does not seem to have occurred to them—so they told Wang to leave the manuscripts where they were.

Not long after, in 1907, the British explorer and archaeologist Sir Aurel Stein arrived in Dunhuang by camel in the middle of a freezing sandstorm. He was in a fine mood because he had just discovered the long-lost westward extension of the Great Wall mentioned in Chinese annals. What happened next still infuriates the Chinese and appears to have shamed even Britain, for in the Central Asian gallery of the British Museum, where many of the manuscripts ended up, it is difficult to find even a trace of Sir Aurel Stein. Stein got wind of Wang's finds and, together with his Chinese assistant, stayed around for several weeks, trying to find a way to weasel some of the manuscripts from Wang. Stein, it must be said, had as much respect for ancient manuscripts as anyone, though for scholarly reasons rather than for religious ones. He truly believed that to acquire the manuscripts and take them to India, and then to London, was to rescue them from oblivion and possible destruction.[1] Moreover, he considered Xuanzang his patron saint because, like the ancient Chinese pilgrim, Stein, too, criss-crossed the dangerous deserts of Central Asia looking for traces of the Buddha and his followers. This was a happy coincidence, because a local artist had just finished murals commissioned by Wang, depicting scenes in the life of Xuanzang. So imagine the impact it had when the very first manuscript Wang drew at random from the pile to allow Stein to examine carried a final colophon that the translation had been done by Xuanzang himself from originals he had personally carried from India.

Stein describes the scene in the little room: "Heaped up in layers, but without any order, there appeared in the dim light of the priest's little lamp a solid mass of manuscript bundles rising to a height of nearly ten feet, and filling, as subsequent measurement showed, close on 500 cubic feet." He managed to talk the dedicated priest out of thirteen thousand manuscripts, seven thousand in Chinese, the rest in other languages. Because Stein could not read Chinese, his selection was on the basis of age and condition more than on the importance of the text. Had he known that a thousand of them were copies of the Lotus Sutra, he might have been more selective. The most famous of all was a copy of the Diamond Sutra. Although there are many manuscripts of the Diamond Sutra in existence, this work is famous because it was block-printed on seven pieces of paper joined together, with a block-print illustration on the first sheet. It bears a date, 864, which makes it the oldest printed book in existence. It can now be seen in the British Museum near the Gutenberg Bible. A Chinese scholar in a National Library of Peking publication describes the Diamond Sutra and adds: "This famous scroll was stolen over fifty years ago by the Englishman Ssu-t'an-yin [Stein] which causes people to gnash their teeth in bitter hatred" (Hopkirk 1980).

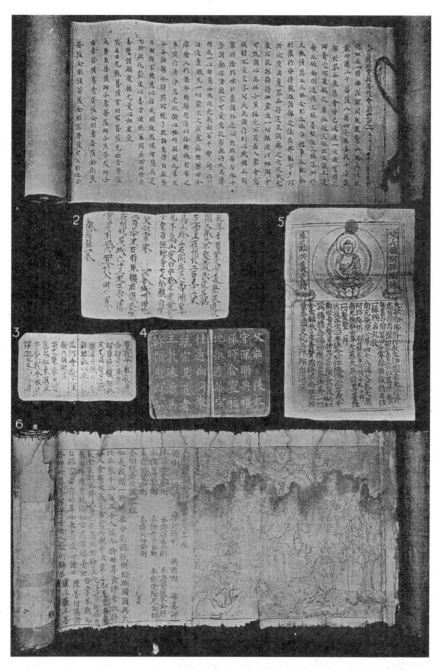

These manuscripts, taken from Dunhuang by Aurel Stein, include a copy of the Lotus Sutra (bottom). It is a roll of block-printed Buddhist texts with a frontispiece from a wood engraving. The book carries a date of A.D. 864, making it the oldest printed book in the world. It is now in the British Museum.

SCRIPTS

The two major families of scripts that dominate in Asia are based on principles different from the Roman alphabet that we use. The alphabet used for writing English is phonetic; theoretically, there is a graph for each sound, both consonants and vowels. In reality, the correspondence between the actual sounds of spoken English and the twenty-six graphs[2] available for writing it is not good. What sound does /c/ correspond to? Is it /k/ as in "picnic"? Or is it /s/ as in "implicit"? We could really use a separate graph for /ch/ as in "church," and while we are at it, we could add a single graph for /sh/ as in "shame," something to stand for the soft /g/ in "corsage" (for people who don't already pronounce it with a /j/), and for the /ng/ in "singing." Perhaps we are most in need of graphs for vowels, such as the different /a/'s in "father," "famous," and "fashion." However, imperfect though it is, the logic of our system is one-sound-one-graph, and vowels count the same as consonants.

We have already seen a different system at work in Burma. That system focuses on the syllable, and the core of the syllable is its consonant. The sense of speech is different in these languages. Speech is made up of so many consonants modified by vowels. In writing speech, you write consonants, then put marks above, below, behind, and in front of it to indicate vowels. So in the Tamil script of South India, /pa/ is written ப, /pa/ is written பா, /pi/ is பி , /pu/ is பு, /po/ is போ, /pai/ is பை , and /pau/ is பௌ. A typewriter for these languages allows you to make a consonant sign, then instead of moving ahead automatically, it sits there while you decide where the vowel marks go.

The syllabic systems of Tamil and Burmese came originally from India. The earliest known Indian script is found on forty-foot-high columns set up by King Ashoka around 250 B.C. to mark the boundaries of his empire and to proclaim Buddhism as the law of the land. This script, now known as Ashokan Brahmi, was deciphered in the nineteenth century by James Prinsep, who worked for the East India Company. A sure sign of its antiquity was the fact that even the Brahmans could not read it. When the first Englishmen saw it, they guessed it might be Greek, but how Greek came to be written on columns in Delhi, Allahabad, and Bihar was anyone's guess. What is usually needed in deciphering ancient scripts is a key text such as the famous Rosetta stone where the same inscription is recorded in both a known script and an unknown one. It turned out that Ashokan Brahmi was not Greek, but an ancestor of Devanagari, in which Sanskrit is written, and there was an intermediate script, now known as Gupta Brahmi, in use during the Gupta Empire from A.D. 319–550. Once Gupta Brahmi was translated, they could work backward to Ashokan Brahmi. The key for Prinsep was a number of stone

This section of an Ashokan column erected around 250 B.C. contains the earliest surviving examples of brahmi, *a forerunner of modern* devanagari.

columns that circle an ancient Buddhist stupa at Sanchi in Central India. He wrote to a friend: "The Sanchi inscriptions have enlightened me. Each line is engraved on a separate pillar or railing. Then, thought I, they must be the gifts of private individuals where names will be recorded. All end in *danam* [i.e., the Brahmi graphs for danam]—that must mean 'gift' or 'given'" (Keay 1988:52). So danam gave him the d, n, and m, and from there he was able to decode the rest.

Below is a line of Brahmi script. You will notice that there is one character per syllable, with a special graph for a vowel that begins a word: u-pa-sa-ka, etc. Noninitial vowels are indicated by modifying the consonants with little added marks.

Brahmi Inscription

Brahmi Inscription: Upasaka-Nagamitaha bariyaya upasika-Silaya lele sagasa, "The Cave of the female lay-devotee, Shila, wife of the lay-devotee Nagamitta, [is given] to the Sangha."

Source: Maloney 1974:37.

For instance, the third graph, $\wedge$, is /sh/. Without any modification, the vowel associated with *sh* is assumed to be a; this is called the "inherent *a*." Thirteen graphs later, it reappears with a little *7* on the top, making it /shi/: λ. The vowel /i/ appears with /mi/ ψ and /ri/ γ . The vowel /e/ is seen in the second /l/: /la/ Ω and /le/ λ, and in /ne/: Υ . With just this much knowledge, you could predict other Brahmi syllables.

It is unknown where Brahmi originated. Some have supposed that the still-undeciphered script of Indus Valley (see chapter 5) may be its ancestor, but most scholars doubt that. It has important resemblances to Semitic scripts of the Middle East, especially in its emphasis on consonants. Semitic scripts in their earliest forms did not show vowels at all; one had to guess that "k-t-b" meant *kitab*, "book." Later, little marks were placed above, below, and beside the consonants to indicate vowels, and this is the form in which it must have been brought to India. But there is no historical trace of its route or date or means of arrival in India. At any rate, this is the script used by Ashoka, and the script of the earliest Hindu and Buddhist texts was later forms of it. All major scripts of South and Southeast Asia descended from Brahmi, but, of course, they had to be adapted to the very different languages that they had to serve. In Southeast Asia, where the materials for writing were until very recently the palm leaf and iron stylus, the graphs evolved in rounded forms that would not damage the leaves. In North India, where pen and ink were used, the distinctive "clothes hanging from a clothesline" style developed, where the line over the top connects graphs for individual words. Such a line, made with a stylus, could damage the palm leaf. Like Brahmi, each consonant graph has either an inherent *a*, or an attached sign to indicate the vowel:

क	कि	की	के	कु	कू	को	कौ
ka	ki	kī	ke	ku	kū	ko	kau

Written Chinese

The word for civilization in Chinese is *wenming*. In written form it is composed of two graphs: the graph for *wen* (writing) and the graph for *ming* (understanding). To be civilized has always been a marked feature of Chinese self-identity; to be civilized was to understand writing. The Chinese have had a fully developed script since at least the fourteenth century B.C., and emergent forms can be traced back six thousand years. The most remarkable fact is that this script has been in continuous use ever since, and the script used in the twentieth century is a direct descendant of the earliest forms.

The discovery of the earliest forms of Chinese writing came about much the same way as the discovery of Peking man fossils: ancient specimens inscribed on bones and tortoise carapaces were classified as dragon bones and ground up as a cure for fever (Chou 1979). In the year 1899, a Peking scholar named Wang Yi-jung was taking doses of dragon bones for his malaria. When he ran short, he asked his house guest, who was also a scholar, to go to the apothecary for a refill. As this man watched the dragon bones being freshly ground, he noticed strange markings on them and had a closer look. He thought the markings looked like old forms of Chinese writing, but they were not immediately readable. Wang and his friend bought all the remaining fragments of bone, and then asked about the source. Over the next few years, this amazing discovery led Chinese scholars to rediscover the ancient history of their own written language. In excavations carried out between 1928 and 1937 at five sites, all around what proved to be the ancient capital of Shang dynasty, Anyang, over twenty thousand specimens were found, and eventually the number grew to one hundred thousand.

The ancient Chinese communicated with their ancestors, and occasionally with a shadowy deity named Shangdi ("Emperor of Heaven"), by writing questions directed to them on the shoulderblades of oxen or on the carapaces of turtles. These have come to be called oracle bones. The questions were written twice, once in the affirmative and once in the negative: "Will Lady Hao be in good health after she gives birth to her baby?" "Will Lady Hao not be in good health after she gives birth to her baby?" These were then heated by holding a red-hot iron to the back of an inscription until the bone cracked. The diviner looked for—and tried to produce—a crack resembling the Chinese character *pu*, signifying an affirmative answer. Thus, the question was conveyed and the ancestor replied.

Knowing how the Roman alphabet evolved is not particularly helpful in understanding any of its written languages, but for an English speaker trying to understand Chinese writing, it is helpful to know how the graphs came to be formed in earliest times.

The Chinese graph is logographic; that is, each graph represents a word, and as we have already seen, in Chinese each word is generally a single syllable.[3] There are very few words like the English word "river" or "elephant" where meaning is carried across two or three syllables. There are two types of logographs in Chinese, simple and complex. Box 3.2 shows some simple ones. The first column consists of ancient forms, the second column their corresponding modern forms, and the third column their pronunciation in Mandarin. A large number of the earliest simple graphs were fairly obvious pictures of the things they referred to: the sun, rain falling from a cloud, a man walking, a woman kneeling, a child with a head large in proportion to its body, a man in a cell, a kneeling man with his hands raised in surrender, etc. Graphs for less easily drawn words

Box 3.2 Simple Chinese Logographs in Ancient and Modern Form

⛒	日	ʈʉ̀	'sun/day'
⌢	雨	y̌	'rain'
⚡	水	ʂuěi	'river/water'
🐟	魚	ý	'fish'
𝄢	人	ʈə́n	'man' (i.e. human being)
𝄢	女	nỹ	'woman'
⛝	口	kʰǒu	'mouth'
⌀	目	mù	'eye'
	眉	méi	'eyebrow'
⅄	木	mù	'tree'
	其	cī	'winnowing-basket'
	子	ʨʉ̌	'child'
	兼	ciēn	'to have two at once' (hand holding two arrows)
	若	ʈuò	'yield, conform'
	東	tūŋ	'east' (sun behind tree)
	囚	ciōu	'prisoner' (man in cell)
	好	xàu	'love' (woman and child)
	妞	nuàn	'quarrel' (two women)
	言	jén	'flute'
	辟	pì	'prince'

Sampson, 1985, p. 24.

could be made by combining them: "love" is the graph for mother plus the graph for child. "Prisoner" is a man in a cell; "east" is the sun behind a tree; "quarrel" is two women side by side; "flute" is a mouth with a reed; and so on. There are a thousand or so of these simple graphs.

A writing system cannot get very far with pictures alone. To make up more words, scribes began adapting words that were picturable to make words that sounded similar (or at least they did in the language as it was spoken at that time). Let's look at how this worked using English rather than Chinese. In English the word "sun" (picturable) sounds like the word "son." You could use the sun graph for both, and let the correct meaning be deduced from context. You could go on with this process:

= sun

= son

= soon

= sung

= sin

= shun

Graphs like this were roughly *phonetic*; a single graph that once stood specifically for a single word came to stand for a whole set of similar-sounding words. But you can imagine that if the system kept on like this, it would eventually get tremendously confusing. So ancient Chinese scribes developed another device for sorting them out. Another set of elements, known as "significs," were developed to combine with phonetics to give the reader a clue as to which meaning was intended. For instance, the graph for "man" could be combined with the graph for "sun" to indicate "son"—i.e., "the man-type of sun." A graph for an open mouth could be combined with "sun" to mean "sung." The mouth and man graphs could also be combined with other elements to create other words. Because of these combinations, Chinese graphs can be learned and remembered more easily than might be imagined, since constituent elements show up again and again.

All these combined elements are written with great elegance in a single imagined square, so they all take up roughly the same amount of space, unlike English words that vary tremendously in the space it takes to write them out. A Chinese graph may have two strokes, such as in the graph for "man," or thirty or more in a very complex graph, but they will both take up the same size square. These are then written in vertical rows beginning on the right hand side. And because of the monosyllabic nature of spoken Chinese, each graph will (usually) be pronounced as a single-syllable word.

One of the virtues of the Chinese system of writing is the very fact that there is no direct connection between the graph and its pronunciation. This means that any given graph can be called by whatever word is used in the various dialects of Chinese, so that it does not matter if all Chinese do not speak the same dialect; they all read the same script. It works much like the numerals in Europe, where the numeral 1 is called "one" in English, *un* in French, *eins* in German, and *uno* in Spanish. This feature may be the single most important factor in the historic unity of the Chinese cultural world.

In the last several decades, the People's Republic of China has attempted two far-reaching reforms of the written language. The first reform is an attempted simplification of many of the old multistroke graphs; this has been received with only so-so success, and has not been adopted by Chinese communities outside the People's Republic of China. The second reform has to do with the way spoken Chinese is transcribed into the Roman alphabet. The old system, known as the Wade-Giles system, involved many digraphs and apostrophes, and was often quite misleading as to actual pronunciation. Mao Tse-tung, T'ang, *ts'ao-shu, jen* (pronounced "run"), etc., are examples of Wade-Giles. The new system, pinyin, is the method Beijing has urged all writers and publishers everywhere to adopt. However, it is questionable whether this new system is really less ambiguous. Most non-Chinese speakers find *qin* and *xia* more puzzling than the Wade-Giles *ch'in* and *hsia*. (In this book we are usually following pinyin except in a few well-known Wade-Giles transliterations.)

Korean and Japanese

Both Korea and Japan were deeply influenced by China when, in the first few centuries of the common era, they began forming state systems. China was the sun and they were moons reflecting her cultural glory. Each copied or attempted to copy major institutions wholesale. Korea tried to become a *sohwa*, a "small China." Among other things, both countries borrowed China's script, having none of their own.

On purely linguistic grounds, this was probably not a wise thing to have done. Chinese writing was wonderfully suited to the grammatically simple, tonal, and monosyllabic nature of the Chinese language, but Korean and Japanese had not even the remotest connection to the Sino-Tibetan family. Korean is one of the Altaic languages (including Mongolian, Tartar, and Turkish), and Japanese may be also, although there is a lot of uncertainty about that right now. At any rate, both languages are polysyllabic, atonal, and highly inflectional; that is, verb forms change by adding a variety of different endings to perform various functions in the sentence. This is something written Chinese does not have the capacity to do.

However, Chinese was the only script available during the critical period. And so both Koreans and Japanese struggled for centuries to make Chinese writing work for their very different languages. The result in Japan was "quite an astonishingly complicated method of making language visible" (Sampson 1985).

There was another factor beyond the language difficulties contributing to the complexity of written Japanese. To quote G. Sampson:

> Japanese society, during much of the period in which the script was developed, was characterized by the existence of an aristocratic class many members of which lacked political power or indeed any serious employment, so that their only role in life was as definers and producers of cultural norms, ways of civilized living. As a natural result, many aspects of Japanese culture, including its writing, were greatly elaborated, made exquisite and intellectually rich rather than straightforwardly functional. (This contrasts with the case of China, which at most periods of its history was a rather down-to-earth, workaday civilization and where the script, for instance, was shaped in the historical period largely by civil servants who had plenty to keep them busy.) (Sampson 1985: 172–73)

This contrast, however, is no longer true. The Japanese writing system, complicated though it is, works fine for one of the most hard-working and technologically advanced societies in the world. Moreover, Japan has one of the highest literacy rates in the world; at 99 percent, it is higher than the United States, France, and many other industrialized nations. And dyslexia is practically unknown.

Let's take it one step at a time. First, Japan adopted Chinese writing along with a whole literature—Buddhist and Confucian texts, poetry, and prose—in Chinese. Inevitably, an enormous number of Chinese loanwords merged into the Japanese lexicon during those first few centuries (from the seventh century on). Even today, when the Japanese need to coin new words, they turn to Chinese roots as we turn to Greek and Latin ones. The graphs, taken more or less directly from Chinese and still used in that form, are known as *kanji*, from the Chinese *hanzi*, "Han characters."

When Japanese tried to write native words and sentences, the problems were immense. While the writing system was still the plaything of an idle elite, ingenious adaptations were created, which made reading a matter of clever decoding and elegant word play. But eventually a syllabic script emerged. The Koreans had invented a syllable system (not Han'gul, an earlier one) in which the first four syllables were *ka-na-ta-ra*, and the Japanese used the first two, *kana*, to refer to their own similar efforts (in the same way, "alphabet" comes from the first two letters of the Greek alphabet). Each kana graph stands for a consonant + vowel combination since almost all Japanese syllables take that form. There are actually two kanas: *hiragana* (plain kana) and *katakana* (partial kana). Both sets were constructed by simplifying kanji graphs, and both are perfect matches for each of the forty-nine syllables of the Japanese language.

In modern writing, all three can be used together. Kanji graphs are used for morphemes like verb roots and nouns. Hiragana is used for inflections at the ends of verbs and nouns (like "-ing" and "-ed" in English) and also to spell out grammatical morphemes that are equivalent to English "of," "the," etc. Katakana is used for loanwords from foreign languages other than Chinese and to spell out foreign names.

Korea went through much the same trials for centuries, but finally, in the fifteenth century, King Sejong (1418–1450) invented a new script. He set up a "Bureau of Standard Sounds" and appointed a group of scholars to create a phonetic (i.e., syllabic) script. By this time, of course, the Koreans were quite familiar with such scripts, which had originated in India and were widely used throughout Asia. In two years, a twenty-four-character system was devised that has been called the "world's best alphabet." It took a while for the script to be accepted, because the educated elite viewed it as a trivialization of Chinese. They called it "vernacular writing" (*onmun*), and for a long time it was used only for the most practical clerical functions, a kind of inferior shorthand. But in this century the script was renamed *han'gul*, "great script," to raise its status, and it is used exclusively in North Korea and widely in South Korea.

NOTES

[1] There was something to this concern. A few years later, four hundred White Russian soldiers were interned in the caves. They did so much damage to the great wall paintings that now Stein's photographs are the only remaining record of them.

[2] In what follows I will use the term "graph" in place of such diverse, and potentially confusable, terms as letter, character, sign, symbol, etc.

[3] The view that each graph represents an idea or concept rather than a word is quite misleading, therefore the term "ideograph" is best avoided.

4

TRIBAL PEOPLES

Majority and Minority Ethnic Groups in Modern Asian Nations

	Nation	Major Groups	Minorities	Percent
East Asia	China	Han (92%) 1.19 billion	55 *minzu* [Tibetan, Miao, Dai, Manchu, Mongol, Uygur, Yi . . .]	8.14% 80 million
	Korea, North & South	Korean (100%)		
	Japan	Japanese (99%)	Ainu Korean (less than 1%)	50,000
	Taiwan	Han (14%) Taiwanese (84%)	10 groups [Amis, Taya, Paiwan, Bunun, Puyuma, Rukai, Saisat, Tsou, Yami, Taroko	1.7% 337,342
Southeast Asia	Vietnam	Vietnamese [Kinh] (87%)	53 groups [Hmong, Yao, Mnong, Jarai, Ede, Bahnar, Kohor, Sedang, Hre, Raglai, Steing, Jeh-trieng, Ma, Cho Ru, Brau . . .]	2% 800,000
	Laos	Lao (50%) Thai (20%)	Phoutheung, Hmong, Yao . . .	23% 800,000
	Cambodia	Khmer (90%)		
	Thailand	Thai (99%)	6 main groups [Karen, Hmong, Akha, Lahu, Lisu, Mien]	1 % 500,000
	Myanmar [Burma]	Burman (69%) [Bamar]	Shan, Chin, Karen, Kachin, Palaung-Wa, Mon, Rakhine, Arakanese, Pao, Naga, Akha Lahu . . .	no reliable statistics; perhaps 20 million
	Malaysia	Malays (60%) Chinese (22%) Indians (8%)	54 groups [Orang Asli (Semang, Senoi, Proto-Malay), Dayak, Bisayah, Kenyah, Kajang . . .]	571,000
	Singapore	Chinese (76%) Indians (6%) Malays (15%)		
	Indonesia	Javanese (60%)	300 groups [Timorese, Papuans, Dyaks, Tana Toraja . . .]	40%
	Brunei	Malay (64%)	Chinese (20%), Tamil (3%), "Indigenous"(8%)	
	Philippines	Filipino (84%)	"Indigenous Cultural Communities [ICC]" 55 main groups [Ifugao, Hanunoo, Ilongot, Kalinga, Agta, Sama, Tasaday, Igorot, Bangsa Moro . . .]	16% 6.5 million
South Asia	India	Hindus (80%) Muslims (11%) Christian (2 %) Sikh (2%)	More than 200 "Scheduled Tribes" [Koli, Bhil, Gond Dafla, Naga, Khasi, Garo, Santhal, Oraon, Munda, Juang, Khond, Savara, Chenchu, Sholega, Toda Kota, Mizo, Andamanese . . .]	7% 51 million
	Nepal	Hindu Nepalis (90%)	Newar, Tibetan, Sherpa, Gurung, Magar, Tamang, Bhotia, Tharu	
	Bhutan	Bhotia		15%
	Pakistan	Panjabi	Sindhi, Pathan, Baluchi . . .	8% 7.7 million
	Bangladesh	Bengali (98%)	Marma, Chakma, Bawm, Mru, Khumi, Lushai, Bunjugi, Pankhu, Murung	1% 1.5 million
	Sri Lanka	Sinhalese (74%)	Ceylon Tamil, Moor, Indian Tamil	

Adapted from Burger 1987; Cultural Survival 1987; Barnes et al., 1995.

Throughout Asia are many peoples living on the margins of nation-states who are dominated by groups ethnically different from themselves. Among these groups are the Santals and Mundas in India, the Akha and Hmong in Thailand, the Tana Toraja and Dayaks in Indonesia, the Kachin and Karen of Burma, and the Dai and Miao of China. These peoples have been captured by more powerful ethnic groups in the process of state building and boundary drawing. They are viewed as problematic in various ways by the nations that have captured them. Tribal peoples may be viewed as impediments to full national integration because they retain non-normative customs, languages, and adaptations. Their citizenship may be in doubt if they maintain strong connections with similar communities across national borders, or if their swidden-style cultivation or pastoral nomadism require them to move their villages frequently. They may be viewed as insufficiently civilized (at worst, they are "wild" or "living fossils"), requiring expensive remedial action on the part of the majority society. Yet, when viewed as indigenous peoples whose present cultures somehow preserve the ancient past, their claims to territory and rights may be seen to have some moral ground. Every modern state has devised policies to deal with these "tribals" or "minorities," and the targeted groups have themselves responded in interesting ways to the kinds of attention, definitions, and policies set by central governments.

Identification of such groups is filled with political difficulties. First, minorities are not necessarily tribal people. The Chinese are a minority in Malaysia, Indonesia, and Thailand, yet they are by no means tribal, nor are the Indians in Singapore and Malaysia, or the Vietnamese in Cambodia. On the other hand, what is a tribe? A century of anthropological research has not resulted in satisfactory concepts, far less consensus, for identifying a tribe. Tribes tend to be defined by what they are not: they are not states. "A tribe is an animal without a central regulative system," wrote Marshall Sahlins (1968) in a famous attempt to define and describe a particular kind of social formation, the tribe. What he meant by that is that the tribe is a simpler system than the state, which has centralized political control and a monopoly on the use of force, yet the tribe is more complex than simple hunter-gatherer bands. Anthropologists working for the World Bank produced the following set of characteristics of tribal societies:

1. geographically isolated or semi-isolated;

2. unacculturated or only partly acculturated into the societal norms of the dominant society;

3. nonmonetized, or only partly monetized, production largely for subsistence, and independent of the national economic system;
4. ethnically distinct from the national society;
5. nonliterate and without a written language;
6. linguistically distinct from the wider society;
7. identifying closely with one particular territory;
8. having an economic lifestyle largely dependent on the specific natural environment;
9. possessing indigenous political leadership, but little or no national representation, and few, if any, political rights as individuals or collectively, partly because they do not participate in the political process; and
10. having loose tenure over their traditional lands, which for the most part is not accepted by the dominant society nor accommodated by its courts, and having weak enforcement capabilities against encroachers, even when tribal areas have been delineated (Kingsbury 1995).

Further difficulties in identifying tribal groups arise when governments for one reason or another are trying to suppress consciousness of ethnic difference. Burma, for instance, which has enormous, well-organized, and territorially based ethnic groups in a state of more or less perpetual armed conflict, has deliberately not taken an accurate census since the last one done by the British back in 1931 (Smith 1995). In its 1970 census Malaysia gave a total "aboriginal" population of seventy thousand for peninsular Malaysia, but since then the category has mysteriously disappeared, and the Orang Asli have been redefined as Malay. Why? The New Economic Policy grants constitutional preference to indigenous Malays over Chinese and Indians. There can, by definition, be no group more indigenous than the Malays.

Other nations, intent on clarifying once and for all exactly who is from what tribe or ethnic group in an effort to rationalize government and to administer "civilizing" or "uplifting" programs, have overclarified to the point of creating identities that never exactly existed before. China, in a concerted effort of social science-*cum*-bureaucratic research, has determined there are exactly fifty-six ethnic groups (*minzu*), no more and no less, including the Han, who are 93 percent of the population, or 1.11 billion people. Different rules apply to the minority *minzu* than to the Han; the one-child policy, for example, does not apply to them, and they have been granted a form of regional autonomy under the 1984 Law on Regional Autonomy for Minority Nationalities.

India has identified more than two hundred tribes speaking one hundred languages scattered throughout the subcontinent. These are registered as "Scheduled Tribes" (there is also a list of "Scheduled

Castes") who are deemed to need protection and uplift. Perhaps they benefit from the many laws intended to protect and assist them, such as India's version of affirmative action (actually a quota system) that reserves seats in national and state legislatures and spaces in universities for them, but most of these advantages prove to be better on paper than in reality. The vast majority of Scheduled Tribes are among the poorest 30 percent of the Indian population (Burger 1987).

In the 1980s and 1990s, a new word has begun to be applied to tribal peoples: "indigenous." Indigenous refers to the original population of a territory, as the Native Americans are the indigenous people of the United States. The term began to be used in the late 1950s when the International Labour Organization adopted a treaty intended to protect "indigenous and tribal" populations (ILO Convention 107). The term made good sense where first applied, such as in North America and the Amazon Basin, where the indigenous people have been there for ten or twelve thousand years, while the colonizing people have been there for a mere two hundred. It seems a little less illuminating when applied to Asia, however. The Orang Asli may have been in Malaysia for ten thousand years, but the Malays have been there for four or five thousand. The Malay term for themselves, *bumiputera*, means "sons of the soil." Who is not "indigenous" in Asia?

However, the term is likely to be with us for a long while, since it is becoming the term of choice in a number of international institutions such as the World Council of Indigenous People and the United Nations Working Group on Indigenous People, and also because minority groups in Asia are becoming politically mobilized around the term.

These examples show the conceptual difficulties and the political stakes for "minorities," "tribes," or "indigenous people," however they are labeled. The rest of this chapter attempts to account for the emergence of ethnic identities within the context of historical political conditions, and then looks closely at one such group, the Hmong.

TRIBE, STATE, AND ETHNIC GROUP

Ethnic Identity

A potential trap was set in the last chapter that we would not want to fall into in this one. We described linguistic groups—dialects, languages, and language families—with very ancient origins. We hypothesized ancient homelands where ancestors speaking the protolanguage must once have lived. We suggested that these languages are related to each other, which implies that modern speakers of them are also somehow related. We traced the spread of these families into new territories. Collectivities with these characteristics are often referred to as ethnolinguistic groups. Identification of such groups, however, has been a scientific enterprise associated with a modern worldview and the interests of the modern state. They may have no reality for the peoples involved unless made real by fairly recent political conditions. Think, for instance, of the surprise it was to speakers of Indo-European languages to discover the relationships among these languages. The Indo-Europeans never had any conceptions of unity or of sharing a common history and culture, and still do not. No more so do the Sino-Tibetans or the Austronesians or the Austroasiatics.

There is another set of collective identities that are genuinely experienced, yet are patently recent, and they have a certain lesson for us. The nation of Singapore, for instance, has existed only since 1965. Its citizens now think of themselves as Singaporeans, but that is an identity that had to be consciously constructed by the purposeful effort of the state in order to transcend older and potentially divisive identities: Chinese, Indian, and Malay. Singaporeanness is explicitly taught in the public schools and promoted in sophisticated public relations campaigns such as the television music video showing a multicultural group of young people singing "One people, one nation, one Singapore. . . ." Similarly, an Indonesian identity emerged during the independence movement from a colony constructed by the Dutch out of a heterogeneous group of islands and peoples. Likewise, an Indian identity emerged in the late nineteenth century as a part of the early Indian nationalist movement.

The point of these examples is that these identities have been constructed in response to particular political conditions in a particular historical period; in this case, late colonialism and the emergence of modern states throughout the region. Because the process is so recent, it is visible to us.

But surely, one might argue, many other identities are not recent at all but ancient and enduring. If by that we mean only that everyone has ancestors going "all the way back," then yes; or if we mean that some people, such as the Han Chinese, developed their collective identities many centuries ago. Just as nationalist identities are phenomena of the last two centuries, and were constructed in traceable ways, so ethnic identities have been constructed. But when, how, and why in each case is only beginning to be understood. Yet we are accustomed to thinking in a certain way about identities that we now refer to as ethnic, without realizing how modern the phenomenon is.

The Colonial Theory of Ethnicity

During the colonial era, a certain theory of ethnic groups and ethnicity emerged. This was the tribal model of ethnicity. The tribal model assumes that originally there were isolated tribes inhabiting a certain territory, speaking a common language, descended from common ancestors, sharing a common culture, more or less integrated in shared social institutions, and having a characteristic mode of adaptation to their environment. These traditions were passed largely unchanged from generation to generation, with the result that at the point where they first encountered outsiders who were motivated to describe them (typically Western missionaries, colonial administrators, or anthropologists), their lifeways could be regarded as preserved modern specimens of ancient cultural systems. Only at the crucial moment of the present or recent past have they suffered destructive encounters with more powerful neighbors, so that while some of these tribal peoples have survived into the twentieth century, they are sadly anachronistic and probably destined for extinction. Here is a not uncommon view:

> The Shendus, Pankhos, Mrus, Murangs, and Bonjugis of the Chittagong Hill Tracts are yet to receive even a peripheral contact with the civilized world. Their way of life is timeless. Their cultural configuration is still intact, the outlines still hard and sharply drawn against the contrasting background of civilization with no sign of dimming. Their religious beliefs and practices completely insulate them against the demands of modernism. Even their economy is antediluvian. (Van Schendel 1995)

After constructing this model of ethnicity, colonial administrators set about clarifying the model on the ground, so to speak. As new peoples were encountered, their tribe or ethnicity was identified (or a label was assigned), generally a term applied to them by other peoples. Maps of their territories were drawn up. Censuses attempted to identify everyone as a member of one and only one ethnic category. An evolutionary model identified the social attainments of ethnic groups in relation to each other (and to the colonial society), and efforts at uplift aimed to educate, convert, civilize, and develop those groups held to be wanting. Political benefits accrued (or didn't) as one was or wasn't a member of targeted ethnicities. Finally, this model was passed on to the modern independent states that emerged from colonial control and has continued to dominate policy in the new states. And so, in a strange way, this mistaken model of ethnicity has become real. For every Asian nation today has its identified ethnic minorities that are regarded as problematic in various ways and toward which governments direct special policies. Members of these designated groups have gone along with it in the interest of political survival.

However, if you read carefully the writings of some observant early travelers in the years before the model I have just described was fully developed, a different picture emerges. In the 1790s, at the very beginning of British control in India, Francis Buchanan traveled in the

Chittagong Hills of what is now eastern Bangladesh (where Shendus and Pankhos are said to await contact with the "civilized world"). He describes a complex ethnic situation in which there were villages inhabited by swidden cultivators belonging to different language groups. There were other villages consisting of a dominant group of one ethnicity together with their debt peons from different groups, and villages where leaders had servants from several other groups. There were chiefs who collected tribute from households belonging to an amalgam of ethnic groups. Because of their style of agriculture (swidden) and because of raids and warfare, all groups were continually on the move. There was no question of isolated tribes living in distinct territories, but instead there were a number of different patterns of multiethnic integration (Van Schendel 1995).

In other words, the isolated, autonomous, and self-conscious tribe of the classical model was a rare phenomenon, not just in the Chittagong Hills, but, as recent historical and ethnographic research has been showing, throughout most of Asia.

Moreover, there are long-term processes by which people change from one ethnicity to another. The 1.11 billion Han Chinese did not achieve those numbers solely by outreproducing the other fifty-five ethnic groups. Over centuries, peoples from other groups have deliberately "Han-ified" themselves as a self-conscious strategy to raise their status and local influence by taking on the cultural practices of the dominant ethnic group of the Chinese state. This process, often referred to as assimilation, is sometimes encouraged by the state and sometimes resisted by it. An example of the latter would be the stigmatized boat people of Guangdong Province, who were required to register as non-Han, Dan people. There was tremendous social pressure against any effort to pass oneself off as Han, yet many tried to do just that. The 1561 *Records of Guangdong Province* gives a typical characterization of the Dan boat people:

> [The Dan] people are peculiar in that people of the same surname intermarry, in that they do not wear hats or shoes, and are foolish, illiterate, and ignorant of their ages. . . . In recent years, those who live in the center of Guangdong are beginning to learn to read. [Some] have moved ashore and, having attached themselves to registered households, are themselves registered in the same way as commoners. There are even some who have succeeded in the examinations. (Ye Xian'en 1995)

In other words, through accumulating wealth, investing in land, and acquiring education, some were beginning to pass themselves off as Han. But this effort was not always successful, and there are records of ex-Dan being convicted and punished for false pretenses.

On the other hand, the state often puts considerable pressure on people to assimilate to the dominant culture. Steven Harrell refers to this as a "civilizing project" in which the state views itself as a superior civilization with a mission to improve the inferior peoples on their periphery (Harrell 1995). The 1945 constitution of Indonesia describes the 1.5 million tribespeople on their thirteen thousand islands as having "social life, economic performance and level of civilization below acceptable standards" (Burger 1987:142). The state views its mission as bringing these people up to acceptable standards. The dominant center of Indonesian power is Java, where ninety million people, or 60 percent of the entire population, live on 7 percent of the land. People on other islands have their own distinct cultures. It was only the Dutch empire that gave legitimacy to Indonesia and established dominance from Java. Official Indonesian policy insists that the many distinct ethnic groups are one political, economic, cultural, and defense unit. There is no self-determination. There are no reserves. Their policy of planned transmigration encourages the resettlement of Javanese in other areas, such as in Irian Jaya, the western half of New Guinea. The population of Irian Jaya is Melanesian, having vastly more in common linguistically, culturally, and historically with people on the eastern half of the island in the independent state of Papua New Guinea than they have ever had, or will ever have, with the Javanese.

China even in pre-Republican and pre-Revolutionary times had a similar viewpoint, as Steven Harrell writes:

> That the attitude of the late Imperial (Ming and Qing) Chinese state toward its peripheral peoples can be characterized as a civilizing project, we have no doubt. From the standpoint of the Confucian worldview, civilization was characterized by *wenhua*, which refers to the molding of the person (and by extension the community to which the person belongs) by training in the philosophical, moral, and ritual principles considered to constitute virtue. . . . It follows that there was a scale of civilizedness, with the most civilized being those who had the greatest acquaintance with the relevant literary works, namely the scholar-officials who served the imperial state and who served as theoreticians of the moral order. Other Chinese were somewhat cultured; their family life, religion, language, and other attributes were similar to those of the literati, even if they had no refinement or direct knowledge of the important literature. Non-Chinese were a step down, being not even indirectly acquainted with the moral principles laid out in the classics. . . . This moral scale of peoples fits in nicely with the continuing historical process of absorption of once-peripheral peoples into the broader category of *Zhongguo ren* (people of the central country), or Chinese. We know that ever since the southward expansion of the Han dynasty (206 B.C.–220 C.E.), regions had been sinified by a com-

bination of Chinese migration, intermarriage, and cultural assimilation of the former natives. (Harrell 1995: 19)

The lesson is that there is nothing "essential," eternal, or primordial
about ethnic identities. These identities come and go; they can be created
where none existed before. They can be constructed internally by a people
who have cause to begin imagining themselves as one people, or they can
be assigned from the outside by people bent on differentiating "them"
from "us." Given sufficient motivation and resources, one ethnicity can be
shed in favor of another. Yet when anthropologist Edmund Leach suggested that ethnic identity can change easily according to the dictates of
economic and political circumstances, another anthropologist, William
Geddes, repudiated this as a dangerous view with no scientific backing
that would be attractive to "proselytizers and administrators of every
faith and political persuasion" (Geddes 1976:11). Geddes was concerned
that this argument was in the interest of dominant groups whose efforts
at state building would assimilate the Hmong and eradicate their culture.
It can be seen that, invariably, issues of power underlie issues of ethnicity.

HOW THE THAI BECAME AN ETHNIC GROUP

The Thai are a case in point. Charles F. Keyes has shown the historical
process by which Thai ethnicity first emerged in the premodern state,
then continued to change in the modern Thai state (Keyes 1995). We
begin with one of those large and complex ethnolinguistic groups
described in the last chapter, the Tai (or Dai). A number of separate Daic
languages and dialects are spoken by people living in southern China,
Laos, Thailand, and northern Burma. The recognition of this category
(the Tai peoples or the Daic language family) is a product of modern
scholarship. Neither in the present nor in the past have speakers of all
these languages had a sense of shared history and culture, nor did they
ever integrate into a single unit of social organization or think of themselves as a people. Rather, the Tai/Dai have always been a large number
of communities interconnected by kinship ties, some with their own
local chiefs, rubbing shoulders with people of other languages and customs (e.g., the Han Chinese or the Khmer of Southeast Asia), and
embroiled in various and shifting political arrangements throughout
the regions they have inhabited.

In the thirteenth century, or even earlier, a few of these Tai-speaking
peoples began experimenting with scripts for writing their language.
They began these experimental scripts with preexisting Southeast Asian
scripts, perhaps Mon, which had been previously adapted from Indic

scripts. Once some Tai-speakers (by no means all) had a means of writing their language, they could begin to produce texts. These texts formed the basis of a sense of themselves as an "imagined community," to use Benedict Anderson's term. Initially these were translations of Buddhist texts; gradually use of the new script expanded to include legends about particular Buddhist monuments or religious orders, myths of ancient places, annals of dynastic lines, and, eventually, histories of the past of particular groups. Thus, by means of a shared script and literature, the past was remembered. That is to say, a selectively constructed past now gave a sense of common descent to a portion of the Tai-speaking peoples and became one marker of their emerging ethnic identity. These were the peoples who, in the fourteenth century, were unified by a prince at the court at Sukhothai and were distributed through a region that would eventually be carved up into the modern states of Laos, Thailand, Burma, and China.

Many other Tai-speakers, especially those in southern China, never shared in this new world of written texts. But as some chiefs began forming courts and supporting Buddhist monasteries and temples, the peoples subject to these courts began to develop a shared identity, which in the beginning was Lao. Though they did not all speak the same language, they used the same script and thought of themselves as different from the Khmer of the powerful competing state nearby at Angkor, which they admired, emulated, and fought.

THE PREMODERN AND MODERN STATE

The old states that centered on the Sukhothai and Ayudhya courts were a far different kind of state than the modern states with capitals at Bangkok, Vientiane, and Rangoon. Modern states began to emerge in the late nineteenth and early twentieth centuries throughout Asia, a process being completed as late as the 1970s in a few places such as Laos. No matter how different these states might be along some dimensions (socialist, democratic, constitutional monarchy, soft authoritarianism, etc.), they have certain features in common, and they differ from premodern states in a few highly significant ways: they have precisely delineated geographical borders drawn on maps and transferred to territories that are internally guarded and defended, and ratified by international law. They have centralized and uniform governments whose authority extends to those clearly demarcated borders, and they exercise control over every individual living within them.

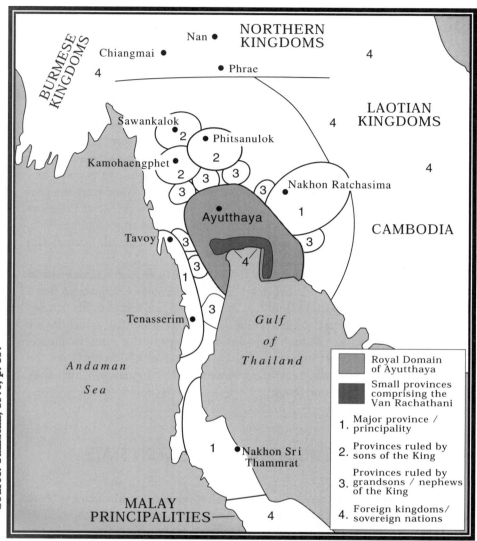

Source: Tambiah, 1976, p. 137

The following appears within the map image:

NORTHERN
KINGDOMS

Nan •

Chiangmai •   4

BURMESE KINGDOMS

• Phrae

4

LAOTIAN
KINGDOMS

4

Sawankalok
2
• Phitsanulok
2

Kamohaengphet •
2   3   3

3

3   • Nakhon Ratchasima

Ayutthaya

1

CAMBODIA

Tavoy   3

3

1

4

3

Tenasserim •   Gulf
of
Thailand

Andaman
Sea

	Royal Domain of Ayutthaya
	Small provinces comprising the Van Rachathani
1.	Major province / principality
2.	Provinces ruled by sons of the King
3.	Provinces ruled by grandsons / nephews of the King
4.	Foreign kingdoms / sovereign nations

1   • Nakhon Sri
Thammrat

MALAY
PRINCIPALITIES —   4

Map 4.1   The Premodern State

But things were different in the premodern state, as a comparison of the two maps will show. While there is also no single type of premodern state (examples will be examined in separate chapters on India, Southeast Asia, China, and Japan), they did not have the characteristics described for the modern state. More typically, a ruler established a court in one place and extended his authority outward from this center as far as strength of arms, bonds of kinship, strategic marriage, and religiously underwritten authority could extend. Beyond that, relations of dependency and tribute were established with local chiefs and their communi-

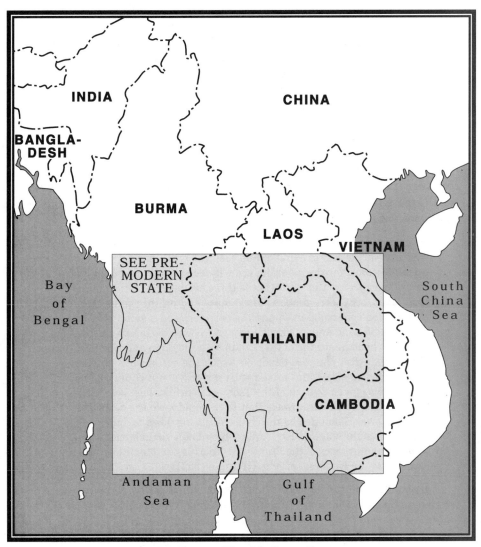

Map 4.2   The Modern State

ties of the same and different ethnic groups and languages. There were not boundaries so much as frontiers; a king might set up stone markers indicating the edge of what he considered his territory, but this was not necessarily the beginning of someone else's territory. Between two strong kingdoms might be a frontier inhabited by any number of weaker chiefs or relatively autonomous tribal peoples, playing off one rival king against the other while trying to maintain a precarious independence.

These bonds of alliance and dependency between kings and outlying chiefs were maintained by political rituals such as those described in the early nineteenth century by S. F. Hannay. In upper Burma there existed various semi-independent groups, some Shan, some Kachin, each with their own chiefs. The Burmese were beginning to take over the authority of the Shan, slipping into traditional political rituals established by the Shan. The way it worked was this: the continuity and spiritual succession of the Shan rulers were represented by spirits (*nats*) of the founding ancestors that were enshrined in the Buddhist monastery at Mogaung. These ancestral spirits, said to have been three brothers in life, bore Shan royal titles. On all state occasions their shrines were brought out and carried in procession on men's shoulders. These provided the occasion for receiving the submission of subordinate chiefs. The ceremony by which the Burmese governor received the submission of local Shan and Kachin chiefs was witnessed by Hannay in 1836:

> The ceremony commenced by killing a buffalo which was effected with several strokes of a mallet and the flesh of the animal was cut up to be cooked for the occasion; each Tsobua [chief] presented his sword and spear to the spirits of the three brothers. . . . Offerings of rice, meat, etc., were made to these nats and on this being done each person concerned in taking the oath received a small portion of rice in his hand and in a kneeling posture with his hands clasped above his head heard the oaths read in both the Shan and Burmese languages. After this the paper on which the oaths were written was burned to ashes and mixed with water when a cupful of the mixture was given to each of the Tsobuas to drink, who, before doing so, repeated the assurance that they would keep the oath. The ceremony was concluded by the chiefs all sitting down together and eating out of the same dish. . . . All . . . by this act virtually acknowledged the supremacy of the Burmese authorities and their own subjugation to the Kingdom of Ava. (Hannay 1837)

By consuming the ashes of the paper on which oaths of loyalty were written along with offerings made to the spirits of the superior prince, the chiefs incorporated into their own bodies tokens of their submission. Such a ritual of political alliance and subjugation has no resonance for us today. We can find nothing directly comparable in today's state administrative apparatus. Smaller chiefs making symbolic acts of subordination to greater chiefs by presenting arms and swallowing written oaths is not the way regions are integrated in modern states. But such were the ways small polities were interconnected in the premodern period.

It was colonialism that brought the modern state to Southeast Asia. The British began taking over territories of Burma piecemeal throughout the nineteenth century, while the French did the same thing from the east, leaving Thailand an independent but pushed and shoved entity in between (see chapter 9). This shattered the emergent cultural unity of the

Lao, as the colonial powers imposed European state models by drawing and defending borders demarcating Laos, Cambodia, Burma, Thailand, and China. Thailand (or Siam) now found itself with unfamiliar borders drawn and enforced by others, and the logic of this European model began to influence them in other ways, too. Every person within those borders was part of the Siamese state.

Siamese elites began to ponder how these people were related. What made them distinct from their neighbors, especially from the closely related Lao of Laos and the Shan of Burma? In 1833 a princely monk named Vajirayana (who later became King Mongkut) discovered an inscription that described a King Ram Kamhaeng of Sukhothai who invented the Thai system of writing. King Ram Kamhaeng now became thought of as the founding ancestor of the Thai people. ("Thai" is used to refer to this emerging ethnic group, now the majority population of Thailand; "Tai" is used to refer to the larger and older ethnolinguistic group identified by scholars.) Though the Thai spoke many different but closely related languages, those differences were forgotten within the borders of Thailand, but remembered between the borders of Thailand and Laos. Their kings, since the eighteenth century centered on Bangkok, became a focal point of Thai identity, maintaining a limited cultural continuity with the premodern state, even as various reforms begun under Rama V (Chulalongkorn) began to reconfigure Thai institutions as a modern state.

Thus we see how the Thai became an ethnic group. Many factors played a part: (1) creation of a script for their language(s) and of a literature that began to be shared by a group larger than local face-to-face communities, who could begin to imagine a large number of people they would never see as sharing a common past and culture; (2) the formation of the premodern state focused on a court and dynastic line; (3) contrasts between the Sukhothai-Ayudhya-Bangkok states (Thai states) and those of Angkor (Khmer), Pagan (Burmese), and Luang Prabang (Lao); (4) the establishment of modern states in the colonial era and the creation by the Thai elites of a national identity for people living within its borders; and (5) adoption of the colonial model of majority and minority ethnic groups.

THE HMONG OF THAILAND

As we have seen, ethnic identity emerges, in one of its scenarios, when two different groups, especially when they are speakers of different languages, look at each other over a period of time and ponder their differences. The Thai, whose ethnic identity as a process of historic construction we have just examined, distinguish themselves from a number of groups collectively labeled hill tribes, who inhabit the northern and western hills, speak non-Thai languages, are not Buddhist, and do not, for the most part, practice wet-rice agriculture. These hill tribes are generally classified in six main groups: Karen, Hmong, Mien, Akha, Lahu, and Lisu. These groups, of course, ponder the Thai and each other and are also engaged in the work of self-definition. One of these groups, the Hmong, we shall look at in some detail.

Who Are the Miao?

As recently as the 1970s, books on the Hmong of Thailand were still referring to them as Miao or Meo. "Miao" is not an ethnonym (the term that a people use for themselves), but the term by which the Chinese have known them (or someone) for several thousand years. Hmong have not lived in the hills of Thailand and Laos longer than a few hundred years at most, and before that, they were most certainly in southern China, where there are at present some 7.5 million people classified by the Chinese as Miao. So, although they are a tiny minority in Thailand (about fifty-eight thousand), they are considered part of one of China's five largest minorities (minzu). The story of the Hmong, then, really begins in China.

The Chinese character that is read as "Miao" is a compound of the characters for "plants" and for "fields." This conveys a meaning of "sprouts," "seedlings," or even "weeds," suggesting "wild uncultivated tribes." Indeed, *miao* was an ancient category appearing in both the *Shu jing*, compiled by Sima Qian (145–190 B.C.), and the *Shi ji*. These refer to a San Miao kingdom existing around the third century B.C., which sounds specific enough, but *miao* was used more generally, along with *man* and *yi*, to mean "barbarians," especially with reference to indigenous peoples living in the southwestern frontier of the expanding Chinese empire. (What the "barbarians" called themselves we have no way of knowing.)

These people, who did not have systems of writing, who did not know the Confucian texts, and who were not centrally organized, were viewed by the Han Chinese as lacking civilization and even culture. The Chinese word for culture, *wenhua*, which is also the word for "writing," or "literary transformation," suggests "the moulding of the person by training in the philosophical, moral, and ritual principles which constitute virtue" in the Confucian system (Harrell 1995). Chinese descriptions of tribal people tend to emphasize their lack of civilization by focusing on the fact that they record events with knots on a string and numbers with notches on a piece of wood. The Chinese saw it as their civilizing mission to bring Chinese control, and with it Chinese culture, to them. Norma Diamond (Diamond 1995) describes how Chinese gazetteers of late Ming and Qing times were attempting to classify different types of barbarians in the Yunnan-Guizhou area. One classification distinguished *Sheng Miao* from *Shu Miao*—literally, "Raw Miao" and "Cooked Miao." "Raw" seems to have meant unassimilated Miao resisting pacification and state control, while "cooked" Miao were more sinified. Sheng Miao thus could be compared to the "Wild Indian" category of American frontier culture.

As the Chinese state was pursuing an active policy of conquest and pacification in southwestern China during the early eighteenth century, they met great resistance from the Miao, an episode that has become known as the Miao Rebellions. This resistance lasted into the nineteenth century and prompted migration of many Miao into Laos and Thailand. This political effort of pacification was accompanied by renewed effort to classify and describe the local populations in a series of publications known as the Miao Albums. These consisted of paintings or block prints with descriptive texts that tended to highlight the loveliness of the women, though acknowledging their easy sexuality and provocative dress, and the aggressiveness of the men. The Hei Sheng Miao are described as treacherous and aggressive people who were conquered once and for all in 1736 but only after half of them were killed a decade earlier.

The process of bringing the southern regions under state control involved moving more and more Han into the area as administrators and settlers, and also "using barbarians to control barbarians." Some Miao (presumably "cooked") were appointed as local officials (*tu-si*) over their own people with responsibility for collecting and presenting annual tribute to the Chinese court. In the late nineteenth century, a Miao became Viceroy of Yunnan, and in the 1930s, a Miao was the military governor of Yunnan.

Ethnology as a recognized social science began in China in the first part of the twentieth century, though it was certainly an arm of government policies of assimilation and control. The Miao were described as of a low cultural level, their religious beliefs were viewed as mere superstitions, and there was little effort to understand or convey the Miao worldview or its social organization, while there was great attention devoted to classifying the various kinds of Miao, very often on the basis of characteristics of Miao women's clothing (Blue, White, Flowery, Black, Red, etc.). Their divisions and subdivisions across a number of prefectures and provinces ballooned into the hundreds.

Things changed after the Communist revolution. With a theory of cultural evolution based on Marx, Engels, Lenin, Stalin, and Mao, the People's Republic authorized an immense effort of scientific research that would identify the "nationalities" of China (using the Chinese form, minzu, of the Russian *nationalnosti*) and rank them on a scale from primitive to slave to feudal to capitalism to socialism. Ironically, having forms of communal land use qualified one as primitive, not socialist, if one was not a collectivized Han farmer. The great diversity of the Miao that had perplexed social scientists in the first half of the century was now glossed over in favor of a theory that all Miao were part of one ancient ethnic category, and that any regional differences that appeared among them were recent divergences from an ancient common pattern. This view takes it as settled truth that their original homeland was somewhere between the Yellow River and the Yangtze River, from where they wandered south and west to their present locations.

Descriptions of Miao continue to emphasize their colorful customs and their differences from the Han and encourage maintenance of some, but not other, practices. Miao religious practices are summed up and dismissed as worshipping spirits, ancestors, and ghosts and wasting lots of money on ceremonies; but their music, dance, and costumes can be retained if not set in a religious context and if they make a good show for tourists and for television as proof that the cultures of the minorities are respected and encouraged (Diamond 1995).

Hmong in Thailand

Almost all the Hmong in Thailand are members of either the White Hmong (*Hmong Glor*) or the Blue Hmong (*Hmong Njua*) (who are known as the Green Hmong in the United States). There are linguistic differences between the two groups, but the dialects are mutually comprehensible. Blue Hmong women wear short skirts woven of hemp that are deeply pleated and have a light blue batik pattern on indigo. White Hmong women sometimes wear a white skirt (hence their name), but most of the time wear dark trousers with a long embroidered sash that hangs down the front and back.

There can be no doubt that the Hmong of Thailand consider themselves one ethnic category distinct from other groups whose villages are interspersed with theirs. Hmong villages may share a hillside with Karen or Akha or Lahu villages, the best land in the possession of whoever got there first. The sense of common identity among Hmong is not expressed in territoriality or in any kind of political organization at a level higher than that of the village, although everyone has kinship ties with people in other villages, and the clans also cut across village boundaries. In this, they are unlike the Karen, who have autonomous territories in the states of Kawthoolei and Kayah in Burma (Myanmar), an active independence movement under the control of the Karen National Defence Organization, and a Karenni Army. In Thailand, however, the Karen are often impoverished, dependent on more prosperous Hmong villages to provide them with employment, frequently working in Hmong poppy fields with payment in opium.

There are now several good studies of Hmong villages, notably a study of two Blue Hmong villages, Pasamliem and Meto, by William Geddes (1976), and of the White Hmong village of Nomya by Nicholas Tapp

(1989). In addition, I spent a short period in the White Hmong village of Chengmengmai in 1987, the source of the photos in this chapter.

When it comes to transliterating Hmong names and words, some authors use the Barney-Smalley system, devised specifically for Hmong. It uses Roman characters but expresses Hmong tones by adding a letter to the end of each word that should not be pronounced as a consonant but as a tone. So "Hmoob" is pronounced "Hmong" in a high tone, "Vaj" is "Vang," and so on. For Hmong, this system is not confusing, since none of their words end in consonants anyway, but it is highly disorienting for non-Hmong readers who are not specialists in Hmong language, so I will transliterate Hmong words in a way closer to their actual pronunciation for English speakers, ignoring tones altogether.

The Transitory Community

A Hmong village is a comfortable array of thatch and bamboo houses frequently situated in a horseshoe pattern on the highest hillside available to them, at least three thousand feet in altitude, four or five thousand if possible. At these elevations, mornings are cool, often beginning with a still mist thickened by smoke from cookfires, which burns away after a few hours. Even in the heat of the day, the temperatures will be ten degrees cooler than on the plains where the Thai live. The first sounds of the morning are rooster calls and people using rice pounders shaped like teeter-totters, hammering out the rice for the day. Women rise early to get at the work that fills their long days, but in moments of leisure they will sit just outside their doorways, embroidering the new clothes for the New Year festival, with a child or two playing nearby.

There are clues to the transitoriness of a Hmong village if you look around. The houses are airy and spacious structures built directly on swept earth with walls of split bamboo and thatched roofs. These are easily packed up and moved. At Chengmengmai all the fruit trees planted around homesteads were younger than five years, and the nearest fields visible from village doorways were already in fallow. People were having to walk a long way to their fields. Chaithong, the shaman, had a four-hour walk to the four *rai* (1.6 acres) he cultivates with his two wives. As the soil near the village wears out and it becomes a day's walk just to reach your fields, you begin to think about packing up and moving to where your fields are.

This simple calculation lies behind the famous mobility of swidden cultivators everywhere. The Hmong are often said to be the most mobile of the hill tribes of Thailand, but the same issues face all of them. The village of Meto, studied by Geddes, was pioneered in 1961 by four men of Tang clan and six men of Jang clan. In 1965 the village had a population of 570. When Geddes returned for a brief visit in mid-1966, a year later, not a single house remained. By 1970, the area of Meto had become "just another jungle valley with few signs of its former habitation." Where did the people go? Almost all the planting area had shifted to the northeast, five or six kilometers away. People had begun building field huts, then improving them until they became like second homes, while they spent less and less time in the village. Eventually, the people abandoned the original village and moved out to the newly developing area. In the process, however, only some members of the old village reassembled at the new one. Others went off in other directions, forming new communities elsewhere.

The great problem of the last few decades, however, is finding new land that is not already in the control of another group. There is virtually no virgin forest left, and population growth in the hills means that there are already claims on almost all the land. The result is that people at Chengmengmai were beginning to talk about terracing their hillsides in order to turn to the wet-rice cultivation practiced in the valleys, which enables one to go on using the same land practically forever. But terraces are expensive to build and maintain, and the people of Chengmengmai will need a dam (which they are looking to the government to build) in order to channel the water.

Hmong tend to idealize the lowlanders' wet-rice system, viewing it as an easier life than their own life in the hills. In this, most of the evidence suggests they are wrong. A compilation of studies on the labor expenditures by foragers, swiddeners, and intensive (plow) agriculturists seems to indicate that in the sort of intensive cultivation required by the wet-rice method, Hmong labor investment will radically increase (Ember 1983):

Hours Worked Per Week			
	average	**men**	**women**
foragers	14		
swiddeners	41	36	46
intensive cultivators	70	63	75

Anthropologist Edmund Leach (1964) described the keen admiration that British administrators had for the terraces of upland Burmese during the early days of British control. It seemed like a highly efficient utilization of land, and they resolved to encourage the highland peoples to extend the practice. But the more encouragement given by the British, and the more political conditions became settled so that agriculture could proceed peacefully, the fewer new terraces went in. Gradually, in fact, people began dissolving back into the forest, returning to ancient methods of swidden cultivation. The explanation proved simple and logical. Terrace cultivation was so expensive and so labor intensive that only the pressure of certain kinds of conditions forced people to it. One of these was chronic warfare, which forced people to cluster around local warlords for protection. Another was the presence of certain trade routes through high passes where warlords could sit and play robber baron, forcing Chinese, Indian, and Burmese merchants to pay fees for safe passage. When the British put an end to both warlordism and robber baron games, the incentive to keep up the terraces was gone.

Today, however, there is a new incentive: population growth in the Thai hills. Therefore, swidden cultivators are again talking about building terraces, and in the more prosperous villages, Hmong and others, one will see a few acres of terraces being put in by farsighted cultivators. Already in 1966, there were three terraced fields in Meto.

Adaptation and Response: Opium

Hmong and other hill tribes are now having to adapt to new conditions of overpopulation in the hills, just as they have had to adapt to other changed circumstances in the past. This kind of flexibility is nothing new, although there is a popular misconception about the "timelessness" of so-called tribal societies and the antiquity of their lifestyles. If any more evidence were needed, opium cultivation by the Hmong would be another example of responding to new opportunities.

In the eighteenth century, extensive opium use began in China. It was not altogether unknown earlier; Arab traders had brought it to China in the seventh century for use as a medicine, and for centuries it was mixed in various concoctions for a variety of ailments and used as a sedative prior to surgery. But it was not smoked until the seventeenth century when the Dutch introduced tobacco smoking from Java, and people soon thought of mixing a little opium with the tobacco for a stronger impact. It is not easy to smoke opium by itself, but gradually the tobacco was omitted as a way was devised to smoke opium by melting little bits over a flame and rapidly inhaling it.

The trade in opium in the eighteenth century was almost entirely in the hands of foreigners. The East India Company grew it in their colony in India and brought it to China to trade for silk, tea, porcelain, and other products desired in Europe (see chapter 9). China soon had a tremendous opium addiction problem, provoking the Opium Wars of 1840–1842 against England. The war resulted in humiliation for China and the opening of the country to as much opium as European traders could bring in, thus both feeding the new addiction problem and draining China's wealth. In response, China began encouraging local production of opium. Suddenly there was a new cash crop opportunity for groups like the Hmong (Miao) of China, many of whom already lived at altitudes above the three-thousand-foot level beloved by poppies. Chinese opium was not

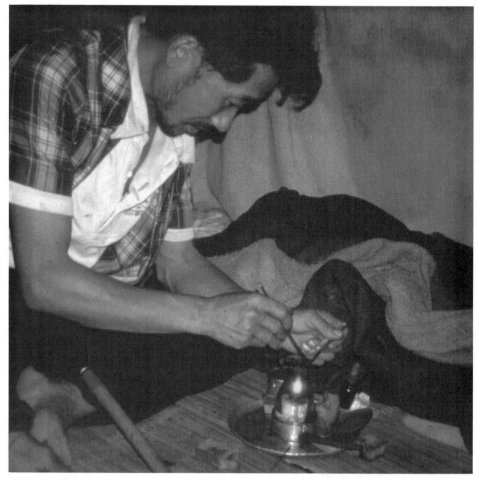

The village's most important shaman, Chaithong, is also addicted to opium. It is legal for him to grow enough to meet his needs—about ten pipes a day. He cuts the raw opium with aspirin and heats it in a tin spoon over an open flame. He then puts it into the pipe to smoke.

as high in morphine content as Indian opium, but it was a great deal cheaper and there was soon a large market for it.

For the Hmong, opium became a crop as important as *padi* (rice). Padi provided subsistence needs and opium provided cash. Both were essential, and the trick was to strike the right balance of the two. Padi does best between two thousand and thirty-five hundred feet; higher than that, it is a little too cool. Poppy does progressively better from three thousand to five thousand feet. It likes cold weather and a gentle rain as it is maturing. But the rain should stop about the time the petals begin to fall so the seed heads do not get wet and the latex drain away when they are tapped. Poppy can grow in the same field for ten years before the soil becomes exhausted, while padi fields, at least in the parts of Thailand inhabited by the Hmong, need ten years of fallow after only two or three years of use. It would seem to make sense to plant a field in rice, then shift to poppy after two years, but this is difficult because rice, being a kind of grass, is almost impossible to clear away sufficiently to allow room for the poppies to grow. The solution, when clearing a new area for cultivation, is to select some fields for rice, others (higher up) for poppy. Maize is planted first in the poppy fields to keep them weed-free, then about August or September, poppy is planted among the maize and harvested in December or January. This gives a bonus of maize, which is neither a subsistence nor a cash crop. Instead, it is fed to pigs, which are important in the ceremonial life of the Hmong and can be eaten or sold. Thus, a poppy economy is actually a poppy-pigs-maize complex.

When Geddes did his ecological study of Meto village, he found most households planting more poppy than padi. The 32 households of Tang clan, for instance, had 245 acres in poppy and only 52 acres in padi. This often meant they did not produce enough padi to meet all their food needs, but the Hmong view was that it was better to plant poppies and use some of the income to buy whatever extra rice was needed by the household.

At harvest time, after the petals have fallen, the seed heads of the poppies are tapped. This is highly labor-intensive work, as each head has to be handled twice. A special three-bladed knife is made by binding together three blades at different angles so each blade will cut a different level into the seed head to tap a different layer of the sap. After the first stroke, the sap immediately begins to ooze, but it quickly congeals without dropping off the head. Four hours later, when the sap is viscous and amber-colored, it can be scraped off with a flat iron blade and wrapped in poppy petals. There can be as many as thirty heads to a plant, though the average is seven or eight. Though each poppy is only tapped once, workers will have to go over each field many times to be sure they have it all.

Since opium production has been illegal since 1957, most efforts to study opium production have been hindered by an understandable tendency on the part of cultivators to underreport production and earnings. Nevertheless, the Thai government estimates 3.25 kg. of raw opium per acre is an average for all producers. Some groups, such as the Mien, tap the poppy heads several times and get much higher yields, perhaps as much as 10 kg. per acre. Using the lower figure, together with data on the amount of land actually under poppy production, Geddes calculated that the 71 Hmong households of Meto village produced 1.3 metric tons of opium in the 1965/66 season. The total value was $59,880, or $843 per household. The richest household, the headman's large extended family of twenty persons, earned $2,968. The Hmong were viewed as richer than other tribes, and even richer than nearby Thai farm families whose average annual income from crops other than opium was $155.

The opium trade has gone through somersaults over the last century as entrepreneurs in and out of government, tribal brokers, and assorted drug lords have waxed and waned in the "politics of heroin." The rural physician Wu Lien-teh wrote: "I often saw mile upon mile of land covered with multi-colored poppy plants in Manchuria, Shansi, Shensi, Jehol, Fukien, Yunnan, and Szechuan, from which the various war-lords hoped to derive needed revenue for maintaining their troops" (Wu Lien-teh 1959: 492). Chinese warlords were not the only military interests supporting themselves with opium in this century. While China fairly successfully put a stop to opium cultivation after the 1949 revolution, France was establishing an opium monopoly over poppy production in Laos and cultivating a Hmong leader, Touby Lyfoung, as their opium broker. When heroin addiction spread like a plague among American GIs during the Vietnam War, the demand was supplied by narcotics rings with excellent connections in the South Vietnamese government. In 1971 Prince Sopsaisana, the newly appointed ambassador to France, arrived at Orly Airport with a suitcase carrying 60 kg. of heroin worth $13.5 million on the streets of New York (McCoy 1972). Ancient Indians knew Southeast Asia as *suvarnabhumi*, the "land of gold," but when Burma, Laos, and northern Thailand are called the "Golden Triangle," it isn't with precious metal in mind.

A little bit of the value added as opium gets processed in factories on the Burma border, then sent through a chain of cities—e.g., from Homong in the Shan State of Burma to Bangkok to New York—can be seen in the following:

10 kg. opium → 1 kg. heroin → $10,000 in Bangkok → $200,000 in New York

The 1990s have been boom years in opium and heroin in the Golden Triangle, with 88 percent of Southeast Asian opium now coming through Burma:

Opium Cultivation in Southeast Asia in tons per year		
	1989	**1993**
Burma	142,700	165,800
Laos	42,130	26,040
Thailand	4,075	2,880

The low figures for Thailand show the success of Thailand's effort to halt opium production and to replace opium with other cash crops among groups like the Hmong. So far there has been a drop in income among those who have gone along with the new policies, since no crop is as lucrative as poppy. The Hmong are changing and adapting once again.

Fathers and Sons

Elsewhere in much of Asia, it is land that holds fathers and sons together in kinship units. A family's wealth, congealed in a single piece of earth, passed from father to son, often for generations, unites them in common cause and is their means of survival and their defense against impoverishment. But the Hmong do not own land in this sense. The claim a father has on his son is not a piece of land to pass on to him. Communities come and go, and sons could readily strike out in search of their own new fields, and sometimes do. More generally, however, it is the case that fathers and sons work and live in close proximity. If not land, then what binds them together?

The bond between father and son transcends death, and this is the organizing principle of social life. The father's welfare in the afterlife depends on how his sons bury him and attend to his needs through ancestor worship. The sons' welfare in life depends on their father's well-being in the afterlife, for he will be in a position to send them good fortune or misfortune. A critical moment in this trans-death relationship is when the time comes for the son to bury his father. The headman of Nomya village attributed his good fortune in having four sons and only one daughter to the favorable alignment of his father's grave. Another villager was less fortunate because a small peak between two mountains made his father's grave less auspicious. The energy of the earth is conceptualized as a great dragon that lies beneath the crest of the highest mountain chains that form its spine. Parallel hills to the left and the right are male (left) and female (right). In order to reach the place from which rebirth occurs, the deceased must be buried in the late afternoon (which is the morning of the spirits) in such a place where it can catch the "dragon veins" before the dragon flies out at night, and so ride it to the otherworld. This place would be on the crest of the highest hills where the parallel male hills to the left are higher than the female hills to the right. Such a burial will favor the living sons and the continuity of the family. The deceased's head should be turned away from the sunrise so he can watch over his family's welfare without being blinded by the light.

This unseverable bond between father and son is the basis of the household, the village, and the clan, a principle often called patrilineal by anthropologists. Patrilineality can mean a great many things, however, and we will want to look closely at how it works among the Hmong.

Most Hmong spend at least part of their lives in extended households, where one or more adult sons and their wives and children live with his parents. Of the seventy-one kinship charts Geddes published for Meto, twenty-six of them were extended families. The largest, composed of twenty individuals, was also the richest family, but the average household was only eight persons. In other societies it is the death of the father that causes an extended family to break apart into its component nuclear families, but among the Hmong it is more typically the reassembling of the village in a new location. Then, a son who has been married a number of years and has many children and perhaps a second wife will build a separate house. Of course, a widowed father or mother will live with an adult son (sometimes called a stem family).

The household is the primary work unit of Hmong society. Production of padi is to meet the needs of the family. There are no other production units in the society—no village-level production, no clan-level production, no private businesses that are not household based. Households hold the fields they work in common, husband and wife working side by side, with the children also contributing, for their work, too, is of economic value. The domestic unit as the principal unit of production is often cited as a marker of societies known as "tribal":

> The domestic groups of tribal societies have not yet suffered demotion to a mere consumption status. Nor is human labor power detached from the family and, employed in an external realm, made subject to an alien organization and purpose. Production is a domestic function. The family is as such directly engaged in the economic process, and largely in control of it. Its own inner relations, as between husband and wife, parent and child, are relations of production. (Sahlins 1968: 75)

Above the household, the most important units within the village are the clans. Hmong say there are about twelve Hmong clans, but in any particular village there will be only four or five. Among the 106 households at Chengmengmai, 51 were members of Yang clan, 21 were Li, 18 were Thao, 15 were Ma, and one was Xiong. The numerical strength of the clans has important political consequences for the village, since generally the headman will be from the largest clan. These clans are patrilineal in the sense that one is a member of one's father's clan, while women change their clan identities at marriage. At death, women are among the clan ancestors who are worshipped by their living descendants.

These clans are not territorial or localized, but are dispersed among the villages of the Hmong people. There is no apical, or founding, ancestor; no clan headman or senior and junior lines; and no genealogies are remembered that would attempt to account for each person's exact tie to everyone else. The clans have sometimes been called surname groups because that is the extent of their social organization. According to Geddes, "We may define clans and their sub-divisions as essentially religious associations conferring rights of community upon their members through the spiritual bonds between them" (Geddes 1976: 57).

A myth told by the headman of Chengmengmai accounts for the origins of the clans. The importance of this myth is apparent from the fact that Geddes and Tapp each record several versions of it that were told to them. Here is the Chengmengmai version:

There was a family who on the first day cleared a field; next day they went to check the work. The field had returned to its original state. So they cleared again. On the third day, the same thing happened. Next day, it all happened again. Then a messenger named Phya Eng appeared to them. He spoke to the youngest brother and said the world would be inundated by a great flood, so it was useless to be clearing the field. He was instructed to find a giant gourd and make a hole large enough for himself and one younger sister to get inside; he must do it by the 15th day of the 9th moon (i.e., the full moon). The rains began and they went in the gourd, closing it off, and bobbed away. Three days and nights rains flooded the world. At the end the water level dropped and they landed on ground. The flood had killed all human life. Procreation was now impossible. Phya Eng reappeared and told the brother and sister that they must take each other in marriage and produce offspring. They said they must not do this, as they were brother and sister, but he promised proof that it was right to do this. He instructed one of them to take a needle up one side of the mountain, and the other to take a thread up the other side, and both to throw theirs down the hill. If the needle landed threaded, it was evidence that they should marry. So they did it, and it turned out as Phya Eng predicted; it was threaded. The couple begged for further evidence. They resisted marrying each other. Phya Eng told them to each take one part of a rice mill and do the same thing from the mountain top. If it lands with the right part on top of the other part, this is evidence that their marriage is proper. And this time again it worked as he said. So they married and after a year the sister became pregnant. When she gave birth, it was not a baby; it was a round mound of green flesh. So Phya Eng was again consulted. He said, no problem; you build a number of small houses. He took the green ball and cut it into many pieces and put them into each house. Quickly they turned into human beings. Each piece became a couple, and these couples were then given the many surnames of the Hmong people.

As a member of a particular clan, your advantages are a sense of relationship and thus rights as kinsmen wherever you meet. "Mere possession of a common name is enough to ensure a friendly reception among people who would otherwise be strangers." If you migrate to a village where members of your clan are already settled, you can expect help from them in settling in. They will give you a field to get you started, and probably feed you until you can survive on your own.

But the nature of the clan as a religious association is most apparent at death. A person cannot be allowed to die in the house of someone of a different clan, so in an emergency any clansman may be called on to accept someone to die in their house. It is village clansmen who conduct the many expensive and protracted ceremonies associated with death and burial. When a man dies, the head of household selects two men, one from the clan of the deceased and one from the clan of the deceased's wife, to organize the mortuary rites. The corpse will be buried in the late afternoon on an auspicious day, which may be from three to ten days later. In the meantime, many tasks must be accomplished. Chandarsi (1976) describes twelve specific tasks that are assigned to relatives, including: preparation of the body; informing relatives in distant villages of his death; preparing enough food to feed the many people who will come for as long as they stay; feeding the dead man himself three times a day; firing three shots from a gun every time he is fed; blowing the pipes and beating the death drum; making a coffin; obtaining the chickens, pigs, and oxen that will be offered; settling the dead man's debts; and selecting the burial site. These tasks are the work of his clan, and of people from other clans who are related to him by marriage. The splendor of a man's mortuary rite is testimony to his greatness in life and to his family's devotion to him. This message is not aimed only at the living community, but to the deceased himself, who must be made content to depart by provision of everything he needs for the journey to the place of his ancestors. Otherwise, disappointed and ashamed, he may stay around and cause trouble for the living, who will only have to go to great expense later on to find the causes, and then make the offerings necessary to induce the ghost to depart satisfied.

On the day of death the corpse is washed by the immediate family and laid out on a stretcher inside the house, with his head toward the main stove, just opposite the ancestral shrine. He is dressed in new clothes with a small red cloth over his face, but the body is not wrapped or treated beyond that. At his head lies a chicken that has been killed by twisting its neck. It will accompany him to the next world. Food, a crossbow, and sword are also laid nearby for the journey.

A long chant known as *tergi* helps the deceased realize that he has died and serves as a kind of verbal map for his journey. It describes the way through the spirit world that the deceased must follow, offering advice on how to prevent being waylaid, and what to do upon arrival at the place of the ancestors. It also teaches the living about the nature of the afterlife.

Tergi begins by expressing the sorrow of the chanter who came to the great stove at the dead man's house and did not find him alive, as in the past, but dead. But since he is dead, here is what he should do. The chant describes the preparations the family has made for the body. They've made a basket for cooking sticky rice, and a stretcher to carry him to the grave; a chicken (or a dog) has been killed to be his companion ("when you eat this chicken you should go with it"), a red cloth covers his face so he will not be ashamed of being dead in front of others, shoes have been provided for the journey, and a thousand rupees for his expenses (in paper money) has been burned.

Thus provisioned, he should head next to the village where he was born to retrieve his placenta from under the main housepost where it was buried on the day of his birth. This is his clothing to be worn to the next world. After nine days' journey, he will come to two gates. He is instructed what to say to the guards in order to be allowed through. Then he will come to villages where Hmong are enjoying normal life. Young people are courting; others are out riding horses, pounding rice, or drinking fresh water. He should not be tempted to join them. Beyond that he will come to more surreal sights. There will be man-eating stones and a tree with eight branches, nine roots, and nine eyes. He should drink the milk of the tree and call it mother and father to make all the sickness of his body disappear. At a third gate he will be asked how he wants to be reborn. A little further is a three-way junction; he should take the middle path that leads to a big river that he must cross. His new parents live just on the other side. That is his destination.

A dramatic feature of every Hmong funeral is the killing of one or more oxen for the mortuary feast, and the splendor of a funeral will be determined in large part by the number of oxen killed and the number of people fed. This is one of the reasons a man wants many children and many wives. An ox must be provided by each of his wives, one ox must come from each of his married sons, and each of his married daughters should contribute to the purchase of a single ox. Other relatives contribute a pig, rice, paper money, alcohol, and incense. On the day before the burial, these people arrive at his house with these gifts, firing a gun twice to announce their arrival. The household fires twice in welcome, and pipes are blown as the large party enters the house. In the evening, all these relatives tell the deceased what they have given him, wish him well on his journey, and then listen to a very long recitation, the *sersai*, which instructs them all on how they should now behave.

On the morning of the burial day, the body is finally carried out of the house and placed in the coffin that is supported on two T-bars specially made for the purpose. Strings tie each of the gift-oxen to the corpse, which the dead man is asked to accept. The oxen are then killed with axe blows to the head, and the internal organs cut out and cooked for a morning meal. The oxen are divided up and distributed according to formula to everyone who has played a role in the funeral rites.

Carrying the corpse to the selected burial site can be a dangerous prospect. The location will generally be a great distance away, on the crest of a hill, selected by geomancy in the process described earlier. There is never such a thing as a Hmong cemetery, for even two bodies buried nearby may quarrel over the land, which becomes their "fields" in the afterlife. The real danger, however, is that the souls of the funeral party may try to follow the souls of the dead man, so the souls of the living are called and ordered to stay in the household when the dead man is taken away. Then a few close relatives carry the coffin to the grave site. Someone in the lead blows the pipes and a daughter of the dead man carries a torch to light the way. In the rear is a man who tosses paper money to spirits along the way for permission to let the dead man pass.

A third of the way toward the burial place, the pipes stop playing and the girl throws away the lighted torch and runs back home in order to confuse the ghost in case it wants to return. A little further, they stop again, and the ghost is told that in his "house," i.e., his grave, there is plenty of food and that is where he should henceforth eat. At the grave site, a bit of sweepings from the coffin are put in someone's shirt, representing the souls of the living burial party that must be collected and brought home. The coffin is put in the grave first, then the body laid inside, and the dead man is told that, if he gets hungry in the next three days, there is money and rice for him that he can cook for himself. On the third day his family will bring him food and build him a "house," a cairn of stones to mark his grave.

This and further ceremonies over the next year have the important function of setting the spirit of the dead into an appropriate new relationship to his former household. On the one hand, any animosity the dead might have toward the family must be headed off by respectful and generous words and gifts. The dead must not come back at inappropriate times to cause trouble. On the other hand, they must come back on certain occasions, especially at New Year, to receive offerings and messages from the family and to bring them good fortune when called upon. In other words, the dead person through these ceremonies is taught how to be a good ancestor. The Hmong do not practice secondary burial, as do many other Southeast Asian peoples, which serves the purpose of processing a decaying body into dry bones and an unhappy ghost into a satisfied and benevolent ancestor. The Hmong accomplish the same goal with a series of ceremonies, food gifts, and invitations to return home for brief visits at appropriate times. Eventually, after a ceremony at the gravesite that cuts the grasses and roots that may be holding the soul in its grave, the dead man will be taken away from his spirit parents and reborn to a new life.

These are the tasks of family and clan in assisting one's departure from life and celebrating the life just finished. One's clan gives a person an identity and community larger than the household and different from the village, both cross-cutting and transcending village society. As we have seen, a village is a transitory thing, whereas a clan is eternal. But clan membership is not enough to satisfy all your needs. You must get your wife from another clan.

"Silver Celebrates the Worth of Women"

A Hmong woman spends her life working hard, but this labor brings her advantages that women in many other societies do not have.

The myth told above describes a primordial couple who are brother and sister but become husband and wife. This myth should not be taken as sanctioning incest, for the brother and sister in the story know it is wrong for them to marry and resist the urgings of Phya Eng to do so, but they are forced to it by necessity if life is to resume on earth. As if proving them right, the outcome is a monstrous mound of green flesh. The theme of going up opposite sides of the mountain, a male side and a female side, found in that myth appears in other myths recorded by Tapp. In one of these, a brother and sister compete for superiority to see who "will be the emperor who guards the dragon." The brother says, "You're only a woman. Your body is for carrying water and bearing children. You cannot govern heaven and earth." Boiling with fury, the sister challenges him to several tests, and in one after the other they come out even. One she devises is a test of strength: "Each of us will have to carry ten measures of copper on the left side and ten measures on the right side." The brother says, "All right, you're the oldest, you go first." The sister is able to carry ten measures of copper and ten of iron, but so can her brother. Then they compete about wisdom: who can learn about the "veins of the slopes" (i.e., the knowledge of geomancy). For this they have to go up the left (male) and the right (female) hillsides, but in this case the brother gets there first. There he catches the "veins of the dragon" and begins riding it, causing the slopes to collapse around him and churning up the land like water, while the sister laments that she has lost everything (Tapp 1989: 155).

This myth seems to be accounting for gender differences, among other things, and several features stand out. The first is how well the sister fares in competition with her brother. She suggests the competition in the first place. She dreams up the tests they must pass. On many of them they come out equal, most strikingly in carrying loads of copper and iron in the test of strength. She is the right hand, he the left. Many people in the world reverse that formula on the grounds that the right hand, the strong hand, the hand that throws the spear or holds the pen, is surely male. But the Hmong logic is that the "right hand toils and the left hand rests," therefore the right hand is female. Or again, "the mountain to the left (male) is the stronger one, the mountain to the right is the toiling one."

So, women are valued for their strength and their ability to work hard, to carry heavy loads, and to make important contributions to the household. The wife is a full partner with her husband in the economic survival of the family. There is no complaining from Hmong men about having to support women who make no economic contributions as, for instance, Indian men may sometimes do. Someday someone may do a close study of the relative labor of Hmong men and women in Southeast Asia, and when they do, they may well find women putting in many more hours than men. Such discoveries are being made in similar societies in other parts of Asia. Carol Ember in an important 1983 article (Ember 1983) amassed evidence that women in horticultural (i.e., swidden) societies work longer and harder than men in these societies, as do women in societies practicing intensive agriculture. She suggests that this is because men devote themselves to politics and protection, leaving women to work in the fields once the hard part of clearing a new field is done. When men get pulled out of cultivation during warfare, if they find women can carry on for the most part without their help, there is little incentive for them to return to the fields.

To have a wife is therefore essential, and she will not come cheap. If a man wants a wife, and wants to claim her children for his family and clan, he will have to pay a brideprice in silver. Traditionally this silver was in the form of Indian silver rupees that circulated for years in the hills of Southeast Asia, supplied by Indian traders settled in the larger towns like Chiangmai. One still sometimes sees these, bearing images of the young Victoria with braids looping around her ears, but these are becoming rarer, since India no longer mints rupees in real silver. Most of the old coins have been melted down and are now traded in the form of ingots or silver neck rings. The value of the silver is generally high, more than the savings of a household accumulated over several years. When Geddes was in Meto, the average was about 350 silver rupees, worth about $200 (in 1965 prices). Cash will not do.

Fathers may sometimes try to arrange these marriages, and child betrothals are occasionally agreed to with the exchange of a bottle of liquor and four silver rupees, but girls are rarely forced into marriages they do not want, and they do not have to stay in marriages where they are not well treated. There are too many opportunities for boys and girls to fall in love and decide they will marry. There is, for example, the famous "courting ball game" played at the New Year, which is unfailingly mentioned in all accounts of the Hmong (and of the Miao in China), an ethnic marker if ever there was one. Gathering in a group of young people, girls on one side and boys on the other, they toss a soft cloth ball in a rather flirtatious way. Afterward, couples may pair off romantically during the freedom allowed during the holidays. Though virginity is formally valued, in fact there is a certain freedom of sexual experience that would be more vigorously prevented in many another society. If a girl becomes pregnant, as frequently happens, she will marry with the payment of silver. If no silver is paid, the child belongs to her own clan.

When the new bride comes to her husband's house, she is introduced to the house spirits and ancestors and becomes a member of her husband's clan. She begins a life of industrious labor, both productive and reproductive. She may well be older than her husband. Geddes found that first wives were on average two years older than their husbands. People said that boys marry when fifteen or sixteen, girls around twenty. This may be the result of the greater sexual freedom that allows boys to become involved with girls already somewhat more sexually mature, followed soon by marriage.

Men are entitled to go right on flirting after they are married, but if they get a girl pregnant, they had better be able to provide the silver to marry her. Men and women have very divergent points of view about polygyny, which a majority of men who survive to middle age will have enjoyed. (Forty percent of Meto households were polygynous.) Women do not enjoy sharing a bed with their husband and another wife, which is how the system works. Being a second wife is less prestigious than being a first, but having a second, younger wife brought in by one's husband is also humiliating. Theoretically, a first wife's permission must be obtained. If she has no children, she will not be in a position to resist. She may, however, be willing since a second wife is expected to do the field work while the first wife can retire to household work. If a woman is very strongwilled she may be able to prevent her husband from proceeding with his plans. While all men hope to have two or more wives, both to increase the workforce of his household and for the prestige of being a man who can afford several wives, they do not wish second-wife status for their daughters.

Another form of marriage is sometimes discussed in the literature on the Hmong: marriage-by-capture. When it happens in Hmong communities in the United States, it is usually treated as rape. When it happens in Thailand, it may not be much more approved, and occasionally the Thai authorities are called in to intervene (Tapp 1989). Geddes describes a case in Meto where a girl of one clan was seized outside the village by men of another clan as a bride for one of their members. The girl was the pretty daughter of an opium addict, who had no other members of her own clan in the village to protect her. The girl escaped and ran home, and a few years later committed suicide by swallowing opium. Marriage-by-capture often appears in the literature as a valid marriage alternative, but in a society like this where the possibilities of marrying a person of one's own choice are fairly good and where elopement is also possible, marriage-by-capture exists principally as a way of forcing a girl into an unwanted marriage. A notable case occurred in 1918 when a Laotian Hmong of some prominence wanted to marry a beautiful girl named May. He paid the girl's uncle to kidnap her. The child of this marriage-by-capture was the well-known Touby Lyfoung, for eight years the only Hmong member of the Opium Purchasing Board. Four years after the marriage, following quarrels and beatings, May committed suicide by the usual method of eating opium.

Spirits, Domestic and Wild

The fields, forests, and hills beyond the village are filled with creatures living their own lives and desiring to be undisturbed by humans. When a man and a snake meet along a trail, they are mutually startled and hurry out of each other's way. Similarly there are spirits of all kinds inhabiting the wild places and wanting to be left alone. When humans disturb their habitations, there may be trouble. A snakebite can threaten one's life; so can a spirit attack. The most powerful and dangerous spirits, according to Chaithong, the shaman at Chengmengmai, are those that inhabit termite mounds and those that live in the great trees in and around Buddhist temples. Spirits in termite mounds cause nosebleeds in children, physical weakness, and illness if you dig into them or even go near them. The spirits in the temples have made themselves resemble the figures in the temple: they have elongated heads and red mouths. The Buddhist images must also have some kind of power, Chaithong supposes, but whether their power is equal to that of the spirits in the trees, he does not know.

There are other spirits closer to home, in the village and even in the house. They have various origins and vaguely known identities. Overlooking most villages will be a large and well-formed tree on a hill where the main spirit of the mountain is invited to take up residence to look after the village. The door, the main post of the house, the large fireplace, and the small fireplace each have their spirits. There is the spirit that lives in the funeral drum. There is Sierglung, once a living human, the useless one of seven brothers, who never did his share of work but lazily spent his days amusing himself. When he fell sick and died, no one cared, and his body was left to be eaten by wild animals. But then his angry ghost came back to take vengeance by killing his brothers and their animals until a shaman advised the family to set up a small shrine inside the house and give him food gifts annually. Since then, all Hmong have a shrine to Sierglung in their house. Sometimes individual subclans or families have spirits of their own dead who for some reason failed to become benevolent ancestors but became angry ghosts bent on spite. All these spirits can become friendly allies in the spirit world if made happy with the regular offering of a chicken or pig.

Spirits are disembodied, but all living things, as their condition for living, have spirits temporarily housed in the body. Souls are sent to the human world to live within a particular body for a fixed period of time, sometimes described as a license with a fixed expiration date. When the time is up, death is inevitable, although under extraordinary circumstances extensions are possible. If a person falls into a coma it may be because his or her time has ended. If the person survives, it is evidence of a struggle and triumph in the spirit world; such a person will surely become a shaman.

The Hmong view the soul as less firmly attached to the body than in the Western view. In the West the senses—sight, hearing, smell, etc.—are viewed as part of the body's perceptual apparatus. The Hmong theory of the self divides things up differently. The soul is a vague composite entity of seven divisible parts: a soul-piece for each eye and ear, plus one in the nose, the mouth, and the heart. All of these can stray from the body, posing a threat to life itself. In other words, the senses are part of the soul rather than part of the body. At death, the souls of the ears, nose, and mouth remain with the body in the grave, but the souls of the eyes and heart go to the afterworld and are eventually reincarnated. In sleep, the eyes and heart may wander and cause dreams.

The complexities of the interconnected worlds of spirits and humans require specialists who can move between these two worlds safely and skillfully. Every village must have one shaman, and most will have several. The most powerful shaman in Chengmengmai was Chaithong, a thirty-eight-year-old opium addict who had two wives and six children. Chaithong's grandfather had been an especially gifted shaman who had been selected by a spirit (*neng*) to become a shaman (*chingneng*). This way of becoming a chingneng is considered extraordinary. Chaithong became a chingneng in the more usual way. He got sick, and an older chingneng was called in to kill the sickness. But he did not get well. He was taken to the hospital and still did not recover. More chingnengs were called, and finally his grandfather said, "If you do not become a chingneng, you will get sicker and sicker." But he was only a ten-year-old boy and the thought frightened him. They used a common divination method to determine whether Chaithong should become a chingneng. He took four pieces of water buffalo horn (made by sawing two horn tips longitudinally) and holding them together, he said, "If they fall all open, I'll become a chingneng," and then he threw them. They fell open. So he began studying with his grandfather.

One of Chaithong's most difficult cases was in a village a few miles downhill where a man lived with his wife, his mother, and his young son. When we arrived by Landrover at this household it was unclear who the

Chaithong demonstrates the most important method of divination used by a Hmong shaman—casting the buffalo horns. Two tips of the horn of a black water buffalo or a black bull are cut in half, each with a convex and a concave side. Questions are posed and the answer is discovered, depending on how the bones land. This is how they landed when it was determined Chaithong should become a shaman.

patient would be. The grandmother had a large goiter that projected six inches from her neck. The young wife appeared to have a cataract in one eye. But it turned out to be the adult son who was the patient. He suffered from epilepsy, and did not seem to be improved by Western medicine that, in any case, they could not afford. Perhaps the problem was evil spirits.

Things were already arranged for the chingneng, and he went right to work. A bench faced the spirit altar. On the spirit altar were a bowl of

The shaman, his face shrouded with a black face cloth and waving strips of red cloth, rides his "horse" into the spirit world to contact those forces directly. An assistant keeps up a steady rhythm on a drum until the climax of the ceremony, hours later, when the final struggle with the afflicting spirit takes place.

A chicken's neck is cut as an offering to the spirits to protect the patient. The spirit gets the life force of the chicken and the family eats the flesh.

padi, puffed rice, and incense. Chaithong put on the *ti hao*, the black cotton face covering that provided sensory deprivation for him as he sat on the bench, or "horse," which he rode into the spirit world. Various noisy implements get the spirits' attention and drive them out: the brass gong that an assistant bangs at a hypnotic rhythm; a set of brass castanets with strips of red cloth that clatter and wave; and a spear tip attached to an iron ring that is his weapon to fight the spirit. The patient sits right behind the shaman, passive and hopeful, as the chingneng fights on his behalf in the invisible world.

This all takes a very long time. For two and a half hours the chingneng chants and gallops, his bare feet pounding the hard earthen floor until a groove is gouged in it. Once he stops briefly, throws the bones four or five times, and makes a report to the household. He smokes a pipe of tobacco and then resumes his journey. The old grandmother waits with a chicken, its feet tied, under her arm. Two more are in a basket waiting. One is taken outside and killed, as promised to the evil spirit. The evil spirit will have to go outside to get it. Beside the chingneng, a coalpot filled with coals has been lighted, and a bucket of water is coming to a boil.

Once in a while the chingneng leaps high into the air with the help of his assistant to contact the benevolent household spirits in his struggle with the evil ones. He becomes hoarse with chanting; his back is cooled with a damp cloth. Sometimes he peers at his opponent through the iron ring with the spear tip. Another hour passes.

Suddenly there is a flurry of excitement. The chingneng is thrown violently from the bench into the hearth, knocking over the pot of boiling water, breaking the coalpot, and filling the whole room with hissing steam and ash. As it clears, we see the chingneng rolling in the coals, fighting with the almost-visible spirit. Then he leaps up and hurls the spear in the direction of the door, as simultaneously the door is slammed shut. The spear stabs into the door with a thud. The evil spirit is defeated and gone.

There is still a bit more work to do in the spirit world; the exhausted, ash-covered chingneng gets back on the horse and chants longer, this time thanking the household spirits for their assistance and restoring their authority. But the tension is clearly relieved; the patient looks dazed but happy. Grandmother whispers something with relief to another old woman. The daughter-in-law and a neighbor stretch a chicken's neck and cut its throat. Blood drains into a cup. Because the coalpot is broken, this chicken, a reward to the household spirits, has to be boiled at a neighbor's house.

The patient then receives the *khlua ki tesh*, the "wrist string," specially braided with three colors of thread, around his neck, wrists, and ankles to bind his beleaguered souls more securely to his body. An *X* in lampblack is drawn on his forehead to disguise him from the evil spirit who may still be lurking in the vicinity for the next few days. And the triumphant warrior, the shaman, relaxes with a pipe of tobacco smoked in an old unexploded steel US 2.7 air-to-ground rocket pod left over from Vietnam War days.

Will the patient be cured of his epilepsy? Of course we wonder. We do know a great deal about the body-as-machine and epilepsy as a disease. Do we know as much about the powers of the mind on the body? We are quite sure of our medical paradigm, but might not other models of human suffering prevail elsewhere, producing different forms of suffering? Or, at the very least, do not we also call priests and healers into hospital rooms to pray over and lay hands on patients attached to ventilators or dialysis machines? Who knows what powers lie behind and beyond the known diseases?

The shaman is both healer and spiritual leader, physician and priest. He diagnoses; divines; tells the future; does war with evil spirits and sends food gifts to the friendly ones; and stands between humans and the chaotic, invisible world that is the cause of all their suffering.

5
INDIA

Chronology of Indian History

2300	**Indus Valley Civilization** (ca. 2300–1750 B.C.)	Urbanization & city planning; worship of "Proto-Shiva" and goddess; wheat and cotton cultivation; trade with Sumer
1500	**Vedic Age** (ca. 1500–450 B.C.)	1500–1000 Indo-European Aryans enter from Northwest 1200? Vedas 1000–450 North Indian conquest and unification ca. 600 *Mahābhārata;* ca. 750–500 *Rāmāyaṇa* of Valmiki 800–600 *Brahmanas* 600–300 *Upanishads* 563–483 Buddha
300	**Maurya Dynasty** (ca. 323–185 B.C.)	326 Alexander the Great invades India 323 First unification of India under Chandragupta Maurya; capital at Pataliputra (Patna) 269–232 Emperor Ashoka
100 B.C. A.D. 300	**Satavahana**	
400	**Gupta** (ca. 4th–6th century A.D.)	"The Classical Age"—Establishment of Temple Worship 399–414 Faxian in India 643 King Harsha's Great Feast (reigned 606–647) 630–645 Xuanzhang in India
500 600		
700	**Pallava** (7th–9th century)	
800 900	**Pala** (ca. 8th–12th century)	
1000 1100	**Chola** (mid-9th–13th century)	1175–1192 Ghurids begin conquest of India
1200	**Sultanate** (1192–1526)	Establishment of Central Asian empire in North India; Islamic culture enters; many new Ramayanas in regional vernaculars Destruction of Buddhist universities; end of Buddhism in India
1300 1400	**Vijayanagar** (1336–1565)	
1500 1600 1700	**Mughal** (ca.1526–1827)	Tulsi Das' *Rāmāyaṇa* in Hindi 1556–1605 Akbar
1800 1900	**British** (ca. late 18th century– 1947)	1757 British victory at Plassey 1757–1858 "John Company Raj" 1857 Anglo-Indian War ("Indian Mutiny") 1858–1947 British Raj
1947	**Republic of India**	

AN "EMPIRE OF THE SPIRIT"?

Our knowledge of Indian society is dominated by the colonial era. Even though colonialism ended in India half a century ago in 1947, there are two major ways in which colonial India is still an issue. The first is the extraordinary impact that colonialism had on India's institutions. The two hundred years of British influence and control, reckoning from the Battle of Plassey in 1757 to the drawing down of the Union Jack at midnight on August 15, 1947, turned India into a modern state and left no social institution unaltered. Terms like "traditional India" and "the timeless caste system" are virtually meaningless, though they are sometimes carelessly used by those who view the colonial era as long gone and irrelevant. When we go to India now, as tourists, scholars, or business people, we go to an India transformed by the colonial encounter.

Colonialism also dominates our knowledge of India in the colossal legacy of colonial scholarship about India. India did not have the indigenous tradition of historiography that China had, as we shall see in chapter 7. If it had, that would have been the starting point and foundation for modern and Western models for writing India's history. Indian historiography, to the extent it existed, was limited to genealogical pedigrees of local rulers to prove they were descended from Vishnu or the sun, or to ballads extolling the victorious battle of one ruler over his enemy. While such sources are not worthless and have recently been used with good effect by ethnohistorians, they were not sufficient to have prevented whole eras and empires from disappearing from history. Indus Valley civilization, the Mauryan Empire, King Ashoka, and Buddhism's origin and spread throughout India all vanished without a memory. When in 1976 in China the huge burial army of the First Emperor (221–206 B.C.) was rediscovered archaeologically, it was not really comparable to the rediscovery of Mohenjo-Daro in northwest India in 1924, because there were Chinese histories aplenty describing Qin Shihuang, but there was not a trace in any Indian text to provide a parallel account of Indus Valley civilization.

It was not that India had no intellectual class that might have been writing history; far from it. It was just that they had much more important matters on their mind to write about than the goings on around them. There was the nature of the soul and the nature of the universe. There were the fabulous doings of divine characters like Shiva, Krishna,

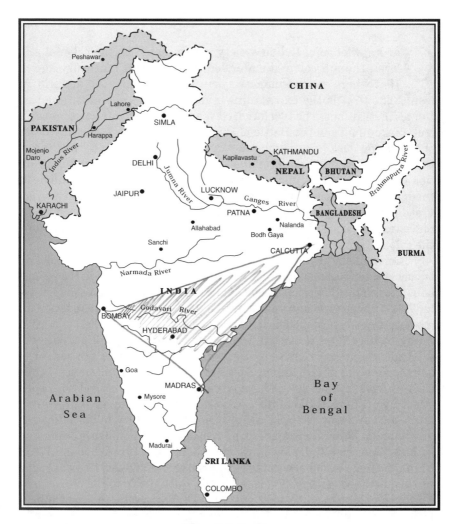

Map 5.1 India

and Kali. There were legendary stories to be told at enormous length in the *Ramayana* and the *Mahabharata*, treated as history and whose historicity has yet to be seriously addressed. And if little serious attention was paid to the doings of actual kings and actual ordinary persons, there was lengthy and sometimes brilliant reflection on how kings and kingdoms *should* be ordered, how society *should* be organized, how humans *should* conduct themselves. These were not ivory-tower philosophies, in many cases, but texts taken seriously, applied to real life. They were authoritative in the sense that society in many intriguing ways altered itself to be what the texts asked of it.

Since the mode of thinking about the world that we call historical was not a form of thought indigenous to India, when British adventurers, traders, and eventually administrators gradually usurped power in India, they quickly began to apply Western historical methods to this exotic new place. The result was a vast literature of variable quality. We have already encountered the brilliant Sir William Jones in chapter 3, whose effort in mastering Sanskrit led to the discovery of the Indo-European language family and the founding of historical linguistics. That was only one of the discoveries of nineteenth-century scholarship. Discovery after discovery was reported in periodicals like the *Journal of the Asiatic Society of Bengal*, in travel accounts by the score, in the voluminous gazetteers describing every local region in minute detail written by overworked local officials, and in multivolume surveys such as A. C. Cunningham's *Archaeological Surveys of India*, which ran to twenty-three volumes. It has sometimes seemed they discovered it all and said it all.

A perennial topic was the caste system. Its complexities fascinated the British, while its inequities appalled them—even as they inserted themselves at the apex of the hierarchy, bounding themselves off with rules of separation like any other caste. The caste system was the elephant and they the blind men trying to take its measure, determine its nature. Were the castes so many tribes, each with its own history and customs, trying to preserve ethnic identity in close interconnection with other tribes? No, that was too simple, since the caste system was also a division of labor: Unlike self-sufficient tribal cultivators, the castes were deeply interdependent economically. Above all, they were interdependent ritually. Powerful landowning castes could not get their sons and daughters married without ritualized services up and down the hierarchy. Brahmans could not maintain sufficient purity to chant the Vedic mantras without washermen to remove impurities from their clothes, barbers' wives to remove birth pollution, and sweepers to clean their latrines. Everyone depended on the Brahmans to perform their essential life-cycle rites. The logic that best accounted for the hierarchy of castes was a ritual logic. Brahmans, not kings, were at the top.

The puzzling secondary position of kings and the subordination of political power to ritual authority became the caste system's most intriguing feature. As kings were toppled one by one in the East India Company's spreading control—here a principality annexed, there a *raja* reduced to tax collector—British scholars consulted with Brahmans about how this society, which they now had to govern, worked. It seemed to be a system of weak kings and powerful Brahmans. It seemed to be a civilization in which power and economics were subsumed under religion. It seemed to be an "empire of the spirit."

In the process of ruling it and writing about it, the "timeless caste system" was being reconstructed. "Colonial intervention . . . removed the politics from society and created a contradictory form of civil society—with caste as its fundamental institution—in its place" (Dirks 1989b:61). Kings were deposed or reduced to figureheads while real power was transferred to the British. But this new form of power, being alien, was ignored by scholars writing about Indian society who wanted to know about the "traditional" system and found it inviting to render invisible the impact of their own usurpation of power.

In this chapter, we will of course look at the caste system as it is now in postcolonial India. But in looking at the premodern state, we will attempt to reconstruct it before its colonial alterations began.

THE MORAL SOCIETY

The world's earliest states, emerging in the second and third millennia B.C. in Egypt, Mesopotamia, India, and China, were the first to face the questions that all states, including modern ones, have got to face: How to mobilize power effectively? How to survive past the first generation? How to manage the force that created the state without immediately destroying it? How to get and keep the loyalty of diverse groups drawn together in the state?

The family, village, and tribal solidarities that long preceded the state had their moral codes, often implicit, which seemed as natural as the growth of plants in sunshine and rain or the springtime birth of calves and lambs. But as states emerged out of competition, conquest, and domination, a new social formation had appeared for which there was no natural model to provide for harmony and continuity. Both China and India sought ways to conceptualize these new concentrations of power that would legitimate the rule of a monarch and divert attention from the privileged classes that now had to be supported. The family was a natural metaphor that both societies made use of. The king would be a father to his people, using the military might by which he conquered them to protect them; the people would be his children who owed loyalty and obedience and could expect justice from him. (The metaphoric potential of motherhood in state ideology was apparently less fruitful.) But an ideology of the family writ large could go only so far in underwriting state power.

Rama, the hero of the Ramayana and India's greatest (and mythological) king, as he prepared to obey the command of his father that sent him into a fourteen-year exile on the day on which he was supposed to be crowned king, said: "There is no greater act of righteousness than this: obedience to one's father and doing as he bids" (Pollock 1986). He was thus modeling a son's moral obligation to his father and a subject's obligation to his king. The word translated as righteousness is dharma.

Dharma: The Moral Order of the Cosmos

Some concepts, generally the most important ones, cannot be easily translated. If there is a key concept for understanding Indian society, it is the concept of dharma, which we will simply call by its Indian name.

Dharma has a wide range of meanings deriving from the Sanskrit root *dhr*. It means the essential foundation of things, and so signifies "truth." It means that which is established, customary, or proper, and so signifies "traditional" or "ceremonial." It means one's duty or responsibility, hence "moral obligation." It means that which is right, virtuous, or meritorious, hence "ethical" (Malony 1987). It means, in sum, both "the way things are" and "the way things should be."

Though mostly from a somewhat later period, the concept of dharma is found in the very earliest Indian text, the *Rg Veda* (1200 B.C.), where we hear about the gods engaged in dharma when they separate day from night, make one season follow another, and make the rains fall. The gods do not create the universe but maintain its good order through their ceremonial acts, their vows, and their ascetic practices. And later, in the Laws of Manu, which ordain how humans should conduct themselves in moral society, those who support dharma are promised "fame in this world and incomparable happiness after death" (Manu 2.9). Thus, both humans and gods are responsible for maintaining dharma.

Every social category and life stage has its own dharma that contributes to the fundamental goodness and order of the cosmos. There is a term, *svadharma*, which means "one's own" (sva-) dharma, but this does not imply an individualistic, personal sense of values such as Westerners typically mean by such phrases as "This is what I stand for" or "These are my own personal values." Svadharma means an individual's moral obligation *given one's position in the social order*. There is the dharma of kings (*rajadharma*), the dharma of women (*stridharma*), the dharma of one's class (*varnadharma*), the dharma of one's life stage (*asramadharma*), the dharma of one's caste (*jatidharma*). The moral order of society is composed of social categories, not of individuals. The *Dharmashastras* (the "science of dharma") were lawbooks expounding on dharma for the various classes of people.

Dharma has its opposite: *adharma*.[1] Adharma means "immorality" or "unrighteousness" or against the natural order inherent in the universe. A person may conduct himself in an adharmik manner. A society may lapse into disorder, wickedness, chaos. A society where people do not live by the dharma of their class, gender, life stage, and caste is a chaotic, immoral society. The concept of dharma holds society to an ideal that it cannot always meet, and its sympathy for reform is generally limited to reinterpreting change in terms of ancient values.

It was the work of the centuries from about 700 to 300 B.C. to find ways to link dharma to the state and to stabilize the early kingdoms that all too easily fell into bloody conflict.

The First Civilizations

The first urban society in India emerged in the Indus Valley around 2300 B.C. This was the world's third civilization, a thousand years later than Egypt and Sumer in Mesopotamia. Indus Valley was in contact with Sumer via a land route stretching from oasis to oasis across the Iranian Plateau, and via a much easier coastal route in the shallow waters of the Arabian Sea and up the Persian Gulf. India was the fabled source of peacocks and monkeys, ivory and gems, spices and incense. The cities of Indus Valley were dependent on the great Indus River for a water source and for transportation. They grew wheat and cotton, were the first to weave cotton into cloth, and brought their raw materials by river to the two great cities of Mohenjo-Daro and Harappa.

The first civilizations did not emerge quickly but required a long evolution out of farming communities whose growth and increased productivity supported the nonproductive elite that dominated them. Box 5.1, "Characteristics of Civilization," identifies some of the primary and secondary features associated with early civilizations. The political structure of a civilization is the state, where power is centralized in a monarch or oligarchy. Society had grown more complex, with new forms of specialization and stratification. The king gathered around him a full-time warrior class; priests who functioned as advisors, diviners, and intercessors with the gods; and a nobility composed of the king's family and lineage that grew larger and more powerful by the generation. All these people had to be supported by the agricultural classes. Older studies sometimes talk about the "surpluses" produced by early states that allowed nonagricultural classes to emerge as if surpluses were some kind of natural phenomenon growing out of agricultural technology. The facts are much less pleasant. Independent cultivators were turned into peasants, tied to the land by various devices that squeezed them for surpluses to support the growing nonproductive elite. A percentage of the harvest, often 25 percent or 50 percent, was demanded, which forced peasants to work harder and find ways to grow more, because their own subsistence needs remained the same. It was political coercion, not simply improved agricultural technology, which squeezed out an extra portion of grain to be passed upward as taxation.

5.1   Characteristics of Civilization

Primary Features

The State:

- Centralized authority in a monarch, king, emperor, or oligarchy
- Stratification of society with an aristocracy, priesthood, military, and peasants
- A tax/tribute system for redistribution of surpluses upward

High population densities
Expanded food production to support economically unproductive classes
Urbanization: villages, towns, and a few true urban centers with populations of 7,000 to 10,000
Full-time craft specialists

Secondary Features

Monumental art and architecture
Long-distance trade
Codified law
Writing systems
Mathematics and astronomy
Religion in the service of the state
Bifurcation of folk culture and court culture, with court-sponsored arts and intellectual traditions

In the meantime, urban densities formed around the king's court and in a few trade centers, so that along with villages there is a hierarchy of urban spaces: towns and one or two major cities. In the earliest cities, ten thousand was a lot of people; by 2500 B.C., there are cities with populations close to one hundred thousand. Cultural and intellectual life began to diverge from village culture in the urban centers of privilege in the courts of early kings. Specialists of all sorts elaborated their own cultural domains: a few carpenters turned into architects and engineers, building palaces, temples, and mausoleums for their royal patrons; ministers codified the law; priests pondered the old myths and rites, raising new philosophical questions. They gazed at the stars and developed astrology and astronomy. Mathematics grew out of useful practices like engineering and astronomy. Royal courts sponsored new forms of art: theater, music, dance, and poetry. Most interesting of all, perhaps, is the development of new uses for religion: The power of the state needed to be legitimated somehow; new forms of religion emerged in the service of the state.

Note that a civilization is something more than a state. States are political formations that can come and go rather quickly, and most will not form a true civilization around themselves. A civilization includes enduring cultural traditions that can be maintained and passed on from generation to generation even when political centralization has lapsed, whereas a state is a centralized social system that is much more vulnerable to spinning into disorder at the death of a powerful leader or collapsing into bitterly contested struggles for leadership that end in fragmentation. So civilizations can outlast particular states. Indian civilization has survived through eras when no state could be said to be functioning or when only small regional states existed. Similarly, Chinese civilization has stretched across eras when the state itself disappeared in periodic chaos.

Indus Valley Civilization (2300–1750 B.C.)

Indus Valley is the mystery civilization of Asia. While its two major cities, Mohenjo-Daro and Harappa, have been extensively excavated and now lie exposed once again to the blistering sun of Pakistan (see box 5.2, "A Most Curious Object"), almost everything we would want to know about the people and their culture remains unexplained. Perhaps these people were ancestors of the Dravidians, who are now the vast populations of the southern Indian states of Tamilnadu, Kerala, and Mysore. There are a few tiny tell-tale pockets of Dravidian-speakers stranded in the Indus Valley region of Baluchistan, though now the languages of the northern states are all Indo-European. They certainly had a well-organized and centrally planned society, but what kind of political order was responsible for this is not clear from the archaeological record. They had a script, but what ideas were captured by it is unknown because the script has never been deciphered. The religious ideas that motivated their lives have left traces only in rough sculptural form, and so the connection to later Indian ideals remains conjectural (Fairservis 1975).

The cities of Mohenjo-Daro and Harappa were the most modern cities of their time; there was a genius of civil engineering and public works. The cities were built on a grid plan, with a broad north-south street bisected by narrower east-west streets. Houses built on these streets were often large and multiroomed with windowless exterior walls, inner courtyards, and flat roofs. This house style remains prominent in much of India to this day, allowing family life to be lived in inner privacy in the courtyard and, on hot nights and cool winter days, on the rooftop. Many of these houses had private interior wells with outlets in several rooms of the house. Bathrooms were built against an exterior wall, with sloping floors and chutes that drained bathwater to the lane outside. From there, sewage was disposed through brick-lined covered channels to cesspits outside the city. This water and sanitation engineering was unmatched anywhere in the world prior to the last couple of centuries.

5.2   A Most Curious Object

In the winter of 1872–3, while touring the Punjab, Cunningham investigated Harappa, on the Ravi river. It was 'the most extensive of all the old sites along the Ravi', and, according to Charles Masson who discovered it on his way to Afghanistan, it boasted the ruins of a vast brick castle. Cunningham found plenty of bricks, several mounds of them in fact, but no castle. Nor was he altogether surprised. Standing amongst the mounds, he could hear the trains rattling along the new Lahore-Multan line. More than a hundred miles of track had been ballasted with bricks from Harappa.

> The most curious object discovered at Harappa is a seal . . . which was found along with two small objects like chess pawns, made of dark brown jasper. . . . The seal is a smooth black stone without polish. On it is engraved very deeply a bull, without hump, looking to the right with two stars under the neck. Above the bull there is an inscription in six characters which are quite unknown to me. They are certainly not Indian letters. . . .

The seal itself found its way into the British Museum where it was joined by one or two others which came to light during the late nineteenth century. But no further progress was made in probing their significance. . . . Certainly Sir John Marshall attached no immediate importance to them. For twelve years after his appointment as Archaeological Director, no one visited the place. When one of the Department's staff finally visited Harappa in 1914, it was just to survey it. He did indeed recommend that the main mound be excavated, but it was not until 1921 that work started. In that year, more pottery and more seals were discovered, as well as a number of stone implements. But still the significance of these finds was doubtful.

But the breakthrough was imminent. A year before, R. D. Banerji, one of Marshall's Indian recruits, had been travelling in the sand wastes of Sind 400 miles south of Harappa and near the mouth of the Indus. At a place called Mohenjo-daro, he stopped to investigate a ruined Buddhist stupa and monastery, both built in brick, and he noticed in their vicinity several other promising-looking mounds. Two years later a trial dig got under way. Some engraved pieces of copper and some seals were found. One of the seals depicted what was thought to be a unicorn; all bore pictographic letters which Banerji immediately recognized as belonging to the same class as those on the Harappa seals.

In 1924, Marshall compared the finds from Mohenjo-daro with those from Harappa, and recognized that they belonged 'in the same stage of culture and approximately to the same age, and that they were totally distinct from anything known to us in India.' In a report to the *Illustrated London News* in 1924 Marshall could not conceal his excitement.

> Not often has it been given to archaeologists, as it was given to Schliemann at Tiryns and Mycenae, or to Stein in the deserts of Turkestan, to light upon the remains of a long forgotten civilization. It looks, however, at this moment, as if we are on the threshold of such a discovery in the plains of the Indus. Up to the present our knowledge of Indian antiquities has carried us back hardly further than the third century before Christ. . . . Now, however, there has unexpectedly been unearthed, in the south of the Punjab and in Sind, an entirely new class of objects which have nothing in common with those previously known to us. . . .

John Keay, 1988, pp. 165–68.

This photo shows the citadel at Mohenjo Daro after excavation. In the distance is visible a Buddhist stupa from a later era.

A society that is technologically advanced enough for this kind of town planning and sanitation engineering surely, one might suppose, would be able to write its language. Contemporary civilizations had this knowledge: Sumerians had developed cunieform and Egyptians had hieroglyphics, both of which can now be read. Early Chinese civilization, which developed later, also had a script that can be read today. But Indus civilization does not appear to have advanced far along this route, a tremendous handicap to us when it comes to attempts at understanding this early phase of Indian history. All known samples of Indus script come from some four thousand seals and a bit of graffiti on pottery. These seals were terra-cotta rectangles an inch or two in dimension that would leave an impression in wax and may have been used as a wax seal on parcels. There were a total of 419 signs, with 200 in frequent use. This is too many for an alphabetic script like ours, and not enough for a logographic one like Chinese. Most probably it was syllabic. But there are no long texts; the longest string of characters is a mere twenty-one signs, and the average is more like five or six (Fairservis 1975). Thus, it is unlikely that the script was used to express complex ideas in religious texts or historical

This seal, less than two inches wide, is one of hundreds found in Indus Valley sites. The characters on the top have never been translated. Many of the seals, like this one, show a bull before what may be a sacrificial post, suggesting that in Indus Valley bulls were objects of sacrifice and perhaps also of worship.'

accounts. The best guess at present, based partly on the fact that Indus seals have been found in Sumer, is that the inscriptions were names of merchant families used to identify goods in long-distance trade.

When it comes to religious ideas, again we have to guess on the basis of intriguing clues. The seals that bear the puzzling inscriptions also contain pictures of animals that were important then: the humped bull, tiger, camel, antelope, and elephant. Often animals are depicted tethered to an ornamented post as if about to be sacrificed, and one shows a woman about to be sacrificed, her arms raised in supplication. A frequent figure is the horned god, a male sitting in a cross-legged pose with his hands on his knees and wearing a headpiece of buffalo horns. In one, two worshippers kneel beside him with hooded cobras towering over them. This deity so resembles the later god Shiva that he is often referred to as the Proto-Shiva. The frequency of religious themes on the seals could sustain a religious, rather than commercial, function.

Other hints of later Hindu practices are the many female images, possibly goddesses, which far outnumber male images. They are often crudely made of terra-cotta, as if constructed for popular use or to be discarded after brief use at a festival. These mother goddesses are lavishly decorated with layers of necklaces, bangles, and belts; have fabulous fan-shaped headdresses; and are bare-breasted. Perhaps this is how women of the Indus Valley dressed. In later times, the Indus Valley goddess, who had a partner in the Proto-Shiva, was temporarily eclipsed by the male deities of the Aryan pantheon, but she ultimately reemerged as the primordial Shakti, who takes form in Kali, Durga, Saraswati, and other female deities. A few better-made male images were also found, one assumed to be a priest, another remarkably (but impossibly) Greek-looking from the realism of his torso.

Most puzzling of all is the question of how Indus Valley civilization was organized. Though it spread across a vaster region than either Sumer or Egypt, a thousand miles from west to east, with over one thousand towns and two or three great cities so far excavated or located, there is precious little evidence of strong centralized government beyond the indirect evidence of the well-laid out cities. No palace complex exists where a great king might have lived and held court. No great temple complex bears testimony to a cult of the divinities depicted on seals and in terracotta statuettes. There is no evidence of rivalry between states or of warfare. The closest to a structural center of power that has been discovered is a pillared hall with many tiny adjacent rooms called by archaeologists an "assembly hall" located at the highest points at Mohenjo-Daro and Harappa. There is little to suggest the residence of a great king here, but it just might be the center of a priesthood, whose monks lived in the cubicles and functioned as a powerful oligarchy in worship of a god and goddess, ordering society through their ritual authority, and enforcing a rational plan in the laying out of the cities and maintaining water and sewage systems. What seems most powerful in Indus Valley civilization is not monarchical authority so much as some kind of cultural authority, the existence of a conceptual plan for human social life that got peacefully recreated wherever people settled and formed villages and towns.

The Vedic Age (1500–450 B.C.)

For Indus Valley civilization we have ruins but no words; for the Vedic Age, we have words but hardly any ruins, at least for the formative first thousand years. But this vast resource of texts tells us, directly or indirectly, a great deal about the people who entered India in the centuries following the decline of the great cities of the Indus Valley. We must remember that a state can dissolve and cities fall into ruin while a civilization is kept alive by rural populations that go right on living much as they always did. What makes the early post-Indus culture a puzzle for historians is that a new ethnic group, the Indo-European Aryans, apparently entered India from the northwest, conquered and intermarried with the local people, and eventually established a series of small kingdoms across North India. They brought a very different culture with them, whose most important religious ideas are contained in four texts, the *Vedas*. The cultural tradition that finally emerged must have been a syncretism of the new Aryan culture with older Indus culture, but who contributed what to the mix has not been sorted out.

The Aryans, like the Hittites and Greeks to whom they were ethnically related, were a society of Bronze-Age tribal warriors who herded cattle and were organized patriarchally under tribal chieftains called rajas. They worshipped male gods whose names were widely known to Indo-Europeans, as evidenced by the appearance in Hittite texts of about 1400 B.C. of Indra (Indara in Hittite), Varuna (Uruvna), Mitra (Mitira), and the Naksatras (Nasatiya). Like the Greeks, they moved into a region where more advanced urban civilizations were already in decline. Their religion of transcendent gods of the heavens encountered and partially replaced the earth goddesses of agricultural peoples. And like the Greeks, they brought epics of heroic and embattled kings that were composed early in the first millennium B.C. and written down much later. The Mahabharata, like the *Iliad*, is an epic tale of bloody warfare among related princes; the Ramayana, like the *Odyssey*, is the tale of a long exilic journey in territories of mythical beings, ending with a joyful return home. The kidnapped Helen of Troy, whose abduction leads to the Trojan War, has her counterpart in the abducted Sita, whose rescue dominates the Ramayana.

For the first five hundred years, the newcomers made themselves at home in the upper and lower reaches of the Indus. They wrote of encountering empty cities and dark-skinned people called *dasas* whom they scorned and fought. For the next five hundred years (from about 1000 to 450 B.C.), they moved eastward, discovered the great Ganges system, and began setting up small kingdoms all across North India. Certain of these kingdoms became famous in the great epics. Indraprastha (now Delhi) and Hastinapur were the capitals of the Pandavas and Kauravas in the Mahabharata. Kosala, the capital city of which, Ayodhya, was Rama's kingdom, and Mithila, the capital of Sita's father, King Janaka, figure in the Ramayana. Kashi was the ancient name of modern Banaras, sacred to Shiva. And Pataliputra, the easternmost kingdom of the Vedic Age, was the first kingdom to conquer the others and establish an empire that stretched from Bengal to the Indus, the Mauryan dynasty, in 323 B.C.

The most ancient "texts" of the Aryans were too sacred to write down, even after a script was devised late in the Vedic Age. The Vedas were *sruti*, "heard" scripture, directly revealed words of the gods or of the cosmos, and they were passed down orally from teacher to disciple, just as they are today, three thousand years later, as young Brahmans memorize whole books by precise formulas of rote learning intended to ensure that even if passages are not well understood, they will nonetheless be passed on in linguistically perfect form. Eventually, Brahmans made their peace with writing and wrote the Vedas down, but the Vedas still exist mostly as oral texts chanted at rituals. The oldest Veda, the Rg Veda, is a collection of 1,017 poems in Sanskrit so archaic that some of it is not fully translatable. The oldest portions may have been composed as early as 1200 B.C.

"The Creation" (see box 5.3, "Two Myths from Rg Veda") is a very early speculation on the perennial puzzle of the origin of the universe. What could have existed before all that presently exists came into being? How could what exists now have arisen? It hypothesizes a primordial condition when there was no space, no sky, no night or day, no life, and, therefore, no death. The forces of creation imagined in the Rg Veda are heat ("That One arose through the power of heat") and desire ("desire came upon That One in the beginning"). It raises the possibility that gods might have created the cosmos, only to reject it: "The gods came afterward with the creation of the universe." But a more shadowy, unnamed entity called only "That One" arose through heat, and then, through the flush of desire, the "first seed of mind" was planted. The creative power of heat and the existence-maintaining properties of desire would continue to be fundamental assumptions of Indian thought for the next three millennia. We do not hear that this One in the high heavens is any of the known gods such as Varuna, Mitra, or Indra. There is no idea about this One at all. That One knows and desires, but does not create. Already we find nuclear ideas of later Hinduism: multiple gods vs. a prior, more abstract sense of God; desire as the central fact of existence (with its opposite, desirelessness, associated with nonexistence); and the priority of mind over the material.

"The Cosmic Sacrifice" seems to be describing a later phase of cosmos making. The gods now exist and what do they do up in the heavens? They make sacrifices. Another divine figure, Purusha ("the sacrifice born at the beginning"), is bound "as the sacrificial beast." One is reminded of Indus Valley seals with the bull tied to the sacrificial post. The division of the sacrifice brings the essential components of the phenomenal world into existence. From the melted fat of Purusha were made beasts of the air, the forest, and the village.

5.3   Two Myths from Rg Veda

The Creation

There was neither non-existence nor existence then; there was neither the realm of space nor the sky which is beyond. What stirred? Where? In whose protection? Was there water, bottomlessly deep? There was neither death nor immortality then. There was no distinguishing sign of night nor of day. *That One* breathed, windless, by its own impulse. Other than that there was nothing beyond. Darkness was hidden by darkness in the beginning; with no distinguishing sign, all this was water. The life force that was covered with emptiness, That One arose through the power of heat.

Desire came upon That One in the beginning; that was the first seed of mind. Poets seeking in their heart with wisdom found the bond of existence in nonexistence. Their cord was extended across. Was there below? Was there above? There were seed-placers; there were powers. There was impulse beneath; there was giving-forth above.

Who really knows? Who will here proclaim it? Whence was it produced? Whence is this creation? The gods came afterwards, with the creation of this universe. Who then knows whence it has arisen? Whence this creation has arisen—perhaps it formed itself, or perhaps it did not—the One who looks down in it, in the highest heaven, only he knows—or perhaps he does not know.

Rg Veda 10.129

The Cosmic Sacrifice

When the gods performed the sacrifice with Purusha as the offering, spring was the clarified butter, summer the fuel, autumn the oblation. They anointed Purusha, the sacrifice born at the beginning, upon the sacred grass. With him the gods, perfected beings, and sages sacrificed. From that sacrifice in which everything was offered, the melted fat was collected, and he made it into those beasts who live in the air, in the forest, and in villages. From that sacrifice in which everything was offered, the verses and chants were born, the meters were born from it, and from it the formulas were born. Horses were born from it, and those other animals that have two rows of teeth; cows were born from it, and from it goats and sheep were born.

When they divided Purusha, into how many parts did they apportion him? What do they call his mouth, his two arms and thighs and feet? His mouth became the Brahmin; his arms were made into the Kshatriya (warrior); his thighs the Vaishyas (the people); and from his feet the Shudras (servants) were born. The moon was born from his mind; from his eye the sun was born. Indra and Agni came from his mouth, and from his vital breath the Wind was born. From his navel the middle realm of space arose; from his head the sky evolved. From his two feet came the earth, and the quarters of the sky from his ear. Thus they set the worlds in order.

There were seven enclosing-sticks for him and thrice seven fuel-sticks, when the gods, performing the sacrifice, bound Purusha as the sacrificial beast. With the sacrifice the gods sacrificed to the sacrifice. These were the first dharmas. These very powers reached the dome of the sky where dwell the perfected beings, the ancient gods.

Rg Veda 10.90

Wendy Doniger O'Flaherty, 1988.

Humans, however, come from the division of the body of Purusha. Perhaps the most significant feature is that the first division of humans at the very creation was not by gender (as in "male and female created He them") but by social classification: the mouth became Brahmans (priests), the arms became Kshatriyas (warriors), the thighs became Vaishyas (the people), and the feet became Shudras (servants). This four-category classification known as the *varna* system, the basis for the caste system, was created by sacrifice at the very beginning of the universe.

Finally, in this myth we see the gods in the heavens doing the same work as Brahmans on earth. They perform sacrifices. Everything comes from it. And it follows that if you want to keep the cosmos in good order, sacrifice becomes essential. That is the duty of Brahmans, whose principal activity during the Aryan period (as well as in the present) was performing the many required sacrifices. Their central feature was the burning of the sacred fire with offerings of *ghi* (clarified butter), certain kinds of grain and wood, and sprinkles of water, along with chanting the appropriate Vedic verses. These rituals were always done on behalf of a householder or king, the *yajman*, who cannot perform the sacrifice himself.

The sacrificial flame itself, which is the embodiment of the god Agni, is the transforming power of the cosmos. What makes fire sacred? Fire is the sun, the source of heat and life. It is terrestrial fire, a piece of the sun on earth. It is the household fire, which cooks the food that nourishes us. It is lightning, the mediating fire that connects the sky and the earth. Fire is life, for the sun makes things grow. Finally, at death, a bit of fire brought from the cooking hearth lights the funeral pyre that burns the body and releases the soul.

A Tale of Two Kings: The Premodern Hindu State

The kingdoms that arose in North India in the first millennium B.C. established certain ideals for the Hindu polity that had far-reaching influence throughout the subcontinent and into Southeast Asia in later times. Two ancient Indian kings, one mythical, one historical, stand out as models of the Indic monarch. The actual king inherited India's first great empire, enlarged it through bloody conquest, then transformed it by institutionalizing a new state religion throughout his domain. The mythological king, assuming he *was* mythological, never actually ruled anywhere, but his reputed reign is regarded as India's golden age, while the historical king was totally forgotten in India (though not outside of India) within a few centuries and had to be rediscovered in the nineteenth century by British scholars. The kings I am referring to are Rama (of the Ramayana) and Ashoka (269 to 232 B.C.).

Rama: Hero of the Ramayana. Rama's story is told and retold in hundreds of versions throughout India and Southeast Asia, in poetry and prose, almost always as a public event (see box 5.4, "The Ramayana"). It is constantly being performed in villages and urban areas, as in the past it was performed in court. It is chanted by pandits reading from a text, enacted by traveling troupes of actors, or performed by puppets. For the last 150 years, the Ramayana has been presented as an annual "theatre of hyperreality" at a site across the Ganga River from Banaras (Schechner 1993). In nightly episodes lasting a month, Rama's fourteen-year exile is reenacted by actors and followed by audience-pilgrims who literally journey from site to site where all the critical pan-Indian locations, from Ayodhya to Sri Lanka, are reproduced around the palaces and gardens of the Maharaja of Banaras and the town of Ramnagar. The actors who play Rama, Sita, Lakshman, and Hanuman are *svarup*, "forms" or incarnations of the divine figures themselves, worshipped with garlands and *pranams* (respectful folding of hands or touching of the feet) at the end of each performance. At the end of the last episode, when Rama and Sita have returned triumphally to Ayodhya to begin the glorious reign of Rama, the actors' feet become black and blue with reverential touching. Before the final performance of farewell to Rama and Sita, they are carried by royal elephants to the palace, where the Maharaja of Banaras, dressed simply as a devotee of Rama, washes their feet, and garlands and feasts them. These royally sponsored reenactments have been going on in India since at least the second century B.C., and spread to Southeast Asia where even today scenes from the Ramayana may be seen on the inner side of the great wall surrounding the royal palace in Bangkok.

5.4 The Ramayana

The King of Lanka, a ten-headed demon named Ravana, has won a promise by the gods that he cannot be conquered by any divine or demonic force. Dismissing as impossible the notion that any mortal could destroy him, he thinks he is invincible. At the same time, in the city of Ayodhya, King Dasharatha is having a special sacrifice to provide him with a male heir. Immediately his three queens give him sons. Eldest is Rama, son of queen Kausalya; Queen Kaikeyi gives birth to Bharata; and Queen Sumitra gives birth to twins, Lakshman and Shatrughna.

Rama's career as a warrior begins when as a young man his teacher-sage Vishvamitra leads him and Lakshman to the nearby kingdom of Mithila, where they encounter King Janaka in the middle of a great sacrifice. Janaka stops to welcome the princes from Ayodhya and tells them about the miraculous birth of his daughter, Sita, found when the king plowed a furrow in the earth. Because of this miraculous birth he has vowed she will only be given in marriage to a hero who can pull the bow of Shiva, which is in his keeping. Many princes and kings have come, failed to pull the bow, and in their humiliation waged war. Rama is shown the bow; he pulls it so hard he breaks it, and thus wins Princess Sita's hand in marriage.

Not long after, King Dasharatha resolves to retire, and arranges for the coronation of Rama. As Rama is beloved by the citizens of Ayodhya, there is great rejoicing as the day approaches. But Dasharatha's youngest queen, Kaikeyi, fearful that her fortunes will decline when Rama is king, plots against him. Dasharatha owes her two favors, which she now claims. First, he must banish Rama to the forest for fourteen years, and second, her own son Bharata must be put on the throne. Dasharatha is grieved, but must fulfill his vow. Rather than resort to force of arms to keep the throne, Rama insists on fulfilling his father's vow and accepts the banishment. Bharata, loyal to his half-brother, places Rama's sandals on the throne and rules as regent until Rama returns. At first Rama plans to take only his brother Lakshman, but Sita insists she can never be happy if separated from her husband and that the forest will be a better place than the palace if she is with her husband. Finally Rama agrees to take her, too. As the people of Ayodhya weep, Rama, Lakshman, and Sita depart.

Many adventures occur in the forests and jungles that they traverse in their wanderings. A demoness named Shurpanakha falls in love with Rama and threatens to eat Sita. Lakshman cuts off her nose. She flees to her brother, Ravana, and tells him of the cruelty of Rama and the beauty of Sita. Ravana decides to kidnap Sita for himself, and carries her off to his kingdom in Sri Lanka. Desperate to find Sita, Rama encounters a monkey prince named Sugriva, who has also lost his wife under similar circumstances. They resolve to help each get the other's wife back. Particularly helpful is Sugriva's minister, Hanuman. It is Hanuman who comes to Rama's aid, discovering the location of Sita, under guard in a grove near Ravana's palace. He witnesses her constant refusal of Ravana's advances, creeps in to present her with a signet ring belonging to Rama, and promises to soon rescue her. Hanuman allows himself to be captured in order to enter the court of Ravana; there they set his tail on fire. The quick-witted monkey manages to escape, sets the city on fire with his burning tail, and returns to Rama with his inside knowledge of the Lanka capital.

Now the monkey army, led by Rama, Lakshman, and Sugriva, begin their assault on Lanka. They build a bridge across the strait so the army can cross. There is a huge battle with tremendous loss of life on both sides. At the end, Rama and Ravana meet in hand-to-hand combat, and Ravana dies at Rama's hand.

Sita's virtue is now in question. Did she or didn't she remain chaste while in Ravana's control? She insists on undergoing a test of fire; she enters the fire and emerges unscathed in proof of her virtue. Then Rama and Sita return triumphantly to Ayodhya, whose citizens light candles to welcome them, an event repeated every year at the fall holiday of Divali. Rama rajya begins; Rama now rules over Ayodhya in years of peace and well-being. The perfection of Rama rajya is marred only by the renewal of gossip about Sita. Rama's one weakness is to give in to these rumors and banish Sita, once again, to the forest. There, she lives in the shelter of a sage and gives birth to twin sons, Lava and Kusha. She remains, even in banishment, the loving and loyal wife of Rama, teaching her sons to sing the praises of their father. Finally she returns to the earth from whence she came, and Rama lives many years in private loneliness without Sita until he finally ascends to heaven.

A televised serial in 1987 had over 80 million viewers, the most watched program ever on Indian television. Paula Richman (1991:3) describes the reactions of viewers:

> It was not just that people watched the show: they became so involved in it that they were loath to see it end. Despite the fact that Doordarshan, the government-run network, had only contracted with the producer for a year's worth of episodes, the audience demanded more. In fact, sanitation workers in Jalandhar went on strike because the serial was due to end without depicting the events of the seventh, and final, book of the Ramayana. The strike spread among sanitation workers in many major cities in North India, compelling the government to sponsor the desired episodes in order to prevent a major health hazard. . . . Many people responded to the image of Rama on the television screen as if it were an icon in a temple. They bathed before watching, garlanded the set like a shrine, and considered the viewing of Rama to be a religious experience.

After transforming India's television audience into a devotional congregation for a year, the Ramayana lent its expressive capacity to a more ominous event. On December 6, 1992, Hindu mobs led by right-wing, religiously motivated political parties—the Bharatiya Janata Party and the Vishva Hindu Parishad—demolished a sixteenth-century mosque said to have been built by the first Mughal emperor, Babur, over the birthplace of Rama in Ayodhya, setting off Hindu-Muslim riots across India in which more than five thousand people were killed.

What can account for the grip that this 2,500-year-old story has on the imagination of twentieth-century Indians? Some kind of *energia*, or "social energy"—the ability of a text to cause a "stir in the mind" (Greenblatt 1994)—is at work here. A text that has such life, age after age, is certainly a many-stranded thing; each generation and class brings its own set of historical circumstances and preoccupations to a narrative that invariably has fresh expressive capacity to energize a new age. Earlier in the century, Gandhi used the symbolism of *Rama rajya*, "Rama's reign," to mobilize Indians around a vision of a new golden age of an independent India, using a hymn to Rama as a nationalist rallying song. The Ramayana may have had its greatest surge of popularity during the thirteenth and fourteenth centuries as Central Asian invaders stormed across North India; Indians identified these rapacious aliens with the evil King Ravana, and their own Hindu kings were identified with the deposed but finally vindicated Rama.

However, during the era when the Ramayana was composed and had its first audiences—sometime between 750 and 500 B.C.—it was surely addressing different social concerns. As we know from all the epics that describe life in those times (the Ramayana, the Mahabharata, and the

Harivamsa), it was a violent era of bloody succession fights and conflict between small kingdoms. Kingdoms built by strength of arms had not found ways to moralize the exercise of power. The other great epic from this period, the Mahabharata, is the most pessimistic of all, describing a war of apocalyptic proportions with horrible weapons of destruction that ends with eighteen million corpses and the death of every principal character. King Dhritarashtra, in desolation, says: "This world is savage. How can one understand the savagery of this world?" and Bhishma replies: "You are part of it." Only in this century has anything close to the Mahabharata's apocalyptic vision occurred, when forty million people lost their lives during World War II.

The Mahabharata cannot imagine a dharma for a kshatriya (warrior) other than this one:

> [The kshatriya] must always be ready to slaughter the enemy, he must show bravery in battle. . . . The kshatriya who conquers in battle most effectively wins the [higher] worlds. Killing is the chief dharma of one who is a kshatriya. There is no higher duty for him than to destroy enemies. . . . [A kshatriya] who would satisfy the claims of his dharma, a king in particular, must fight.
>
> Mahabharata 12.60.13–18

The most famous and beautiful section of the Mahabharata is the *Bhagavadgita* (the "Song of God"), where the warrior-prince Arjuna halts in his chariot, filled with dread at the coming battle where he must kill his cousins or be killed by them. The god Krishna has taken the form of his charioteer and urges him on, giving him moral justification for it:

> I am time grown old, creating world destruction
> set in motion to annihilate the worlds;
> even without you, all these warriors
> arrayed in hostile ranks
> will cease to exist.
> Therefore, arise and win glory!
> Conquer your foes and fulfill your kingship!
> They are already slain by me.
> Be just my instrument,
> The archer at my side! (Miller 1986)

But the Ramayana has a new vision for kings. Its author, Valmiki, writing the Ramayana for kshatriya patrons, suggested a different dharma for kshatriyas. Rama rejects "the kshatriya's code (rajadharma) where unrighteousness and righteousness go hand in hand, a code that only debased, vicious, covetous, and evil men observe" (Pollock 1986:68). Rama is the first kshatriya prince to renounce *artha*, power. When palace intrigue puts his succession into jeopardy, instead of plunging into warfare to claim his rightful throne—the Mahabharata solution—he goes into a fourteen-year exile, living like an ascetic in the wilderness. On his return to Ayodhya at the end, purified by his suffering in exile, empowered by his asceticism, and made wise enough to govern, Rama ushers in a utopian age of peace, abundance, and righteousness.

Of course, there never was such an age, except in the imagination. The bloody centuries between the writing of the Ramayana (750–500 B.C.) and the first imperial unification in 323 B.C. provoked fundamental rethinking of the meaning of human existence and the nature of order in the cosmos and in society. There was profound questioning of the efficacy of the Brahmanical rites, rooted in the Vedas, which led to questioning of everything connected to life in society, from the family to the kingdom. Renunciation of society, already seen in Rama's voluntary acceptance of exile to the wilderness, in search of truth beyond society's (dis)order became common, and in Indian thought two great alternatives for meaningful human existence emerged: life in society and life outside of society. Even princes faced this choice, many of whom renounced, including most importantly Prince Gautama, who became the Buddha. We shall return to these issues later in this chapter.

In 326 B.C. Alexander the Great marched his armies across the five rivers of the Panjab, assaulting the front lines of Indian war elephants and infantry with his Macedonian cavalry and flaming arrows, defeating every raja who stood up to him. It was only disarray in his own hinterlands that caused him to stop at the Indus and turn back in the same year. He left behind him Greek generals who founded kingdoms in the upper Indus that survived for centuries (most importantly, a major city called Taxila), and left untouched an empire that was growing in the far east of the Ganges with its capital at Pataliputra. Much of what we know about this empire comes from reports by a Greek ambassador, Megasthenes, and from inscriptions left by the third ruler of the Mauryan dynasty, Ashoka.

Ashoka: The Forgotten King. Ashoka's life seems to have been filled with all those ambiguities of rajadharma that we have just seen. He inherited an empire extending from the Panjab to Bengal that had been unified by conquest carried out by his grandfather, Chandragupta Maurya, and expanded this empire southward by the same methods. Three principal sources describe Ashoka's reign and the manner in which the Mauryan Empire was governed. The first was an amoral, Machiavellian treatise called the *Arthashastra* ("The Science of Governing") said to have been written by Kautilya, a Brahman advisor to a Mauryan ruler thought to have been Chandragupta Maurya. Kautilya attempted to define the state just as I did at the beginning of this chapter. For Kautilya, it was a state when there was a king, his ministers, a territory, a fort, a treasury, an army, and allies. This practical treatise does not exactly describe a Rama rajya; rather, it describes a repressive civil and military bureaucracy sustained by spies, soldiers, and bureaucrats, where one fourth to one half of all crops were paid into the imperial treasury (Wolpert 1993:58–59). The treatise urges the shrewd king to make war on any other king he thinks he can defeat, and warns the king against trusting anyone, least of all his own administrators. "Bureaucracy," Wolpert concludes from his reading of Kautilya, "with all its mixed blessings, was thus obviously no recent Western import to Indian soil, and may have had indigenous roots in Harappan society" (Wolpert 1993:59).

However, two other sources present a different picture. These consist of a series of inscriptions on rocks and pillars put up by Ashoka across his empire, and several pious texts about the life of Ashoka, most importantly the *Asokavadana* ("The Legend of King Ashoka").

By the time the pillars that Ashoka erected along the periphery of his empire in the third century B.C. began to draw British interest in the nineteenth century, they were no longer associated with the name of Ashoka, nor could anyone read the inscriptions, which were in two kinds of forgotten scripts. (It was actually Ashokan brahmi; see chapter 3 for a sample.) Some thought the script looked a little like Greek, and for a while, there was a theory that Alexander the Great had come as far as Delhi. However, when more pillars began to turn up as far away as Bihar, it was clear some other explanation was needed. Eventually, over thirty columns were found in various conditions (Keay 1988). These had met various fates; one was gently pulled down, transported by ship up the Ganges, and erected on the third story of a Mughal mansion in Delhi, where it stands to this day. Others came in handy for cannon practice, and a couple served to support a bridge British engineers built over a silted-up river. In the seventh century, Xuanzang claimed to be able to read these pillars, but his translations have proved incorrect. For within a few centuries of Ashoka's time, knowledge of Ashokan brahmi was lost, and Hindus were referring to the pillars as "Bhima's walking stick" (Strong 1983). It was James Prinsep who finally cracked the code of Ashokan brahmi in the nineteenth century.

Some of the character of Ashoka can be read in the columns and rock edicts. His conversion to Buddhism is attested to by the Thirteenth Rock Edict (see box 5.5, "The Words of Ashoka"), where he regrets the suffering of Kalinga caused by his conquest, declares his devotion to dharma, and urges that dharma be accepted throughout his empire and proclaimed beyond it. In the "Legend of King Ashoka" we learn he was rejected by his father, King Bindusara, because of his ugly skin, despite the prophecy of a wandering ascetic that he would be a cakravartin, a "wheel-turning" monarch, that is, a great king who rules the whole world according to dharma. He succeeded in becoming king, but his cruel streak soon became apparent. After beheading five hundred of his ministers on a whim

This is one of more than 30 pillars erected by King Ashoka around his vast empire, proclaiming dharma. This one, bearing inscriptions in brahmi, was removed from its original site and carried upriver to be erected on the third floor of a Mughal prince's mansion, where it stands to this day.

5.5   The Words of Ashoka from the Thirteenth Rock Edict

When the king, *devanampiya* ("Beloved of the Gods," i.e., Ashoka), had been consecrated eight years, Kalinga was conquered, 150,000 people were deported, 100,000 were killed, and many times that number died. But after the conquest of Kalinga, devanampiya began to follow dharma, to love dharma, and to give instruction in dharma. Now devanampiya regrets the conquest of Kalinga, for when an independent country is conquered people are killed, they die, or are deported, and that devanampiya finds very painful and grievous. And this he finds even more grievous—that all the inhabitants. . . suffer violence, murder, and separation from their loved ones. . . The participation of all men in common suffering is grievous to devanampiya. Moreover there is no land, except that of the Greeks, where groups of brahmans and ascetics are not found, or where men are not members of one sect or another. . . .

For all beings devanampiya desires security, self-control, calm of mind, and gentleness. Devanampiya considers that the greatest victory is the victory of dharma; and this he has won here and even five hundred leagues beyond his frontiers in the realm of the Greek king Antiochus, and beyond Antiochus among the four kings Ptolemy, Antigonus, Magas, and Alexander. Even where the envoys of devanampiya have not been sent men hear of the way in which he follows and teaches dharma, and they too follow it and will follow it. Thus he achieves a universal conquest, and conquest always gives a feeling of pleasure; yet it is but a slight pleasure, for devanampiya only looks on that which concerns the next life as of great importance.

I have had this inscription of dharma engraved that all my sons and grandsons may not seek to gain new victories, that in whatever victories they may gain they may prefer forgiveness and light punishment, that they may consider the only victory the victory of dharma, which is of value both in this world and the next, and that all their pleasure may be in dharma. . . .

Modified from Wm. Theodore De Bary, ed., 1958, p. 144.

and burning alive five hundred women in his harem, he began to be called Ashoka the Fierce (Chandashoka). He employed an executioner who contrived to carry out all the tortures of the Buddhist hells right here on earth. One day Ashoka's executioner imprisoned a Buddhist monk, with plans to execute him the next day. But during the course of the night—spent meditating on the teachings of the Buddha—the monk achieved nirvana, breaking the bonds of existence. When on the following day the monk was thrown into a cauldron of human blood, urine, and excrement, the executioner could not get the fire to burn. Instead, the monk floated tranquilly on a lotus blossom in the midst of the filth and horror, and when Ashoka arrived to witness the execution, the monk began a display of stunning superhuman powers. Ashoka begged for an explanation. "I am the son of the Compassionate Buddha who has cut through the tangles of worldly inclinations," the monk informed him. "I am detached from all modes of existence" (Strong 1983:217). He told Ashoka of a prediction by the Buddha that one hundred years after his *parinirvana*, a cakravartin named Ashoka would spread his teachings by distributing his relics far and wide. "But instead you have built this place of suffering." Hearing these words, Ashoka put his hands together in repentance: "Forgive me this evil deed. Today I seek refuge in the Sangha, the Buddha, and in the Dharma[2] that is taught by the noble ones." Ashoka's next act was to distribute fragments of the Buddha's body throughout the world in eighty-four thousand stupas (a number connoting totality). From then on he became known as Dharmashoka.

As Dharmashoka, he was both cakravartin, "world ruler," and Buddhist layman. Who could better support the Buddhist monks than the king who has the entire treasury at his disposal? Ashoka enacted his rajadharma by many acts of religious donation (*dan*) to the *sangha*, culminating every five years in giving away all his worldly possessions as dan.

Though Rama was not historical and Ashoka was, that distinction means a good deal less than the fact that both kings were larger than life to subsequent ages through sacred texts held to be about the "really real." They provided moral-political models for later rulers coming to thrones through conquest, sometimes rising ignobly from highway banditry, or getting their start as tax collectors under the Mughals, and needing to moralize or legitimate their rule. The biographies of Rama and Ashoka presented a scenario for just rule. A Hindu king wished to rule like Rama. A Buddhist king wished to rule like Ashoka. And later rulers did emulate them, as we see from Xuanzang's eye-witness account of King Harsha (A.D. 606–647).

King Harsha lived during India's Classical Age, a great Hindu-Buddhist king whose capital was at Kanauj. At the end of the year A.D. 642, he invited to his capital all the disciples of all schools of thought—Brahman, Buddhist, and Jain—as well as all the subordinate rajas of his empire. Thousands came on elephants, chariots, palanquins, and foot. First he feasted all the vassals and the best of the Buddhist monks, Brahmans, and Jains, presenting them with new robes and golden dishes filled with coins. Eighteen days of religious debate and interpretation of sacred texts followed, with winners proclaimed and honored. Then came Harsha's *mahadan*, or "Great Almsgiving," held every five years in the manner attributed to Ashoka. On a large field at the junction of the Ganges and Jumna Rivers, all the monks and Brahmans of Harsha's kingdom were said to gather for seventy-five days of dan in which Harsha gave away his entire royal fortune. On the first three days, the gods were worshipped with dan: Buddha, Surya (the sun god), and Shiva. On subsequent days, dan was given to monks, Brahmans, Jains, the poor, orphans, and the destitute. Ultimately, five years' worth of royal accumulation was distributed, reserving only the military strength of the king to defend his kingdom (his horses, elephants, and weapons of war). He gave away every personal adornment until he had to beg his sister for an old cloth to cover his nakedness. Then he prayed to Buddha: "May I, in all my future births, continue always to give thus, so that I may attain salvation" (Mirsky 1964:100–103). At the end, the eighteen subordinate chiefs joined the king in acts of dan by distributing their own wealth to redeem the king's jewels and royal robes and presenting them back to him as gifts. When they finished, Harsha was as rich as before.

This pattern of establishing kingly authority through the giving of gifts, which often took the less extravagant form of providing support for Brahmans and endowing temples, became the essence of statecraft until British times and did not fully disappear even then. Lower-ranking chiefs established relationships with kings by sharing in the granting of royal gifts, as we have just seen Harsha's vassals doing. As Dirks writes about the Pallava kings and their hierarchical relationship with lower-ranking chiefs: "They received honor by participating in the granting of royal gifts (dan). In so doing, they entered into a relationship with the Pallava king predicated on the sharing of the king's sovereignty. That is, they became active and necessary participants in the central royal ritual; the sovereignty of the Pallavas that was predicated on their divine origin was shared with the chieftains who embodied similar virtues on a lesser scale" (Dirks 1989a:29).

Gradually, Buddhism disappeared from India, and the picture we see of Harsha honoring Buddhists as well as Brahmans, the Buddha as well as the Hindu gods, simplified into the older pattern of raja as chief patron of the Brahmans. At the same time, rajas began attempting to trace their genealogies to the gods—Vishnu or Indra or Surya or Shiva—emulating Rama's incarnation of Vishnu. As all good things flow from the gods, so the flow of gifts from the king established his authority and redistributed his sovereign substance to his people.

From *Dan* to Tax Collection

As the British moved into India, they brought different assumptions about the relationship of kings to subordinate chiefs and to peasants. They surmised that it was about tax collection, or that it should be. Efficient tax collection would take a reasonable share of each harvest, pay the tax collector a fee for his efforts, and flow into the state treasury to be disbursed for public works and payment of civil-service salaries. To the British, the state was a secular system based on a commercial logic of assets, income, and cash flow. What they found was a grossly disordered system of titles and honors, where temple rituals presided over by kings were affairs of state and where lower chiefs gave gifts to higher ones and were given territories in return. At every turn, whole villages and districts were simply given away to Brahmans or temples or military retainers, so that the ratio of actual revenues to theoretical revenues could be 25 percent or less. The Collector of Tirhut in the late eighteenth century wrote disapprovingly of this system:

> Raghava Singh [Maharaja of Darbhanga] by large presents to the Nawab Mohabat Jan acquired the lease of Tirhut at one lakh of rupees [Rs. 100,000] and a full confirmation of his title of Raja. He also paid annually a nazarana of 50,000 rupees to Raja Darnidhar, the Nawab's Dewan, which, together with other valuable presents annually repeated, secured to him the quiet possession of that [region]. (Stevenson-Moore 1901:44)

The system of Indic kingship—morally based on dharma and practically articulated through the hierarchical exchange of gifts and the redistribution of the king's authority downward, a system practiced for over two thousand years—was declared incompetent and corrupt, and the British set about amending it.

THE CASTE SYSTEM

Indians, like everyone else, are born into families and communities that already at birth define who they are. These communities will further shape the individual they are to become. One of these identities, however, has no real equivalent in any other society in the world. This identity specifies certain innate attributes shared with other members of the same community and locates that community in a hierarchical structure of the society as a whole. If a man is born a Brahman, for example, he is held "by nature" to be capable of learning the Vedas and performing the Vedic rites on behalf of others; he is naturally a calm and spiritual person. A Rajput is a lusty, martial sort of fellow, proud, quick to perceive an insult, and prone to heavy drinking. By tradition and innate capacity, he is a warrior and ruler, a descendant of Rama himself (Hitchcock 1959). In any local area, people identify the various groups, their own included, by such summarizing characterizations. In the West, we might call such a description a stereotype, but that would be to miss the essence of what Indians, particularly Hindus, mean by jati, or "caste" in English.

Beyond such traits as spiritual or martial temperament, members of the same jati are believed to share many other fundamental characteristics that come to them coded in their very blood and bones. These include tendencies toward certain character strengths and weaknesses, certain livelihoods, and certain codes for conduct (Marriott & Inden 1977). It helps to understand that the word jati at its most general means "kind," as in "kind of being" or "humankind"; it can mean "race," "tribe," "gender," and even "genus" and "species." So, the different castes of Indian society are of the same order of difference as the various biological species. Just as cows, tigers, dogs, and snakes have their own distinct character, food preferences, mode of livelihood, appropriate actions for their kind, and distinct breeding populations, so Brahmans, Rajputs, Baniyas, Lohars, Nai, and Bhangi have their separate and distinct character, food preferences, mode of livelihood, moral code, and marrying community. It is no more appropriate for Rajputs and Brahmans to intermarry than it is for tigers and cows to mate with each other. All these uniquely different animal and human species, or jatis, are the right and good order of nature and the cosmos, created at the cosmic sacrifice of Purusha and maintained, more or less, throughout the ages by the right conduct of living beings. This is dharma, the moral order of the universe.

This viewpoint does not dichotomize nature and culture (animals vs. humans) as does the Western view, but hierarchizes all beings in a ladder of higher and lower categories. The higher a group, the closer to perfection it is. Though any particular existence is confined to one or another of these categories, life flows through all of them. Humans in their various lifetimes may be incarnated in any of the human categories and may endure some existences as animals, ghosts, or demons. This long-term view characteristic of Hinduism, which spans hundreds of lifetimes, promotes moral and spiritual striving toward improvement. All beings, including animals and the gods, are in theory striving for spiritual perfection, for future existences that are better than the present one, and ultimately for escape from the cycle of life entirely. It is action, or *karma*, that determines the fate of the soul from one existence to the next.

The Cycle of Existence
gods
cows
rishis
ascetics
Brahmans
Kshatriyas
Vaishyas
Shudras
Untouchables
animals
ghosts
demons

Discussion of Indian sociology, it is clear, can quickly turn to Indian metaphysics; we will keep the focus on society in this section and turn to religion in the next.

The Varna System

In the myth of the "Cosmic Sacrifice" (see box 5.3, "Two Myths from Rg Veda"), we saw that the original primordial sacrifice of Purusha by the gods carved him into pieces that became the Brahman, the Kshatriya, the Vaishya, and the Shudra. These four social categories appeared early in the Aryan age, or may even have entered India with the Aryans. The Brahmans, or priests, and the Kshatriyas, or warriors and rulers, remained much the same over time. Vaishyas, in Aryan times, were conceptualized as commoners, but came to be the commercial castes. Shudras, once servants, became the many agricultural and artisan castes. In the Aryan age, these were probably more like classes, or varna; a classification system that attempted to conceptualize what must have been a tremendous cultural diversity in ancient India. There were the Aryans, themselves class-stratified; there were the Harappans or Dravidians, known to the Aryans as dasa, who must also have been stratified in some way; there were various tribal peoples—certainly more then than now—who were remote from the emerging states; there were Greeks, Central Asians, and other ethnolinguistic groups. The physical types were nearly as diverse as their customs, yet somehow all these groups came to be functionally interlinked without losing their separate identities in the Mauryan and Guptan empires, and the varna classification stretched to fit most of them.

The varna system became more rigid as time went on, yet it always had a certain fluidity to absorb new groups in the category most suitable to its conceptual structure. When the warlike tribal group known as Gujars came plundering in from Afghanistan, they were assimilated to the varna system as Kshatriyas. When humbler slash-and-burn cultivators were absorbed by expanding small states, they found occupational specializations and continued to cultivate, and were classified as Shudra. When, however, those specializations were of the most menial and polluting sort, such as scavenging, removing the filth of others, or dealing in the carcasses of dead animals, these people were considered too low, too inferior, too impure to be absorbed into any of the four varna categories. They were avarna, nonvarna, or, to use the English term, untouchable. On these people fell all the suffering of a system meant to preserve the good order of the original cosmic sacrifice.

Between 200 B.C. and A.D. 200, this social system was codified in a moral code book, or Dharmashastra, attributed to Manu (see box 5.6, "The Laws of Manu"). This work, which in the beginning was partly descriptive of what actually *was* happening and partly prescriptive, defining what *should* happen, came to have immense influence. As Brahmans interpreted it and kings enforced it, society became more rigorously shaped by its prescriptions.

Already in Manu's time, the logical model equating human groups with animal species had a perplexing flaw: the jatis lacked the barrier against successful mating that animals have biogenetically. Humans of different castes can and do mate and reproduce, regardless of how disap-

5.6   The Laws of Manu

v. 74. Brahmans who are intent on the means of gaining union with Brahman and firm in discharging their duties, shall live by duly performing the following six acts. . . .

v. 75. Teaching, studying, sacrificing for himself, sacrificing for others, making gifts and receiving them are the six acts for a Brahman.

v. 76. But among the six acts ordained for him, three are his means of subsistence: sacrificing for others, teaching, and accepting gifts from pure men.

v. 77. To the Kshatriya, three acts required of Brahmans are forbidden: teaching, sacrificing for others, and the acceptance of gifts.

v. 78. The same are likewise forbidden to a Vaishya; for Manu . . . has not prescribed them for men of those two castes.

v. 79. To carry arms for striking and for throwing is prescribed for Kshatriyas as a means of subsistence; to trade, to rear cattle, and agriculture for Vaishyas . . .

v. 80. Among the several occupations the most commendable are, teaching the Veda for a Brahman, protecting the people for a Kshatriya, and trade for a Vaishya.

v. 81. But a Brahman, unable to subsist by his peculiar occupations just mentioned, may live according to the law applicable to Kshatriyas; for the latter is next to him in rank.

v. 82. If it be asked, "How shall it be, if he cannot maintain himself by either of these occupations?" He may adopt a Vaishya's mode of life, employing himself in agriculture and rearing cattle.

v. 83. But a Brahman, or a Kshatriya, living by a Vaishya's mode of subsistence, shall carefully avoid the pursuit of agriculture, which causes injury to many beings and depends on others.

v. 95. A Kshatriya who has fallen into distress may subsist by all these means; but he must never adopt the mode of life prescribed for his betters.

v. 96. A man of low caste who through covetousness lives by the occupations of a higher one, the king shall deprive of his property and banish.

v. 97. It is better to do one's own duty incompletely than to perform completely that of another, for he who lives according to the law of another caste is instantly excluded from his own.

v. 99. But a Shudra, being unable to find service with the twice-born and threatened with the loss of his sons and wife through hunger, may maintain himself by handicrafts.

v. 100. Let him follow those mechanical occupations and those various practical arts . . .

v. 123. The service of Brahmans alone is declared to be an excellent occupation for a Shudra;

v. 126. A Shudra cannot commit an offense, causing loss of caste, and he is not worthy to receive the sacraments; he has no right to fulfill the sacred law of the Aryans, yet there is no prohibition against his fulfilling certain portions of the law.

v. 127. Shudras who are desirous to gain merit, and know their duty, gain praise if they imitate the practice of virtuous men without reciting the sacred texts.

Georg Buhler, trans., 1886, pp. 401–430.

These men of the Kahar caste are carrying a Brahman bride to her husband's house.

proving Manu and others may be. The great diversity of actual jatis came to be explained as the result of an ancient miscegenation between the four varnas. Bhangi, the sweeper caste, is said to be descended from a Shudra and a Brahman woman. Kahars, a caste of palanquin bearers, are descendants of a Brahman and an outcaste woman. Chamars, the leatherworkers, are offspring of a fisherman and an outcaste woman. By asserting descent from an intercaste marriage, the low and avarna castes lay claim to a higher origin and greater social dignity than they currently enjoy. At any rate, it is not the varna categories but the many hundreds or thousands of jatis that are the true, significant social entities within which Indians are born, marry, and die. A Brahman cannot marry just any Brahman; a Maithil Brahman must marry another Maithil Brahman and not a Kanyakubja Brahman; a Rajput marries another Rajput, not a Jat or Gujar, even though all three groups are Kshatriya. Even the many untouchable jatis observe this same rule of like marrying like: a Chamar does not marry a Balmiki or a Dom.

One sometimes hears that the caste system has disappeared or that it was abolished by the Indian constitution. This is untrue. A good 98 percent of Indians still marry within caste, as is immediately apparent from reading the matrimonial advertisements in most Indian newspapers where very modern families search for spouses in arranging marriages for their offspring. The caste system still dominates life in rural areas, where 80 percent of Indians still live. Modern electoral politics ignores castes as voting blocs at their peril. However, Part III of the Constitution of India does abolish untouchability and makes most of the older forms of discrimination a legal offense. These include restricting access to wells, bathing places, roads, temples, and public places. The Untouchability Offenses Act of 1955 put teeth into the constitution by providing fines or imprisonment for these offenses. These reforms have removed most of the more egregious discriminations, such as preventing members of unclean castes from getting an education, requiring them to shout or ring a bell warning upper castes of their approach, and forbidding women of these castes to cover their breasts.

Yet the old prejudices remain in subtle ways. Once when I was living in Meerut, my apartment came with the services of a young Bhangi woman to clean for me. Every day she headed straight for the bathroom and cleaned in a whirlwind of splashing water and vigorous scrubbing with her stiff broom. In the bedroom, I was required to come along behind her to lift the edges of blankets so she could sweep under the bed without polluting the bedding. She did not enter the kitchen at all, for this is the place where family meals are cooked, the purest center of any Hindu household; no unclean persons allowed there. (This would go for the wife as well during her monthly period.) When I gave her a cup of water, she placed the cup in a niche in the outer compound wall, assuming no one from my household would ever drink from that cup again. She laughed in delight when I had squashed a fat lizard in the shutters; it was her job to remove dead things. But when, conscience-stricken, I tried to explain that as I was an American, there was no clean and unclean here in my house, but rather she and I were equal, her face clouded in perplexity and doubt, and she slowly shook her head. I realized that when in India, I would have to live by their rules.

Pure and Impure

The hierarchical structure of beings assumes greater purity the higher one goes up the hierarchy, and less purity the lower one goes. Impurity seems to adhere to organic processes of waste and decay. Coming into contact with bodily effluvia or dead animals makes a person temporarily polluted. Some castes have the obligation to deal with these things as a livelihood; for instance, sweepers clean everyone's latrines. Leatherworkers deal with dead animals. Doms deal with dead humans. Therefore, they are permanently polluted and have the lowest places in the hierarchy.

Concern for the polluting effects of bodily processes accounts for a whole set of practices. The left hand is the "hand of pollution" because it is used for washing oneself with water after defecating and is therefore never used for eating; one eats with one's right hand. Saliva is polluting, once it has left one's mouth, and therefore traditionally Indians did not use silverware but carefully tossed bits of food into their mouths to prevent saliva from contacting the fingers. On ritual occasions, as in the past, meals are eaten from banana leaves, a kind of natural paper plate that is discarded after one use. Musical instruments that require blowing into them cannot be played by people of high caste, leaving that occupation open to the lower castes and to Muslims. Licking stamps and envelopes pollutes them and is best avoided.

Food and water are pollution prone, since impurities—like electricity—transfer easily in a water medium. Boiled rice is less safe than rice fried in oil. Eating is a dangerous time, all in all, because food can bring impurities into one's body. There is a whole set of foods, *kachcha* foods, which are so vulnerable to pollution that they are rarely shared with people of lower castes, boiled rice most of all. On the other hand, *pakka* foods are safer, ceremonial foods that can be shared at feasts: deep-fried breads, milk-based foods like yogurt and ghi (products of the cow), and raw foods. Milk is so pure that it can be safely taken from anyone providing you can be sure it has not been diluted with water.

Death pollution strikes everyone related to the dead person, usually for a period of eleven days; at the end of that period, male kinsmen must bathe and shave their heads in order to lift the death pollution. Birth is another highly biological time, filled with bodily fluids that are polluting and require the work of women specialists of several castes, but this is considered "happy pollution" and does not affect so wide a range of kinsmen.

Pollution falls heavily on women during their menstrual periods. They do not bathe or brush their hair or renew the *bindi* on their foreheads; they may not enter their kitchen or temples, but must sit on the front porch for four days, and will even wave the children away because they are unclean. At the end of four days they can bathe and put on clean clothes.

There is greater laxity these days with many of these observances; they tend to be followed with greater care in rural than urban settings, and among orthodox high-caste families than among the lower castes. One place where the high castes still adhere to these practices is among the orthodox Maithil Brahmans of Mithila.

The Castes of Mithila

Mithila is a culturally conservative region of north Bihar, lying just south of Nepal and the Himalayas between the Gandak and the Kosi Rivers before they flow into the Ganges. You might remember Mithila as the home of King Janaka and Sita, the place where Rama came to pull Shiva's

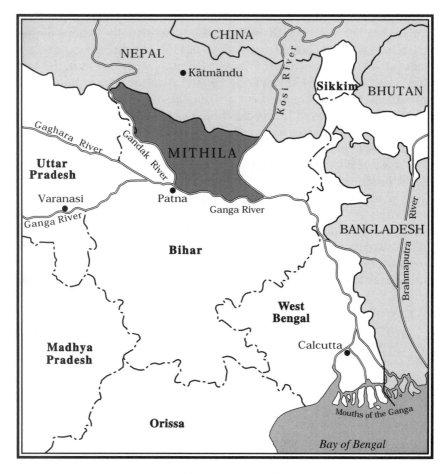

Map 5.2 Map of Mithila

bow and win the princess. A dynastic marriage linked Mithila[3] and Rama's kingdom of Kosala. During the colonial era, most of this land belonged to Darbhanga Raj; at 4,400 square miles, it was one of the largest of the zamindari[4] estates of British India. The Maharaja of Darbhanga was a Maithil Brahman, the most powerful caste of this region. Both before independence and now, whether measured by political power, by wealth and the control of land, or by status in the ritual hierarchy of castes, Maithil Brahmans dominate in Mithila.

There are several dozen principal castes in Mithila, but the major ones are shown in the box below, in rank order as perceived by a Brahman informant. When multiple informant views are compared from various levels of the hierarchy, there is disagreement about the precise ranking of castes near each other, who often compete for precedence by refusing to accept food or water from each other, thus claiming higher status. For example, Rajputs and Kayasthas each claim to outrank the other; here the Brahman informant takes the side of the Kayasthas.

The informant, a Maithil Brahman, has this to say about the other castes: Bhumihars are petty landlords who claim to be Brahmans but are lower because they have taken up agricultural pursuits and given up priestcraft. Maithil Brahmans serve as their priests for domestic rites. Kayasthas are record keepers for landowners and village surveyors and accountants. They are "famous for spending lavishly and do not hoard money like Bhumihars." The one hundred thousand Rajputs in Mithila are not native to the area, but came during the Mughal Era and became *zamindars,* which is why the Brahman counts them as lower than Kayasthas, even though Kayasthas are technically a superior type of Shudra.

The next few castes are the middle agricultural castes, "clean castes" in ritual terms, upwardly mobile in political and economic terms, now pushing against Brahman dominance and gaining power in local and state government. Yadavas are by far the largest caste in the region, at one eighth of the total population. They are herdsmen and cultivators and consider themselves related to the god Krishna, who was also a cowherd. The Chief Minister of Bihar, the top spot in state government, and formerly always in the hands of Brahmans, is now a Yadava. Dhanuk is another large agricultural caste, though originally they were archers; they are considered a "clean" caste from whom Brahmans can take water, and therefore they often are employed as servants by Brahmans. Koiri are considered industrious cultivators and among the best tenants in the area, but Brahmans will not take water from them, and therefore their status is lower than the Dhanuk. Mallah are boatmen and fishermen, and thus are considered lower than the chief agricultural castes above, although there is a slight anomaly here, for Brahmans will take water from them, but not from Koiri.

Principal Castes of Mithila and their Traditional Occupations

Maithil Brahman—priests, scholars
Bhumihar—agricultural zamindars
Kayastha—scribes
Rajput—zamindars
Yadava—herders of cows and water buffalo
Kewat—agriculture; servants
Dhanuk—agriculture; once archers
Koiri—vegetable gardeners
Mallah—fishermen and boatmen
Dusadh—agricultural laborers; "thieves"
Chamar—leatherworkers
Musahar— "rat eaters"
Teli—oil makers
Pamaria—singers and dancers
Mali—garland makers; vaccinators
Dom—basketmakers

This Maithil Brahman is chanting the genealogies at siddhanta, *a ceremonial affirmation of agreement to marriage between the fathers of the bride and groom.*

Then there are the unclean castes. Dusadhs are among the most stigmatized of the large castes, but are also economically very important as agricultural laborers and are gaining real political power in North Bihar because they form a large voting bloc with increasingly powerful leaders. The British knew them as a "caste of thieves" and in some of the larger villages posted special police stations to keep a curfew over them at night. A Brahman informant says, "On the principal of 'set a thief to catch a thief,' they monopolize the position of village watchman." Chamars carry away the carcasses of dead animals and make sandals, drums, soccer balls, and bicycle seats out of the leather. Musahars "eat rats, snakes, and lizards," and are "expert at getting hidden crops from rat holes." Mali make garlands for temple worship, and have a special relationship to the smallpox goddess, Sitala; prior to the arrival of the modern clinic, a form of raw vaccination was performed by members of this caste with pus taken from the previous year's inoculations, which induced in children a mild case of fever and smallpox, from which patients usually recovered. Finally, Dom are basket makers and assistants at cremation grounds. This account leaves out some other important but smaller castes, such as Nai, barbers whose wives function as midwives; Dhobi, washermen; and Kumhar, potters. All these castes perform essential services, practical and ritual, for the superior castes of the region.

Above all, the Maithil Brahmans dominate politics, education, social life, and culture in Mithila. Historically, they gradually moved into Mithila from other places to the west, welcomed with gifts of land from earlier Kshatriya kings. When Turks ran out the Hindu kings in the fourteenth century, they set up a few Brahmans as local officials and representatives, and these Brahmans slowly turned themselves into rajas, enacting rajadharma as elsewhere in India: practicing statecraft by giving dan in the form of land gifts to temples, to Brahmans, and to their own loyal followers. Over centuries, these gifts-in-perpetuity turned a large population of village Brahmans into small landlords. Finally, as landowners they functioned in their villages as the dominant caste, a kind of local-level raja, distributing patronage on their own, although these Brahman landowners always retained their Brahman traditions as well.

The *Jajmani* System

It is in the village that the caste system as a very practical division of labor is most visible. Whichever caste is the principal landowner (zamindar) in a village plays a central role in the village economic system. These may not necessarily be kshatriyas; they could be Brahmans, Shudras, or even Harijans.[5] The term jajman means the person who sponsors a rite and employs a Brahman to officiate; it has come to mean the patron in patron-client relations in a village. The persons with most resources for sponsoring all kinds of events and employing a wide range of services are the major landowners.

In previous centuries, village economies were largely moneyless economies, and the exchange of services for grain was an essential mechanism for survival. So the principal landowners sublet fields for a share of grain or employed laborers at harvest and paid in grain. Most castes had some kind of economic link to the landowning families; Brahmans performed their rites, barbers shaved them, barbers' wives delivered their babies, potters made their pots, carpenters repaired their houses, dhobis washed their clothes, sweepers cleaned their latrines, etc. These were not do-it-yourself farm families as in the Old West; these were do-it-for-each-other families, forming tightly knit communities linked by complex and multidimensional economic and ritual ties, the true ties that bind. Payments were not made for immediate services, which would then close an exchange and cancel out a debt, but were done according to a long-term cycle of exchanges. At harvest, each jajman's service providers would know exactly how much grain was due him. There were other expectations as well: a *dhoti* or two every year, a hand-me-down sari or bangles from the zamindar's wife, a specific amount of oil, gifts on the birth and marriage of a son or daughter, and so on.

In recent years, as the cash economy has reached deeply into villages, most of these relationships have shifted to a pay-for-service system, but often traditional services continue to be provided on ritual occasions. At a recent *shraddha* (funeral memorial) in Ujjan Village in Mithila, an occasion where several hundred people must be feasted, the Mahapatra (funeral Brahmans) performed the rites, Chamars made special funeral shoes, the Nai shaved the men's heads and faces, Sokhan provided banana-leaf plates, Kewats carried water, Kumhar made small terracotta cups and bowls, Dom made serving baskets, Yadavas provided yogurt, Mallahs provided fish, and Bare provided betelnut. All these service providers were repaid in gifts, grain, and cash.

Dangerous Exchange of Substances

The Brahman who described the various castes of Mithila frequently referred to taking water or not taking water from castes lower than his own. The exchange of substances is one of the great preoccupations of the castes. Exchanges are both *essential*, because the caste system is a functional division of labor, and *dangerous*, because the castes are separate, self-contained units in danger of contamination from beings lower than themselves in the hierarchy of perfection.

Every exchange involves the transfer of particles from giver to receiver. As we have already seen, when the king distributes dan, part of his royal substance, which comes ultimately from the gods, flows with it. All good things from the gods are elevating to humans because any substances flowing from gods to humans are sure to be beneficial. Likewise, anything received from a Brahman will bring particles of the Brahman's superior substance with it. One can always accept a gift of food or water from a superior; this is why Brahmans are often employed as cooks in public places; anyone can eat from their hand.

Exchanges with an inferior are a different matter, because particles of the inferior flow upward with it. For this reason, people will not share food with persons of a lower caste; inferior substances will flow upward and pollute them. However, Dhobis can wash the clothes of Brahmans and Kayasthas, and Musahars can clean their latrines, because polluting biological substances of superiors will not hurt them, and they thus perform an essential service for the superior castes, helping them maintain their ritual purity and restoring them to an auspicious state.

There are times when one might want to give gifts upward, passing on one's own inferior substance. Getting rid of some of one's own sin and inauspiciousness can be accomplished by giving gifts to superiors, who will absorb it safely if they are powerful enough and willing. The gods will do this for humans, so people give gifts of food and wealth to Kali or Vishnu, who consume a little of it and leave the leftovers to be consumed by the giver. These auspicious leftovers of the gods are called *prasad* and will be taken home and shared with family members and friends. Manu states that one of the duties of Brahmans is "accepting gifts from pure men." In so doing, the Brahman absorbs some of the inauspiciousness of the giver. This is why most rites end with the feeding of Brahmans; by eating, the Brahman absorbs the inauspiciousness and sin of the ritual donors who thus get the full benefit of their sacred rites. But there is some "poison in the gift," as Gloria Goodwin Raheja puts it (1988), and Brahmans will only perform this function for the pure castes. The most inauspicious of rites are funeral rites. During the funeral, the relatives of the deceased, in order to be free of death pollution, must give gifts to Brahmans, transferring the death pollution away from themselves and onto the Brahmans. But most Brahmans are reluctant to take on such pollution, and so in every area, some Brahmans specialize in this work, but pay the price by being ranked as the lowest of Brahmans and being shunned by others.

Taking substances from a superior is sometimes called "respect pollution," but actually one can only be improved through contact with a superior being. Children touch the feet of their parents to show respect, and anyone may touch the feet of a higher-status person for the same reason. A woman touches her husband's feet and eats the leftovers from his plate, which are prasad to her. Devotees sip water in which the sandals of their guru have been dipped. Even the products of the cow are purifying for humans. The most purifying substance of all is *panchgavya*, a mixture of five products of the cow: milk, yogurt, ghi, dung, and urine. Drinking this can purify a person of his worst sin.

THE DHARMA OF WOMEN

It is always culture that determines the nature of men and women. More specifically, as Sherry Ortner has argued (1996), the rise of the state produced institutions and belief systems that radically altered relations between men and women. The patriarchal extended family emerged as the state's lowest-level unit; male heads of household became responsible to the state for their women and junior males. This was the first true emergence of patriarchy. Among elites, hypergamy, or the marrying up in rank of daughters, became a common ideal in marriage. The king, of course, set the pattern, accumulating wives partly as one category of treasure of the realm, partly as a way of making bonds of kinship with subordinate chiefs whose loyalty was politically necessary. Mughal Emperor Akbar, for example, had five thousand wives, and his motives were clearly not merely libidinous (see box 5.7, "The Imperial Harem of Akbar"). According to the contemporary account in the *A'in-i Akbari*, "His Majesty forms matrimonial alliances with princes of Hindustan, and of other countries: and secures by these ties of harmony the peace of the world." The account then goes on to describe the good order in the emperor's enormous household; despite the assistance of chaste women, writers, cash keepers, porters, and guards, "His Majesty does not dispense with his own vigilance, but keeps the whole in proper order," a model for simpler patriarchal households throughout his realm.

This pattern then generalized among elite classes; if a man could give his daughter in marriage to a higher-ranking family or lineage, he forged superior kinship alliances for himself, as well. Daughters of high rank accumulated at the top of the status system, some destined to go unmarried because there was no man higher in rank to give them to. Hypergamy placed a premium on the girl, a lower-ranking prize that had to be made more valuable through additional gifts of dowry, through personal adornment, and through her sexual purity. In this social environment, the "female purity complex" emerged, in which women's virtue is seen as a problem for the men of her family. State societies constructed elaborate ideologies about the nature of women and created models for them to emulate and institutions for the protection of their virtue.

In this formally posed photo of an Indian extended family, the statuses of the various family members can be read in their positions and dress. The elderly head of household is the man seated in the center; his wife sits beside him, her head modestly covered. His adult son, beginning to take over many of the family responsibilities, stands to the right. The two young women on the left whose heads are uncovered are daughters of the household. The veiled figure in the background is the son's wife and young child; she ordinarily would not come onto the verandah in her father-in-law's presence, but an exception has been made for this photograph.

In India, a woman's truest nature and best potential is embodied in the virtuous Sita. The life experience of most women is to be kept sheltered by their male kinsmen, first in their father's house and village and then after marriage in their husband's house and village, as Sita was protected by her husband, Rama, and her brother-in-law, Lakshman. But the princess of the Late Vedic Age had a great deal more adventure in her life than did later women, for whom the protection of males is symbolized by the curtain, *parda*. Women live in parda, or in seclusion, behind the curtain.

Conservative Muslim women literally wear the curtain whenever they leave the house, in the form of the full-body wrap known as the *burqa*. Hindu women use the end of their saris to cover their heads when

5.7 The Imperial Harem of Akbar

His Majesty is a great friend of good order and propriety in business. Through order, the world becomes a meadow of truth and reality; and that which is but external, receives through it a spiritual meaning. For this reason, the large number of women—a vexatious question even for great statesmen—furnished his Majesty with an opportunity to display his wisdom, and to rise from the low level of worldly dependence to the eminence of perfect freedom. This imperial palace and household are therefore in the best order.

His Majesty forms matrimonial alliances with princes of Hindustan, and of other countries: and secures by these ties of harmony the peace of the world.

As the sovereign, by the light of his wisdom, has raised fit persons from the dust of obscurity, and appointed them to various offices, so does he also elevate faithful persons to the several ranks in the service of the harem. . . .

His Majesty has made a large enclosure with fine buildings inside, where he reposes. Though there are more than five thousand women, he has given to each a separate apartment. He has also divided them into sections, and keeps them attentive to their duties. Several chaste women have been appointed as *daroghas*, and superintend over each section, and one has been selected for the duties of writer. Thus, as in the imperial offices, everything is here also in proper order. The salaries are sufficiently liberal. Not counting the presents, which his Majesty most generously bestows, the women of the highest rank receive from 1610 to 1028 Rs. per month. Some of the servants have from 51 to 20, others from 40 to 2 Rs. Attached to the private audience hall of the palace is a clever and zealous writer, who superintends the expenditure of the Harem, and keeps an account of the cash and the stores. If a woman wants anything, within the limit of her salary, she applies to one of the cash-keepers of the seraglio. He then sends a memorandum to the writer, who checks it, when the General Treasurer makes the payment in cash, as for claims of this nature no cheques are given.

The inside of the Harem is guarded by sober and active women; the most trustworthy of them are placed about the apartments of his Majesty. Outside the enclosure the eunuchs are placed; and at a proper distance, there is a guard of faithful Rajputs, beyond whom are the porters of the gates. Besides, on all four sides, there are guards of Nobles, Ahadis, and other troops, according to their ranks.

Whenever *Begams*, or the wives of nobles, or other women of chaste character, desire to be presented, they first notify their wish to the servants of the harem, and wait for a reply. From thence they send their request to the officers of the palace, after which those who are eligible are permitted to enter the Harem. Some women of rank obtain permission to remain there for a whole month.

Notwithstanding the great number of faithful guards, his Majesty does not dispense with his own vigilance, but keeps the whole in proper order.

Abu'l Fazl 'Allami, 1927 [ca. 1590], pp. 45–47.

they go out, or may have the entire rickshaw swathed in a sari, but for the most part, living in parda means not going out, but rather staying in the courtyard of one's own household, and even out of sight of the senior men of the household. Servants and children can be sent to shop or carry messages. Household architecture has been shaped to the needs of parda; throughout much of India a house is built around a central enclosed courtyard where the women and children stay. There are women's quarters, the *zenana*, and men's quarters, the *mardana*. In Mithila, a household is a compound of four small buildings arranged in a square around the central courtyard. The men's house is to the east, opening onto the village lane; this is the threshold between the public life of the village that is the men's world and the private domestic life of the women inside. Guests do not get beyond the front verandah.

As a man is defined by the career preordained as the caste's occupation or by another career he may choose to take up, a woman's career is her husband. "Career," of course, is too Western a term; let us use dharma instead. Stridharma, the dharma of women, is devotion to one's husband. A woman's life is to serve her husband and give him children; her virtue protects him; he is her lord. The very word for husband, *pati,* means both husband and lord. At marriage she becomes a *pativrata*, one who has "taken a vow to her husband/lord." She worships him by eating the left-overs from his plate as prasad. She may fast on Tuesdays to ensure his long life. While he lives, her life is filled with auspiciousness and good things; when he dies, she is plunged into an ascetic widowhood.

A young girl's life is for the most part a time of joyous freedom in her father's house and village. She does not have to cover her head and she may well be free of the household tasks that will be her lot in adulthood. Eventually, her father will begin to worry about settling her future; he will have to arrange her marriage. In previous generations, this had to be done before puberty, as it was a sin for a father to let his daughter reach sexual maturity in his household, but legislation now forbids (without having exactly stopped) marriage before age sixteen.

A father will begin by making cautious inquiries among men of his caste, seeking a prestigious marital connection in a distant village. Far more attention is paid to the prestige of the family the daughter is given to than to the boy himself and whether the two persons will be happily married. The negotiations will include coming to terms over dowry. Daughters do not inherit wealth when their fathers die, but receive their share at marriage, which is transferred to their husband's family. As India continues to prosper with economic development, the dowry system has intensified. Dowry generally includes a cash payment, gifts to the son-in-law, and clothing and jewelry to bedeck the bride. Cash payments have become astronomical in recent years. The bride's father may be required to pay several *lakhs* of rupees[6] in cash and gifts, which frequently include refrigerators, motor scooters, automobiles, televisions, or four years' university tuition for the groom.

In the last few years, as consumerism has grown, Indian society has had to struggle with a new form of greed made possible by the old tradition of dowry. A young bride comes into her new family as a "Lakshmi," a goddess of wealth, bringing money and consumer goods. The groom's family may make further demands on her father, a new form of extortion with the bride held hostage. When the father's resources run out, a "kitchen accident" occurs in which she burns to death in a kerosene fire. Most major Indian cities have several such "accidents," called "dowry deaths," a week, most of which are never prosecuted. The husband then marries again, getting a new dowry.

When a girl marries, her life is transformed. She moves to a strange house in a strange village to begin life with a man she did not meet until her wedding. This transition is both fearful and romanticized, for Indians are socialized to fall in love after the wedding, not before. The wedding rites initiate her *suhag*, the auspicious state of a woman with a living husband, no longer a virgin, not yet a widow. It connotes full adult sexuality, all the beauty and glamor of a woman whose arms and ankles jingle with bangles, whose forehead is red with auspicious red powder (*sindur*) in the part of her hair, whose body is clothed in colorful saris, whose womb is productive with life (Raheja & Gold 1994; Brown 1997).

As a young bride in her husband's household, her delight in suhag is tempered by the necessity of submitting to the authority of all women senior to her, which includes first of all her husband's mother, and then all the wives of her husband's elder brothers. These large extended households are built around a core of fathers and sons; daughters marry out to other villages, wives marry in from outside. These can be warm and happy family communities with lots going on all the time and never a shortage of companionship, but they also have their built-in tensions, which are best handled by careful lines of authority and codes of conduct to protect the vulnerable. The young bride is vulnerable to possible sexual predation by older men of the family, and so avoidance patterns require her to stay away from them if at all possible or to keep her head completely veiled in their presence. Men will cough politely as they enter a room to give her an opportunity to slip out; they will convey messages to her through a child.

A woman is considered blessed if she dies before her husband. But if she becomes a widow, parts of the funeral rites for her husband will include the formal beginning of her widowhood. Such rites frequently include breaking the wife's bangles, washing the red powder out of the part in her hair, and robing her in a white sari. The more extreme forms of ascetic widowhood have been modified in recent years, but as recently as 1996 I met young widows in Mithila who were wearing the white sari and avoiding all auspicious occasions such as weddings.

Widows have sometimes chosen to follow their husbands in death rather than to live for many years as a widow, an act which has Hindu sanction, although practiced only in a few castes and very rarely since it was outlawed by the British in 1829. *Sati* sprang into a great national controversy in 1987 when an eighteen-year-old Rajput girl named Roop Kanwar committed sati by joining her husband of one year on his funeral pyre. Technically a woman does not commit sati but becomes a sati through this act. The word sati means "inner truth"; it is the strength of her vow to become sati that is believed to cause her body itself to ignite on the funeral pyre as she holds her husband's head in her lap. The sati of Roop Kanwar immediately became a cause célèbre. Educated young Rajput men viewed it as a return to their old standards of valor by a heroic young Rajput woman, and they immediately formed a "Committee for the Defense of the Religion of Sati" (Sati Dharma Raksha Samiti). Much of the debate revolved around the question of whether Roop Kanwar's act was voluntary (as most witnesses claimed) or was forced (according to some reports, she was found hiding in a shed as she got an inkling of what was in store for her, was dragged out, drugged, and "helped" onto the funeral pyre) (Hawley 1994; Oldenburg 1994). Indian feminists protested that either way, it did not matter; sati should not be glorified and no one should profit from it through the temples that are built afterward on the site of a sati.

A sati becomes a *satimata*, a "mother sati" or goddess, and a shrine is built on the site of past satis, to which people come from far to worship a woman who has so perfectly fulfilled her dharma as a woman and her vow (pativrata) to her husband. Sita, who went through the fire to prove her purity as a wife, is sometimes held to be the first sati, though the flames proved her purity by not burning her. The other myth-model of a sati is Parvati (also known as Sati), whose father insulted her husband, Shiva, by not inviting him to a feast. In protest against this insult, she flung herself into a fire, and the grief-stricken Shiva stumbled throughout India carrying her corpse, leaving portions of her body here and there across North India, where temples sprang up in her honor. But as one feminist Indian scholar, Veena Talwar Oldenburg, says in a contesting interpretation of the myth: "Her act did not signify piety toward a husband but wilfull protest against a father. So the Sati myth cannot really qualify as the inspirational myth for sati" (Oldenburg 1994:163).

HINDUISM

Upanishadic Thought

In the many small kingdoms that dotted North India during the Late Vedic Age, kings gathered intellectuals, Brahmans, and sages at their courts; a new sophistication was emerging from court culture and early urbanization, and new philosophical questions began to emerge that questioned the ritualism of the Brahmans and puzzled about such questions as the nature of the self, the soul's fate after death, and the nature of the cosmos. The texts that record these new speculations are known as the Upanishads, the most philosophical of all early Indian texts, which were being written between 700 and 200 B.C.

A bit of the flavor of these discussions is captured in the Katha Upanishad. A prince named Nachiketa calls Yama (Death) to him and asks: "After death, does a man still exist?" Yama stalls. Even the gods have trouble with this question, he said; wouldn't you rather have gold? Fair maidens? Chariots? Music? The world-weary Prince Nachiketa says, "These things last only until death. And they wear out the sense organs. Besides, wealth doesn't make a man happy. Even kings know that." Yama sighs and admits that Nachiketa has wisdom; he is seeking truth-knowledge. So Yama agrees to reveal the truth that is such a great secret that hardly anybody knows it.

Brahman (Brahma or Paratma). Who is the greatest god? The polytheism of the Aryans made this question inevitable, and people tended to select favorites, or insist that one deity was only a form of a higher one. But a more abstract and encompassing view emerged: Brahman.[7] Brahman was the unknown god behind all the known ones, so unknowable that one could only talk about him in metaphors: He is the foundation of the universe, the firstborn, the soul of all the gods, born in the form of breath, created with the elements, the place where the sun rises and sets, realized only by the mind, the unmanifest, he contains all the gods.

Atma. Yama's greatest secret was that each person has an inner soul, the atma. Again, it is described metaphorically: it is not born, it does not die, it has not sprung from anything, it is smaller than the small, greater than the great, it is hidden in the hearts of all living creatures, it goes everywhere, it dwells in impermanent bodies but is itself bodiless, it is a subtle essence, it is a part of Paratma (the "Great Soul"). We sense it in deep, dreamless sleep, the still center of the self, when all the sense organs are closed off from the outside world. Yama's answer to Nachiketa is, The atma goes on after death because it is a part of eternal Brahman.

Maya. Death lives in the manifest world, or maya. All things that come into existence must die and then come into existence again. The atma and Brahman are eternal, but nothing else is; all the rest is transitory and therefore illusory. Nothing lasts.

Karma. Death belongs in the physical world because of karma. Karma is activity. Acts are not solitary events but are connected to each other by long chains of action and reaction. To exist in the material world is to act; it is the very condition of our existence. We must eat, move, speak, listen, think; our bodies demand it. This is a law of the universe: All action comes from someplace and goes someplace. This is also a moral law, for good action produces good results and bad action produces bad results.

Our embodiedness is a matter of three bodies, all governed by karma: First, there is the physical body with its senses pointed outward to the world, to food, to comfort, to pleasure. Our senses keep us in interactive exchanges with the world. Second, there is the "subtle body" inside: the emoting, longing, watching, caring, thinking, desiring body; our "psychological selves," we might say. Remember in the creation myth, desire was the originating force of the cosmos; and desire as karma keeps existence going on endlessly. Only desirelessness can bring an end to existence. Third, further inside—we come to metaphors again—are the "karmic seeds" deposited by past actions in past lives, the "causal body" that has caused this new life to sprout from the actions of the previous existence. The atma hardly has a chance against such embodiment. No wonder atma goes undetected in most people.

Samsara. All that action of the physical body gives life to the karmic seeds; all those actions await their results. The sages did their best at metaphorizing how this might happen. It is another kind of biological continuity. So, when you die, your atma with its karmic seeds gets reincarnated in another body, and it all starts over again: more senses, more desiring, more actions, more suffering. This is the cycle of reincarnation, or samsara.

Yama revealed the whole secret to Nachiketa: There is a way to escape the karmik hold on oneself, but it is extremely difficult and only a few ever succeed. If one could only escape the body and the controls of karma, the atma would finally be freed to be reabsorbed in Brahman, and there rest eternally in blissful repose, returned to the source of all things. The task is to escape the body *in this life.* The senses, all turned outward, must get drawn inward. Stop the activities of the senses; draw the mind inward. Try to achieve a continuing state of dreamless sleep. So all the disciplines of the ascetic are aimed at that; it is a discipline much like an athlete's, but aimed at inner control. A whole host of ascetics withdrew from society to seek this enlightenment and escape from rebirth. They practiced long hours of meditation, often accompanied by withdrawal to places where the world's hold is lessened, such as a mountaintop, a holy spot along the Ganges, a temple, a cave, or an inner room. Frequently they tested the success of the struggle against and triumph over the senses with flagellation, stilling the heartbeat, exposure to extremes of heat and cold, elimination of food. The great yogis who practiced these forms of asceticism, known as *tapas*, were said to build up an inner heat that gave them supernatural powers. The sati who sits on the funeral pyre with her husband's head on her lap has also generated this kind of supernatural heat: she bursts into flames and ignites the wood herself. At death, the yogi hopes to have finally escaped from rebirth to be re-absorbed into Brahman, a state known as *moksha*. For this reason, Hindu ascetics, who may be seen by the thousands at every sacred place in India, particularly along the Ganges and in the Himalayas, are buried or thrown into the river uncremated, for there is no longer an atma needing release from the hold of a body; it has already returned to Brahman.

Ascetic practice did have its strong allure and many people did—and still do—renounce life in society, for despite its renunciation and its abstractions, asceticism is a highly active form of religion, a full-time vocation. However, these ideas proved too abstract to be satisfying to the majority. Most people were not prepared to renounce society. Like people everywhere, they were deeply embedded in life and culture and tended naturally toward forms of religion that engaged them actively. They preferred to enjoy its benefits, living passionately in the world. For people with passions who are living complicated lives, devotion to a god whose image (*murti*) can be seen, whose biographies can be known, was much preferred over a formless god that could only be grasped with metaphors. As a woman ascetic living in Rishikesh said to me when I asked her if her goal was *moksha*:

> Oh, no, no, no. No! I have no desire for moksha. I'm happy for any number of births to be Lord Krishna's devotee. Birth after birth after birth, if I could go on worshipping him I would be grateful! Because the job of being a beloved of Lord Krishna is far superior to any moksha that can be offered by anyone. In fact the opposite: I'd rather *eat* the sweet than *become* the sweet. Moksha is becoming the sweet. The bhakta prefers to keep sucking the sweet.

This passionate devotion to a god of form is known as *bhakti*. During the same centuries when Upanishadic thought was emerging, the old Vedic gods were merging with indigenous deities and taking new forms. Of these, three became the focus of bhakti devotionalism: Krishna, an *avatar* (incarnation) of Vishnu, the main deity of the Mahabharata who later further developed in the intensely erotic *Gitagovinda* of Jayadeva; Shiva, the fearsome, ascetic god who sits in meditation on Mt. Kailash, letting the Ganges flow to earth through his matted locks (he may already have been present in the Indus Valley as the horned god who merged with the Vedic Rudra to become the Lord of the Dance of later Hinduism); and

Shakti, the great goddess who takes forms both fearsome and lovely. Some of her forms—Kali, Durga, Chinnamasta, Chandi—are powerful, untamed, and unmarried deities who are sexually aggressive and dangerous. Their hair flows wild, they drink blood, they dance on corpses in the cremation ground in the middle of the night. The fact that devotees call such goddesses *Ma* (mother) suggests a psychological ambivalence, an erotic, incestuous infatuation toward strong and devouring mothers and a fear of female sexuality more generally. Other goddesses—Parvati, Saraswati, Lakshmi, Sita—are tamed and domesticated through their marriage to male gods.

Besides these three, there are many, many others. Yet most Hindus will assert that ultimately God is One, that all forms (*rupa*) are part of the Formless (arupa) One, and that beyond existence is nonexistence, and that is the location of ultimate truth. Still, the focus of society—dharmik society, where kings ruled and men and women married and reproduced within their appropriate castes—was on form, on the incarnated, on this Kali Yuga (the present decadent epoch). During the Gupta Age (A.D. 320–550), when North India was again united from the Indus to Bengal under kings who took names from the Mauryan Empire (more Chandraguptas, but no Ashokas), temples began to be built to house the murtis of the gods. The murtis were themselves "houses," splendid sculptures in bronze, stone, papier-mâché, and terra-cotta, to which the gods were called in "eye-opening" ceremonies. In the Vedic Age, worship had been done outside, under the heavens, so the gods, who were not generally represented in figurative form, could watch. Even the Buddha was depicted in friezes only by signs of him—the tree of enlightenment, his teaching seat, the wheel of dharma—rather than by images, which did not emerge until the Gupta Age.

BUDDHISM

Rediscovering Buddhism

In 1819, a British captain was riding across fields in Central India at a place called Sanchi toward a low hill in the distance. At the top there was a circular stepped pyramid about 554 feet in circumference with a colonnade of pillars, spaced eighteen inches apart, encircling it, and gates at the north, west, and east. There were sculptures everywhere, all topsy-turvy, many of them defaced; some were Hindu and Jain gods, but what surprised the captain was the presence of Buddha images amongst the more familiar Hindu deities. Was it possible that Buddha had once been worshipped here? But where were Buddhists today? Everywhere but India: in Nepal, Tibet, China, Burma, Thailand, Ceylon, Japan.

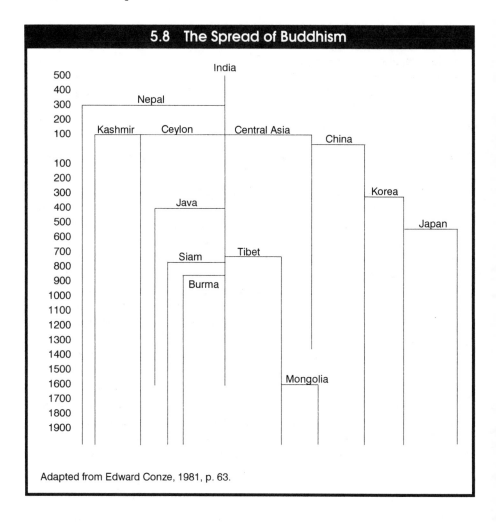

5.8   The Spread of Buddhism

Adapted from Edward Conze, 1981, p. 63.

Traveling in Burma in the 1790s, Francis Buchanan was told by devout Buddhists that the Buddha had been an Indian from Bihar. Later he worked in Bihar, where there was a town called Bodh Gaya, which means "Buddha went." There were several old temples in poor condition that were served by Brahmans. People in the vicinity worshipped many Hindu gods—and also images of Buddha, who was "an incarnation of Vishnu." Every now and then strange-looking foreigners would arrive, often accompanied by servants, to reverently tour the ruins. One such pilgrim said these ruins had been built by "Dharma Ashoka, King of Pandaripuk." No one had any idea who Ashoka was, or what place Pandaripuk had been (Keay 1988).

In the 1830s, two travel journals of ancient Chinese pilgrims were translated into English and read with astonishment in India. Between A.D. 399 and 414 Faxian had traveled to India seeking Buddhist texts to take back to China. This was the height of the Gupta Age, and Buddhism was thriving. All North India was at peace, and Faxian was able to travel from one vast Buddhist monastery to another, some of them with thousands of monks. He wrote: "The kings are firm believers in the Law. When they make their offerings to a community of monks, they take off their royal caps and along with their relatives and ministers, supply them with food with their own hands. That done, the king has a garment spread for himself on the ground and sits down on it in front of the chairman; they dare not presume to sit on couches in front of the community" (Legge 1886). But in his search for Buddhist texts, Faxian was disappointed, for in most places dharma was being transmitted orally from master to pupil without the aid of texts. Finally he did find a few of them, which he copied. He stayed three years, long enough to learn Sanskrit and make some of his own translations to take back. His careful descriptions amounted to a map of Buddhist India with site plans of all the main shrines.

Three hundred years later, Xuanzang made much the same journey, but now things had changed. Buddhism was in retreat. Many shrines were in ruins. In Kashmir and Bengal, Buddhists were being persecuted. Xuanzang wrote of his grief at the empty spaces where Buddha had once taught; his grief was shaped by his sense that Buddhism was going into decline. Over the next several hundred years, two factors would bring the Buddhist era to a close in India: the reembracing of Hinduism and Brahmanism by Indian kings—King Harsha was as much a Hindu as a Buddhist—and the incursions of Muslims of Central Asian origin. Muslim historians described "shaven-headed Brahmans" who were put to the sword. What the Muslims took to be a whole city and fortress were actually Buddhist monasteries and colleges. A great library was scattered, images were wrecked, and as a result many beautiful Buddha images seen in museums all have missing noses, ears, and arms. This was the end of organized Buddhism in India; those who survived fled north to the Himalayas, south to Sri Lanka, or east to Burma or China, and historic amnesia spread over India.

The Four Periods of Buddhism

Buddhism has persisted for twenty-five hundred years, undergoing profound change during that time. Each of these phases resulted in the production of new sacred texts, all claiming to be the words and teachings of Buddha himself. We can identify four periods (Conze 1988):

The First 500 years: "Old Buddhism" (500–1 B.C.). The period begins with the life of Buddha himself and encompasses the Mauryan

Empire. During this time, beliefs and practices that became identified later as Hinayana ("Lesser Vehicle") Buddhism emerged, and this is the form of Buddhism that went to Southeast Asia as Theravada Buddhism ("The Way of the Elders"). King Ashoka converted to Buddhism and spread it throughout his empire by edict and beyond it by sending out missionaries, including his own son to Ceylon. He built stupas to house relics of the Buddha and endowed monasteries. Buddhist iconography during this period remained symbolic: the empty throne, the sacred Bodhi Tree, a footprint, the wheel of dharma, but never representation in human form.

During this period, the focus was typically Indian in its preoccupation with what we might call psychological questions: Suffering is a psychological state and salvation comes from control of one's own mind. Buddha was the first and greatest teacher who discovered these laws and passed them on to his disciples, leaving an "open hand" when he died, all his insight passed on for others to learn. The perfected saint was the *arhat*, one who, like Buddha, had achieved extinction of desire and would no more be reborn in this world.

The Second 500 Years: Mahayana Buddhism (1 B.C.–A.D. 500).

Great changes take place in Buddhist thought. To realize in oneself the true nature of things is the path to salvation. Fully enlightened saints are raised to the status of *bodhisattvas*, beings who halt on the brink of extinction for eons to bring salvation to others. Rather than being venerated as dead teachers, eternal bodhisattvas such as Amitabha, Avalokiteshvar, and Maitreya, are now objects of worship, barely distinguishable from deities. Rather than full-time ascetic practice, salvation is brought by these bodhisattvas to devotees who cast their faith in them; they are saviors. It is no longer believed there was just one Buddha; there were many Buddhas, and full Buddhahood is possible for anyone. In these new forms, Buddhism begins its conquest of the rest of Asia, traveling to China, Japan, and Korea by one route, and to Southeast Asia by another.

Monasticism is at its peak with vast monasteries filled with new art forms. Many of these monasteries are dug into rocky cliffs, as at Ajanta and Dunhuang. Wealthy lay devotees earn merit by commissioning paintings and sculpture, which is truly at its peak during this period. In the upper Indus region, a Greek-influenced kingdom known as Gandhara is particularly important in these developments. Gandhara lies at the crossroads on the way west to the Mediterranean and north to Central Asia and China. Here Buddhism meets Greek sculptural traditions, alive with sensuous realism. Buddha with his ascetic's topknot and semi-lidded eyes looks remarkably like the Greek god Apollo. He wears a toga draped in the Hellenistic style. He has on Athenian sandals and is flanked by Corinthian columns. These influences go all the way to China and Japan, where

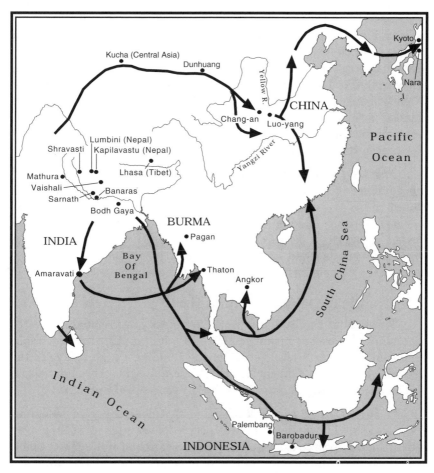

Map 5.3   Route of Dispersal of Buddhism

Buddhism becomes associated as much with high culture as with renunciation.

The Third 500 Years (A.D. 500–1000). This is the period of the rise of Tantric Buddhism in India, Nepal, and Tibet; while in centers outside India, Buddhism takes on creative new directions, particularly Ch'an (China) and Zen (Japan) Buddhism.

Tantra sees harmony with the cosmos as the key aim of enlightenment and uses magic and occult methods to achieve it. The ideal man is the *siddha*, who is so much in harmony with the universe that he has no material constraints on him, and thus has extraordinary powers, able to manipulate cosmic forces within himself and outside himself. In India, Tantra developed a "Left-Handed" and a "Right-Handed" form. Both forms assert that the goal of spiritual striving is to transcend all the multiplicity of maya, the manifest world, into a state of perfect unity with the cosmos. This is symbolized by male-female dualism, which can be transcended by a discipline of meditation and rituals in which the unity of the self with the cosmos is enacted through sexual union with a partner. The "Right-Handed" forms did this only symbolically, but the shocking "Left-Handed" forms did it literally. The art of Tantra was full of sexual images, most notably the famous Yab-Yum, a male and female figure locked in energetic sexual embrace.

The Last 1000 Years. There has been little change during the last thousand years. Buddhism has been in a holding pattern. Everything is bound to decay, according to the teachings of Buddhism, dharma included. Japanese Buddhism marked the year 1052 as the beginning of the age of *mappo*, a period of the total degeneration of Buddhism, after which individuals could no longer hope to achieve Buddhist enlightenment by their own efforts but would have to depend on a savior.

The Three Jewels of Buddhism

Throughout the Buddhist world, devotees have recited the words that Ashoka uttered on his conversion as a way of making their own spiritual commitment: "I take refuge in the Buddha, I take refuge in the Dharma, I take refuge in the Sangha." These are the "Three Jewels," a mnemonic device that summarizes the key concepts of Buddhism.

"I Take Refuge in the Buddha . . ." Among the many renouncers of society who wandered between sacred river sites and Himalayan retreats in the sixth century B.C.[8] was the son of a chief of the Shakya tribe in the foothills of the Himalayas. His name was Siddhartha Gautama, son of a warrior chief who grew up in wealth and privilege and had a beautiful wife, Yashodhara. Nevertheless, with all the good things life could offer, he had an existential crisis in his twenties that changed his life. While traveling outside his palace, he encountered four sights whose cumulative effect was to stun him with the inevitable suffering of the human condition. A feeble old man made him see the inevitability of old age; a burning corpse exposed him to death; and the sight of a hideously deformed leper revealed the horror of disease. A fourth sight planted in his mind the first hope of an escape: a wandering ascetic offered a radical alternative to passive acceptance of old age, suffering, and death. The birth of a son seems to have signaled his entrapment in life and spurred him to take action. Telling no one, he shaved his head, put on the simple robe of an ascetic, and left his home forever in the beginning of a search for spiritual liberation.

Searching for a spiritual teacher, a guru, he traveled south toward the small kingdoms growing up along the Ganges. His first teacher taught him a form of meditation that led to a kind of trance state, or "state of nothingness." Siddhartha quickly learned this method and soon surpassed his teacher, but found it unsatisfying, since such a state had no moral dimension and was no escape from old age, sickness, and death. He had several other teachers and joined a group of ascetics who were soon thinking of themselves as his followers. Their practices included severe physical punishment that endangered their lives. After several years and growing expertise in these methods, Siddhartha realized that physical torture was no more spiritually liberating than physical pleasure. Again he had to leave.

He began to eat normally again and wandered on, coming to a small river in south Bihar. He stopped on its banks for several days, meditating under a fig tree. During one of these long nights of meditation he came to a profound new insight into the truth of the human condition. This was his True Awakening, or Enlightenment. He had achieved nirvana in his lifetime. The place where this occurred became known as Bodh Gaya, which became a place of pilgrimage, and the tree became known as the Bodhi Tree, or Tree of Enlightenment. Gautama himself became known as Buddha, the Enlightened One. He was thirty-five years old.

The Buddha lived for forty-five more years until his parinirvana, final extinction, a long lifetime with time enough to make a great impact and establish a large following. He first reached out to the five companions he had broken with over the futility of self-torture. In the Deer Park not far from Varanasi (Banaras) he preached his first sermon on the "Four Noble Truths." Soon he had a core of forty-five young followers, who moved among the towns along the middle Ganges, teaching to an ever-growing number of laymen and renunciants. The Buddha spent the last two decades of his life settled in Shravasti, the capital of Kosala, living a communal life that would become the monastic tradition of Buddhism. At the age of eighty, he fell sick and died with his grieving followers around him. His body was cremated, and the ashes distributed to local rulers who enshrined their portion in ten stupas.[9]

It should be clear that the Buddha was not a deity but an exemplar. He was the first to discover these great truths and teach them to others. At least from the point of view of early Indian Buddhism, Buddha's role was that of spiritual master par excellence.

"...*I Take Refuge in the Dharma*..." What was the insight that came to the Buddha under the pipal tree? Whatever it was—and it is difficult to convey in words, for it is beyond knowing through words—it is the core of his teaching, now called dharma.

Buddha came to see the world as characterized by three qualities: *anitya, duhkha,* and *anatma. Anitya (anicca* in Pali) is the characteristic of impermanence. Not only does everything that comes into existence eventually go out of existence, but even one's own subjective states of mind are always shifting and changing. This is because all things that exist are but temporary compounds of smaller elements, and all compounded things must decay.

Duhkha *(dukkha* in Pali) is the characteristic of suffering or sorrow. The first sermon of the Buddha on the "Four Noble Truths" focused on duhkha. It borrowed its rhetorical form from an ancient medical formula in which first you state the nature of the illness, then the conditions that give rise to the illness, then whether there is a cure, and finally the means of the cure (Skilton 1994). Thus, the First Noble Truth simply states: Life is full of suffering. The Second Noble Truth states the condition that gives rise to suffering: not fate, not malevolent spirits or angry gods, but human desire. We are in inner bondage to our cravings, our trying to hang on to things and people, our longing for wealth, prestige, and love of others. The Third Noble Truth states whether there is a cure: Yes, cessation of suffering, which is known as nirvana, is possible. The Fourth Noble Truth declares the means of the cure: an Eight-fold Path of morality, meditation, and wisdom.

Anatma *(annata* in Pali) is the characteristic of the absence of selfhood. We saw earlier the Katha Upanishad's description of the atma, which by Buddha's time was a widely accepted view of the pure, subtle, and eternal self or soul that passes from one lifetime to the next to the next until final absorption in moksha. But Buddha's teachings about impermanence (anitya) quickly brought into question the doctrine of the eternal atma. The transitory combination of elements that make up any object—a leaf, a chariot, a human being—has no essence beyond the temporary combination of parts. As the monk Nagasena argued before the Greek King Menander, there is no chariot apart from its wheels, axle, seat, reins, or spokes. Take those apart, and there is no "essence" left. No more is there any eternal atma once a human body falls into death and decomposition. Nevertheless, each new thing that arises is conditioned by previous states, so that karma or action does still have consequences in the Buddhist view.

"... I Take Refuge in the Sangha." The *sangha,* the community of monks, grew out of that population of wandering ascetics who had renounced society to seek spiritual liberation. The custom grew among Buddha's followers to gather together during the three months of the rainy season in a single place, often provided by a lay follower of Buddha

5.9 Buddha's First Sermon: The Four Noble Truths

According to Buddhist tradition, Buddha preached his first sermon after achieving Enlightenment in the Deer Park outside the city of Varanasi. This sermon was the fundamental Four Noble Truths of Buddhism, which set in motion the "Wheel of Dharma" throughout the land and the world.

Thus have I heard. Once the Lord was at Varanasi, at the deer park called Isipatana. There he addressed the five monks:

There are two ends not to be served by a wanderer. What are these two? The pursuit of desires and of pleasure which springs from desire, which is base, common, leading to rebirth, ignoble, and unprofitable; and the pursuit of pain and hardship, which is grievous, ignoble, and unprofitable. The Middle Way of the Tathagata [one of the titles of the Buddha] avoids both these ends. It is enlightened, it brings clear vision, it makes for wisdom, and leads to peace, insight, enlightenment, and Nirvana. What is the Middle Way? . . . It is the Noble Eightfold Path—Right Views, Right Resolve, Right Speech, Right Conduct, Right Livelihood, Right Effort, Right Mindfulness, and Right Concentration. This is the Middle Way. . . .

And this is the Noble Truth of Sorrow. Birth is sorrow, age is sorrow, disease is sorrow, death is sorrow; contact with the unpleasant is sorrow, separation from the pleasant is sorrow, every wish unfulfilled is sorrow—in short, all the five components of individuality are sorrow.

And this is the Noble Truth of the Arising of Sorrow. It arises from craving, which leads to rebirth, which brings delight and passion, and seeks pleasure now here, now there—the craving for sensual pleasure, the craving for continued life, the craving for power.

And this is the Noble Truth of the Stopping of Sorrow. It is the complete stopping of that craving, so that no passion remains, leaving it, being emancipated from it, being released from it, giving no place to it.

And this is the Noble Truth of the Way which Leads to the Stopping of Sorrow. It is the Noble Eightfold Path—Right Views, Right Resolve, Right Speech, Right Conduct, Right Livelihood, Right Effort, Right Mindfulness, and Right Concentration.

Wm. Theodore De Bary, ed., 1958, pp. 98–99.

---

in a grove or forest clearing. These became months of building solidarity, rereading the Sutras, practicing meditation, and instructing new followers of the Buddhist path.

Living in community raised some of the same kinds of problems facing people who did not renounce society. Individuals did not always get along. Spiritual aspiration could turn competitive. Pride could creep in. Above all, the body's sexual urges had direct and indirect ways of resisting efforts to suppress them. Therefore, soon after Buddha's death, a set

of rules for the spiritual community, called the *Vinaya,* developed. It consisted of 227 prohibitions in order of seriousness; the first four were
abstention from all sexual intercourse, from theft, from destruction of life
even down to a worm or ant, and from claiming any superhuman powers.
Offenses against these rules resulted in expulsion. Other rules forbade
handling gold and silver, engaging in trade, drinking alcoholic beverages,
sitting or sleeping more than eight inches from the ground, and eating
any meals after noon.

ISLAMIC CIVILIZATION IN INDIA

No personality radiates from Indian history with the vibrancy of Akbar.
He was a contemporary of Elizabeth I, and part of a new cultural strand
in India for whom the actions of kings were worthy themes to write
about; therefore we know a great deal about him. At the age of thirteen,
in 1556, he inherited the Mughal Empire, founded by his grandfather
Babur. By his twenties, he had consolidated and expanded the empire
by conquest north and south so that, by his death in 1605, his domain
stretched from Afghanistan to Bengal, from the Himalayas to the Dec-
can. But India has had conquerors aplenty; it is not Akbar the warrior
who leaps from the pages of history, but a vivid spirit whose actual face
is known from dozens of paintings and whose life and times were
recorded in admiring detail by contemporary writers. His biography, the
Akbarnama, was written in his lifetime by Abu'l Fazl and illustrated by
court painters chosen and personally overseen by Akbar himself. The
nineteen-year-old emperor is at the epicenter of one scene in which a
charging bull elephant chases another across a pontoon bridge. Holding
himself by a bare foot hooked under the harness of "Sky-Rocket," the
meanest, wickedest elephant in India, Akbar has driven him against an
equally aggressive elephant, now fleeing in defeat. The pontoon bridge
breaks under the fury of their charge, throwing men into the water on
either side, while others rush to pull the emperor from the danger he
has put himself in.

Akbar maintained a workshop of over a hundred artists who
painted episodes from past and recent history, recorded scenes of Hindu
life, and exhaustively illustrated events from the Mahabharata, Ramayana, and Harivamsa, which Akbar had translated for the Muslim elite.
He sat for his own portraits and also had all his noblemen sit for theirs,
so that paintings of the emperor holding *darbar* (audience) are filled with
faces that really sat before the emperor. But the masterpiece was the biographical Akbarnama, a work in twelve volumes with fourteen hundred
illustrations that took fifteen years to complete (Welch 1978:40). These
remarkably detailed paintings are all the more amazing for being minia-

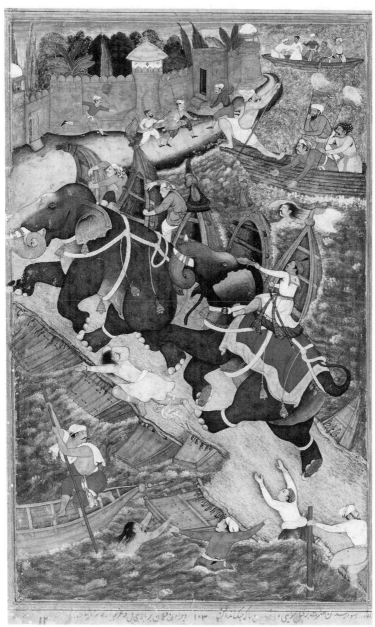

In "Akbar Restrains Hawa'i," one of the scenes from the Akbarnama (ca. 1590), we see the great Mughal emperor in the vortex of the action, driving his elephants across a pontoon bridge against the enemy. Warriors falling into the turbulent waters contrast with Akbar's aggressive control from the center of the action. In a companion painting, his ministers watch in alarm from the shore.

tures. The scene of Akbar and the two elephants is only 13 inches by 8 inches. They were painted in opaque watercolor with brushes made of a few hairs plucked from kittens or baby squirrels, fitted on the fingertip of the artist. The glint of sunlight burnishing a North Indian scene was accomplished with pounded gold mixed with a little silver or copper.

Akbar was the greatest of the "Great Mughals," a line of brilliant, long-lived, cultured, often enlightened, and frequently cruel rulers whose zenith was the four men: Akbar, Jahangir, Shah Jahan, and Aurangzeb. Their four reigns spanned the years from 1556 to 1707. After the death of Aurangzeb, weaker men followed, who were hounded by the growing influence of the British. The last of the Great Mughals, Bahadur Shah, was little more than a pawn during the Anglo-Indian War (a.k.a. "The Great Mutiny") of 1857. He died in exile in Burma. However, these rulers, who were Muslims and creators of the great synthesis of Indian and Islamic civilization, were not the ones who brought Islam to India.

The Islamic Conquerors

The Islamic conquest of India happened in three phases over eight centuries. It began during the period from 711 to 1206 when a series of adventures by military chiefs of Turkish and Afghan background took them into Sind, then the Panjab, and further and further east. Most of these early efforts caused severe social crisis in India—felt particularly harshly by Buddhist monasteries, where easily identifiable "infidels" were slaughtered in great numbers—but failed to establish enduring kingdoms. These conquests were launched from Persia, which had already created a high culture that blended the Islamic faith with science, art, and literature in the Persian language. The Persian-Islamic influence would greatly enrich India culturally over eight centuries despite the humiliating and often brutal conquests India had to endure in the process.

The second phase of conquest, generally called the Delhi Sultanate, lasted from 1206 to 1526, when a series of dynasties ruled from the new capital at Delhi. These were Afghan and Turkish military lords from Inner Asia and their clients, who jockeyed for power among each other, as first one, then another managed to control Delhi. During this period, Muslim scholars, scribes, Sufis, poets, and intellectuals flocked to India, seeking the patronage of the new regimes. The earliest phase of conversions occurred at this time, though they were limited in number. It is likely that the Turkish elite opposed the conversion of the Hindu nobility, should the nobility have been so inclined, since Islam was the faith of the ruling class and large-scale conversions would have increased competition for the foreigners. Converts came largely from the peasantry who worked on lands owned by the Islamic elite and by the mosques. In addition, noncaste tribal peoples on the fringes of the caste system now had a way to be absorbed into Indian society other than as avarna. They could convert to Islam.

The third phase of conquest was the Mughal Empire (1526–1858), established by Akbar's grandfather Babur. Under the Mughals, the synthesis of Persian and Indian heritages culminated in the brilliant cultural achievements of the imperial court. Among the most visible of their accomplishments were great works of architecture, also a synthesis of Muslim and Hindu motifs. Great mosques and palace complexes were built in Delhi, Agra, Ajmer, Allahabad, and Fatepur Sikri. Most famous of all is the Taj Mahal, built by Shah Jahan, the "Engineer Badshah," as a mausoleum for his wife Mumtaz. All the Great Mughals except for Aurangzeb ruled their Hindu subjects with a good degree of respect for cultural and religious difference, in part because they were a relatively small elite imposed on a vast Hindu populace, and in part because the most popular form of Islam in India, Sufism, had so much in common with Hinduism that the line between the two faiths was easily blurred.

Islam began on the Arabian Peninsula early in the seventh century when an illiterate member of the Quaraish tribe, recently arrived in Mecca, began receiving visions from God. At that time the Ka'aba, the great temple in Mecca, housed hundreds of idols; but the messages received by Muhammad proclaimed the singularity of God. When he began to teach the message of his visions, he was hounded out of Mecca, fleeing to Medina in 622. This is the first year of the Muslim calendar, and the date generally given for the founding of Islam.

The angel Gabriel continued to give revelations to Muhammad over a period of twenty years, and although the original, a tablet guarded by angels, is believed to remain in heaven, the earthly form was pieced together by followers under the third caliph, Uthman (644–655), as the authorized version of the Qur'an in 114 chapters. The Qur'an is supplemented by the Hadith, a collection of stories about what the Prophet or one of his followers said or did under certain circumstances and that provide moral guidance for Muslims facing similar problems in later centuries. Thus a complex of customs, or Sunna, have become the orthodox Islamic tradition, the culture of Islam. This sacred order continued to be the topic of scrutiny and controversy, as Muslims attempted to apply the Qur'an and the Hadith to social life and make law conform to sacred prescriptions and proscriptions. Out of this debate emerged a holy law known as the Shari'a, similar to the Laws of Manu, which attempted to regulate social life for Hindus. In India, Muslims developed their own version of the Shari'a known as the Hanafi Law.

No faith coming to India, it would seem, could be more contrary to the outlook of Hindus than Islam. For Hindus, the world is illusion; for Muslims, the world is "dread reality." Each lifetime is followed not by another lifetime but by eternal salvation in heaven or eternal damnation in hell. God is not infused through all reality, taking many shifting forms, but is the Creator who stands outside the fallen creation. Allah is unchanging, eternal, omniscient, omnipotent. Yet there were variations among Islam's major sects—Sunni, Shi'a, and Sufi—and not surprisingly, it was Sufism, the sect that had most in common with the Hindu-Buddhist worldview, that was responsible for spreading Islam in India. Sufi was a twelfth-century mystic order in which saints resembling Hindu *sanyasis* traveled through India preaching an ecstatic and mystical form of Islam. Popular religious culture became a mixture of Muslim and Hindu practices as Sufis adopted Hindu ceremonies, devotional songs, and yoga techniques (Lapidus 1988:449). Poetry expressing the yearning for and love of Allah was not unlike the bhakti devotionalism of Hinduism. In the process of adopting Indian languages, music, and poetic forms, Urdu was born, a literary version of Hindi that became a Muslim language for India. Sufis spread the idea of a universal hierarchy of saints and the practice of veneration of tombs. Shrines emerged as centers of worship, which led to the accumulation of properties granted by state authority. Yet, the Mughals never attempted to establish an orthodox Islamic state and were occasionally criticized by a handful of vocal, orthodox Muslims on the fringes of the court for being too cosmopolitan, too cultured, and too cozy with the Hindu elite (with whom they intermarried extensively). "[It] was not state control of doctrine, teaching, or judicial administration, nor a history of well-established schools of law and *ulama*, but one of numerous autonomous and competitive Muslim religious movements" that was the legacy of premodern Indian-Islamic organization (Lapidus 1988:463).

NOTES

1   This is an Indo-European linguistic feature parallel to "theist-atheist" where the addition of a- or an- reverses the meaning of the noun.
2   These are the "Three Jewels" of Buddhism: Buddha himself, Buddha's teachings (dharma), and the monastic community (sangha).
3   Then, Mithila was a city, the capital of Videha; now, Mithila is the name of the region.
4   A zamindar was a landowner. The term could be used for small and great landholders, but in some parts of British India major zamindars called themselves raja or maharaja, titles that the British also frequently bestowed.
5   Gandhi's term for "untouchables," meaning "People of God."
6   One lakh equals 100,000 rupees. As of this writing, the value of one dollar is about forty rupees; so one lakh is over $4000. A typical middle-class monthly income is Rs. 1500 to 3000; so a dowry of two lakhs might be eight years' income.

7 Not to be confused with the priestly caste of Brahmans.

8 Dates for the Buddha's life vary. Sri Lanka chronicles place it at 563 B.C.; a mainland tradition puts it at 450 B.C.; more recent research puts it at 485 B.C. (Gombrich 1984).

9 And a few centuries later, as we have seen, Ashoka opened these stupas, removed all but a fragment from each, and built 84,000 more stupas (or at least quite a lot) throughout his empire.

SOUTHEAST ASIA

Chronology of Southeast Asian History

	BURMA	THAILAND	CAMBODIA	VIETNAM	INDONESIA
3600					
1600	BRONZE AGE		N E O L I T H I C		
1000					
100 BC			DONG SON 6th–2nd C. B.C.		
0 AD					
100					
200					
300	PYU AND MON KINGDOMS (300–900 A.D.)		FUNAN 3rd–6th C. Beginning of Indian Influence		
500		DVARAVATI PERIOD			BRONZE AGE
600			CHENLA 6th–8th C.		
700			PRE-ANGKOR 7th–9th C.		CENTRAL JAVANESE 8th–10th C.
800		SRIVIJAYA 8th–13th C.		DAI-LA 8th–10th C.	
900	PAGAN PERIOD		ANGKOR PERIOD		EASTERN JAVANESE
1000	9th–13th C.	LOPBURI 13th–14th C.	9th–13th C.	DAI-VIET 11th –12th C.	10th–16th C.
1100					
1200		SUKHOTHAI PERIOD 13th–15th C.		TRAN 11th–12th C.	ISLAMIC PERIOD 13th C.–Present
1300	SHAN-THAI 1287–1760	AYUTTHAYA 14th–18th C.			MAJAPAHIT PERIOD
1400			LAOS 14th–Present	LE 15th–18th C.	1293–16th C.
1500					
1600					
1700		BANGKOK PERIOD late 18th–20th C.			
1800	ALAUNGPYA 1760–1885				
1900					

The diversity of Asia is most evident in Southeast Asia. No empire ever united or even pretended to unite all its peoples, its peaks and valleys, or its vast island chains, though plenty of rulers claimed to be god-kings of the whole world. The ten nations of modern Southeast Asia—Vietnam, Cambodia, Laos, Thailand, Burma (Myanmar), Malaysia, Singapore, Indonesia, the Philippines, and Brunei—are coming to think of themselves as a geopolitical region with important interests in common, but this is a phenomenon of the twentieth century. The mainland region, excluding northern Vietnam, together with Java and Bali, came early under Indian cultural influence, with god-kings whose palaces were models of the Himalayan abode of Hindu gods—an influence that lasted over a millennium and is still clearly visible today. Northern Vietnam for many centuries was China's southernmost province, with the first written forms of its language in Chinese characters and an elite who quoted Confucius and ran its bureaucracy in the Mandarin manner. Southeast Asia includes two great archipelagoes, themselves collections of hundreds of islands of tremendous diversity, both of which had political unity forced on them by colonialism. The Dutch created "Indonesia" out of several western islands where states had existed in the past—especially Java and Bali—and a number of central islands that are home to tribal folk who never formed states and never wished to join the states of others; and an easternmost province, Irian Jaya, which belongs culturally to New Guinea. The second archipelago, the Philippines—"300 years in a Catholic convent and 50 years in Hollywood"—was longest-colonized of all, first by the Spanish who sailed in from the east across the Pacific with shiploads of gold dollars from their Mexican colony, and then in this century by the United States.

FOUR STAGES OF SOUTHEAST ASIAN HISTORY

Although Southeast Asia's history and prehistory are not yet well known, certain broad phases can be identified: the prehistoric period, from 2500 to 150 B.C.; a period of Indian cultural influence, beginning about A.D. 100 and lasting until A.D. 1300; a period of Chinese and Islamic influence, from roughly 1300 to 1750; and the period of Western colonial intervention, from 1750 until the fairly rapid extinguishing of colonial control in the decades following World War II. Although there has been a great deal of archaeological research in recent years, there is no site

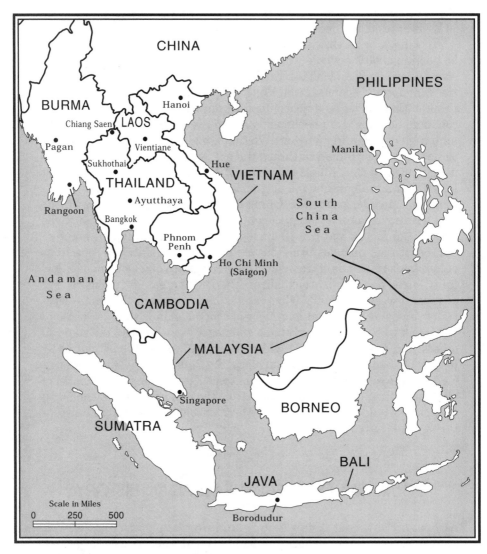

Map 6.1   Southeast Asia

or region where there is a single comprehensive sequence connecting prehistory and historical periods (Hutterer 1982). This is a critical gap, because just how the early civilizations of Southeast Asia emerged, and what kinds of societies provided their platform, is of enormous interest, yet little can yet be said with certainty about this transition.

Early scholars assumed that prehistoric Southeast Asia was a syncretic place, fashioned out of influences borrowed or imposed from China and India, thus accounting for names like "Indochina," "East Indies," and "Further India." However, there is growing evidence that in prehistoric times, Southeast Asia was far from a recipient of higher cultures to the west and north, but an innovative region where important advances in agriculture, metalwork, and pottery manufacture were made—and sent west and north. And in the early Indianized states, an older view that imagined intrepid Indians—traders, warriors, Brahmans, or monks—carrying their culture into Southeast Asia is being replaced by a view that Southeast Asians themselves actively sought out Indian ideas and constructed their states on an idealized model of Indian kingship.

The Prehistoric Period 2500–150 B.C.

One fact to keep in mind is that Southeast Asia in the prehistoric period included southern China. As the prehistory of east and southeast Asia unfolds with the work of archaeologists, there is a tendency for modern nationalist interests to be rooting for all the best and earliest discoveries to come either from China or from mainland Southeast Asia. But these borders were not relevant during the Neolithic and Bronze Age periods. The Han Chinese did not begin to incorporate the region south of the Yangtze until the first millennium B.C., that is, after the prehistoric period we are considering here (Bellwood 1992). In cultural and linguistic terms, a single integral region stretched from south of the Yangtze to the South China Sea, including Tai, Tibeto-Burman, Miao-Yao, and Austroasiatic groups that still inhabit both sides of the current border. It was, according to Bellwood, in southern China that Neolithic technology—food cultivating, pottery making—developed, and this successful new adaptation fueled the population growth and expansion southward and into the islands of Southeast Asia via sea routes, most significantly the route from Taiwan to the Philippines and into Indonesia, which carried the Austronesian languages into their vast diaspora (see chapter 3).

The "cultures" of prehistoric Southeast Asia are known to us only through archaeological sources, where the word "culture" has its own meaning, both more and less precise than when the same word is used by historians or cultural anthropologists. A "culture" to archaeologists is the assemblage of objects and evidence left behind in sites, always a pathetically scant sample of all that the "culture" (historian/cultural anthropolgist sense) had once been. Archaeologists are trained to carefully examine these assemblages in their site contexts, compare them with assemblages from other sites, near and far, and make cautious but informed inferences about the actual culture that once thrived in that region.

One fact is clear about Southeast Asian prehistoric cultures: water was no barrier to communication. Straits and seas did not isolate folk into so many discrete, unique, and insulated societies; rather, from 40,000 B.P. forward, large numbers of Southeast Asians traversed vast stretches of water, so that most "cultures" (archaeologists' sense) span waterways, linking, for example, Taiwan-Philippines-Timor, or Malay Peninsula-Sumatra-Borneo, or even Borneo-New Guinea-Fiji.

The earliest of these across-the-seas dispersals took Australo-Melanesians into Australia and New Guinea around 40,000 B.P. By 9600 B.P., another broad "culture," known as the Hoabinhian, was distributed from Burma to southern China to Malaysia and parts of Sumatra. These were preagricultural foragers whose pebble tools are their most distinctive cultural feature at this distance in time.

By 3000 B.C., Neolithic (that is, food-producing) cultures were well established on the Khorat Plateau of northeast Thailand, and probably in other alluvial sites on the mainland. Rice itself was probably domesticated in southern China around 5000 B.C. (see chapter 2). Rice cultivation is not found outside low alluvial basins until after about 500 B.C. The phenomenon of dry-rice swidden cultivators in the hills is apparently recent; three teams of archaeologists have scoured the hills of Thailand looking for evidence of ancient dry-rice cultivation without turning up anything (Bellwood 1992:122). The Neolithic assemblage typically includes domesticated cattle, pigs, fowl, dogs, cultivated rice, and flooded fields.

The Neolithic assemblages are joined by bronze working by 1100 B.C., when we find industrious metalworkers casting copper and tin in open-hearth furnaces. They used both the lost-wax methods and bivalve molds made of clay strengthened with rice chaff. At the site of Ban Na Di is a cemetery with many burials wrapped in mats, and a child covered with a crocodile skin. The dead were sent off with grave goods like necklaces and bracelets made of shell or shell beads. Quickly made figurines of unbaked clay in the form of cattle, pigs, dogs, other animals, and humans suggest concepts of an afterlife where these companions will be needed.

These metalworking Neolithic societies reached a new cultural height about 600 B.C. in a densely populated and stratified society centered on the Red River in northern Vietnam, known as the Dong-son culture. Here, skilled artisans began to fashion a wholly unique and beautiful bronze drum that has become the distinguishing feature of the culture. These drums stood on splayed feet, with bulbous upper sides and a flat tympanum. They were highly ornamented with scenes that hint of the culture where these drums resounded: warriors wearing feather headdresses, houses with raised platforms, and longboats with a drum in a cabin or amidships. Around the upper perimeter were friezes of birds, deer, and other animals, along with intricate geometric patterns. They were cast in one piece, including their lavish ornamentation, by the lost-wax method. Over two hundred of these Dong-son drums have been found

These huge bronze Dong-son drums, a triumph of late Neolithic technology, were manufactured in the Red River region and traded widely throughout mainland and island Southeast Asia.

in Vietnam, Cambodia, Thailand, the Malay Peninsula, and in Indonesia, almost everywhere but Borneo and the Philippines. However, they seem to have been manufactured only in the Red River region and traded to other areas. Dong-son drums are frequently found in burial sites, which give additional evidence of a stratified society in the variations of wealth buried with the dead. One hundred bronzes were found in one grave, and some very wealthy persons were buried in coffins of lacquered wood.

When we turn to insular Southeast Asia, we have much less to work with in terms of archaeological evidence for the pre-Indic period, because conditions are less favorable for preservation in the tropics. However, the archaeological record is clear about the sudden appearance around 2500 B.C. of a new culture whose distinguishing feature is a red-slip and incised pottery. Along with these pots are found shell beads and fishhooks, a tool of agate for drilling shells, and obsidian flakes. These finds undoubtedly represent the arrival of the daring, seafaring Austronesian-speaking people, who moved south from Taiwan to the Philippines, to Sulawesi, and to Timor, covering thirty-five hundred kilometers in less than a thousand years (Bellwood 1992). Here they pioneered cultivation of taro, yams, and other tropical crops. These same peoples moved out into the Pacific across five thousand kilometers of islands from New Guinea to Samoa and Fiji, where the culture is known by the term "Lapita" and the people became the Polynesians.

Besides their red-slip pottery, it is their burial practices that distinguish the pre-Indic cultures of insular Southeast Asia. In caves in Tabon, Philippines; Niah Cave in Sarawak; and at Long Thanh in southern Vietnam, large burial jars with fitted lids containing human remains have been found. Jar burials, not always in caves, have been found more widely in Java and Bali, and the famous but poorly understood Plain of Jars in Laos may also be from this era. About 1.5 meters in height, the jars appear to have been used for burial in the first century B.C. (Bellwood 1992). During the Vietnam War many were destroyed, and no significant research has been done there since the 1930s, so the famous jars are another puzzle waiting to be solved. Most of the jars that have been closely examined appear to be cases of "secondary burial," a practice still widely followed in island Southeast Asia. The dead are first cremated or allowed to decay rapidly, then the cleaned and processed bones are placed in a small jar inside a large jar that also contains grave goods of iron and bronze.

All of these developments were indigenously Southeast Asian. However, in the last few centuries of the first millennium B.C., a scattering of intriguing foreign objects make their appearance. In the Sa Huynh (southern Vietnam) site, objects from China and India are found. In burial jars in Java and Bali, there are glass beads from India. In the late prehistoric period, there are trading centers in the Philippines where Chinese traders come, and most intriguing of all is a recently excavated site at Sembiran, on the coast of Bali, that appears to have been a trade station with ties to Arikamedu, on the Indian coast near Pondicherry, which was an Indo-Roman trade station. "When all these finds are put together they hint very strongly of the oldest direct evidence from Southeast Asia for the trade in spices that linked the Roman Empire, India, and Southeast Asia in the first centuries of our era" (Bellwood 1992:133).

Period of Indian Cultural Influence A.D. 100–1300

In May 1992, newspapers and television around the world flashed an indelible scene from Bangkok: King Bhumipol seated on a sofa while in front of him two men in suits, the Prime Minister and the leader of the democracy movement, are on their hands and knees before him. There had just been a violent showdown between a military-dominated government and democracy activists in which soldiers had opened fire on civilian protesters, killing dozens of them. The submission of the Prime Minister and the leader of the opposition brought an immediate end to the confrontation, and shortly after, the Prime Minister resigned. A prominent Thai said of the king: "He is the unifying force of Thai society. He is the one who is a check on the system. He can tell us whether we are going in the right direction or the wrong direction. He is the standard of morality, of righteousness" (Shenon 1995). That is, the king is a *dharmaraja*. Like Ashoka, he is a king of righteousness.

How did the kings of Thailand gain such immense moral power? How did they come to constitute themselves dharmarajas, modeling their kingdoms after those of India?

When Europeans began arriving in mainland Southeast Asia in the late eighteenth and early nineteenth centuries, they were surprised to find, so close to China, cultural practices that seemed more Indian than Chinese. Peasants wore wraparound sarongs in the South Indian fashion rather than the trousers of the Chinese peasant. They wore turbans, not straw hats. They carried their goods on their heads, as in India, not on the two ends of a pole, as in China. They ate with their right hands, not with chopsticks. They played musical instruments very similar to the Indian sitar. They wrote their languages in scripts clearly related to the South Indian scripts and ultimately descended from Ashokan Brahmi. The elephant was the sign of royalty, as in India, not the dragon, as in China. They worshipped Indian gods like Shiva and Vishnu; they had a version of the Ramayana called in Thailand the *Ramakien*; and they venerated the Indian teacher, Buddha (Chandler 1992). Above all, Southeast Asian states were clearly Indic states, legitimated with an Indian cosmology and enacted with Indian symbols of authority.

The pre-modern states of Southeast Asia had a unique vision of territoriality, one of two principal types. The first vision imagines and draws distant lines, often demarcating them with walls, always defending them with troops. This is the model of Hadrian, building and defending a wall across central Britain. It is the vision of Qin Shihuang, building the world's greatest expanse of wall to bound off the Middle Kingdom from the irrelevant lands and peoples beyond. The second model, the *mandala*, is a vision of the state as a circle with a center of concentrated power, virtue, and sanctity, a pivot not only on the terrestrial plane, but an axis linking earth and heaven, at whose center dwells a figure of supreme power, at once warrior, king, and god. Ultimately the model of the state as distant lines to be drawn and defended prevailed, but the latter vision of the state had hundreds of proximations over a fifteen hundred-year period in Southeast Asia, both on the mainland and in the islands.

The state as mandala was an Indian conception, as was the widespread word for such a state, *nagara*. Nagara, in India, is a perfectly ordinary word for town, but in Southeast Asia for two millennia it was the very word for civilization, a "sacred city," the powerful central energy node of the archaic state, the mandala. Geertz claims there were hundreds or thousands of nagaras in Indonesia alone in a continuous process of state formation and dissolution, and as many more on the mainland of Southeast Asia. But we will focus on the most successful ones, those known to us through Ashoka-like inscriptions on columns by which kings proclaimed their authority; through accounts of travelers, most often Chinese; through stupendous archaeological remains, some of the most fabulous on earth; and through texts, though fewer than historians would wish, left behind on palm leaves and parchment.

A long-debated question has been how Southeast Asia came to be Indianized. Were Indians responsible for Southeast Asia's Indianization? Did they operate like the Chinese, who annexed territories further and further south, establishing a military post north of the Tonkin Delta in 214 B.C. and by 111 B.C. controlling most of the north? For a thousand years, Vietnam's northern region was China's southernmost province, known to them as Giao Chi. But the answer is no; Indians never set out on any expeditions of conquest in Southeast Asia, and there was never any political connection between the two regions.

Indians did, however, go to Southeast Asia to trade, as we have already seen. They called Southeast Asia Suvarnabhumi, the "Land of Gold," and the Indonesian islands, which Europeans called the "Spice Islands," Indians called *suvarnadvip,* the "Islands of Gold." Indian traders were also trading to the west with Rome, as the Arikamedu site, excavated by Sir Mortimer Wheeler in 1955, has shown. But when Roman Emperor Vespasian prohibited the exportation of gold in A.D. 69, that may have been a turning point, intensifying Indian trade with Southeast Asia. Most likely Indian traders set up semipermanent trade establishments near local chiefs, maintaining links with home, sending home for brides. They would have brought Brahmans to their distant settlements to perform life-cycle rites for them, and these Brahmans would have brought the sacred works in the Sanskrit language—the Vedas, the Dharmashastras, the Puranas, the Ramayana, the Mahabharata—with them. These were the first books, and the first writing, Southeast Asians saw. These Brahmans would, in other words, have been carriers of India's high culture.

But it is unlikely such persons could have imposed Indian culture on Southeast Asian rulers. Southeast Asia was Indianized, as Lansing argues (1983), not by the arrival of Indians bearing civilization, still less by Southeast Asians going to India (though both of those things surely happened), but by the power of Indian ideas. These powerful ideas included a mathematical astronomy that made possible a calendrical system that located the human world in the divine cosmos. The "vision of a vast and orderly cosmos" permitted both the far-reaching metaphysics of Hindu and Buddhist thought and required integration of the human realm into an overall theory of cosmic order. That is, it contained a theory of the state that was naturally attractive to rulers all over Southeast Asia. It is easy to imagine the appeal of these ideas to a ruler who had conquered his enemies; commanded the loyalty of troops and vassals, villages and persons; and could claim to control a vast territory—was he not like Indra in his heaven? Was such a man not a god-king? This new theory of the state functioned to legitimate the state by converting military conquest and political dominance into cosmically meaningful categories.

Although Indic ideas came to Southeast Asia with all their multiplicity of gods, sects, and epics, and in both Hindu and Buddhist variants, the major regional nagaras tended to emphasize either Hindu or Buddhist strands. We would not want to overstate this distinction, as the cosmological underpinnings were similar in both cases. The monuments built by Hindu and Buddhist monarchs tended both to feature a central raised structure, but for Hinduized monarchs such as those at Angkor, they housed the lingam of Shiva, Shiva's phallic icon, while for Buddhist monarchs they were stupas housing relics of the Buddha. In both cases, these were centers of concentrated cosmological power where royal authority fused with sheer divinity.

The major locations of these Indianized kingdoms with predominantly Hindu cosmologies were Funan, Bali, Angkor, and the Thai kingdoms of Sukhothai, Ayutthaya, and Bangkok.

Funan. The lower Mekong valley and delta was where the first Indianized kingdom, known to the Chinese as Funan, emerged between the first and sixth centuries A.D. Two Chinese diplomats, Kang Dai and Zhu Ying, visited Funan from the southern Chinese state of Wu with orders to seek information regarding trade with India. Kang Dai's report, though lost, was quoted at length in later Chinese chronicles, such as the *Liangshu* (History of the Liang Dynasty). They tell of an Indian Brahman named Kaundinya who was said to have married a local Naga princess and founded the ruling house of Funan, "changing the rules according to the customs of India." Kings had adopted the Indian honorific -*varman*, meaning "protected by," in names such as Jayavarman and Gunavarman. Texts on columns were written in both Sanskrit and ancient Khmer. A footprint of Vishnu was venerated. And everywhere princes undertook the drainage of marshlands, the building of irrigation channels, and the digging of reservoirs.

Archaeologists have supplemented our knowledge of Funan. At sites like Oc Eo, excavated by Malleret in 1944, a large canal completed eighteen hundred years ago is clearly visible from the air, and five ramparts and four moats were found on excavation. Thriving trade with both

India and China is evidenced by exotic trinkets: Chinese mirrors, rings and seals with Brahmi script from India, and even Roman coins, dated to the reign of Marcus Aurelius, A.D. 161–180.

Bali. The most enduring of the Indianized nagaras of Southeast Asia is Bali's, which survived into the twentieth century and in some ways survives still as a richly Hindu ceremonial culture focused on village temples, the only Hindu state outside South Asia. The state itself disappeared in gunfire and flames in 1906:

> The Dutch army appeared, for reasons of its own, at Sanur on the south coast and fought its way into Badung, where the king, his wives, his children, and his entourage marched in a splendid mass suicide into the direct fire of its guns. Within the week, the king and crown prince of Tabanan had been captured, but they managed to destroy themselves, the one by poison, the other by knife, their first evening in Dutch custody. Two years later, in 1908, this strange ritual was repeated in the most illustrious state of all, Klungkung, the nominal "capital" of traditional Bali; the king and court again paraded, half entranced, half dazed with opium, out of the palace into the reluctant fire of the by now thoroughly bewildered Dutch troops. It was quite literally the death of the old order. It expired as it had lived: absorbed in a pageant. (Geertz 1980:11–13)

Bali in its heyday was, as Geertz sees it, a "theater state," where great theatrical rites—cremations, tooth-filings, temple dedications, pilgrimage, and blood sacrifices—drew together the people, the priests, and the rulers in a single sociopolitical ritual drama. Where others have argued that royal cults exist for the purpose of legitimating a particular political order, it is Geertz's view that "mass ritual was not a device to shore up the state, but rather the state, even in its final gasp, was a device for the enactment of mass ritual" (Geertz 1980:13). And Lansing (1991) has more recently supported this view somewhat indirectly by demonstrating that Bali's vast, terraced irrigation system is not the work of political rulers but of a separate hierarchy of water temples, water temple festivals, and water temple priests. That is to say, the rulers of Bali were doing little of a practical, bureaucratic nature to justify their existence. Rather, they were busy reproducing the world of the gods here on earth.

Angkor. The middle Mekong between Phnom Penh, the modern capital of Cambodia, and the Tonle Sap, the great freshwater lake that quadruples every year from monsoonal floodwaters that cause its tributary to the Mekong to temporarily reverse course, has been the heartland of Khmer civilization since the sixth century. Here the kingdoms of Chenla developed between the sixth and eighth centuries A.D., followed by the brilliant Angkor state from the ninth through thirteenth centuries. As a nagara, from which its name derived, Angkor was unrivaled. Each of the twenty-five rulers of the Angkor dynasty built his own temple-palace-

6.1 The King of Angkor Goes Out

In the year I spent in Cambodia I saw [the king] go out four or five times.

When the king leaves the palace, first comes the cavalry, leading his escort, followed by an array of standards, banners, and music. Next comes a troupe of palace girls, anywhere from three to five hundred, dressed in flowered material, their heads garlanded with flowers and holding large candles lighted even in broad daylight. After them come more palace girls bearing the royal utensils of gold and silver and an assortment of all kinds of ornaments whose usage I don't understand. Then come the palace girls who, armed with lance and shield, form the king's private bodyguard; they, too, form a troupe. They are followed by carriages ornamented in gold and drawn by goats and horses. Ministers and nobles mounted on elephants look straight ahead, while clustered around them are their many, many red parasols of rank. After them in palanquins, carriages, and on elephants come the king's wives and concubines; they have more than a hundred parasols decorated in gold. Behind them comes the king. Holding the precious sword, he stands on the royal elephant, whose tusks are encased in gold. More than twenty white parasols, gold-trimmed and with golden handles, surround him. A great many elephants form a cordon around the king and the cavalry guards him.

If the king leaves the palace for a nearby visit, he uses only a golden palanquin, which is carried by four palace girls. Most of such visits are made to a small gold pagoda before which is a gold Buddha. Those who see the king must prostrate themselves and touch the ground with their foreheads. They call this obeisance *san-pa*. Anyone who fails to show proper respect is seized by the attendant guards, who punish the offender before releasing him.

Twice each day the king holds an audience to conduct the affairs of government. There is no set procedure. Whoever desires to see the king—either officials or any private person—sits on the ground and awaits him. After a little while, one hears, far off in the palace, distant music; outside they blow on conchs to announce his approach. I have heard that he uses only a gold palanquin and does not come from very far away. An instant later, two palace girls lift the curtain on the Golden Window and the king, sword in his hand, appears. All those present—ministers and people—clasp their hands together and beat their foreheads on the ground. As the sound of the conchs ceases, they can raise their heads. At the king's pleasure, they may approach and sit down on a lion skin, which is considered a royal object. When all matters are disposed of, the king retires, the two palace girls let the curtain fall; everyone rises. Thus one sees that, though this country is barbarous and strange, they do not fail to know what it is to be a king.

Zhou Daguan, on his visit to Angkor, August 1296–July 1297
Jeannette Mirsky, 1964, pp. 232–33.

mausoleum complex on the northern bank of Tonle Sap. An Angkor king was first of all a warrior-king, rising from amongst other chieftains, defeating some in battle and winning the admiring fealty of others, and binding them to him through gifts of land and gifts of honor; a palanquin with gold stretchers and four gold-handled parasols went to ministers of highest rank. Finally came bonds of kinship as he accepted wives from allied chiefs. We still can see these warrior-kings depicted in bas relief on royal compound walls, Suryavarman reviewing his armies, his best general mounted on a great war elephant.

But they were also more than warrior-kings. When Jayavarman II came to power in 802 after a period of captivity in Java where he saw a god-like king rule from a sacred court, he followed up his conquest of his rivals by establishing the royal lingam—emblem of the god Shiva in the form of his phallus—in a temple-pyramid called Rong Chen. Many centuries later, in nineteenth-century Bali, Indic kingship would require of the king "to project an enormous calm at the center of an enormous activity by becoming palpably immobile" (Geertz 1980:130). But in ninth-century Angkor, kings had too much work to do, as sovereign-warriors as well as god-kings; it was Shiva's lingam that was housed, sacred and immobile, in the divine center of the kingdom, which was simultaneously a replica of Shiva's Himalayan abode and the center of the universe.

The terraced monuments replicating Hindu conceptions of the abode of the gods in the marshy flatlands of central Cambodia required enormous resources of land, labor, and wealth. Land and labor could be expanded by conquest, by taking of slaves, and by corvée labor. Additional wealth was required through taxation, but Angkor had no monetary system. Taxes were paid in rice and other primary produce. Land registers were maintained by officials who determined the amount of produce owed on the basis of the quality of land. Land irrigated from royally sponsored irrigation canals could get two or three crops per year, and was consequently assessed at more than a rain-fed upland field. Peasants were required to produce double what they needed to survive in order to pay taxes. For specialist classes, taxes were paid in honey, wax, sugar, spices, salt, medicine, livestock, feathers, rhino horns, ivory, sandalwood, and cloth. A stone inscription from the Temple of Preah Khon describes the provisioning of the temple: "The king and the owners of villages have devoutly given 5,324 villages, totaling 97,840 men and women, 444 chefs, 4,604 footmen, cooks, and others, 2,298 servants, of which 1,000 are dancers, 47,436 individuals making sacrificial offerings" (Freeman & Warner 1990:112). All this wealth was needed, plus slave and corvée labor, to keep the construction projects going and to maintain a court ceremonial designed to sustain a god-king in his heaven-on-earth capital.

Angkor's rulers built their monuments to Shiva in the ninth and tenth centuries; to Vishnu in the following century; and finally began to

Depicted here is the great causeway leading to the central structure of Angkor Wat. The compound was laid out as a cosmological model of the universe, with the causeway the access to heaven. In the great palace/temple ahead resides the devaraja, the god-king, in his "Himalayan" abode.

favor Buddha from the twelfth century on. The greatest achievement of all, Angkor Wat, was built by Suryavarman II for Vishnu. Its central sanctuary originally contained a Shiva lingam, Suryavarman's royal icon, but in later centuries it became a place of pilgrimage for Theravada Buddhists, so it now contains images of the Buddha—surrounded by bas reliefs of the voluptuous *apsaras* who once fluttered in delight around Shiva's lingam.

Seeing Angkor Wat from the air makes immediately visible what it was designed to be: the largest man-made model of the cosmos ever. A moat 1400 by 1600 yards is the ocean surrounding the world. A single causeway crossing the moat into the heart of the cosmos, the summit of Mount Meru (where reposed the Shiva lingam), is the route between earth and heaven. Concentric enclosures around "Mount Meru" represent mountain chains encircling the central continent. Angkor Wat was constructed so that if you stand in front of the western entrance on the spring equinox, the beginning of the year according to Hindu astronomy, the sun rises directly over the central tower. From there throughout the year it illuminates the fabulous bas reliefs carved on the inner wall of the third gallery; in the spring, light falls on depictions of the creation with the churning of the Ocean of Milk; on the side of the setting sun is the terrible battle of Kurukshetra, the pivotal event of the Mahabharata, whose themes of conflict and doom seem to have been on the minds of Khmer kings.

One length of bas relief shows two ranks of soldiers, the disciplined Khmer regulars in perfect formation contrasted with an unruly crowd of Thai mercenaries, some gabbing to men behind them, others leering drunkenly out of the bas relief. Yet the Thais' day came. Angkor went into decline as the Thai began their expansion on the Khorat Plateau, stealing their vassals and depriving Angkor of essential sources of land, people, and wealth. Sukhothai, founded by Angkor, declared its independence in the thirteenth century; in the next, it conquered Angkor. Irrigation systems fell into disuse, reservoirs silted up. And in the great temples, seeds of the strangler fig fell and rooted, growing in crevices and expanding, until like gigantic tusks they ripped stone blocks apart, toppling roofs and towers, inviting the jungle to take back the monuments of the Angkor kings.

The Thai: Sukhothai, Ayutthaya, Bangkok. The Chao Phrya Valley has been the principal domain of the Thai (Siamese) people. It is the location of modern Bangkok and the site of the most recent and still surviving Cakri dynasty of Thailand. Thai kingdoms were founded after 1300, but before the coming of the Thai, there were earlier kingdoms. On the Khorat Plateau of what is now Northeast Thailand, a dry, raised region without the alluvial features that made hydraulics such key activities in other mandalas, the Siamese state emerged. Even earlier, between A.D. 200 and 950, there were kingdoms involved in trade with India and China known as Dvaravati. Both Chao Phrya and the Khorat Plateau site reveal a preponderance of Buddhist themes, in contrast to the Hindu influences in Cambodia, Bali, and southern Vietnam: stupas, bas reliefs with Buddhist scenes, and ordination halls. We return to these Theravada Buddhist states in the next section.

The Period of Chinese and Islamic Influence, 1300–1750

The Hindu-Buddhist prince and peasant were the most common social types in Southeast Asia by the fourteenth century, and the mandala was the idealized state. The principal exception was Vietnam, where from the Red River south along the central coast there was a series of small chiefdoms or kingdoms not properly called mandalas, as they were strongly influenced by Chinese conceptions of the state, with Confucian bureaucracies and Chinese-style rituals and burials. Vietnam was often under direct control by China, particularly in the North. However, movements of ideas and peoples after the fourteenth century gave to the region two new cultural types: the Muslim trader and (as we have recently come to speak of them) the Confucian capitalist.

Chinese and Muslim traders came out of civilizations with radically opposed views of the trading life. In Confucian China, merchants were parasites living off the honest labor of others. Society needed traders to distribute production, and many did become wealthy, but they were always stigmatized by the Confucian establishment. By contrast, in Islam, commerce was a gift of Allah, and his prophet, Muhammad, was actually a caravan trader. Many statements from the Qur'an convey Allah's approval of trade:

> It is He who has made the sea subject [to you] that you might eat fish from it and that you might extract from it ornaments to wear; and you see ships ploughing in it that you might seek [profit] from his abundance and that you may give thanks. (16:14)

The establishment of Muhammad's state in Medina in 622 led to an astonishing expansion of well-organized tribal armies motivated as much to control the lucrative trade routes of Asia and North Africa as by the truth of Islam. Only four years earlier, in 618, the illustrious Tang dynasty had been founded in China. Trade soon brought the two civilizations into contact, certainly along the ancient Silk Route, now once again open and thriving, but also via the southern maritime route through the Indian Ocean and the South China Sea. Arabian and Indian merchants sought China's silks, ceramics, and porcelains; in exchange they provided jade, ivory, frankincense, and Persian silk. Over the next few centuries, as Arabian tribes conquered the Middle East and North Africa, leading to establishment of the Abassid Empire (720–1258), Chinese trade under Tang (618-906) and Song (960–1280) benefited from new shipping technology: keels, rudders, sails, new navigational techniques, and increases in vessel size. A shift to a money economy made possible large-scale investment in surpluses for export. The Song "economic revolution" put Chinese paper, silk, textiles, ceramics, porcelain, iron, and steel into international trade (Risso 1995). Most of this trade was conducted along the southern shipping routes through Southeast Asia.

The Chinese Diaspora. Remarkable as it may seem, the arrival of sweeping Chinese influence in Southeast Asia may be traced to the burgeoning strengths of a tribal people thousands of miles to the north in the arid lands cut off from the warming tropical influences by the Himalayas. These people were the Mongols.

In 1206, Genghis Khan succeeded in unifying the unruly Mongol tribes at an historic meeting on the Kerulen River where they conferred on him the Mongolian version of a title that by now will sound familiar: Universal Ruler. The title was not cakravartin, but *genghis khan*. He, too, conceived his mission as divine, setting out with his sons and generals to conquer the world. He came far closer than any Southeast Asian *rajadeva* (god-king) to doing so.

Genghis Khan himself pierced the Great Wall, but it was his grandson, Khubilai Khan (1215–1294), who completed the conquest of China. He chose Beijing as his winter capital, then began moving down the Yangtze, taking city after city. Capturing the Song navy, the Mongols became, for the first time, a maritime power. In 1285 and 1287, Mongols conquered Hanoi. In 1287, Khubilai's grandson, Timur Khan, occupied the Indic state of Pagan in Burma.

These Mongol invasions in southern China set in motion a stream of refugees who fled south, hopefully out of harm's way. The invasion of Nanchao in Yunnan Province in 1253 impacted the Dai, among others, who began moving south in large numbers into territories dominated by the Khmer. Rather than sinicizing Khmer territory, however, this movement ended up Indianizing the Thai, Lao, and Shan.

It was in the island areas that enduring Chinese influence began most to be felt. Sumatran and Javanese traders were quick to send envoys to Khubilai's capital, seeking preferred-port status. This led the Javanese into risky competition in Javanese seas with Mongol fleets, and for a time it seemed the Mongol empire would include Java. But the new Javanese state of Majapahit first defeated, then reestablished friendly trade relations with China in 1293. They also opened trade relations with Western Europe through Venice, making Javanese ports essential centers in the early phases of the world economy.

Although China's central government went through periods of convulsive withdrawal from all foreign connections, as when Ming emperors banned all overseas trade with a policy in which "not even a little plank was allowed to drift to the sea" (Blusse 1989), this did not stop the southeastern provinces from a trade they had engaged in for centuries. Two regular routes were plied by Chinese junks outfitted by prominent Chinese families with capital from their landed estates. One route went along the mainland coast from Vietnam to the Malay Peninsula to western Java. Another route went via Japan, down the Ryukyus, Philippines, and eastern Indonesian islands, ending in Manila (Andaya 1992). In a number of these locations, small overseas Chinese trade communities had settled by the sixteenth century or earlier. These Chinese communities became the commercial entrepreneurs in places like Bangkok, Singapore, Kuala Lumpur, and Djakarta in the twentieth century. As minority communities specializing in trade, these diaspora Chinese were visible and frequent targets of envy and animosity. In some places, like Bangkok, they took Thai names and attempted to assimilate into Thai society. In other places, like Singapore, Kuala Lumpur, and Djakarta, they remained visible as a Chinese ethnic minority and often retained their ties to China. It is these, especially the Chinese of Singapore, who have come to be identified among Asia's "Confucian capitalists."

Islam. Unlike Buddhism in Southeast Asia, which was associated with land-based empires ruled by cakravartins, Islam spread among maritime trade communities. In the fifteenth century, Melaka's (Malacca's) population of fifty thousand to two hundred thousand persons consisted primarily of Muslim merchants of many ethnicities: Gujaratis, Bengalis, Javanese, and Chinese (Risso 1995). A Hindu chief named Parameshvara converted to Islam and changed his name to Megat Iskander Shah. His control of the center of trade ensured that his kingdom would flourish, and with it, Islam. From here, the faith spread throughout the Malay world, joining it to a great religious community stretching from the Middle East through India and Southeast Asia. Converts took Arab names, thereby enhancing a growing Muslim identity that transcended their original cultures. Melaka was not the only coastal, Islamic trading center; these trading classes spread to other islands and to Java itself, threatening the older Indic "theater states" with "a tangled crowd of foreigners and locals . . . unassimilable to the Indic world view" (Geertz 1968:39). In the fifteenth and sixteenth centuries, the balance of power began to shift to these newcomers whose faith was in Allah. Mosque and market replaced temple and court as centers of sociopolitical power and cultural growth. The Melaka sultanate provided Southeast Asia with a prototype Malay state different from the theater state of the Indic model, yet in many ways also a moral, exemplary center. The sultan was the source of all honors and the defender of the Islamic faith.

Muhammad's teachings provided a formidable contrast to the Indic worldview with its rich symbolism. Islam was simple to the point of asceticism. The many gods of Hinduism were reduced to one God, Allah. Where the rich and powerful Hindu raja was allowed many wives, a rich and powerful Muslim sultan or merchant could have only four. Drinking and gambling were prohibited. Religious practice was simplified to the Five Pillars, all obligatory: the confession of faith, repeated over and over ("There is no God but Allah and Muhammad is his Prophet"); the five daily prayers; fasting during specified periods; the once-per-lifetime pilgrimage to Mecca (*hajj*); and the religious tax, or alms. The smoky clutter of images, offerings, and clanging bells that make a Hindu or Buddhist temple a place of such symbolic density was replaced by the austere mosque, little more than a large room where many worshippers can gather on their knees in prayer.

Despite this simplicity, Islam was not a world-rejecting religion like much of Hinduism and Buddhism. The fact that Muhammad actually formed a successful state, unlike Jesus and Buddha, meant that the Islamic state was normative, a part of Islam from its very origin. There developed an early emphasis on the administration of the law, or Shari'a, based on the Qur'an. The benefit of the Shari'a was that wherever Islam spread, converts shared a common law to govern their lives, even if they had no actual Islamic state to enforce this law. This law potentially included governance even of commerce. The Qur'anic admonition "fill the measure when you measure and weigh with balanced scales" led to the market inspector, who checked weights and measures, oversaw local transactions, approved medical practice, and insured that bazaar folk observed prayers and fasts (Risso 1995).

In this new, post-Indic, Southeast Asian environment, Islam grew into something quite different than it had been in its Arab, North African, and Central Asian forms. Even though Islam was a universal religion with a common sacred text and law, it took very different forms as it adapted to cultures as far apart as Morocco and Indonesia. Clifford Geertz's classic little book, *Islam Observed*, describes the different spiritual climates in the two civilizations. In Morocco, the Islamic conception of life came to mean activism, moralism, and intense individuality; while in Indonesia, Islam's view of life, newly planted in Indic soil, emphasized aestheticism, inwardness, and the radical dissolution of personality (1968).

The conversion story of Kalidjaga, the culture hero who is said to have brought Islam to Indonesia, shows more than a touch of Hindu-Buddhist piety (see box 6.2, "The Conversion of Kalidjaga"). The spiritual transformation of a debauched thief takes place after decades of yoga-like meditation beneath a tree, a familiar Indic sort of inner enlightenment. He then went on to introduce the *abangan* form of Indonesian Islam, a complex of ideas and practices that was dominant for over four centuries. Its central event is the *slametan*, a communal meal given by Muslim households for all men in the immediate neighborhood. Almost any event can be the pretext for a slametan: a birth, wedding, funeral, Islamic holy day, name changing, illness, circumcision. After a formal speech and Arabic prayer, a meal is quickly eaten, and it's over. Its purpose is to protect from malevolent spirits that may want to upset us, to seek well-being, and to honor a host of spirits, animals, gods, ancestors, and other beings not generally a part of canonical Islam. At the same time, it functions to enhance equality and solidarity among the men of the neighborhood, who may or may not be relatives, friends, or equals in an absolute sense.

In the late nineteenth century, Muslims in Indonesia, so undifferentiated from earlier Indic mysticism and Malay *adat* (custom), reconnected with Middle Eastern orthodox Islamic sources. Qur'anic schools sprang up, devoted to correct doctrinal understanding of the Divine Law. Islamic

6.2 The Conversion of Kalidjaga

Kalidjaga is said to have been born the son of a high royal official of Madjapahit, the greatest and last of the Indonesian Hindu-Buddhist kingdoms. He left the failing Madjapahit capital as a young man, moving to one of the liveliest of the arriviste harbor states, Djapara. When Kalidjaga arrived in Djapara, he was a fairly accomplished ne'er-do-well named Radan Djaka Sahid. At home he had been an habitual thief, not averse to stealing from his own mother in order to drink, whore, and in particular, gamble. When his mother's money was gone, he abandoned her impoverished and set out to steal from the general public, becoming finally a highwayman of such renown that men were afraid to go to the market in Djapara for fear of being held up by him.

It was at this time that Sunan Bonang, said by some informants to be an Arab and in any case a Muslim, came to Djapara. He was dressed in gorgeous clothes, draped with expensive jewels, and his cane was of solid gold. As he walked the streets of Djapara thus set out, he naturally attracted the professional attentions of Radan Djaka Sahid, who stopped him and, brandishing a dagger, demanded his jewels, his clothes, and his golden cane. But Bonang was not afraid, and indeed he simply laughed. He said, "Don't always be wanting this thing and that thing and the other thing; desire is pointless. Do not be attached to worldly goods; we live but for a moment. Look! There is a tree of money."

And when Sahid looked behind him he saw that the banyan tree had turned to gold and was hung with jewels, and he was astounded. In fact, he became instantly convinced that material goods, the things of this world, were as nothing compared to the power of Sunan Bonang. Then he thought to himself, "This man can turn trees into gold and jewels and yet he does not seek riches." And he said to Bonang that he no longer wished to rob, drink, wench, gamble, and so on; he wanted only the sort of spiritual knowledge that Bonang had. Bonang said, "All right, but it is very difficult. Do you have the strenth of will, the steadfastness, the endurance?" When Sahid said he would persist till death, Bonang merely replied, "Wait here by the side of the river until I come back." And he went on his way.

Sahid waited there by the side of the river for years—some say ten, some say twenty, others even thirty or forty—lost in thought. Trees grew up around him, floods came and covered him with water and then receded, crowds passed him by, jostling him as they went, buildings were built and torn down, but he remained unmoved in his trance. At length Bonang returned and saw that Sahid (he had some difficulty locating him amid the trees) had indeed been steadfast. But instead of teaching him the doctrines of Islam he merely said, "You have been a good pupil, and as a result of your long meditation you now know more than I do," and he began to ask him questions, advanced questions, on religious matters, which the uninstructed pupil answered immediately and correctly. Bonang then gave him his new name, Kalidjaga—"he who guards the river"— and told him to go forth and spread the doctrine of Islam, which he did with unsurpassed effectiveness. He had become a Muslim without ever having seen the Koran, entered a mosque, or heard a prayer—through an inner change of heart brought on by the same sort of yoga-like psychic discipline that was the core religious act of the Indic tradition from which he came.

Clifford Geertz, 1968, pp. 25–29.

reform movements begun in Egypt and India reached Indonesia. In the early twentieth century, a pilgrim returned from Mecca and founded the Muhammadijah sect—vigorous, modernist, orthodox. These new Muslims, influenced by reform and counterreform and feeling connected to an international Islamic brotherhood, are known as santris. Thus revitalized, Islam in Indonesia and Malaysia is a culturally and spiritually vigorous dimension of Southeast Asia's continuing complexity.

THERAVADA BUDDHISM AND THE THAI STATE

The Siamese kingdom of Ayutthaya was profoundly Buddhist, as was (and is) its successor in Bangkok. How it came be Buddhist was described by a Thai monk in the Jinakalamali Legend recounting the founding of Ayutthaya (Tambiah 1976). It was written in Chiangmai in 1516 by a monk named Ratanapanna. It tells the whole history of Buddhism in India and Sri Lanka, culminating with the monk Sumana visiting Sri Lanka and then bringing Sinhalese Buddhism to Sukhothai. Quite naturally, the legend includes reference to Siamese competitors to the east, Angkor, and to the west, Pagan (Burma), characterized as incompletely Buddhist states. According to the Jinakalamali, King Anurudha of Pagan went to Lanka on his magical steed, while the rest of his party followed by boat. There he acquired two treasures of Theravada Buddhist piety. The first was four copies of the *Tipitaka*, the Buddhist Canon; the second was the Emerald Buddha.

Each major region where Buddhism has flourished has produced its own canon—the Sanskrit Canon, the Chinese Canon, the Tibetan Canon. The Pali Canon is the version of the Buddhist scriptures that was written around 20 B.C. at the Mahavihara monastery in Anuradhapura, Sri Lanka. Theravada Buddhists believe that this canon was established by the Third Council of Ashoka, and thus is the oldest and most authentic of all Buddhist texts.[1]

The Emerald Buddha has a more mysterious past. According to the Jinakalamali, the monk Nagasena (who was advisor to the Greek king Menander) wished to propagate Buddhism by making an image of the Buddha that would be indestructible. Indra heard this wish and went to Mt. Vibul where the chakravartin had seven precious stones with supernatural powers. He offered Indra an emerald with the same powers as these jewels, which Indra gave to Nagasena. King Anurudha put these two treasures in separate boats for the risky sea journey back to Pagan, but only one boat arrived safely. The boat carrying the Emerald Buddha and two copies of the Tipitaka was blown off course and ended up in

Angkor Thom, the Khmer capital. Eventually, however, Ayutthaya received the Tipitaka from Pagan and the Emerald Buddha from Angkor, and thus became a more complete Buddhist civilization than either of its predecessors.

The Emerald Buddha, despite its mythological history, really does exist; it became the premier symbol of the Thai state. Historians have traced its path southward with each successive kingdom, first in Chiangmai during the reign of Tilokaraja, then to Sukhothai, then to Ayutthaya, then to a period in Laos, and finally in 1778 to Bangkok, where it may be seen today high on a mountainlike structure in the chapel of the Grand Palace. It protects and is venerated by the Cakri dynasty; four times a year, King Bhumipol ceremoniously climbs up a great ladder to wash the Emerald Buddha and change its robes according to the seasons. Though kings come and go, the Emerald Buddha is the eternal monarch of the Thai kingdoms, as seen in the fact that oaths of loyalty to the reigning monarch are sworn before it. Many rulers had Buddha images that protected the princes and their capital and symbolized the polity; if a king was dethroned, his Buddha image was taken to the conqueror's capital as a kind of hostage—after he had taken an oath of vassalage before it—and kept in a subordinate though respected position near the ruler's own Buddha image.

The relationship between the state and Buddhism underwent a shift in Thailand from the pattern of god-kings of Hinduized Angkor. When Jayavarman was crowned cakravartin of Angkor, he was proclaimed a devaraja, a god-king, an incarnation of Shiva here on earth. But in Sri Lanka, as the Jinakalamali tells it, the cakravartin put on the sacred crown at the request of the Buddhist priesthood in order to look after the Buddhist religion. The difference can be seen in the conduct of King Ram Kamhaeng of Sukhothai. It is said he invented a script for the Thai language; he was also a dharmaraja in the style of Ashoka. He transacted affairs of state on a stone throne called the Manansilapatra, but on *uposatha* days he invited monks to come to the palace to teach the *damma*, a custom said to have been started by Ashoka. At the end of each year's rainy season retreat, he took ordination as a monk himself, donning the yellow robe and pronouncing his resolve to attain Buddhahood. Between times, of course, he had to lead military campaigns and transact other affairs likely to impede his full enlightenment (Tambiah 1976).

The Grand Palace in Bangkok is a living example of the conjunction of symbols of royal and cosmic authority that every Southeast Asian nagara attempted to produce. The Emerald Buddha reposes there, high in its splendid, gem-studded chapel, protecting and representing the Cakri dynasty. There is also the Great Chedi, or stupa, housing relics of the Buddha. To be in the presence of sacred relics of such power confers merit on the visitor and sanctifies the capital and the kingdom. A third source of power is the relics of dead kings of the Cakri dynasty, enshrined in urns high up on narrow lotus towers. Royal funerals became part of the institution of sacred kingship, converting a living king to a bodhisattva, something more than the exemplary Ashoka ever claimed for himself.

The death of a king plunged the country into crisis, not only in Thailand, but everywhere a king represents the state. For when the king dies, what happens to the state? The symbolism of the decaying body of the dead king is potentially politically dangerous. The crisis in Thailand was not only symbolic but literal, since there was invariably a struggle over the succession, made worse by the huge number of wives, and thus sons, a Thai king frequently had. Rama IV, the famous King Mongkut, had over a hundred wives and several hundred children. The royal funeral, along with the coronation of the new king, developed as an elaborate ceremonial refocusing on the capital that helped to prevent usurpation of the throne by ambitious princes or secession of vassals who might choose the time of instability to go their own way. According to Metcalf and Huntington (1991), royal funerals accomplished three things. First, they refocused attention on the center, which claimed to replicate the cosmos on earth, maintaining good order, better not mess with it. Second, royal funerals produced a "charismatic stockpile" of royal relics to be stored in the national palace-temple. And third, the new king was crowned halfway through the lengthy rites for the dead king, thus helping to stabilize his control.

The king's body underwent the process of secondary burial common throughout Southeast Asia. At death, the body was washed, dressed in splendid robes, and briefly displayed before being put into a large golden urn with its knees drawn up to its chin. The new king put the crown on the head of the corpse and everyone bowed in obeisance. The urn was stored in a special hall for at least one hundred days, while the body quickly decomposed in the tropical heat, the liquids of decomposition collecting in a golden vase beneath. In the meantime, the heir was crowned.

After a suitable period, there is a grand procession of the urn to the cremation ground. The urn is opened and the remains are cleaned and washed with perfumed water by the new king. The remains are then wrapped in white cloth, the color of death, and placed on an elaborate funeral pyre, yet another Mount Meru with concentric terraces leading to four tall columns supporting a conical spire, all carved and gilded. At sundown, the fire is lit and it burns all night with the addition of spices to produce a suitable fragrance. In the morning, the royal family takes small fragments of bone from the ashes to be worn in golden lockets by the king's children. The rest of the bones are bundled and carried in state to the palace to be enshrined as royal relics. The ashes go to a monastery. In this way, the king's final transformation into a bodhisattva is accomplished, and the succession to the reign of the new king in completed.

This gilded angel is guarding the temples, residences, and sacred relics of the royal compound in Bangkok. Notice that Southeast Asian angels, like Western angels, have birdlike characteristics, but with tail feathers rather than shoulder wings. In the background is a descendant of the tree of enlightenment from Bodh Gaya, India.

The Buddhist Ramayana

A visitor to Bangkok would be unlikely to miss visiting the royal palace of the Cakri dynasty on the bank of the Chao Phrya River in the heart of the city. One of the most important structures in the palace complex is the Temple of the Emerald Buddha, which, as we have already seen, is a central icon of the Thai kingdom. Along the galleries surrounding the central altar is a set of murals of astonishing beauty: gilt and polychrome scenes from the Ramayana in a Thai incarnation. The residences of Rama and Ravana are multiroofed and flame-tipped Thai palaces. Rama and Hanuman wear silken Thai clothing and aristocratic Thai headpieces. But what is this Hindu story doing in such a thoroughly Buddhist kingdom?

One does not need to look far for further evidence of the importance of the Rama story in Thai culture. The most important king of thirteenth-century Sukhothai took the name Ram Kamhaeng, "Rama the Strong." Every king of the Cakri dynasty founded in Bangkok in the late eighteenth century has taken the name Rama, from King Rama I through the present King Rama IX. The Cakri dynasty named itself after Rama's weapon, the discus, because one epithet for Lord Rama is Phra Cakri, "royal discus," a name taken by Rama I before he became king. The central Thailand kingdom from the fourteenth through eighteenth centuries named its capital Ayutthaya, the Thai version of Rama's North Indian capital city Ayodhya. Scenes from the Rama story are found in Ayutthaya in the ruins of Wat Phra Rama.

The earliest known form of a Thai Rama story is *Dasaratha Jataka*, which may be nearly as old as the original Indian version by Valmiki (Reynolds 1991). Indeed, some scholars have argued that the Thai version is older. There is an equally old Laotian version called *Phra Lak / Phra Lam* (Lak = Lakshman, Lam = Rama). In these ancient versions, the author is said to be Buddha, and the story is a jataka, one of a large number of Buddhist stories about the events in the life of Buddha in previous incarnations.

These very Buddhist versions played important roles at Sukhothai and Ayutthaya, although little is known about these periods. In 1767, Burmese armies destroyed Ayutthaya, and appear to have also destroyed all previous copies of the text. When Rama I (1782–1809), a devout Buddhist, restored order by founding a new capital city at Bangkok, his task was to reconstruct the religious and cultural life of the nation. After defeating the Burmese, he revised the Buddhist canon, codified the laws of Ayutthaya, and commissioned a committee of poets to rewrite the Rama story in a version known as the Ramakien. Rama I himself wrote an epilogue in which he describes the Rama story as a celebrative account that should make hearers mindful of impermanence. In other words, it is a colorful adventure of life in this world, but in the Buddhist context, these transient affairs should be taken lightly for ultimately they are only delusion.

Perhaps because the available texts during the rewriting of the Ramakien were Sanskrit ones, the Ramakien is closer to the Ramayana, with its Hindu themes, than the earlier more Buddhist texts. Gone is the assertion that Buddha is the original teller of the story; gone the view that Rama is an earlier incarnation of the Buddha. Instead, Shiva is the creator god in the background who urges Vishnu to take form as the prince from Ayodhya to save the world from chaos. This theme must have felt profoundly significant to the warrior who sent the Burmese packing and restored the Thai kingdom to a new period of peace and prosperity—under the name Rama I.

In this new version, Ravana, the evil ten-headed king of Lanka, is called Totsakan, meaning "ten-necked." Hanuman is perhaps the favorite figure of the story, a dashing spy and warrior devoted to rescuing Princess Sita but stopping to seduce other beautiful women along the way. The Ramakien was written to be read or performed, particularly as a court drama in a genre known as *lakhan nay* that was performed only by women (Bofman 1984). During the reign of Rama I, these performances sometimes cast his own dancers in the roles of Rama's warriors, and the followers of his brother, who was his constant competitor, in the roles of Totsakan's warriors. Such casting upped the "energia," or social weight of performances, to the point where social reality overcame theatrical fantasy in pitched battles that resulted in the deaths of performers (Reynolds 1991).

Rama I commissioned murals from the Ramakien on the gallery walls of the Temple of the Emerald Buddha. Fifty years later, they were refurbished by King Rama III. On the 100th anniversary of the founding of the Cakri dynasty, they were again refurbished, by Rama V. Rama VII renewed them on the 150th anniversary, and during the 1980s, they had their most recent renewal to mark the 200th anniversary of the Cakri dynasty.

BUDDHISM AND POPULAR RELIGION

Anyone who has ever noticed that Americans who consider themselves Christians may also check their horoscopes, get their palms read by Madam Ruby, dress up like Dracula on Halloween, or espouse personal ethics that emphasize competition, success, pursuit of wealth, and materialism already knows that a canonical religious tradition may mix, in practical life, with an assortment of other religious practices of obscure origins. Yet we sometimes express astonishment that in Theravada Buddhist societies, people's actual religious practices depart considerably from the life advocated in the Theravada texts.

The relationship between Buddhism and non-Buddhist forms of Thai religion, or "spirit cults," has been explored by anthropologist Stanley Tambiah, who worked in the Northeast Thai village of Baan Phraan Muan (Tambiah 1975), a few miles from the Mekong River. Historically, Baan Phraan Muan has always been on the frontiers of competing states—Sukhothai, Ayutthaya, Angkor, Bangkok, Phnom Penh—and has no doubt been influenced by them, and even by larger influences reaching those states from Burma, Sri Lanka, India, and southern China.

Baan Phraan Muan is not identical to, but probably typical of, most Thai villages in the region. The relation between formal Buddhism and lay members of Buddhist society is represented in the spatial organization of the typical village, called *baan* in Thai. The baan will be composed of many households clustered in a not particularly orderly fashion along several narrow lanes. Someplace on the periphery of the village is a *wat*, or Buddhist temple, comprised of several sections. The most accessible part of the wat for laymen of the village is the *sala*, a large wooden building where monks preach to villagers, where village meetings are held, and where the village school may hold its classes. A more restricted building is the *bood*, where laymen are generally not admitted. Here is where ordination of monks takes place and monks hold their own private services, such as confession. Finally, most restricted of all, is the *khuti*, or dwellings of the monks. Between the wat where the monks represent Theravada Buddhism in the most classical, canonical sense, and the village of lay Buddhists, where Buddhism mixes with many unorthodox and pre-Buddhist traditions, there exists a complicated interdependence.

One of the immediate and obvious interconnections between village and wat, layman and monk, is in their interdependent modes of livelihood. Monks, who are strictly forbidden to engage in any agricultural activity, are wholly supported by lay villagers—whose livelihood comes from agriculture. Many of the resources that flow from laymen to monks do so through wat ceremonies that are closely linked to the agricultural cycle. Each of the three major seasons of the agricultural cycle—planting and transplanting, the growing season, and the long harvest season—is marked by rites in which laymen and monks are collectively involved, engaged in spiritual and material exchanges.

However, the emphasis shifts from season to season: from the first expected sprinkles of the rainy season when the first planting is going on, through the three months of rain ending in October (a period that may include an extra month on each end of the rains), after which harvest will commence, is the "high Buddhist" period. The central event is the three months' rainy-season retreat for monks, a practice begun in the first few centuries of Indian Buddhism and rigorously maintained ever since. Major merit-making rites occur on Khaw Phansa, when monks gather at the beginning of the retreat in July, and Org Phansa, when they come out at the end. During this period of piety and asceticism, while the rice is growing, marriage is forbidden. This time of nonfertility and asceticism is the appropriate time for honoring the ancestors at Bun Khaw Saak, "Merit with puffed (i.e., dead or infertile) rice." Finally, a few days after the monks come out, there is a major merit-making ceremony, Bun Kathin, in which villagers of Baan Phraan Muan honor the monks by dragging decorated palanquins and flags through the streets and giving gifts to the *wat*.

During the second half of the year, through the harvest and beginning of field preparation in spring prior to the next rains, village ceremonies shift their emphasis to celebration of life, fertility, and sexuality. The role of the monks and Buddhism is muted (but not absent), while other spiritual powers are invoked.

At the great harvest festival in February called Bun Phraawes, the main deity is not the Buddha but a serpent spirit whose name is Phra Uppakrut. Canonical Buddhism does not acknowledge the existence of shadowy spirit entities like the Naga, Phra Uppakrut, or Tapubaan, the village guardian spirit; angels (*thewada*); spirits (*phii*); or the soul (*khwan* and *winjan*), yet all these spirits are linked to Buddhism in practice and sometimes in their own mythology in Baan Phraan Muan.

For instance, who exactly is Phra Uppakrut? According to villagers, he is a Naga (cobra) whose mermaid mother gave birth to him after Buddha, in an act of questionable propriety for a monk, forced his seed into the water where she swallowed it and became pregnant. Being the son of Lord Buddha, he later was ordained as a monk. The monks also have a story about who Uppakrut was. At the Third Buddhist Council convened by Ashoka, the monks gathered but had no one to preside. Phra Uppakrut, who was in the water meditating, was invited to serve in this role. On the way, he encountered a king who let loose an elephant to attack Uppakrut in order to test his strength. He vanquished the elephant, then went on to preside over the council and resolve controversies about the Dharma (damma), thus contributing to the success of Buddhism. Every year in Baan Phraan Muan, Phra Uppakrut is invited to Bun Phraawes to renew his role as defender of Buddhism and protector against storm, lightening, murder, and other acts of Mara (Tambiah 1975:168–75).

Even though the principal deity is a snake, Bun Phraawes is a major *wat* rite for making merit, chiefly through listening to sermons and recitations of Buddhist texts and stories. From the audience's point of view, the benefit is more than merit to be accrued toward the next life; it is also meant to ensure a good, healthy life and plentiful rain. Thus, Buddhist and non-Buddhist themes and goals intertwine.

A couple of months later is the festival called "merit from firing rockets" (Bunbangfai). According to villagers, this festival has nothing to do with Buddhism, yet even here, links to Buddhism can be found. Again the principal deity is neither the Buddha nor even Phra Uppakrut, but a benevolent guardian spirit of the village who has his own shrine on the outskirts; his name is Tapubaan, "grandfather of the village." There is also the spirit or phii of a Buddhist novice who has his own small wooden statue in the wat right beside the image of Buddha. This phii is offered only vegetarian offerings of rice and sugar, since he is a dead monk, but Tapubaan is a meat-eater and drinker who is given chicken, pork, liquor, and hot curries. The rockets are fired specifically to pay honor and, in return, to receive prosperity and good rains from a third spirit who resides in the swamps. This spirit, Chao Phau Tong Khyang, gets angry if he doesn't hear the rockets and withdraws his protection, allowing all kinds of misfortune to afflict the villagers.

It should be clear from the above descriptions that the actual needs of ordinary villagers cannot be met solely by Buddhism. Buddhism does not offer rain, good harvests, prosperity, fertility, good health, or protection from misfortune. Buddhism's gifts are important but limited. It offers a tranquillity in the face of whatever good or ill life does bring; it offers a theory of rebirth (and a means of achieving a good next life through a system of accumulating); it allows for filial piety through the possibility of transferring merit to one's ancestors; and it allows an alternative life course of ascetic withdrawal from society to focus on meditation and achievement of nirvana (*nibbana*). Buddhism attends to death, but not life; it takes care of one's funeral but not one's marriage. It involves itself with cessation of life and desire, not with fertility and procreation.

The Soul and Other Spirit Entities

Despite the Buddhist doctrine of *anatma* (anatta), Thai have a rather complicated view of the soul. Like other East and Southeast Asians, and unlike Indian and Western views, the soul is multiplex and not well fixed inside the body. There is first of all the khwan, which is actually composed of thirty-two separate essences associated with different parts of the body, such as the sense organs. The khwan is associated with the full vigor of one's life force; it can get frightened and slip out of the body, leaving the owner in a perilous state of decline leading to death if it is not recovered and tied firmly to the body with strings at the wrist.

Though the khwan comes and goes, there is another spirit-essence that is fixed until true and final death—the winjan. The winjan is less the focus of interest and rites in life, but is the essence that goes on to a new existence after death. All winjans become phii but will go on to one or another heaven or to new lives unless death comes unexpectedly or violently and appropriate death rituals are not conducted. In that case, they may become dangerous to people or may enter them as evil spirits that then have to be cast out by the village exorcist.

The fate of one's soul after death motivates ordinary lay people to merit-making actions that ensure a good rebirth. Box 6.3 shows "The Worlds of Theravada Buddhist Cosmology." Existences cycle through all these worlds, and any one is a possible destiny of the soul in the next life. One mostly desires a good rebirth in another human existence, but one of the six heavens would also be a delightful, if somewhat more remote possibility. Above all, one wishes to avoid returning as an animal, a ghost, or a demon, or languishing in one of the increasingly dreadful hells. The merit that ensures a good destiny is accumulated not simply through good deeds but by participation in temple rites and giving gifts to monks. It is necessary to counteract *baab*, demerit or sin, which also accumulates according to the laws of karma (*kamma*). At death, *bun* (merit) and baab are weighed, and the soul's destiny is determined.

The free-floating phii are dangerous and cause suffering. They have a kind of opposite number in benevolent angels, thewada, who flutter down from heaven if called by the village priest (not monk); for example, to bless a marriage. Thewada were never human and are always on the side of good fortune and protection. The heavens have other residents of importance to Thai besides thewada. There are the gods, mostly the old Hindu deities like Indra, who go on residing in their heavens, though overshadowed by the shining figure of Buddha, who is not a god but a pure and omniscient, transcendent human. With his death, or parinirvana, which is frequently depicted in Buddhist art, he became extinct, but his teachings remain to instruct not just mortals but the gods as well, who are also working out their liberation. Though Buddha is not a god, his relics, clothing, jewels, and texts have tremendous power to help humans; they are "fields of merit" where humans can improve their own accumulation of merit toward the next life. There is also the dangerous figure of Mara, Buddha's great demon antagonist who tried to tempt him as he sat meditating under the Bodhi Tree and continues through the aeons to tempt people to sensual pleasures and thus to death and destruction.

The Monkhood

On the other side of the village, in the secluded bood and khuti, sections of the wat where laymen do not go, the Buddhist monk (bhikku), bound in his single piece of saffron-colored cloth, is governed by rules laid down in the early period of Indian Buddhism. The rules of conduct, the *Patimokkha*, are a part of the first book of the Pali Canon, the *Vinaya Pitika*.

6.3 The Worlds of Theravada Buddhist Cosmology

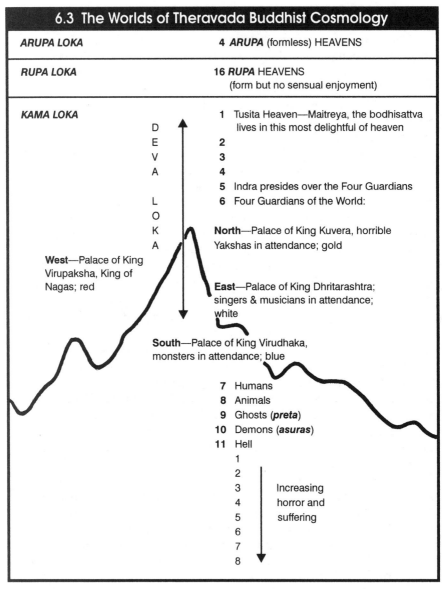

ARUPA LOKA	4 ARUPA (formless) HEAVENS
RUPA LOKA	16 RUPA HEAVENS (form but no sensual enjoyment)

KAMA LOKA

D
E
V
A

L
O
K
A

1 Tusita Heaven—Maitreya, the bodhisattva lives in this most delightful of heaven
2
3
4
5 Indra presides over the Four Guardians
6 Four Guardians of the World:

North—Palace of King Kuvera, horrible Yakshas in attendance; gold

West—Palace of King Virupaksha, King of Nagas; red

East—Palace of King Dhritarashtra; singers & musicians in attendance; white

South—Palace of King Virudhaka, monsters in attendance; blue

7 Humans
8 Animals
9 Ghosts (**preta**)
10 Demons (**asuras**)
11 Hell
1
2
3   Increasing
4   horror and
5   suffering
6
7
8

Lay people are not totally exempt from these rules. They must abstain from taking life, stealing, committing adultery, speaking falsely, and consuming liquor. These are the *panch sila*, the Five Renunciations. On Buddhist ceremonial occasions, they will abstain from three more things: eating after midday; witnessing music, song, and dance; and using scents and garlands. And a final two renunciations may be observed by very pious, and usually elderly, lay people who are more intent than others on their next life: using seats or beds above a certain height and receiving gold and silver (Tambiah 1975).

But for the monk, there are 227 specific rules to be followed. These rules appear to be aimed primarily at avoidance of all forms of sensual enjoyment and living in harmony within the monastic community.

A monk who commits a serious case of theft, who commits homicide or incites to suicide, who engages in sexual intercourse, or who falsely claims to be an *arhat* (a fully enlightened monk with supernatural powers) will be expelled from the monastery. These are extremes of all that monks are pledged to abjure: sexuality, greed, violence, and pride in spiritual accomplishment.

A large number of rules are aimed at guiding a monk in the practice of asceticism, while still fulfilling his somewhat contradictory obligation to accept gifts from lay people to advance their merit-making. He must not accept gold or silver (though it can be given to the wat). He can accept only simple robes, and only as many as he actually needs. He is explicitly forbidden certain luxury items like silk rugs, rich foods, beds, and upholstered chairs. He must not spend more than two or three days in the company of a layman. He must not eat food between noon and the next morning, though he may and should accept his morning meal (usually a ball of rice wrapped in banana leaves) from laymen. He must never ask for more food or for rich food.

Another set of rules guards the monk against sexual impropriety. He must not have any form of physical contact with a woman, nor make any salacious comments, nor be alone with a woman, nor sleep under the same roof as—even if in another room—or accept a robe from a *bhikkuni* (nun). When a woman offers a gift to a monk, they will avoid eye contact, and they will avoid hand contact by placing the gift on a cloth. Masturbation is equally forbidden.

Life in the monastery can be intense and is as filled with potential for dissension as any other close domestic relationship. The monk must avoid any act that would lead to discord in the monastic community. He must not gossip, eavesdrop, make false accusations against another monk, resist admonishment, threaten or provoke another monk, or disparage any of the teachings of the Buddha. There are special times set aside for confessions, accepting a penance, and being either reinstated or forgiven, depending on the severity of the offense.

Only a small minority of Buddhist monks in Southeast Asia are lifelong monks. A majority of men spend some time as a member of a monastic community. This tradition may have emerged historically from the fact that access to literacy and learning was available only in wat schools run by monks; boys were sent to the wat to learn to read and write, and then proceeded to become novices, usually around age eight. Nowadays, with universal education in state-sponsored schools, this function of the wat is dying out, but young men still enter the monastery as a kind of rite of passage into adulthood and marriage. It can also be done as a form of filial piety to pass merit to a deceased father, mother, or grandparent to help their soul on its journey. They may take ordination at the established time, the beginning of the rainy season, and stay only until the end, three months later; or they may stay for a year ("the first year for the mother") or two ("the second year for the father").

Like all important life transitions, the passage from layman to monk does not go ritually unmarked. It takes a two-day rite of ordination to turn a Buddhist layman into a monk, during which his family provides for the new, but simple, needs of the monk-to-be and passes him over to the monastery. These material needs include an ochre robe, an umbrella, a begging bowl, slippers, a razor, a lamp, and a spittoon. His head is shaved as the sign of his renunciation, especially of sexuality, and then he is dressed in the white robe of a novice.

It has long been noted by anthropologists, perhaps most significantly in the work of Victor Turner (1967), that a person in the midst of a rite of passage is in a kind of liminal status, "betwixt and between" their old status and their new status. In such transitional phases, special symbols, conditions, acts, and terms apply. In the case of the Buddhist novice who has shaved his head and changed his clothing, and thus discarded his old identity, but who has not yet donned the ochre robe or entered the monastery, his transitional state is called *Nag* (which, you will remember, refers to the cobra-son of the Buddha). The spirit of Nag is called into his body (*sukhwan* nag) with chants that remind him of his filial obligation to pass merit to the mother who bore and raised him. As in the story of the Nag, Phra Uppakrut, whose mother was a mermaid and whose father was the Buddha, the Nag plays an ambiguous role, suitable to the ambiguous state of the novice, as would-be monk and protector of Buddhism. There is another myth that a snake once disguised himself as a man so he could become a monk, but his true nature was discovered and the Buddha expelled him. The snake begged that at least he should be remembered by calling every initiate a Nag, and so it has been done.

On an overcast day in July 1987, I arrived at Wat Po in Bangkok on the day of Khaw Phansa (the "into" retreat), the only day of the year when monks are ordained. Monks and novices were busy cleaning up after the candle ceremony the night before, with most of their energy going into cleaning the many Buddha images in preparation for the coming rainy-season retreat. At about 8:30 in the morning, a party of several families arrived, led by a highly enthusiastic "cheerleader" who led the families in congratulatory shouts of "*chai-yo!*" as they circumambulated the main chapel three times. Family members carried plastic-wrapped commercially prepared bundles that are the standard gifts for monks. Each of these bundles contained an ochre robe, soap, matches, tinned fruit, tissue

The two men in white carrying lotus blossoms are about to be ordained as Buddhist monks for the duration of the rainy season. After circumambulating the temple three times, along with their families, they enter. They will take vows of obedience to the Vinaya rules and then exchange the white robes of the novice for the orange robe of the monk.

paper, incense, detergent, toothpaste and toothbrush, and candles—items somewhat more personal than are traditionally prescribed. At the rear of this party were the two "Nags"—a young unmarried man of nineteen and a middle-aged man whose wife walked in front of him. They were both wearing white clothes and carrying an unopened white lotus blossom in their folded hands. A final member of the party brought up the rear, holding a large umbrella over the heads of the initiates.

After circumambulating the chapel three times, they halted at the entrance to have their feet washed by family members and to toss away a handful of coins as a further sign of renunciation of wealth. There was a scramble to catch these coins, which bring good luck for life. Inside, a huge image of Buddha dominates the chapel. The space in front of it is divided into two sections; on the right is a raised platform large enough for a hundred monks to sit on, and on the left is a lower level where laymen and family members sit. With their new orange robes carried folded in their arms, the Nags ascended the dais and bowed deeply before the officiating monk. They were then instructed in the rules of monkhood, questioned about their spiritual qualifications for monkhood, and blessed. The officiant then bestowed their new robes on them by laying the robes around each novice's neck. The novices withdrew to a private space behind the dais to don the orange robe of the fully ordained monk. A bell rang, announcing this final transition. When the men returned, they joined the seated monks while their families came forward to present gifts to the wat. The initiate's wife carefully laid her gift on a handkerchief. The most important gift is the begging bowl by which the monk will collect alms. It is made of stainless steel with lengths of twisted orange cotton as a carrying strap.

The last major act was the water ceremony. The families gathered into two groups, each person touching another person to form a human chain, with the first person holding a small silver vase ready to pour water into a cup. At a precise moment in the chanting, the first person dipped the tip of a finger in the water, thus beginning the automatic transfer of merit around the chain of family members. Lastly, the water was taken out and poured on a tree in the courtyard.

Although a chief mark of ordination is renunciation of wealth, it is not inexpensive to take ordination at a major wat like Wat Po. One hundred baht[2] is given to each monk who witnesses the ceremony (there must be at least five); good quality begging bowls cost from 1200 to 1500 baht; robes are 700 to 800 baht; and the prepackaged gift sets are 300 to 400 baht. The total cost thus is in the neighborhood of 3200 to 3700 baht.

Women in Theravada Buddhism

Women cannot now be ordained as monks, though they could until it was forbidden in A.D. 456. In 1932, a monk secretly ordained two women monks in Thailand, but he was forced out of the sangha for this, and the two women disrobed (Swearer 1995:154). There is currently a strong movement under way in Thailand toward founding orders for women similar to the move toward ordaining women in American Christian churches. In 1971, a Thai woman named Voramai Kabilsingh traveled to Taiwan to receive ordination, then returned to found Wat Songdharma Kalyani, a monastery for women near Bangkok. However, the Thai sangha does not recognize her ordination (Swearer 1995:154).

One does often see white-robed, shaven-headed women who are erroneously referred to as nuns. These "women in white" (maechi), mostly old and poor, follow a lifestyle similar to that of monks, but are not ordained and are not "fields of merit" for lay people. They must support themselves from their own or their family's income, or by selling Buddhist charms on the fringes of wats (Van Esterik 1996).

One of the most compelling explanations for the low status of women in Buddhism links it to the freedoms women have traditionally had in other, worldly domains of the culture. The very earliest Westerners to visit Thailand commented with surprise on the public roles of women in economic activity, from plowing fields to buying and selling land to running the bazaars. Men, on the other hand, were busy with nothing but "sitting or lying, playing, smoking and sleeping," according to Simon La Loubere, a seventeenth-century traveler (Kirsch 1996:13). In the premodern economy, international trade was controlled by royal monopolies, while women ran the small-scale, internal trade in market and bazaar. As the Thai economy began to modernize in the nineteenth century, the king leased or sold his monopolies to merchants, but these tended to be neither Thai men nor women, but Chinese immigrant trading families. Thai women continued in their control of small-scale economic activity. In the twentieth century, the Thai economy has become more complex, but women are still found in unexpectedly high numbers as owners or managers of large- and middle-sized firms, as market sellers, hawkers, and market gardeners (Kirsch 1996:27–29), while Thai men are dominant in "power occupations": high-ranking government officials, professionals, office staff, medium-rank government officials, and clerks. Kirsch's contention is that Buddhism devalues these world-attached roles, leaving them to women, while idealizing Buddhist values of asceticism, renunciation, and worldly nonaction, and reserves these roles for men.

However, in non-Buddhist, island Southeast Asia, many of the same points can be made about the division of labor between men and women:

> Another reason that Westerners tend to view women throughout Southeast Asia as having "high status" is that women are usually the ones who deal with money and control family finances, and often become traders. Instead of doling out spending money to their wives, men tend to receive it from their wives. Traditional wet-rice agricultural requirements and the division of labor in harvesting and rice-hulling also gave poor women considerable scope for earning cash or being paid in kind, although mechanized harvesters and hullers have reduced the ability of poorer women and men to earn. . . . Throughout the area, there is a customary distinction between men's and women's tasks and labor, but Robinson's comment on Soroako, South Sulawesi, can be generalized to other societies of the area: "In the peasant economy it seemed a way of organizing tasks, and did not entail a means of one group appropriating surplus from another." Moreover, in many of these societies either spouse will substitute for an absent husband or wife in the event that he or she is unable to perform some task; and when a couple divorces, husband and wife split evenly what was acquired during their time together. Thus women's financial circumstances in this part of the world appear relatively favorable, at least if contrasted with women's circumstances in much of India and China. (Errington 1990:4)

Since women have relative equality and high economic participation throughout Southeast Asia, even in non-Buddhist regions, Theravada Buddhism cannot be either cause or effect in any simple way.

NOTES

[1]Pali is the vernacular version of Sanskrit that was used for public and religious discourse in the early Buddhist centuries; this became the sacred language of the Buddhist countries of Southeast Asia.

[2]One U.S. dollar equaled 27 baht at the time these figures were collected.

7

CHINA

Chronology of Chinese History

Date	Period	Developments
4500	**Neolithic** Yangshao, Longshan, Liangzhu Culture **XIA** (2200–1700)	Walled settlements, wheel-thrown pottery
1700	**Shang** (1700–1100 B.C.)	cities of 10,000; bronze; glazed pottery; silk; writing; horse chariot
1100	**Zhou** (1100–221 B.C.) Western Zhou (1100 B.C.–771 B.C.) Eastern Zhou (771–221 B.C.) Spring & Autumn (722–481 B.C.) Warring States (403–221 B.C.)	"Golden Age" of feudalism cast bronze coinage; stamped gold coins; glass; wrought iron; crossbow Confucius (551–479) Great Wall begun; Grand Canal begun
221	**Qin** (221–206 B.C.)	First imperial unification under the "First Emperor," Qin Shih Huang; destruction of Confucian texts Tomb of First Emperor at Xian [Chang-an]; Completion of Great Wall
206 B.C. A.D.	**Han** (206 B.C.–A.D. 220) Western Han (206 B.C.–A.D. 9) Wang Mang Interregnum (A.D. 9–21) Eastern Han (A.D. 23–220)	Sima Qian, "Grand Historian" restoration of Confucianism communication with West 65 A.D.—White Horse Temple, first Buddhist monastery; paper; porcelain; tea; coal; wheelbarrow
268	**Western Jin** (268–317)	gunpowder
386	**6 Dynasties**	block printing; 399 Faxian to India; 401 Indian monk Kumarajiva; 466 First Buddhist persecution; 574 second persecution
581	**Sui** (581–618)	Beginning of "Golden Age of Buddhism"
618	**Tang** (618–906)	617–645 Xuanzang to India; 690–705 Empress Wu Peak of Buddhism; paper money, canal locks; Chang-an greatest city in the world beginning of Japanese cultural borrowing 864 Diamond Sutra, oldest printed book in the world meritocracy
906	**5 Dynasties** (906–960)	
960	**Song** (960–1280)	movable type printing; Neo-Confucianism; 1130–1200 Zhuxi; *Family Rituals*; examination system; spread of footbinding
1200	**Yuan** (1280–1368)	Khubilai Khan conquers China, 1279; beginning of Mongol control; capital established in Beijing; embrace Tibetan Lamaism; rebuild Great Wall; Marco Polo (?)
1368	**Ming** (1368–1644)	
1644	**Qing** (1644–1912)	Jesuit Mission Emperor Kangxi (r1661–1722) Pu Yi, Last Emperor
1912	**Republican Period**	Sun Yatsen, Chiang Kai-shek
1949	**Communist Period**	Mao Zedong, Deng Xiaoping

Talhe state is shattered; mountains and rivers remain." These poetic words, written twelve hundred years ago, express both a sense of the eternity of the Chinese landscape and the yearning for a stable centralized state that has characterized Chinese culture for over two millennia (Van Slyke 1988:43). More than any other people in human history, the Chinese have achieved a continuity of social and cultural identity even during periods when the state itself collapsed into anarchy or was grabbed by alien conquerors.

To imagine a comparable achievement in the West, suppose the Greeks of Homer's time (900 B.C.) with their small territorial chiefdoms, survived through the golden age of fifth-century Athens when Socrates, Plato, and Aristotle lived and wrote; then all the small Greek city-states and chiefdoms were conquered and unified by Julius Caesar, who carried this culture north and west through all of Europe, founding a state that continued to survive as "Greek" for the next twenty-one hundred years, so that even now, all the peoples of Europe comprise one Greek nation. Suppose further that all the languages derived from Greek and Latin came to be identified as mere dialects of Greek, allowing everyone to believe that in some sense they all speak the same language. Imagine further that as other ethnic groups came into the orbit of Greek culture, they assimilated and came to call themselves ethnically Greek, abandoning their earlier French, German, Danish, Swedish, and other ethnicities. (We shall allow England to be Japan in this scenario, retaining its distinctive identity but borrowing extravagantly from Greek culture.) The capital remains at Athens for long centuries, then perhaps shifts after a period of social disunity or conquest to Rome or Paris or Berlin, but it continues to be a Greek society. During the invasion of "Greece" (Europe) from 1237 to 1242, suppose the Mongols succeed in conquering the whole continent and ruling for several hundred years, eventually becoming as Greek as everyone else, losing their separate cultural identity. And throughout these two millennia, the social philosophy of Socrates is continually elaborated, becoming a kind of civil religion throughout this vast realm. Something much like this hypothetical European history is what actually occurred in China.

A cultural unity among the Han Chinese is already apparent in Neolithic archaeological sites in North China. As long ago as 5000 B.C. Neolithic farmers were asking questions of their ancestors by inscribing on oracle bones the earliest versions of the script still in use today. These oracle bones were the shoulder blades of the oxen that they used to plow their fields. The characters grew more elaborate in subsequent centuries, beginning with forty characters during the Neolithic and reaching four thousand characters by the Shang dynasty (Chou 1979). Writing and literacy early on became to the Chinese the supreme marker of civilization. It was the possession of civilization, in their view, that distinguished them from all other known peoples.

The Zhou dynasty text *Li Chi* provides a kind of ancient Chinese ethnographic classification of peoples in a system of "Five Regions." At the center was the "Middle Kingdom" (*Zhongguo*), i.e., the Chinese themselves, the people who had texts and thus civilization, who could record their history and communicate with their ancestors in writing. On their periphery to the north, south, east, and west were peoples lacking civilization. Their "wild" cultural state was evident in the physical markers describing them: their hair was unbound, they tattooed their foreheads or their whole bodies, they ate raw food, they did not eat grain, they wore skins of animals, and they lived in caves. One group even had their feet turned in upon each other (Legge 1885). Part of the great enterprise of Chinese civilization was the project of civilizing these barbarians, which gradually they accomplished, turning them into Han (Harrell 1995).

The philosophy that eventually provided the civil religion of Chinese civilization, the role that Socrates played in my hypothetical example of a Greek Europe, originates in the teachings of a fifth-century B.C. Chinese sage named Confucius. The writing and texts that were held to be so morally improving that civilization itself was identified with them (*wen*) were in large measure the writings of Confucius and his followers throughout the centuries.

Wen, however, implied more than an advanced culture; wen also implied social institutions for preserving harmony and insuring a well-ordered polity. The state was the instrument for advancing and protecting Chinese civilization. States did sometimes shatter, as in the poignant words of Tu Fu, writing from such a period of *luan*, or social chaos. But such periods filled the Chinese with dread, and Chinese history is a chronicle of triumphs over disorder and turmoil by strong and virtuous dynastic founders who restore order and receive the Mandate of Heaven for their dynasties. Such exemplary periods never last for more than a few centuries before incompetence, corruption, disloyalty, or conquest cause their decay, hence their loss of Heaven's mandate to rule. Each dynasty may be seen as a new experiment in ordering Chinese society, in seeking improved institutions that will better meet the needs of the state, hence the people. Always, however, there was the assumption that there could be only one "Son of Heaven," one emperor, to whom all the people looked for moral guidance and benevolent rule. Regional movements and competitive secessionist states were relatively rare, partly because emperors experimented with ways to prevent regional contenders for power from emerging. As Fairbank writes: "the central myth of the Confucian state was that the ruler's exemplary and benevolent conduct manifesting his personal virtue (*te*) drew the people to him and gave him the Mandate. This could be said as long as rebels could be suppressed, preferably by decapitation" (Fairbank 1992:111).

Suppression of rebels by decapitation suggests the nonideological side of the strong Chinese state. Although such ideological systems of thought as the Mandate of Heaven, the te or mystical store of power of a ruler, and Confucian social ethics provide the moral underpinnings of the Chinese state, there was always also the state's coercive fist. This is *wu*, which means force or military order. Confucius may have preferred a state based on the wisdom and virtue of a fatherly ruler and the moral cultivation of filial subjects, but because virtue often fails, social order may also be imposed and defended by force.

Events of the late twentieth century do not contradict these fundamental patterns of Chinese society. Even with the dialogues going on inside China today regarding the future relationship between socialism and capitalism, there is a surprising degree of consensus regarding the validity of a strong central authority that provides moral leadership for the people. Mao Zedong had tremendous moral authority that has been criticized for its cultic qualities and its excesses during the Cultural Revolution. But many thoughtful Chinese now worry about the moral vacuum of capitalism and look back with a certain nostalgia on the social morality of Mao's teachings contained in these words:

> We must all learn the spirit of absolute selflessness. . . . A man's ability may be great or small, but if he has this spirit, he is already noble-minded and pure, a man of moral integrity and above vulgar interests, a man who is of value to the people. (Mao Zedong 1965)

As Mao articulated a communist morality that had strong resonance with themes of Confucian morality while also governing a coercive state, destroying enemies of the state, and suppressing dissident views, he and the Chinese Communist Party were following a very old pattern. We turn now to the establishment of these patterns in ancient times.

THE BEGINNINGS: SHANG, ZHOU, AND QIN

The Chinese have always been interested in their past—worship of ancestors is worship of origins—and have put extraordinary effort into recording history in dynastic chronicles, gazetteers, travel accounts, and official records. The twentieth century has provided a phenomenal growth of knowledge about the origins of Chinese civilization from a new source, as archaeology has opened to view palaces and tombs of the earliest dynasties. But the names of these ancient kings are not new to us; archaeology confirms the existence of rulers already chronicled in the first century B.C. by China's "Grand Historian," Sima Qian (145–89 B.C.). It was Sima Qian who rescued the name of Confucius from oblivion after the First Emperor, Qin Shihuang (221–206 B.C.), attempted to obliterate Confucian teachings and texts. He gathered together all the older documents that were available to him as court historian and archivist to his Han dynasty emperor to write the *Shi Ji* (Records of the Grand Historian), an enormous work that would require two to three thousand pages for a complete English translation (Wills 1994).

The Grand Historian wrote of three earliest Chinese dynasties: Xia, Shang, and Zhou. His accounts of Xia and Shang are so filled with fabulous stories that modern historians tend to discount them and begin their own historical accounts with Zhou, the dynasty in which Confucius lived. After all, what can you make of the founder of Shang dynasty, born from a mother who became pregnant after swallowing the egg of a black bird? Sima Qian seems to have told the stories as they came to him without passing judgment on their credibility. He had quite a lot of more concrete things to report about specific kings, their characters and actions, and their capital cities.

"The Ruins of Yin"

Three and a half centuries after Sima Qian died, grave robbers plundered a royal tomb in an area long known as the "Ruins of Yin" in the lower Yellow River valley. They found strips of bamboo with writing on them, which made a handy torch for the robbers while they carted off treasures. Some, however, were rescued; these turned out to be a chronology of Shang kings and became known as the *Bamboo Annals*. Sima Qian's *Shi Ji* and the *Bamboo Annals* have long been the best sources on Shang dynasty. But for three thousand years, fear of ghosts and respect for the graves of the ancestors prevented any serious efforts at investigating the "Ruins of Yin," leaving to twentieth-century archaeologists the discovery of the Shang dynasty (1700–1100 B.C.). The scholar Wang Yijung tracked dragon bones to the town of Anyang in the first years of this century and discovered what proved to be the royal archives of Shang dynasty. This touched off a frenzy of treasure hunting as well as some of the best archaeological research done anywhere in the world by Western and Chinese scholars.

First excavated in 1928, the Shang capital of Anyang is now one of the most important archaeological sites in the world. It is actually seventeen different sites near the modern town of Anyang. One of these sites is the major palace complex; another is the royal cemetery. Several sites are bronze foundries where magnificently ornamented bronze vessels were manufactured. Nestled everywhere are humble workshops and residences of artisans and commoners. The old annals identified twelve kings of Shang, one of whom was burned to death when Zhou invaders conquered Anyang. Imagine the delight of archaeologists to find, along with a thousand humbler graves, the remaining eleven royal tombs at Anyang.

These tombs are not monumental in the Egyptian sense, nor even structures at all, but huge burials about ten meters deep, with long ramps leading down into the grave. The ramps on the north and south were longer, giving the burial pits a cross shape. A wooden chamber was built at the bottom, with the coffin, also of wood, in the center. Most of the wood has disintegrated, along with the bodies of the kings, but other materials remained. The kings were buried with sacrificial victims, often decapitated and laid out in rows, with their heads arranged tidily elsewhere. Sacrificed dogs protected the entrances along the ramps. Some tombs were better protected; at Royal Tomb 11, eight chariots complete with two horses and two armed charioteers each were interred on the ramps. This king was accompanied to the afterlife by 160 decapitated victims.

In 1976, a new royal grave was discovered, the first one that had never previously been plundered. It was the final resting place of Fu Hao, the favorite consort of the second Anyang king, Wu Ding, in the thirteenth century B.C. Lady Hao's name was already known from oracle bone inscriptions, one of which asked whether she would be in good health after giving birth to her baby. That is typical enough, but Wu Ding also wants to know whether he will have success against the Qiang tribes when he sends Fu Hao at the head of the army. This extraordinary thirteenth century B.C. woman was surrounded by 440 bronze ceremonial vessels, mirrors, bells, and weapons; 590 jades; 560 objects of bone; 7,000 cowry shells, which were probably used as currency; sixteen humans; and six dogs.

At the end of the 1936 digging season, archaeologists stumbled on a trove of inscribed tortoise shells, which were so compacted after millennia underground that they could not be removed one by one without damaging them. Instead, they were removed en masse—a three-ton block of 17,096 shells so well preserved that the vermilion sketches put on before they were incised could still be plainly seen. This was the vast official archive of Wu Ding's reign.

These finds, together with nearly one hundred thousand written texts from the oracle bones, enable us to know a great deal more about ancient Chinese civilization than we know about Indus Valley, whose script remains undeciphered, not a single name known, and only a few elusive clues about the nature of their society and religion inferable from the excavations.

The Uses of Bronze

Surely it is appropriate to use the terms "state" and "civilization" to describe the Shang period. The consolidation of power in a single authority and the elimination or absorption of competing polities, and the extraordinary works of art and wealth monopolized by the nobility are evidence of this. The Shang state consisted of numerous walled towns, called *yi*, controlled by the great clans of the nobility. The state (*kuo*) consisted of a hierarchy of nucleated places; the royal city, the walled towns of the nobility, and the unwalled hamlets of common folk, who continued their earlier Neolithic pattern (Keightley 1982). Meanwhile, Shang rulers systematically expanded their domains, founding new towns by sending out populations to settle and begin farming the new region.

Extreme variations of wealth are apparent in tombs and homes, from the palatial residences of great kings to the humble quarters of commoners. Bronze was the key to this difference in wealth. The Shang state sponsored copper and tin mining, and royal establishments monopolized bronze manufactures that, with jade and silk, were the main items of prestige accumulation. Bronze was used for two principal purposes. Weapons, in the form of swords, arrow tips, spears, and execution axes enabled the elite to dominate militarily, maintaining internal control and prosecuting offensive action against external enemies. And bronze was the material for manufacturing the objects necessary to communicate with the ancestors, the spirits, and Heaven: heavily ornamented bronze vessels with tripod feet were used to offer them wine, meat, and other specialties from human society and thus tie them into continuing reciprocal relations with living people. These, too, were the prerogative of the ruling class. A third logical use of bronze comes to mind: bronze tools, like adzes, axes, chisels, and plows, for use in agricultural production. However, surprisingly few such tools have been found, and those that have were mostly found in royal graves. Keightley believes that even bronze tools were used for ceremonial purposes, such as ritual plowing of the first fields (or the king's fields) in spring, in digging royal graves, and in constructing the coffins and inner walls of the tomb. Thus, use of bronze was the monopoly of the state, and particularly of the king, who already was known as the Son of Heaven.

COMMUNICATING WITH HEAVEN

The king's legitimacy rested on his unique capacity to communicate with Heaven. His own royal ancestors resided there, where their te, their mystical store of power and virtue, remained available to shower blessings on their living descendants. These ancestors also had access to other heavenly powers that could assure well-being and harmony for all living members of the state. These heavenly powers were sometimes projected into a vaguely conceived "Heavenly Emperor," Shangdi, but conceptions of Shangdi never congealed into a single high creator god as known in the West. When Shang kings died, they became themselves ancestors who would henceforth rule from heaven. Thus, their tombs had to be filled with all the treasures a newly arrived king-ancestor would need, the first of centuries of gifts they would regularly receive from their living descendants. Their obligations to earth and their powers now were greater than ever.

The record of Shang kings' communications with Heaven can be read on the oracle bones in inscriptions up to fifty characters long. Most tended to be practical questions: "Will we get anything when we hunt at Kuei? Will we not get anything when we hunt at Kuei?" The heated metal prod was applied to the reverse side; with a "plop" the crackle-response would appear; and later, perhaps, the end result reported: "On that day we hunted and killed one tiger, 40 deer, 164 wolves, 150 fawns, and a couple of foxes" (Chou 1979). Such accounts give an indirect glimpse of the life of the king and the nobility; it would have been quite a hunting party that killed so much wildlife.

Of course ordinary people did not live like this. Although the nobility were organized in large patrilineal clans held together by wealth, high status, and collective worship of ancestors, commoners had not these mechanisms by which to maintain memory of long-term kinship connections. Their families were small, their ancestors forgotten after a few generations. Few grave goods accompanied their dead; the elegant bronze vessels for giving libations to ancestors were too expensive for them, and probably restricted in any case as a prerogative of great families. Patricia Ebrey writes: ". . . kings were obliged to offer sacrifices of several kinds of meat to their founding ancestor and four most recent ancestors each month; lords, officials, and officers (*shi*) could make progressively fewer and less varied offerings to progressively fewer ancestors. Commoners were not to make sacrifices of meat, but they could offer vegetables to deceased fathers once each season" (1991a:52).

Idealized Zhou Feudalism

To the west of the major Shang centers were a number of tribal chiefdoms who alternately fought with and tolerated each other. They made alliances with the powerful Shang through tribute and vassalage. The Zhou tribes were among these groups. But Shang rulers gradually became weaker, while the Zhou became stronger, and in about 1040 B.C.,

Zhou conquered Shang and established a new capital in the west at Chang-an (now Xian).

Where Shang kings had justified their rule through worship of their own divine ancestors, the Zhou invented the Mandate of Heaven (*tianming*). Although Heaven was not imagined as a creator god or as a divine personality, Heaven was on the side of righteousness and good government. According to Zhou revisionism, Heaven had withdrawn its support from the decadent Shang and bestowed it on them, thus creating the motif of the wicked last emperor of a dynasty gone bad and the virtuous founder-emperor of a new dynasty. This made the Zhou king the new "Son of Heaven." In his mediating role between Heaven and earth, he represented Heaven on earth in his obligation to provide good government; and he represented earth to Heaven in annual imperial rituals. He worshipped in the "threefold kneeling and ninefold prostration" to Heaven. Twice a year, at the summer and winter solstices, the king gave a feast for Heaven of wine, soup, various delicious dishes, and animal sacrifice. In the spring he sacrificed on the Altar of Agriculture and ploughed the first furrow of the year (a custom still performed by the emperor of Japan and the king of Thailand). If things went well, it was proof that the Mandate of Heaven continued with him. Thus the Zhou established moral grounds as the test of legitimacy, which became the orthodox view to the present. The symbolic power of these Zhou royal rites remained central in imperial political theater through all dynasties down to the Qing (see box 7.1).

Zhou dynasty survived almost eight centuries (1040–256 B.C.), the longest-lasting dynasty in Chinese history. During the first two and a half centuries, called Western Zhou because the capital was at Chang-an, new forms for organizing the state were worked out by the new elite class, which consisted of the new Zhou leaders and the former Shang nobility who had merged into a single class. For Zhou kings it was easier to capture a region than to govern it. Kinship ties of loyalty, rather than bureaucratic organization, were the cement that held society together. In theory, all the territory conquered by the king belonged to him, but in order actually to control his territories, he gave his male kinsmen the right to colonize and govern lands in his name. These bonds of fealty were ritually enacted. At Chang-an, the Zhou king established an altar to the God of the Soil on the west side of his palace gate and an altar to his ancestors on the right side of the gate. When a younger brother or nephew established a vassal state, he took a clod of earth from the Son of Heaven's altar to his own capital and built his own local altar to the God of the Soil. In performing rites to his local God of the Soil, he acknowledged the supremacy of the Son of Heaven at Chang-an. But he built a shrine to his own ancestors on the right side of his gate. There was little military force emanating from the capital to hold these vassal states to the center; it all depended on these bonds of loyalty, ritually enacted.

7.1   Cosmological Theater in the Forbidden City

Confucius said, A virtuous ruler is like the Pole Star that remains fixed while all other stars circle reverently around it. When the Imperial palace was begun in Beijing in 1410 during Ming dynasty it was laid out as the earthly plane of this cosmological structure. As the Pole Star is fixed in the north of the heavens facing south, the Forbidden City was located in the northern (yang) part of the city facing the south (yin) side, theoretically linked to Heaven by a cosmological axis with the Pole Star at Heaven's end and the Son of Heaven at earth's end. The emperor, representing earth, wears earth's color, yellow (the color of the soil in the Yellow River basin). In the Hall of Supreme Harmony, the emperor always sat on the north facing south toward his ministers, nobles, and subjects at the Great Audience three times a year and the Regular Audience three times a month.

The Son of Heaven was the only man on earth who could enact the mediating rites for all human society (i.e., for Zhongguo, the Middle Kingdom). Just before sunrise on the night of the winter solstice he sacrificed on the Altar of Heaven; at the summer solstice he sacrificed at the Altar of Earth. At the spring equinox he sacrificed at the Altar of the Sun, and at the Altar of Agriculture; after cutting the first furrow in a ritual field just outside the city, farmers throughout the empire could begin their planting. The Empress picked the first mulberry leaves of spring so that women throughout the empire could begin silkworm cultivation. At the autumnal equinox he sacrificed at the Altar of the Moon.

The city was laid out on the five points of the compass with the fifth point being the center of the earthly cosmological plane where the Son of Heaven dwells. The city is a series of cities within cities, each surrounded by a wall. The Forbidden "City" itself is actually a jumble of palaces, gardens, pavilions, and gates, though inside lived several thousands of the emperor's children, empresses, consorts, and eunuchs. For them, the Forbidden City was a pleasure palace . . . and a prison, for they rarely could leave. It nests within the old city laid out like the old Zhou capital, with an Altar of Land and Grain on the west side of the gate and the Imperial Ancestral Temple on the east. This was the structure that was replicated in every Zhou vassal state for centuries.

All gates and altars on the north are devoted to Earth, and on the south to Heaven. The Altar to the Sun is in the east, where the sun rises, and the altar to the Moon is in the west where the sun sets. The Gate of Heavenly Peace (Tienanmen, now Tienanmen Square since the gate was removed) is matched in the north by the Gate of Earthly Peace.

During Ming times, there was vast population growth, resulting in a quadrupling of the size of the city. When Manchus took over during Qing, the old Ming capital became the Manchu district, and the newer suburbs became the Han-Chinese district, all surrounded by walls.

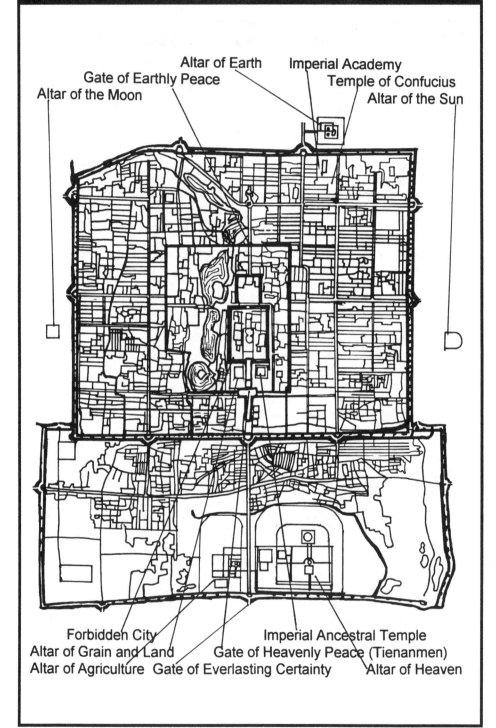

Altar of Earth   Imperial Academy
Gate of Earthly Peace   Temple of Confucius
Altar of the Moon   Altar of the Sun

Forbidden City   Imperial Ancestral Temple
Altar of Grain and Land   Gate of Heavenly Peace (Tienanmen)
Altar of Agriculture   Gate of Everlasting Certainty   Altar of Heaven

Ancestor worship thus had powerful political significance; only aristocratic lineages were entitled to worship their ancestors, and an elaborate code of rules linked complexity of ancestral rites and number of generations of ancestors that could be worshipped to a family's rank in the Zhou state. Commoners were not entitled to worship ancestors beyond three generations, could not offer meat, and could worship only once each season. Ancestor worship throughout Chinese history changed in response to changes in the state and in the nature of elite classes, as we shall see.

During the last five centuries, called Eastern Zhou because the capital moved to Lo-yang, it all began to unravel. Thoughtful people looked back on those early decades of Western Zhou when the feudal system still worked as a golden age.

The early Zhou system of linking vassal states to the king through bonds of loyalty and ritual action gradually dissolved as those many secondary states grew larger and more powerful than the Zhou king himself. It was an easy matter to forget the old loyal bonds and begin to act autonomously; a prince had his own shrine to the God of the Soil and his own ancestral shrine outside his palace door. At one point, over 170 states were operating independently, forming alliances against stronger states and absorbing weaker states until they began to eat one another up. This era, known by the ironically poetic name of Spring-and-Autumn Period (722–481 B.C.), gave way to the Warring States Period (403–221 B.C.), when the competing states had worn each other down to only seven. It was not surprising that people looked back with longing on the peaceful times when all states lived harmoniously under a single king.

Clearly the Zhou golden age was over. However, great strides were made in other areas of social life. Iron, a metal strong enough to make plows that could be pulled by oxen, was discovered, an invention that fueled another phase of the agricultural revolution and another round of population increase. The canals and irrigation works that had been going on for a very long time got a new boost; new areas came under intensive cultivation. A wealthy merchant class began to be documented in the oldest records, but since merchants produced nothing and only made their wealth by the suspicious and undervalued process of trading things for other things, they were put at the bottom of the emerging class system:

> warrior-administrators
>
> peasants and primary producers
>
> artisans and secondary producers
>
> merchants

This class structure remained the frame of reference into the twentieth century, when even the Communists, who received their aversion to the

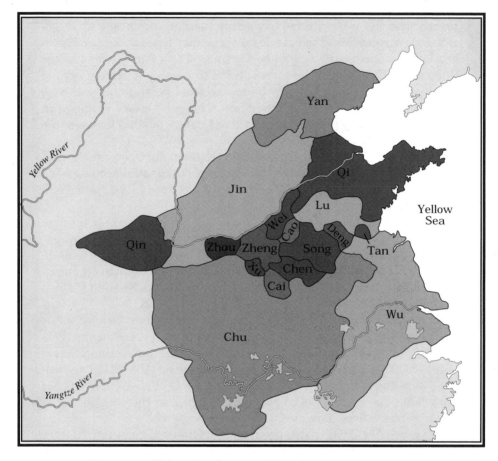

Map 7.1   China During the Warring States Period

bourgeois merchant class from both Chinese tradition and Marx, tried to eliminate the market system from society.

But the greatest gains were intellectual. During the same century that Socrates and Plato were laying down the philosophical foundations for the West, and the Buddha was teaching a new path to salvation in India, Confucius was creating a civil religion for Chinese society.

Two Sages: Confucius and Laozi (Lao Tzu)

The times favored ruthless men of action, opportunists ready to use the arts of wu (war) for gain and glory. But everybody had to live in the chaotic conditions they created, including two men whose thoughtful reflections long outlived the brief gains of conquest. Laozi and Confucius (Kongzi), the two preeminent philosophers of ancient China, may have lived at roughly the same period. Their philosophies are opposite in many ways; Laozi's is so different from Confucius that he seems almost Indian in his insistence on realities behind appearances and on relativizing society's structures and demands.

The historian Sima Qian gives biographical sketches of both men. Some scholars have questioned whether Laozi was a single person or a composite of a number of hill-dwelling sages living disdainfully apart from society. His name, Lao, means something like "old wise one," a term often given to legendary sages. According to the Grand Historian, he was the keeper of the imperial archives for the Zhou kings at Lo-yang at the time when the emperor was becoming irrelevant and society was decaying around him. Sima Qian describes a visit by Confucius, and later followers record a number of their encounters, which turned out differently depending on who was telling the story. As Zhou further declined, Laozi resolved to retreat to the mountains of the west, but at Hangu Pass the gatekeeper begged him: "As you are about to leave the world behind, could you write a book for my sake?" So he wrote a work in two books, setting out the meaning of the way (*tao*) and virtue (*te*) in five thousand characters, and then rode off and disappeared without a trace. The result was the *Tao Te Ching*.

Confucius lived to the east in the state of Lu (Shandong Province) where for a while he held high office. Sima Qian makes a tragic hero of Confucius as well as of himself in the autobiographical portion of the *Shi Ji* (Watson 1958:170). Both men were profound critics of the society of their times; one might use the modern term "dissident" to describe them. For while deeply loyal to Chinese civilization, they criticized—delicately—corruption, unjust punishment, and uncontrolled aggrandizement by political leaders. (Sima Qian once unwisely defended a general who was in disfavor with the emperor. For this offense he was sent to the "Room of the Silk Thread" and castrated. A man of his station would normally commit suicide under such humiliating circumstances, but, as he explains in his history, he stayed alive in order to complete this great work.)

In Lu, Confucius attempted to implement good government, but neighboring rulers plotted his overthrow. Entertainers and dancing girls were sent to distract the Duke of Lu from his responsibilities. Confucius resigned in disgust. For ten years, he and a band of disciples wandered from state to state seeking an opportunity in government service where they might apply their ideals, but they encountered opponents wherever they went whose arguments are recorded as lengthy speeches by Sima Qian. Toward the end of his life, Confucius returned to Lu, resigned to political failure, and lived out his life peacefully writing and teaching his disciples. Only after his death, Sima Qian records with bitter irony, did Confucius achieve the respect he deserved. The Duke of Lu, who ignored him in life, sent an extravagant eulogy to be read at his funeral, recorded in its entirety by Sima Qian.

Confucius and Laozi shared a contempt for their times, but disagreed philosophically on what was called for. Laozi was a mystic who attempted to relativize society much as Hindu renunciants did, holding that society was the sphere of manifest reality—metaphorized as "the ten thousand things"—but true reality was beyond: it was the source, the uncarved block, the Way, the tao.

> *The Tao begot one.*
> *One begot two.*
> *Two begot three.*
> *And three begot the ten thousand things.*

Confucius also spoke of the tao, but in a less metaphysical way than did Laozi, giving it less centrality in his philosophy, which focused instead on the morally perfectible person.

For Laozi, the relationship between the "uncarved block" (the tao) and the "ten thousand things" is or should be a natural, harmonious common identity. "The ten thousand things carry yin and embrace yang. They achieve harmony by combining these forces." All manifest things form a unity with the tao; because they come from that Nameless Source, they model it and operate by its same principles. There should be no tension between them. However, Laozi did not view the ten thousand things as dangerous illusion, as Hindus did, but as good and natural manifestations of the tao. The only danger was in forgetting the Source beyond; trouble comes from thinking the ten thousand things exist in and of themselves, disconnected from their Source.

7.3 The *Tao Te Ching*

The *Tao Te Ching* is said to be the most-often translated of all Asian texts. It far surpasses the *Analects* of Confucius for eloquence, coherence, and meaningfulness in translation. Individual translations vary tremendously, however, as the following selections of the first, and most famous, verse show:

The Tao that can be told is not the eternal Tao.
The name that can be named is not the eternal name.
The nameless is the beginning of heaven and earth.
The named is the mother of ten thousand things.
Ever desireless, one can see the mystery.
Ever desiring, one sees the manifestations.
These two spring from the same source but differ in name;
  this appears as darkness.

Darkness within darkness.
The gate to all mystery.

Gia-Fu Feng and Jane English, transl., 1972, p. 3.

The tao that can be told is not the eternal Tao.
The name that can be named is not the eternal Name.

The unnamable is the eternally real.
Naming is the origin of all particular things.

Free from desire, you realize the mystery.
Caught in desire, you see only the manifestations.
Yet mystery and manifestations arise from the same source.
this source is called darkness.

Darkness within darkness. The gateway to all understanding.

Stephen Mitchell, transl., 1988.

The way that can be spoken of
Is not the constant way;
The name that can be named
Is not the constant name.
The nameless was the beginning of heaven and earth;
The named was the mother of the myriad creatures.
Hence always rid yourself of desires in order to observe its secrets;
But always allow yourself to have desires in order to observe its
  manifestations.
These two are the same
But diverge in name as they issue forth.
Being the same they are called mysteries,
Mystery upon mystery—
The gateway of the manifold secrets.

D. C. Lau, transl., 1963, p. 57.

There are ways but the Way is uncharted;
There are names but not nature in words:
Nameless indeed is the source of creation
But things have a mother and she has a name.

The secret waits for the insight
Of eyes unclouded by longing;
Those who are bound by desire
See only the outward container.

These two come paired but distinct
By their names.
Of all things profound,
Say that their pairing is deepest,
The gate to the root of the world.

R. B. Blakney, transl., 1983, p. 53.

What difference should this viewpoint make to the person living in the world? You should not forget that you, too, come from the tao:

> *Empty yourself of everything.*
> *Let the mind become still.*
> *The ten thousand things rise and fall while the Self watches their return.*
>
> *They grow and flourish and then return to the source.* (Feng and English 1972:18)

Since the Self is also one of the ten thousand things, you, too, have a natural way of being:

> *Better stop short than fill to the brim.*
> *Oversharpen the blade, and the edge will soon blunt.*
> *Amass a store of gold and jade, and no one can protect it.*
> *Claim wealth and titles and disaster will follow.*
> *Retire when the work is done.*
> *This is the way of heaven.*(Feng and English 1972:11)

Traditionally the eighty-one verses of the *Tao Te Ching* were divided into two sections, the Tao (one to thirty-seven) and the Te (thirty-eight to eighty-one). Te is usually translated as "virtue," which in English has lost most of the impact it once had. It is written as a compound with the character for person and the character for heart; it implies inner strength of character, or even a mystical store of power in the person of extraordinary virtue and wisdom. It is often used with the founder of a new dynasty, or the sage-ancestors of society. In focusing on te in the second half of the *Tao Te Ching*, attention turns to rulers and the state. "All things arise from tao. They are nourished by Virtue (te)."

The role of rulers to use their *te* is depicted in verse thirty-nine:

> *These things from ancient times arise from one:*
> *The sky is whole and clear.*
> *The earth is whole and firm.*
> *The spirit is whole and full.*
> *The ten thousand things are whole and alive.*
> *Kings and lords are whole, and the country is upright.*
> *All these are in virtue of* [the te of] *wholeness.*
>
> *The clarity of the sky prevents its falling.*
> *The firmness of the earth prevents its splitting.*
> *The strength of the spirit prevents its being used up.*
> *The fullness of the valley prevents its running dry.*

The growth of the ten thousand things prevents their dying out.
The leadership of kings and lords prevents the downfall of the coun-
try.

Therefore the humble is the root of the noble.
The low is the foundation of the high. (Feng and English 1972:41)

Laozi does not question the right of rulers to exist, but reminds them
of the natural limits of their powers within a universe ordered by the tao.
He trusts the tao in all things to make society function well: "If you want
to be a great leader, you must learn to follow the tao. Stop trying to control. Let go of fixed plans and concepts, and the world will govern itself."
Or more simply and memorably, there is the image of the fish: "Governing
a large country is like frying a small fish. You spoil it with too much pok-
ing."

For Confucius, the central concept was not tao, but *ren:* man or
humanity. "It is man that can make the Tao great." Ren is even less translatable than tao and te. It carries the sense of human moral perfectibility,
of human potential, of the potent goodness of human beings who have
been loved, nourished, and appropriately socialized. Confucius believed
that humans are born with the potential for great goodness, and it is
within a well-ordered society that human goodness flourishes.

The *Analects* of Confucius, where his words are held to be preserved
most authentically, has little of the poetry of the *Tao Te Ching*. If one goes
to the *Analects*—as to the Bible or Koran—expecting to hear the voice of
divine authority, one will be disappointed. They are mostly pithy statements from a man who made no claims of divinity. Interpretation of his
words was what later Confucian scholarship was all about. His ideas are
most often embodied in little stories, such as the following:

> Zizhang asked Confucius about humanity [ren]. The Master said:
> "Whoever could spread the five practices everywhere in the world
> would implement humanity." "And what are these?" "Courtesy, tol-
> erance, good faith, diligence, generosity. Courtesy wards off insults;
> tolerance wins all hearts; good faith inspires the trust of others; dil-
> igence ensures success; generosity confers authority upon others."
> (Leys 1997:86)

The commonsense decency in this explanation of ren might mistakenly portray Confucius's thought as little more than platitudes, which
indeed is how he often comes across in older translations. But his thought
is far more subtle, and far more Chinese, than merely an exotic version of
the Golden Rule.

If Ren is a state of moral awareness and cultivation, one achieves
ren through *li*. Li is the distinctly Chinese concept giving Confucian
thought the tremendous impact it had in Chinese civilization. The follow-

ing passage from the *Analects* shows Confucius trying to explain the behavioral aspect of ren:

> Yan Hui asked about humanity [ren]. The Master said: "The practice of humanity comes down to this: tame the self and restore the rites [li]. Tame the self and restore the rites for but one day, and the whole world will rally to your humanity. The practice of humanity comes from the self, not from anyone else."
>
> Yan Hui said: "May I ask which steps to follow?" The Master said: "Observe the rites in this way: don't look at anything improper; don't listen to anything improper; don't say anything improper; don't do anything improper."
>
> Yan Hui said: "I may not be clever, but with your permission, I shall endeavor to do as you have said." (Leys 1997:55)

What could li mean in the above passage? Translators attempt to make Confucius (or anyone being translated) speak English, but there are different "deep habits" of the two languages that make translation more difficult than just finding the right English word. So Confucius may sound pompous or theatrical when a translation is too close to the original. Li is sometimes translated as "decorum" or "etiquette" or "ritual."

Most recent scholarship has focused on li as "ritual." The character for li is a compound of characters for a ritual vessel and an altar stand. The original rites meant by li were ancestral rites and court ceremonial, but the term came to mean all kinds of formal, patterned behavior. Li, as ceremonious conduct, is the behavioral expression of the inner moral quality of ren. "It regulates one's daily life and interactions with others, channels emotions properly, distinguishes civilized patterns of behavior, and maintains the political order" (Chow 1994:10). When Confucius said in the passage quoted above, "to subdue oneself and return to li is ren," he was suggesting that through self-governing by ritual, one transforms one's own nature. Thus ritual is righteous action, a remedy for moral crisis.

The thing that a Westerner might object to in ritual—that its form is prescribed by society and the past—is what makes li so very Confucian. Westerners are apt to describe ritual as empty and thus inauthentic to the self, which merely goes through the motions. But for Confucians, the authority of society and the ancients is what constitutes morality, and the rituals that have come down from them to us are empowered by that authority and by Heaven itself. Zhu Xi said: "Ritual is the manifested authority of Heavenly principle." There is no value in any authentic selfhood that does not come from these sources. The young may be born with the potential for goodness, but that potential is not fulfilled in a vacuum. It is fulfilled in the moral forms given by society.

It is the rituals of social life that bind society together, and bind individuals to the social order. It is the same li that structures society into a hierarchy of authority and power. "The order that li ought to bind together is not simply a ceremonial order—it is a sociopolitical order in the full sense of the term, involving hierarchies, authority, and power. The li must themselves support this authority and power" (Schwartz 1985:68). This fundamental and far-reaching system is summarized in the "Three Bonds": official to monarch, son to father, and wife to husband. Li governed them all. Family and state were part of the same moral structure; all were ordained by Heaven. The man of virtue, who fulfilled li and ren, Confucius called by the term *junzi.*

Prior to Confucius, this was a title given to the hereditary nobility, a word meaning "prince," but Confucius held that any morally cultivated person could become a junzi; thus it took on an individualistic, achieved sense. (Victorian translators used "gentleman," another archaism to modern ears.) The junzi conducts himself morally and according to li in all his roles: as son, as father, as husband, as official. Women should also conduct themselves according to li, which limited their opportunities to daughter, wife, and mother. Much later, in the eighteenth century, Confucians began to obsess about women, and a cult of women's purity arose, although Confucius himself had very little to say about women.

These two philosophers, Confucius and Laozi, provided the dominant strands coming down from Eastern Zhou to later ages. It may have been the extraordinary influence of Sima Qian's great history, the *Shi Ji,* which kept them alive after the brief dark times to come in the Qin dynasty. Sima Qian brings their differences alive in stories, probably apocryphal, about their meeting. According to him, Confucius once went to Lo-yang to consult with Laozi about the li of the ancients. Laozi scoffed that the ancients were now nothing but decaying bones. He said, "I've heard that merchants keep their goods buried deeply to make it look as if they have nothing, and that a junzi will pretend to be stupid. So give up your pretenses, your mannerisms, and your extravagant claims. They won't do you any good. That's my advice to you." Confucius returned to his students and said: "I know that birds can fly and fish can swim and beasts can run. Snares can be set for things that run, nets for those that swim, and arrows for whatever flies. But dragons! I shall never know how they ride wind and cloud up into the sky. Today I saw Laozi. What a dragon!"

If, to Confucius, Laozi with his lofty indifference to society, was an ungraspable dragon, Confucius's legacy to Chinese civilization was far greater. His teachings became a civil religion that formed the moral foundation for Chinese civilization throughout the ages. But this did not happen immediately. His followers over the next several centuries kept his teachings alive by compiling his sayings and writing extensive commentaries on his insights. Eventually his tomb became a shrine, a center

The immense Kong family, all descendants of Confucius, maintain a vast forest of a graveyard in Qufu, where graves go back to Zhou Dynasty. Confucius himself is buried in the hillock behind the stone column bearing his name. In front of it is a stone alter on which his descendants have sacrificed cattle, sheep and pigs for seventy-seven generations. Kong Decheng, the most senior living male of the lineage, now lives in Taiwan.

where lectures, festivals, sacrifice, and worship were conducted by his later followers, including princes and ministers from Han times onward, right up to the present. But before Confucian teachings came to dominate social values, a major political upheaval was to occur: the conquest of all the small, bitterly contesting domains and the founding of "China" as a centralized state under the genius of Qin Shihuang.

The First Emperor and the Unification of China

The First Emperor has always had a venerable place in Chinese history, but he came alive in our age in 1974 when members of an agricultural commune were digging a well not far from Xian. Thirteen feet down they were astonished to encounter a life-size terra-cotta warrior. This was not the first time farmers had encountered buried warriors. In 1914, as a farmer and his son were digging a well in the same place, a terra-cotta warrior emerged from the mud. As they kept digging, they broke through

The army of Qin Shihuang was discovered by farmers digging a well in 1974. The terra-cotta army, more than 1,100 of them (and possibly 5,000 more), were a replacement for the living companions in the journey into the otherworld who accompanied earlier rulers. Qin himself remains respectfully unexcavated in his tomb nearby.

a watertight layer into an empty chamber, causing the water to suddenly drain away. Thinking they must have uncovered a demon, they dug the warrior out and left it to decay in the elements. But by 1974, Chinese farmers were less worried about demons. Excavations began two years later, and eventually eleven hundred warriors emerged into daylight after twenty-two centuries. They were the army of Qin Shihuang.

This site has only been partially excavated, awaiting better methods as archaeology continues to mature as a science, and also out of respect for the dead emperor. Probably an additional five thousand soldiers are still buried. But the world has been astonished over those already excavated. Two hundred are the vanguard of the emperor's army, armed with crossbows. There are squads of spearmen, and files of archers, some resting on their knees. There are chariots, infantry, and cavalry, the horses and chariots at half-size scale. Most remarkably, each face is unique, as if every soldier had stood for his own sculpture. This diversity, however, results from the ingenuity of ancient Chinese craftsmen, who worked from a number of separate molds for eyes, mouths, noses, beards, head shapes, and the like. By mixing and matching, they made thousands of distinct individuals. Though the emperor's actual tomb has not been opened, ancient historians described its contents:

> The tomb was filled with models of palaces, pavilions, and offices, as well as fine vessels, precious stones, and rarities. Artisans were ordered to fix up crossbows so that any thief breaking in would be shot. All the country's streams, including the Yellow River and the Yangzi, were reproduced in quicksilver and by some mechanical means made to flow into a miniature ocean. The heavenly constellations were shown above and the regions of the earth below. (Dersin and Hagner 1993:84)

Who was the man for whom this astonishing tomb was built? By the third century B.C., the many competing small states had worn themselves down to six main survivors, each heavily armed and capable of fielding armies of not less than one hundred thousand men. The westernmost of these domains was the large state of Qin, which encompassed the old center of Western Zhou. New ideas had been implemented in Qin to reduce the power of the hereditary aristocracy by creating a bureaucracy of appointed officials dependent on the king for their power and survival. The ruler of Qin set out to conquer the other kingdoms, accomplishing this by 221 B.C. He gave himself the name Qin (for his state) Shih ("First") Huang ("sovereign," a replacement for *wang*, "king"), the First Emperor, and his name became the name for China itself (Qin = China). He imagined he was founding a line of emperors to be numbered consecutively forever. By the Third Emperor, his dynasty was ripped apart by violence, but the title *huang-di* remained a title for the Chinese emperor until 1911.

He ruled only a little over a decade; so brief a reign might be dismissed as a historical blip had he not accomplished a restructuring of China whose basic outlines remained until the twentieth century. Determined to reduce the power of local lineages who might later on form separatist regional states, he divided the realm into thirty-six districts. To administer these regions, he rejected the old aristocracy and instituted a meritocracy of men who had earned his respect by their work for him and had no power bases other than the emperor's approval. This new class of administrators was appointed by the emperor and responsible to him. If they displeased him, they were easily removed. He attempted to solve the problem of the existing elites in the old feudal states by forcing 120,000 of these families to move to his capital. Qin saw that primogeniture—passing all a family's property to its eldest son—was a means of accumulating wealth and consolidating power across a number of generations. To reduce such dangerous concentrations, he required families to divide their property when male children came of age (Chow 1994).

Those huge standing armies out in the old states were defanged by confiscating and melting down their weapons, then using the metal to create twelve enormous human statues weighing thirty-two tons each. Believing that people needed clear laws, he codified them and had them inscribed on pillars. Believing laws were obeyed if penalties were severe, relatively light offenses (by current standards) brought flogging, mutilation, forced labor, castration, and decapitation. The emperor himself—as lawmaker, chief executive, and court of last appeal—was above and outside the law. He began the systematic registration of the entire population, encouraging families to adopt surnames by which they could be identified over subsequent generations; this new custom served to reinforce the patrilineal principle in kinship organization and made it easier to form descent groups based on patrilineality.

By the second century B.C., written Chinese had taken many forms, and texts from one place were often unreadable in another. To further unify his state, Qin had the script regularized across the country, which accounts for the fact that today, however diverse Chinese "dialects" might be, all literate Chinese read the same script. But Qin was determined they would not be reading the Confucian texts. Considering Confucius's thought too soft-headed and dependent on individual goodness, he had these books burned. When scholars objected, several hundred were buried alive.

Recognizing the importance of trade and communications, he regularized weights and measures, built five thousand miles of roads, and connected the various pieces of northern walls into the "Great Wall." (Not the one tourists visit today, however; that one was built during Yuan dynasty.)

The First Emperor was thus an organizational genius as well as a cruel ruler who has been remembered with both pride and horror. He accomplished in 221 B.C. what Chandragupta Maurya accomplished in India just one century earlier: the first imperial unification of the northern portion of the country. In subsequent centuries, both countries would suffer "barbarian" (in India, *mleccha*) invasions from Central Asia and would be linked to each other by Buddhist values and text-seeking monks and masters for centuries. Chandragupta's grandson, Ashoka, became a model of the ideal Buddhist king throughout much of the Buddhist world, but his example carried little weight in China. Instead it is the conflicted model of Qin Shihuang, the organizational genius, whose governmental forms imposed on China persisted down to the overthrow of the Qing dynasty in 1911 (Dull 1990:55).

EMERGENCE OF THE CONFUCIAN ELITE (*SHENSHI*)

Every large state struggles to keep control of its outer regions, while regional powers want autonomy to solve their own problems. Believing that the greatest danger comes from a powerful center, the founding fathers of the United States created constitutional limits through the tripartite structure of the federal government and by giving to states all powers not specifically allocated to the center. Even so, there are periodic ebbs and flows as Washington finds ways to grant itself greater power and then shifts it back to the states. In China, the problem has always been viewed the other way around; periods of social chaos are identified as those when the center is weak and the regions are strong.

After the excesses (and successes) of Qin, the Han dynasty (206 B.C.–A.D. 220) had to backpedal a bit on the regional kingdoms, for regional loyalties had been partly responsible for the downfall of Qin. Since much of the old Zhou aristocracy had been destroyed, a new one emerged in Han and Tang dynasties out of the "meritocracy" instituted by Qin. As part of the continuing struggle to limit the power of outlying territories, emperors began to raise up new councilors on the basis of merit and gave them authority over provinces. But always regional military and economic power reaccumulated. Pig farmers and slaves became imperial councilors and founded lineages, joining the new aristocracy. David Johnson (1977) writes about several hundred great aristocratic clans that composed the top stratum of society from Qin to Tang, some of whose genealogies were preserved over a thousand years at Dunhuang. Patricia Ebrey is able to trace the fortunes of the Po-ling Ts'ui family for nearly a millennium from Tang times until they disappear from the scene in the early tenth century (Ebrey 1978).

Because the newly appointed bureaucrats regularly managed to turn themselves into an aristocracy capable of eclipsing the emperor, Han emperors began maintaining private secretarial staffs to keep themselves informed. As this private secretariat slowly expanded into a central executive branch of the bureaucracy through Han and Tang dynasties, many of the palace councilors were scholars who came from the Hanlin Academy, which had been founded as a center of revived Confucian studies. This was a critical juncture in establishing Confucian scholarship as the basis of the future bureaucracy.

A new stage began with Song dynasty (960–1279). The emperor's private secretariat had continued to grow, with real power in the hands of five to nine grand councilors who supervised the burgeoning administration. As it grew, it required an expanded pool of educated persons to fill it. The world's first civil service system emerged to provide this talent. It was a three-stage process. Exams were given every three months at the prefecture level, for which youths all over China spent years studying, achieving this first degree around the age of twenty-four. Those who passed went on to the metropolitan exam in the capital. If you were good enough to pass that exam, the last stage was a palace examination, even occasionally administered by the emperor himself. Every three years, about six hundred men were granted the most prestigious degree, the "Presented Scholar" (*jinshi*). The average age for passing the second level was thirty, and for passing the third level was thirty-six—not unlike the B.A., M.A., and Ph.D. degrees today.

The social significance of these bureaucratic changes was immense. A whole new elite class emerged, whose philosophy was Confucianism (*ru jiao* in Chinese, meaning "the doctrine of the literati"). This elite was composed of two main privileged groups. One was the *shen* (official-gentry) who had passed all the exams, held degrees, and held government positions. But as the scholar class grew, it far outstripped the actual available government posts to be filled; nevertheless, a classical education continued to be the hallmark of the gentry class. Learned men outside government were the shi (scholar-gentry). Together the shen and shi formed a large and influential class that vastly expanded over the next three dynasties—Song (960–1279), Ming (1368–1644), and Qing (1644–1911).

Handbooks prepared for magistrates recommended gaining their cooperation in administering local areas, for the shi class was the link to the common people; "the learned and virtuous scholars are exactly the ones to rely upon in persuading the people to follow the instructions of the officials," held one handbook (Chang 1955:32). They could also stir up trouble if annoyed. Their privileged status was signified in dress. They wore black gowns with blue borders, with various additional markers of rank, up to the nine pythons embroidered on the chest of officials of first rank. Only the gentry could wear sable, fox, or lynx. If a commoner needed to address a member of the gentry, he checked the buttons on their hats. The simple silver button of the lower gentry required "Excellency" (*lao ye*). Gold buttons indicated holders of high academic degrees and titles; the wearer of a hat with a gold button, a flower ornament, a ruby, and a pearl was an official of highest rank. All such titled officials were "Great Excellency." Gentry privilege went beyond wardrobe; if they committed offenses, they could not be humiliated by punishment. If a commoner injured another commoner, the penalty was ten lashes; if a scholar-official, seventy lashes. Commoners could not testify against gentry in lawsuits. Scholar-officials paid lower taxes or were exempt altogether; they could not be required to perform corvée labor or engage in manual work.

Because benefits of membership in this class were immense, membership required passing at least the first level of examinations. Sons were set to work studying hard to pass the examinations that led to official appointments. The expansion of the class of scholars was assisted by the invention of the book made with cheap paper and woodblock printing (Chinese characters carved in wood were preferable to the European movable type).

We know something about life in the schools of Sung China (Lee 1977). When a boy was five or six, his family decided whether he was bright enough to warrant the expense of a classical (i.e., Confucian) education. (Girls could not sit for examinations. We return later to the life women led during these years.) The rich hired tutors. Sons of poor relatives might be allowed to study with these rich boys. The tutors were often young men further along the examination path. An advanced scholar who needed an income might rent a room or set up in a Buddhist temple and recruit pupils from local families. Men who failed the later stages sometimes made a career of tutoring younger boys. There were a few government-sponsored elementary schools, such as one in Kaifeng with more than a thousand pupils.

Of course, most peasant boys went straight to the fields, and sons of old gentry families had some advantages over a first-generation scholar, much like today in the United States. Sons of scholar-officials might travel with their fathers and inherit their libraries. But in the end, it depended on the hard work, determination, and ability of the boys themselves. They lived lives devoted to examinations. Men might sit for the examinations a dozen times or more before finally passing or giving up. A popular nineteenth-century novel describes a large lineage in which only two of sixty to seventy brothers and cousins entertained guests; all the rest stayed behind closed doors, studying for exams (Chang 1955:171).

The exams were all devoted to the Confucian classics. It was as if the secretary of the interior, of treasury, of state, the state governors, and all public officials were appointed to these positions based on their expertise in the writings of Plato and Aristotle. The system produced generalists, not specialists; what was wanted to govern the state were junzi, morally cultivated gentlemen, not experts in irrigation, international relations, or commerce. "A gentleman is not a pot," reads one of Confucius's obscurer statements. He meant that a junzi is not trained to a particular purpose (a pot), but is a generalist. As Stephen Owen wrote recently: "The same question resurfaced in the People's Republic of China in the 1950s, transformed into the 'Red versus expert' controversy, which asked whether public projects should be managed by good communists or by specialists. To the surprise of no one who knew the Chinese tradition, it was concluded that 'not pot' communists would be the sounder choice" (1997:38).

Much as the middle class (or bourgeoisie) that emerged in the West in the nineteenth and twentieth centuries on a capitalist economic base constructed a new set of moral, religious, and cultural values, so the gentry developed its own moral, political, and educational preoccupations. They came in the form of a social conservatism seeking to discover and restore ancient moral practices, particularly in the domain of kinship. These were sufficiently new, and sufficiently based in Confucian ideas, that the Sung transformations have come to be called Neo-Confucianism. Two features of Neo-Confucianism will interest us here: the new interpretations that linked personal and family morality to the state, and the return to emphasis on li in family and lineage ideology. Those changes were triggered by a number of factors, but we will focus on two of them: the Buddhist challenge to Confucianism, and the Mongol and Manchu challenge to Chinese cultural superiority.

The Buddhist Challenge to Confucian Civilization

It is unknown who first brought Buddhist ideas to China, but the earliest positive evidence of its existence there comes from the first century A.D. It is fairly certain that the news of this foreign faith would have come from the oasis towns of Central Asia, where Buddhism took root very early and where many important monasteries flourished, above all at Dunhuang. According to traditional accounts, the Han Emperor Ming woke up one morning and called his advisors to him. A "golden man," a divine being, had appeared to him in his sleep. This must be the Buddha, his advisors marveled. So Emperor Ming sent envoys to India who returned with two Indian masters, a white horse, and the *Sutra in Forty-two Chapters*. They founded the Monastery of the White Horse at Loyang, where it exists to this day.

In its first few centuries at the end of Han dynasty, Buddhism was weak and poorly understood. The Three Jewels of Buddhism—Buddha, dharma, and sangha—were known, but in a simplistic way only. It was a highly sophisticated and varied philosophy, but foreign to Chinese

Beginning in A.D. 493, Chinese emperors earned merit by sponsoring rock-carved images of the Buddha near the old capital of Lo-yang. This colossal Buddha is the grandest of over 2,345 images carved into the rock cliff along the Yi River. Many of the images, carved in deep relief, were hacked away from the rock and carried off by European collectors. Fortunately this one, the grandest of all (the face is said to have been modeled after Empress Wu), was too huge to steal.

assumptions. India was very far away, and there was only a single text, not well translated. Initially, Buddhism was treated like some form of Taoism with its emphasis on purity, simplicity, and nonaction. But as Han began its disintegration because of, as usual, the rise of regional powers that eclipsed the central dynasty, Buddhism came to have broader appeal. For the next four centuries, a variety of small and local dynasties came and went, while the barbarian Toba Turks founded the Northern Wei dynasty in the old heartland with their capital at Lo-yang.

In both the southern Chinese dynasties and in Northern Wei, Buddhist monasteries sprang into existence. In A.D. 400, there were seventeen thousand monasteries and eighty thousand monks and nuns in the south. In the north, Buddhism was even more successful: there were thirty thousand monasteries and a million monks and nuns. The "great age of Buddhism" is the fifth to ninth centuries—Northern Wei, Sui, and the first half of the illustrious Tang dynasty—when emperors themselves converted to Buddhism and lavishly patronized Buddhist monasteries, carvings, works of art, and translations of scriptures. The Toba Turks of Northern Wei embraced Buddhism vigorously, partly as a challenge to the Confucian values of the civilization they sought to emulate and control. These imperial sponsors, and later ones, brought the Indian practice of hollowing out sanctuaries in steep cliffs to China; Dunhuang was one example; the vast stone images of Buddha carved into the hills outside Lo-yang were another.

It was, inevitably, a series of traveling monks—Indian, Chinese, and Central Asian—who did the intellectual work of making the full complexity of Indian Buddhism understood in China. Faxian went to India from 399 to 414 in search of texts he was certain must exist in so learned a land. Although he found a thriving Buddhist culture in which kings respectfully bowed down before monks—something that would never happen in China—he found very few texts. Instead, Indian masters orally transmitted the dharma to their followers. But he learned Sanskrit, one of the few Chinese ever to master that difficult language, and managed to bring a few translations back. Meantime, the great translator Kumarajiva arrived in Chang-an in 401 from Kucha in Central Asia. He introduced Madhyamaka philosophy and joined forces with disciples of the Chinese monk Tao-an in the greatest translation effort in history. A single translation often took four people to divide the work: an Indian monk to orally recite the Sanskrit; another to write it down; another to translate the Sanskrit into oral Chinese; and a fourth to record the text in written Chinese. When Xuanzang returned from India in the seventh century, there was another round of vigorous translation, for by then there were many written texts in India for him to collect. By the eighth century, there was a canon of over a thousand Buddhist texts in good translations, which emperors ordered copied by official bureaus set up for the purpose. This became easier after the eighth-century invention of printing. It was first invented to reproduce charms and images cheaply and quickly, but its potential was quickly grasped. In 972, the first printing of the entire Buddhist canon was done by imperial order. The Diamond Sutra of 864 still exists in the British Museum (see chapter 3).

Religions grow out of the soil of indigenous social patterns and do not transplant easily. In China, the integration of religion and the sociopolitical order had been refined over a millennium. Buddhism was, first of all, a barbarian religion filled with bizarre notions. What did an Indian sage, this Buddha, have to teach a civilization that had Confucius and Laozi? Confucius had placed all emphasis on human life in society. Each person had one life to live, to be fulfilled in the community of family, lineage, and the state. He had refused to speculate on the gods, on Heaven, on the fate of the soul, or whether ancestors were actually sentient and capable of enjoying the gifts that must nevertheless be offered them. But here were Buddhists, denying the existence of all the here and now, proclaiming the utter unreality of all phenomena, plus a host of other outlandish ideas.

Monasticism was particularly un-Chinese. A monk was guilty of cutting off the family line, a sin against the ancestors and the height of social irresponsibility. The exemplary Indian story of Prince Sudana shocked the Chinese. Prince Sudana, like the Buddha himself, renounced his kingdom by giving his father's property away, giving the war elephants to the enemy, and putting his wife and son into the care of others. The Chinese viewed this as not filial, not li, and not ren. Interpreters tried to explain: Sudana realized the world is transitory and wealth and properties do not truly belong to the self, which, incidentally, does not really exist, either. By giving all away and seeking enlightenment, he reached the point of becoming a Buddha. Then he brought salvation to his parents, brothers, wife, son and all mankind. Is this not the epitome of filial devotion and humaneness?

The idea of reincarnation was particularly troublesome. Chinese felt the soul was too tied to the body to survive its death. Further, the idea of reincarnation was a big problem for ancestor worship; how could an ancestor return as someone else's descendant? The concept of the Pure Land eventually solved that problem; instead of reincarnation into another existence, one was reincarnated into the Pure Land, Heaven, a suitable abode for ancestors. Heaven was a Chinese idea; the idea had been around in a vague way forever.

Buddhism in its second five hundred years in India had developed ideas that made it appeal more to the masses than did earlier Buddhism. The Mahayanist notion of salvation through the intercession of bodhisattvas had powerful appeal to all classes. The theory that merit could be transferred from one person to another made this possible. Bodhisattvas could compassionately bestow some of their enormous stores of merit on their devotees. In China, the most beloved of all bodhisattvas was and is Guanyin, the beautiful Goddess of Mercy, portrayed in thousands of paintings and images. Her name means "taking heed of the sound," the one who hears the cries of the suffering world and responds with compassion. In India, she was the male bodhisattva Avalokiteshvar who merged with an early Taoist goddess to become Guanyin. In Japan, she became Kannon. The other well-known Chinese Buddha, the slightly ridiculous "laughing Buddha," developed in late imperial times. He began as the Buddhist messiah Maitreya who became identified with a tenth-century monk named Pu-tai, "Hemp Sack," who had claimed to be an incarnation of Maitreya. "Hemp Sack" replaced Maitreya in the popular imagery of the pot-bellied Buddha who resembles the Hindu elephant-god Ganesh more than he does the great Buddha-to-come.

The most popular Bodhisattva in China is certainly Guanyin, the Goddess of Mercy. She is the Chinese form of Avalokiteshvar, who probably merged with a popular Taoist goddess to become the most beloved Bodhisattva in China.

The *Diantai (Tien-t'ai)* sect made the Lotus Sutra the most beloved of all Buddhist texts in East Asia. Though the central narrative of the Lotus Sutra is the Buddha Sakyamuni revealing a new, more authentic truth, the text was not written in India but in Central Asia some time before A.D. 250. This new truth is that there is only one path to salvation, not three as previously revealed. The one path lies in the heretofore unrevealed fact that everyone—not just monastic virtuosos—have the Buddha-nature and all will be saved and become Buddhas. Nirvana gets redefined; it is not extinction of existence at death, but extinction of ignorance in this life; that is, enlightenment. And this enlightenment comes in the simplest of ways, by casting one's faith in the Buddha. Long passages of the Lotus Sutra describe the people who have already received Buddhahood. There are the traditional hard ways: learning the Law, practicing charity, perfecting self-discipline, enduring forbearance and humiliation. But there are simpler ways: boys at play, making Buddha pagodas in the sand; installing Buddha images in the home; embroidering Buddha pictures; or singing the glory of the Buddha, even with a small sound. The simplicity of these teachings brought Buddhism to the common people and made the Lotus Sutra an icon as much as a sacred text.

One other development needs mention, since it became so important when borrowed by the Japanese. Early in the sixth century, a mysterious Indian meditation master named Bodhidharma visited China. Whatever it was he taught quickly blended with a fundamental Taoist idea: that ultimate truth is beyond words. "The Tao that can be told is not the true Tao." But how can one reach that ineffable truth beyond words, beyond rationality, beyond the ten thousand things that distract us? Obviously all the words printed in books, even sacred ones, are beside the point; in fact, they obstruct the truth. Bizarre new forms of meditation were devised to break through the constructed world of words and reason to reach the intuitive, wordless, "no-mind" reality beyond. They meditated on paradoxes and nonsequiturs in an effort to break down the intellect in a sudden, explosive, obliterating breakthrough to radical unity of being. Ironically, the anti-intellectualism of this approach was of great interest to intellectuals; uneducated people found it unfathomable. Known as Chan Buddhism in China, it still exists and has tremendous cross-cultural appeal today as Japanese Zen Buddhism.

Despite the glory days of Buddhism during Sui and Tang dynasties, Buddhism eventually began to fade. It never really stood a chance against Confucianism. It did not end because of persecution, though there were major persecutions in 446, 574, and 845 when stupas were destroyed, monasteries were looted, and monks and nuns were "secularized" or killed. Even at its height, and with the support of many emperors, state and sangha had a natural antipathy. For one thing, the conceptual structure of the Chinese state did not leave room for institutions existing outside it, as Buddhist monasticism claimed to do. The life of idleness and begging for food was much criticized as parasitic on society; Buddhist monks were criticized for hoarding copper, silver, and gold in ritual objects. The monasteries amassed enormous wealth through gifts from rich donors; they owned huge tracts of land that produced income through the labor of temple serfs and slaves. Using this wealth for money lending and pawnbroking, monks who had taken vows of poverty played a significant role in the development of banking and established commercial enterprises like oil presses and water-powered mills. In Tang times, Buddhists responded to these criticisms with practical ways of enacting Buddhist compassion; they founded clinics and hospitals, provided aid for the poor, and distributed food in famine times. Though the vinaya rules forbade manual labor, gathering firewood and drawing water became a central feature of Chan Buddhism.

With all this wealth, and close ties to emperors and rich patrons, it was inevitable that the sangha would be used for political purposes. Most notorious, perhaps, was Empress Wu, the only woman in all of Chinese history to rule as the supreme monarch. She spent seven years after her husband's death inventing ways to justify her succession (rather than her sons'), then finally did rule from 690 to 705. First, she had a white stone "discovered" in the Luo River that, when cracked open, contained an inscription: "A sage Mother shall come to rule mankind; her rule shall bring eternal prosperity." She then installed her commoner lover as the abbot of the venerable White Horse Monastery. He proceeded to recruit a thousand bodyguards whom he ordained as monks. As abbot, her lover proclaimed that the Great Cloud Sutra had prophesied the reincarnation of the bodhisattva Maitreya as a woman, who would bring an era of peace and plenty. "All her subjects will give their allegiance to this woman as the successor to the imperial throne. Once she has taken the Right Way, the world will be awed into submission." She immediately ordered a Great Cloud Temple to be built in every prefecture of the empire (Wills 1994:142–43). Although Empress Wu appears to have been a good administrator, she was loathed by Confucians for the intolerable innovation of a woman ruling, executing her competitors, and having affairs in old age just like a man. That she could manipulate Buddhist symbols so boldly and successfully was simply one more thing wrong with Buddhism.

In late Tang times, the state was impoverished by civil war and turned to the wealth of Buddhist monasteries to replenish the treasury. At the same time, a more fundamental shift was taking place toward older Chinese values, Confucian ones. As Zurcher writes: "[Buddhism's] decline was a gradual process—it petered out and slowly lost its intellectual vitality and creativity, and its social status, in a world in which the educated elite more and more turned away from it, and in which the best minds were attracted to the examination hall rather than to the monastery" (Zurcher 1984:205).

Buddhism continued to function more marginally in Chinese society. The theme of the messiah, Maitreya, was rich in revolutionary possibility. Secret sects formed, like the "White Lotus Society," which played a role in the downfall of Yuan dynasty. Martial monk-heroes, such as the kung-fu monks of Shao-lin monastery in Honan, became a theme in popular lore (bequeathed to modern action films) and came close to toppling the Qing dynasty at the beginning of the nineteenth century. However, even though the People's Republic of China has liberalized its policies toward religion, most observers of China today view the prospects of a strong comeback of Chinese Buddhism as unlikely.

Neo-Confucianism

In the eleventh century, Zhuxi wrote in the part of *Family Rituals* devoted to funerals:

> Do not perform Buddhist services. . . . If heaven's palace does not exist, then that's that. If it does, then men of virtue will ascend there. If hell does not exist, then that's that; if it does, then inferior men will enter it. Contemporaries, when a man dies, pray to the Buddha. This is assuming one's parent was not a person of virtue but an inferior person who had accumulated bad deeds and sins. Could there be a less kind way to treat one's parents? And if in fact one's parents had accumulated bad deeds and sins, how could they escape the consequences by your bribing the Buddha? (Ebrey 1991a:79–80)

That Zhuxi wrote his famous *Family Rituals* at all was part of the Confucian backlash. Patricia Ebrey, the translator, describes the work as "a militantly Confucian book to combat Buddhist rites and other non-Confucian practices." The glitz of Buddhist culture—all the temples, images and icons, works of art, and showy festivals—prompted a Confucian response. Confucianism had mostly dwelt in the home, in public courtesies, in the texts, the examination halls, and in the discourse of the intellectual class. But in A.D. 630, at a time when there were well over fifty thousand Buddhist monasteries, Emperor Dang Daizong ordered all counties and prefectures to erect temples for the worship of Confucius. The most famous one of all was at Qufu, in Confucius's own home town in Shandong Province. In 1684, Emperor Kangxi described visiting Qufu and meeting Confucius's sixty-fourth-generation descendant and being shown the wall where Confucius's ninth-generation descendant hid the *Classics* when Qin Shihuang burned all the books. During the Cultural Revolution, Qufu would have been destroyed by Red Guards but for the intervention of Zhou En-lai. It is once again a place of pilgrimage, now for

"Confucian capitalists" from Korea, Japan, Taiwan, and Singapore. It would probably be as great a mistake to write off Confucianism in the twentieth century as it was in the seventh century.

During Kangxi's visit early in Qing dynasty, Confucius's descendants had a problem that was a typical preoccupation of the gentry during the seventeenth century. They had maintained their large lineage ties so diligently, for so many generations, that they had now run out of burial space in the family cemetery. There was simply no room to expand into lands registered to others (Spence 1974). They were the classic great lineage idealized by the Confucian elite throughout the centuries, although the actual existence of such lineages varied tremendously throughout Chinese history. Beginning with Sung dynasty, it had another period of flourishing, and Zhuxi's *Family Rituals* had as great an impact on this movement as did Manu's *Dharmashastra* in India (see chapter 5). This movement was fueled during Song as an answer to Buddhism; and during Ming and Qing as an answer to successful invasions by Mongols and Manchus.

It may be a little hard to understand how China, at a cultural peak during Song dynasty, could have been so easily conquered first by the Jin, then by the Mongols (1279). Chinese intellectuals, looking back on their own history during Ming and Qing, also brooded about it, but came to a different conclusion than modern historians. For the latter, the explanation, or part of it, lies in the emphasis on high culture, on virtue, and on peace in the thought of the shenshi, and the disdain in which wu, force or military prowess, was held. Warfare and military might were what had always troubled society from antiquity on; the well-ordered, ideal society was a society at peace. The military was so devalued by the Confucian elite that it does not even have a place in the four-class structure: *shi* (scholar), *nong* (farmer), *gong* (artisan), and *shang* (merchant). (Incidentally, compare to the Indian version: Brahman [priest], Kshatriya [ruler, warrior], Vaishya [merchant], and Shudra [artisans, farmers].) There, also, the intellectual has highest place, but warriors come second.) The brightest young men would not dream of going into the military; they studied for exams to become scholar-officials. Even the great technological invention of gunpowder, permitting the tossing of small bombs and fire lances at the nomadic enemy, was never integrated into a larger military strategy capable of keeping them out of China. All this meant that China was easy prey to aggressive tribal societies who made war a way of life.

China's Yuan dynasty had its roots in a great gathering of Mongol tribes on the Kerulan River in Central Asia in 1206. One of the Mongol chiefs, Genghis Khan, was confirmed as universal ruler or Great Khan over all the Mongol tribes—the Mongol equivalent of Qin Shihuang's great unification in 221 B.C. Most of Eurasia would feel the impact of the

Mongol Empire: Genghis Khan's sons and grandsons spread out in all four directions, establishing Khanates in Russia along the Volga, in Turkestan, in Persia, and, of course, in China. His grandson Khubilai Khan ruled a China that had a much different shape than it did during Tang times. During Tang, China stretched westward along the Silk Road all the way to the Aral Sea; during Yuan dynasty, China pulled in on the west but stretched north to Lake Baikal. (During both periods, Tibet was not in the picture.) The Mongols made aggressive strikes at Japan, Java, and Burma, creating the turmoil in the south that set tribal groups like the Tai moving into Southeast Asia (see chapter 6). Needing a capital more central to his empire, he chose Beijing in the far north of modern China to become his new capital. Laid out in the classic style of the Chinese imperial capitals at Chang-an and Lo-yang, it remains the capital to this day.

The Mongol Empire was a religiously diverse place; there were Muslims, Buddhists, Nestorian Christians, and now Confucians. Khubilai Khan embraced Tibetan Buddhism but was tolerant of other faiths. Confucianism now came to have a strong ethnic component; it was the faith of the Han Chinese.

Perhaps, given the fact that the Confucian paradigm of the civilized state left warfare and military might out of the scheme, it will not be surprising that many scholar-officials went to work with great diligence and loyalty to their Mongol sovereigns. Yes, they hated them; they were "pockmarked and foul-smelling"; one did not want to be downwind of them. Yet as de facto rulers, they had the Mandate of Heaven. Langlois (1978) describes the life of one high-ranking official, Yu Chi, in great detail. He helped the nine Mongol rulers whom he served understand the Confucian *Classics*, hoping this would lead to better administration of the realm. He covered over an ugly struggle among three brothers for succession to the throne by drafting an edict announcing the winner, laying "a polished veneer of Chinese civility and brotherly deference on the surface of the violent power struggle that had taken place." It was not the gentry, but peasants who brought down the Mongols; peasant rebels led the movement that overthrew the Yuan dynasty after only 88 years; Ming, a Chinese dynasty, survived 276 years, then was severely destabilized, again by peasant rebellions. Manchurians (more barbarians) were invited to Beijing to throw the rebels out, but decided to stay and found Qing dynasty.

Scholars analyzing their own history were perplexed: Why did barbarians so easily conquer China? From Song through Qing, situations were somewhat different and a variety of analyses were put forward, but a major theme of all of them was "nativist," a return to the morality and the social structures of antiquity. The Confucian revival that began during Song dynasty reached its peak in the wholesale social reform movement led by the gentry during Ming (1368–1644) and Qing (1644–1912). This movement, imagined as a return to the social morality of antiquity, required a flurry of scholarship to discover what morality had actually been during Zhou and Han dynasties. What were the "authentic rituals" of the sages? It came to focus on three core values: filial devotion expressed in family and lineage rituals, loyalty to the monarch, and wifely fidelity that became a cult of female purity (Chow 1994).

THE CONFUCIAN MODEL
FOR KINSHIP AND GENDER

The Chinese family system has had to respond to innumerable pressures over the centuries, not least in the turbulent decades of the last half-century. Any kinship system is molded by a variety of forces. Family is, at bottom, the basic social unit of human survival; it must be an all-purpose institution for reproduction, child-rearing, emotional support, and care for the elderly. During most of human history it has been the basic unit of production and consumption, playing a fundamental economic role. Through marital ties, it links groups together. It may become a family militia in troubled times. Thus, economic, military, and political factors are conditions families must respond to by formulating strategies for survival, for prosperity, and for achievement of prestige. Finally, family cultures are products of specific historic ideologies; families receive from the past sets of ideals—kinship ideologies—for organizing biological relationships. These ideals may or may not be realizable in particular periods under particular circumstances, and they can change over time. It is essential to understand the ideals that people hold and try to emulate, as well as the conditioning factors that determine the empirical shape of families at given historical moments.

In China, patterns for organizing kinship have been decisively shaped by Confucian ethics. The moral imperative of *xiao*, filial devotion, carried obligations between fathers and sons further in China than perhaps in any other Asian society. Even in Japan, to which these concepts were carried, loyalty to one's lord might require a suicide that left one's parents destitute. But for Confucians in China, as Rozman has put it, the debt to one's parents can never be repaid. The stories of the son who devotes his life to carrying his blind father on his back, or the daughter who carves out a bit of flesh to make a broth for her starving mother illustrate the depth of these filial emotions. The debt goes on after death, in continuity owed the parents by producing at least one son to continue the family line, and in revering them as ancestors with gifts, reports on current goings-on in the family, and, especially among common folk, invitations to return for holidays.

The ideology of the family was decidedly patriarchal in that control of resources and the structure of authority were in male hands. Ebrey identifies four key features of Chinese patriarchy: (1) The conception that property, especially land, belongs to the family, not the individual. (2) This property belongs to the men of the family, and must be divided equally among brothers if divided at all. (3) Fathers have legal authority over women and children, including the right to arrange the marriages of their children, sell their children, and dispose of their labor. (4) These structures are underwritten by the notion that women are morally and intellectually less capable than men and therefore must be under male control (1990:204).

The hierarchies that characterized Chinese society at large began in the family; everyone had a unique place in a domestic hierarchy whose two organizing principles were age and gender. Xiao applied proportionately to relations between elder and younger siblings. Respect is due to anyone older than oneself, including the twin who was born five minutes ahead of you; even kinship terminology distinguishes elder brother and younger brother. Traditionally and ideally, all the sons of a man continue to live with him in a patrilocal joint family until he dies, at which time the sons divide the property equally and the process starts over again. This family, called *jia*, thus has a natural life cycle: a man and his wife have their children, hopefully many; as sons reach adulthood, wives are brought in for them, while daughters are married out to other households. Eventually a number of nuclear families are all living together in one large, well-ordered, and clearly hierarchical household. The men are a tightly bonded unit of fathers and sons. The women who begin as strangers brought in from the outside to share their lives as mothers-, sisters-, and daughters-in-law become the loyal and fertile mothers of the lineage and eventually ancestresses as well.

The benefits of such great households are many. They share a common budget with the expenses of a single household. The eldest male is the chief executive officer of this family corporation, using the capital of several sons' labors to make investments and expenditures for the welfare of the whole. This includes a great house with four connected wings around a central courtyard, perhaps double-storied as well, allowing apartments for each married couple and their children. There will certainly be an ancestral shrine in a prominent location in the main hall. The fund of family capital may be used to buy land, invest in a business, educate the sons, provide dowries for all the daughters, support servants to do much of the labor, and perhaps provide an unofficial second wife, a concubine, for the head of household. Such a family, fulfilling the Confucian ideal, is what most Chinese have aspired to throughout the ages; how-

福蔭堂

In this anonymous mid-nineteenth century painting showing the interior of a Mandarin's house, the values of the scholar-official class are expressed in domestic architecture. We see the formal interior of the ancestral hall, with the youngest descendant being nurtured by two women of the household. The scrolls, forming a paired couplet, read: "Planting three oaks in the courtyard produces excellent descendants [right]; Keeping the five classics in the home raises it to high rank [left]." The two women repeat the symmetry of the couplet, while the young boy embodies the intention of both lines.

ever, empirical studies suggest that this ideal has never been within reach for most Chinese families. The ideal was far more frequently achieved in gentry families than in peasant families. In the best of times, if a family was poor, sons had to leave in search of work; daughters might be sold into servanthood or given as child-brides to other poor families who would bear the cost of feeding them to ensure that farm sons would get a wife at all. Mortality rates, alone, were stacked against the ideal Confucian great family; the chances of a couple surviving to old age with several adult sons and many little grandchildren who survived the perils of infancy was a demographic long shot.

Ancestor Worship

Ancestor worship was not left to custom by the shenshi. Detailed manuals prescribed each movement, garment, offering, and placement of ritual objects. Most authoritative of all was Zhuxi's *Family Rituals* written in the twelfth century. According to French missionary Jean-Francois Foucquet (1665–1741), it was to be found in every home in China, second only to the *Analects* in popularity (Ebrey 1991). This manual was comparable to the *Book of Common Prayer* that was the liturgical order of worship for Anglican Christians from the middle sixteenth century to the present. The purpose of family rituals, according to Zhuxi, is to "preserve status responsibilities" and to "give concrete form to love and respect through cappings, weddings, funerals, and ancestral rites." He hoped, he wrote in the preface, that this book might "make a small contribution to the state's effort to transform and lead the people" (Ebrey 1991a:4).

The book begins with detailed instructions on construction of the ancestral hall in the home (see box 7.4):

> When a man of virtue builds a house his first task is always to set up an offering hall to the east of the main room of his house. For this hall four altars to hold the spirit tablets of the ancestors are made; collateral relatives who died without descendants may have associated offerings made to them there according to their generational seniority. Sacrificial fields should be established and sacrificial utensils prepared. Once the hall is completed, early each morning the master enters the outer gate to pay a visit. All comings and goings are reported there. On New Year's Day, the solstices, and each new and full moon, visits are made. On the customary festivals, seasonal foods are offered, and when an event occurs, reports are made. Should there be flood, fire, robbers, or bandits, the offering hall is the first thing to be saved. The spirit tablets, inherited manuscripts, and then the sacrificial utensils should be moved; only afterward may the family's valuables be taken. As one generation succeeds another, the spirit tablets are reinscribed and moved to their new places. (Ebrey 1991a:14)

The ancestors, clearly still members of the family, required almost as much attention dead as they did when they were living. They needed to be checked in on daily by the head of the household, who was to don a special robe and light incense. The offerings shown in the diagram—tea, wine, and fruit—were for the relatively simple fortnightly offerings. On major occasions such as New Year, they had to be served rice, soup, vegetables, and several kinds of meat. The ancestors had to be informed of every significant event in the life of the family. Zhuxi even provided some sample reports. Did a member of the family receive a promotion? Then they should say:

7.4   Zhuxi's Layout of the Offering Hall

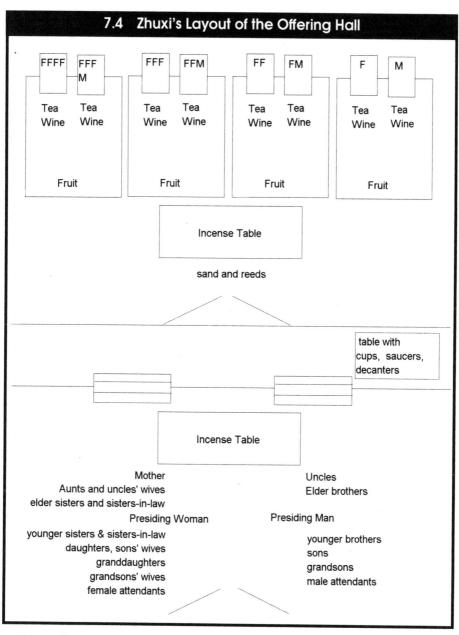

Source: Patricia Ebrey, 1991, p. 13.

> On such a day of such a month we received an edict conferring on such relative such office. . . . A, due to the instructions he received from his ancestors, holds a position at court beyond what he deserves. Through the grace of the sovereign, this honor has been conferred. A's salary comes too late to support his parent, which leaves him unable to choke back his tears. (Ebrey 1991b:19)

Occasionally, reporting to the ancestors was a form of confession. Did you lose your job? You should say you were "dismissed from such a post, that having discarded the ancestral teachings, one is in trepidation and uneasy" (Ebrey 1991b:18).

The most significant feature of this mode of worship is the way in which it reinforced family hierarchies. A Western family might simply gather around the grave of a departed grandfather, probably only once. The Chinese did it in rank order, with men and women segregated. When a man died, his eldest son became the presiding man at all ancestor worship, and his wife became the presiding woman. There might, however, be living family members who were senior to the presiding couple; if so, they stood in front of them, as shown in the diagram. Behind them was everyone junior to them, in rank order. Family hierarchies, impressed on each person's psyche through these somber rituals dozens of times every year, had sacred power. This was the power and force of li.

Though every family needed an ancestral altar in the home, everyone did not have the same ritual obligations. Different ranks of gentry had different authority to perform rites: the higher the rank, generally, the heavier the ritual obligations; and, of course, this was also a matter of prestige. The eldest son worshipped on behalf of his brothers, and this right was passed down in the senior line. The youngest son of youngest sons never did ancestor worship themselves, but had to join the senior men of the family at their household. When the next generation of elders died, the ancestors moved up, too; the ancestral tablets were shifted to the table to the west (to the left), while great-grandfather and great-grandmother's tablets were taken out to the gravesite and burned or, more prestigiously, deposited in the ancestral hall of the larger lineage, if there was one.

Wealth, Power, and Morality in the Large Lineage

In a famous eleventh-century essay, philosopher Xiu Ou-yang urged that the hold of Buddhism should be loosened by local officials promoting Confucian rituals, including weddings, funerals, and ancestral rites. He blamed the decay of these rituals on Buddhism having been allowed to reach into the hearts of the common people. Instructing people in Confucian rituals "not only would prevent disorder but also would teach them to distinguish superior and inferior, old and young, and the ethics of social relations" (Ebrey 1991a:xix). Buddhism's efficient organization in monasteries, temples, charitable organizations, and schools came to be countered by a truly Confucian institution: the large corporate lineage. This form of organization, though sanctioned by the classics, had not been cultivated intensively during the centuries of Buddhism's peak in China. The Confucian reforms of Song dynasty, and later reforms in Ming and Qing, emphasized lineage organization and Confucian rituals. Kinship had work to do, and a revival of the old large lineage took place.

According to the new kinship ideology, the lineage and the state were complementary to each other, not competitive. When lineages diminished in power, argued Ku Yen-wu in 1652, so did the emperor's control over the realm (Chow 1994:84). Remember that emperors from Qin Shihuang on did all they could to minimize the competing power of large regional aristocracies, which were kinship based. Now, it was theorized, Ming had collapsed because of the failure of local resistance to the peasant rebellions and the Manchus had conquered because of the failure of resistance that might have been mounted by powerful local lineages had they existed. If gentry families formed large lineages, these social units could represent the values of the state to the common folk, tutor them in Confucian ideals, and compete with Buddhist institutions. Unlikely as it seems, gentry did in fact go about establishing lineages in these centuries, as the case study of the He lineage will demonstrate.

With the above rationale, strongly Confucian and in the name of the state, corporate local lineages were also found to be effective strategies for economic enhancement. Between the eleventh and nineteenth centuries, powerful lineages emerged at local levels, controlling land and resources, establishing themselves as the ground-level anchor in a chain of links to the emperor through the official appointments of a few of their members, providing stability and morality at county and prefecture levels. These lineages were first studied by British anthropologist Maurice Freedman, who seemed to have said the last word on them in a number of publications in the 1950s (Freedman 1958), but only in the last decade have scholars been able to raise new questions and investigate them in the People's Republic.

A major research endeavor has been under way for several years in the Pearl River delta area by a team of historians and anthropologists, David Faure, Helen F. Siu, Ye Xian'en, and Liu Zhiwei. This area lies in the heart of the vast Hong Kong–Guangzhou development region, now the richest and fastest-developing region of China. In pre-Socialist times there were huge corporate lineages each containing thousands of members and controlling enormous wealth in lineage trusts called *tangs*. These scholars have traced the history of several important lineages and uncovered the territorial bases of their wealth and power. By late Qing (late nineteenth century) people with the He surname were the largest and wealthiest of half a dozen major lineages in the Shawan sands region southeast of Guangzhou in the Pearl River delta. The founding ancestor of He lineage, He Renjian (see box 7.5), settled there in late Song times on fifty acres of land that he soon extended by another fifty acres. His descendants cultivated the river marshes, expanding their holdings in a variety of ways, but most remarkably and successfully by reclamation of the sands deposited naturally by the river. Laborers were hired to drop stones from boats, build dikes, and add upper layers of soil on which fruit trees were grown until the reclaimed land was suitable for cultivation. This land was registered with the government when tax dodging became impossible and then leased out to cultivators of other surnames and to non-Han ethnic groups. The wealth in land was held in a lineage trust, the Liugeng *tang*. By the Republican period in the early twentieth century, He lineage owned over ten thousand acres, one of the richest lineages in the delta, with vast ancestral estates.

It should be pointed out that establishing local wealth was the first step in founding a great lineage. He Renjian began the family fortune, but according to old lineage documents, it was his great-grandsons who built the first ancestral hall to honor this ancestor recent enough to be personally remembered by most people living. The family quickly moved into the shenshi or gentry status, with both degree-holders and wealth. Part of the family fortune was used to educate the sons, and this paid off in the achievement of *jinshi* status by the second generation son, Qilong. Most famous was He Zihai in the fifth generation. He Zihai wrote the first genealogy, going back only five generations to He Renjian, the empirical founder of the local lineage. In citing the glories of He lineage, he wrote: "several tens of descendants have written poetry, practiced the rituals, and served as officials. Other lineages have not been able to surpass this record" (Liu 1995:25). In the same passage, he scoffs at some lineages who were creating fictional ancestors by searching out "reputable and virtuous people of past ages to serve as their ancestors," and refrained from doing so himself. Later descendants during Ming heard rumors of people of He surname elsewhere, most intriguingly at Nanxiong, and as scholar-officials they traveled frequently enough to have visited there and met some of them. However, nothing came of these discoveries immediately.

Besides genealogies, great lineages needed ancestral halls where collective rites to the ancestors could be performed. The first ancestral hall built in the fourth generation was destroyed by warfare at the end of Yuan dynasty, so it fell to the fifth generation in early Ming—the same generation that produced the first genealogy—to build a new ancestral hall. What is significant about the fifth generation is that it was the first to produce scholar-officials of high enough rank to be entitled by law to worship their ancestors farther back than the third generation. Legal prohibitions prevented the rituals and temples that enabled a large lineage

7.5 Construction of He Lineage by Members of the Literati

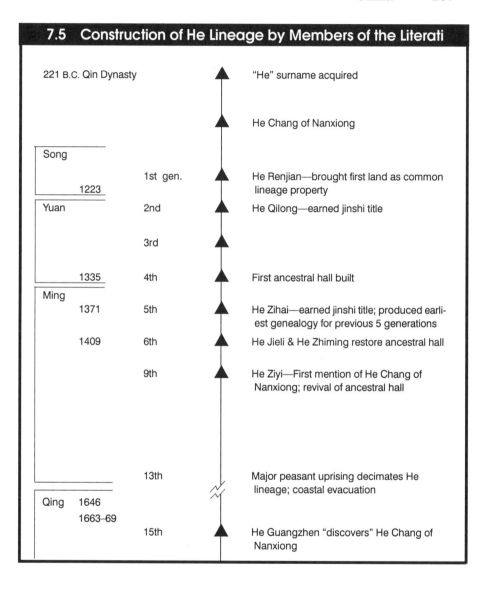

221 B.C. Qin Dynasty			"He" surname acquired
			He Chang of Nanxiong
Song			
1223	1st gen.		He Renjian—brought first land as common lineage property
Yuan	2nd		He Qilong—earned jinshi title
	3rd		
1335	4th		First ancestral hall built
Ming 1371	5th		He Zihai—earned jinshi title; produced earliest genealogy for previous 5 generations
1409	6th		He Jieli & He Zhiming restore ancestral hall
	9th		He Ziyi—First mention of He Chang of Nanxiong; revival of ancestral hall
	13th		Major peasant uprising decimates He lineage; coastal evacuation
Qing 1646			
1663–69			
	15th		He Guangzhen "discovers" He Chang of Nanxiong

to exist at all. The lineage ideology coming down from Song times limited the agnates (members of a patrilineage) who should mourn a common ancestor to five "degrees" or five generations. This model did not produce lineage segments wider than those who shared a common great-great-grandfather, which could be several hundred people but not the huge lineages of thousands of members that were to emerge during Ming and Qing. Such ideologies, the product of the neo-Confucian elite, had the authority of the emperor behind them. People who worshipped their ancestors beyond their station could be punished and their temples destroyed, as the He lineage did to upstart servant lineages who tried to build an ancestor hall in the nineteenth century. Common people generally had no knowledge of their ancestral origins, no lineage organizations, no ancestral halls, and could not name their ancestors four generations back (Liu 1995).

But a new interpretation of the *Classics* allowed an innovation for the gentry; this was the annual worship of the First Ancestor (*shizu*). This provided an institutional basis for a much larger kinship group than previously allowable (Chow 1994). It was not immediately clear who the First Ancestor would be in specific cases, but it generally came to mean the first forebear to migrate to a locale; e.g., He Renjian in 1223. This meant that as generations came and went and the number of He Renjian's descendants multiplied, they did not disperse every five generations but continued to be linked by common worship activities and by shared membership in the ancestral estate. Any number of additional shrines to lower order ancestors could theoretically be built, one for each generation, as was believed to be the practice in the Zhou dynasty, but this was expensive and was only accomplished by very wealthy lineages like the He, who had at least eighty-seven ancestral halls, to publicly demonstrate their solidarity and prestige. By the end of Ming dynasty, the thirteenth generation had been reached, still keeping alive their sense of common descent and still sharing in the growing profits of the ancestral wealth; thus the lineage was corporate in a very real economic sense.

But the transition from Ming to Qing was devastating to the He lineage. The peasant rebellions in the north that led to the Manchu takeover had their version in Guangdong Province; the He chronicler wrote of the "smell of blood" on the Shawan sands:

> The bondservants who had belonged to the various surnames turned upon their masters. . . . Fierce young men in seven villages followed them, set up camps and walled compounds, robbed, and could not be controlled. . . . Every family departed from the village to escape their wrath. . . . They plundered our houses, slew our kin, burned our ancestral halls and turned our pavilions into ashes. (Liu 1995:30)

Social upheaval was followed by natural disaster. Severe floods led to coastal evacuation that lasted from 1663 to 1669. Homes, villages, and ancestral halls were left in ruins, followed by looting and destruction by soldiers and robbers.

As conditions stabilized after 1669, the He lineage had a great deal of rebuilding to do. In 1700, they built a lavish new temple with entrance hall, ritual gate, middle hall, back bedchamber, side halls, bell and drum tower, a kitchen, and servants' quarters. They also began tinkering with the written genealogy and produced a new apical ancestor. Fifteenth generation He Guangzhen uncovered old documents referring to a He branch in Nanxiong and an even older "ancestor," He Chang. He was identified as originally being from Kaifeng, the capital during Later Jin (twelfth century), assigned to a military post in Qinghai, and dying in the service of the emperor in Guangdong. He Chang had everything needed in an ancestor: as an official at the court of the emperor, one could not ask for higher origins or credentials. His Han ethnicity was certain, establishing that the He lineage folk were not non-Han parvenus from the south trying to become Han. And he was the first forebear to establish a line in Southern China, a true *shizu*. Finally, there were He living in Nanxiong to fuse with, and there was already a famous temple built to him because of the virtue (te) that allowed his corpse to flow upstream for thirty li at his death. One could not ask for a better First Ancestor. The details between He Chang and He Renjian were left to genealogists to fill in as best they could.

In this way great lineages were constructed during Ming and Qing dynasties. Several facts are noteworthy: (1) They were constructed post hoc, by descendants who projected their line backward in time according to strategies allowed by existing cultural rules. (2) Large lineages grew by fusion as well as by fission; that is, they sought out distant branches to join with even in the absence of verifiable links, while also growing ever more complex as new generations and new branches emerged. (3) They were subject to state-sponsored Confucian rules about who was entitled to specific rights of worship and group formation. Nongentry families were not allowed to form large lineages, even though a gentry lineage could have segments that included commoners. (4) Even if all the class-based entitlements to play by these kinship rules were in place, it was successful marshaling of economic resources, especially control of land, which enabled corporate lineages to grow large and survive over time.

The advantages of being a member of He lineage are obvious. Members received regular income from lineage holdings; expenses of births, weddings, funerals, and education and examination costs were subsidized by the ancestral trusts (see box 7.6, "He Lineage Worships Its Ancestors"). The lineage maintained armed guards and a defense corps to patrol the sands and protect lineage property and members. They set up schools, hospitals, and orphanages. The lineage was a quasi-government that dominated the official government of the region, with many of its members serving on both sides. The security, prosperity, and prestige benefited everyone.

7.6   He Lineage Worships Its Ancestors

According to the recollections of some older people, about fifteen days after the Qingming festival every year, lineage members would visit the graves in Guangzhou. After lineage heads decided on a date, they sent people to Guangzhou to hire a fleet of colorful boats (known as the boats from Zidong, a village in Nanhal county) in which the literati types would sail to Guangzhou. The rest of the entourage would go in large ferries. Together they formed an elegant fleet, escorted by four armed boats equipped by the He lineage itself. They sailed to Guangzhou in this grand fashion and moored at a berth they had built for themselves. In the evening, they stayed at the four academies, the four martial arts schools, and the Chang-an Inn, all of which belonged to the He lineage; some people would stay at the home of relatives or friends. They would also have bribed the city guards to open the Small Northern Gate in the city wall earlier than usual at the fifth watch (just before dawn) the next day. Almost all the sedan-chair bearers in the city flocked on the occasion to provide service and were paid by the lineage managers. The entire group paraded through the Small Northern Gate to the Grave of the sister-in-law to perform the grave rites. On the third day, they repeated the ceremonies at the graves of He Renjian and others. According to a 1911 record, the lineage spent more than 6,000 taels of silver for the grave visits that year. These extravagant public displays become important rallying points for the collective identity of the lineage as well as for demonstrating to others its power and influence.

Liu Zhiwei, 1995:39

The Family in the Twentieth Century

The last half-century has been a rare historical moment of rapid-fire and sweeping interventions in the lives of a billion people. Prior to the 1949 Communist revolution, forms of kinship we call traditional were in place. These forms survived in Hong Kong and Taiwan, which were unaffected by the revolution. Following the revolution drastic reforms were initiated in the name of socialism under the moral inspiration of Mao Zedong, going much further than comparable movements in the Soviet Union and Eastern Europe. Private property was eliminated; the market was suppressed; all land and labor were collectivized; bureaucratic control by the Chinese Communist Party replaced traditional private entrepreneurial and kinship structures. The full Socialist era lasted from 1958 to 1978. Family and lineage were decisively reorganized during those times; the great lineages were special targets of those reforms. Lineage solidarity was destroyed by assigning each villager to a class category: poor peasant, middle peasant, rich peasant, landlord. The lower statuses were then made to attack, humiliate, and appropriate the property of the rich peasants and landlords who were their kinsmen. Ancestor worship was declared a superstition and forbidden. Cremation rather than burial was encouraged, to save land and to undermine reverence of ancestors. Large expenditures for kinship ceremonials like weddings and funerals were harshly discouraged, and no one could afford them in any case. The marriage law of 1950 prohibited concubinage and child betrothal, which disappeared almost immediately, and permitted women to sue for divorce, prompting two million divorces in the first three years. Putting everyone to work in communes gave women the economic security to take advantage of the new opportunity for divorce.

All of these changes reduced or eliminated the economic logic of the traditional family system, as well as rendering its ideology politically incorrect. Paradoxically, however, some of these changes brought core family ideals within the grasp of many who had never managed to realize them before. Health care and reduced mortality rates meant most people actually had larger kin networks than before. Restrictions on internal migration kept men in their home towns or villages; in the southern provinces of Guangdong and Fujian where large lineages had been most common in the past, these restrictions on movement and collectivization put kinsmen who survived the earlier struggles to work in the same communes, thus preserving them, even though ancestral halls had been turned into work unit headquarters and genealogies had been burned. A few old women still worshipped their ancestors by burning mosquito coils, but most people seemed to give up the old customs rather easily.

The next round of kinship changes offered thrusts in two opposite directions. First, decollectivization returned 80 percent of all agricultural lands to farm families on fifteen-year leases, and rural markets were reopened. Once again, farmers had economic incentives to work hard, invest in their farms, and raise workers. Graham E. Johnson describes the results of liberalization in the Pearl River delta:

> While the full elaboration of all aspects of the operation of lineage cannot be contemplated, many of them are once again practiced. Graves have been repaired, rituals are performed at the graves of apical ancestors, ancestral halls are being restored, ritual feasts occur in the halls once more, lineage libraries are being refurbished, and lineage officers have begun to act as agents for members of the lineage, similar to the way the administrators of lineage trusts intervened on behalf of members in the period before 1949. (Johnson 1993:132)

The other change, however, was the most repressive intervention in private reproductive lives the world has ever seen; 100 million couples were affected. The one-child policy begun in the late 1970s decreed that henceforth, "only half of all families would have a son to carry on the family name, the sibling relationship would disappear, and failure to use contraceptives would be a capital offense" (Harrell & Davis 1993). Through much of rural China, bargaining between village families and local cadres has resulted in softening the enforcement of the one-child policy, though in urban areas, the state has more successfully enforced it. The figures on total fertility of Chinese women from 1965 to 1985 shows the success of this program (Luther et al. 1990), although other factors have been important, especially the embracing of the two-child family as the ideal compromise between traditional values and the one-child policy. The outcomes of the reduction in family size are beginning to be visible, since the first generation affected by the policy is now in its teens. The widespread new phenomenon of the "only child" has resulted in another new phenomenon, the spoiled child. And the traditional Chinese preference for males, which stimulated in vivo gender tests followed by abortion of female fetuses, has produced a shortage of women at marrying age. Now we are seeing responses as varied as urban young women demanding good educations and being choosy about husbands, to the sale of kidnapped girls as brides in remote and impoverished areas.

Total Fertility of Chinese Women	
1965	6.5
1970	6.3
1980	2.6
1985	2.3

Women in Confucian China

The Chinese theory of gender differentiation is founded not in biology—a man's body, a woman's body—but in a more fundamental polarity, that of yin and yang, the complementary binary opposites that are the dynamic of the entire cosmos. The ten thousand things come swirling into existence through the tumbling energy of yin and yang. Gender is only one category of existence; yin is everything dark, cold, female, coarse, water, earth; yang is everything light, bright, heat, male, fire, heaven. Even the soul has a yin part, the *po*, the heavy, material, fetid part that sinks into the earth with the decaying body, capable of becoming an angry ghost; and a yang part, *hun*, the light, spiritual part that floats heavenward and becomes a beneficent ancestor. Male and female bodies, natures, and appropriate social roles all follow from this cosmic dynamic. The rightness of male authority, of patriarchy, is thus derivative of the dominance of the strong, active principle of male yang over the passive gentleness of yin.

This is not to say that gender relations have been unchanging throughout Chinese history, or that they ride above the flux of changing political and economic realities; gender is as susceptible to reconstruction as other domains of culture. We will look at the way in which the nature of the ideal female, and thus the life experience of actual Chinese women, began to change during Song dynasty, producing a pattern in late imperial times a good deal more extreme than in earlier periods.

As we have already seen, various changes in state policy nurtured an ever more defined patrilineal and patriarchal thrust in Chinese society. The spread of surnames aided the remembering of kinship bonds through males, with a corresponding weakening of bonds through female lines. Neo-Confucian revaluation of ancestor worship spread patrilineality more broadly through elite classes and even among commoners, ritually reinforcing ever larger patrilineal descent groups. Confucian values supported by state regulation vested ownership of land in fathers and sons. This Confucian world was a "world authored by men," in C. Fred Blake's phrase (Blake 1994); everything that strengthened it rendered women correspondingly "other" and outside the structure.

For example, patrilineality often renders women nameless and identityless. There is no pool of personal names (like Jim, Shelly, Brad, . . .); everyone gets a surname (Cheng, Li, Wang, etc.) plus two individual names that are generally poetic, descriptive, or even political: Blue Sky, Lotus Blossom, East [is] Red. In a study of naming customs in rural Hong Kong, *New Territories* (1986), Rubie Watson found that men gain a variety of names over a lifetime; a diviner may recommend adding wood, fire, or another element to the name of a sickly child to strengthen him. A man takes a marriage name in a ceremony on the first day of wedding rites. He may earn a nickname from the community that interacts with him; at middle age, if he is successful, he may acquire other names, called courtesy (*hao*) names; and a great man receives additional honorific names at death. These names convey a man's many public identities and achievements; they are recorded on his tablets and in lineage genealogies and so remembered by posterity. But for women, identity is different. A woman is given a name at the age of one month, which ceases to be used when she marries. At marriage, as her husband receives his marriage name, she learns all the kinship terms in her husband's family and will henceforth be called by kinship terms. Her name may never be written down, not on birth certificates or legal documents nor in genealogies or ancestral tablets; it often is not clear what characters would be used if her name *were* to be written down. In old age she is known as *ah po* ("old woman"); when she dies, only her father's surname is written on her tablet ("Family of Lim"). Not even a name survives as testimony of her existence as a person.

The decline in the status of women during Song received further impetus after the conquest of China by the Mongols. The same reforms that brought social conservatism and new preoccupation with Confucian rituals focused moral concern on women. A new cult of women's purity urged widows not to remarry; exhorted women not to read novels, watch dramas, or go out in public; extolled female self-sacrifice in widespread morality tales; encouraged ultrafeminization of women; and supported a widening custom of footbinding. The causes of these changes were various and are in dispute among scholars, but a few likely causes can be mentioned.

The successful Mongol invasion of the thirteenth century, followed by the Manchu invasion in the seventeenth century, each resulting in alien dynasties, put Han Chinese culture on the defensive and generated various cultural responses, as we have seen. What did it mean to be Chinese against Mongol and Manchu rulers? Of what did Chinese cultural superiority consist, if not the political strength to resist invasion? Neo-Confucianism was in part a nativist movement hoping to draw power from the te, the moral strength of the Classical Age. New notions of both maleness and femaleness emerged, according to Patricia Ebrey; male models characterized by barbarian men were replaced by a new literati male "who could be refined, bookish, contemplative, or artistic but need not be strong, quick, or dominating" (Ebrey 1990:221). Hunting declined in popularity. As males moved toward the "effeminate" pole, women became even more delicate, reticent, and stationary. And women became visible symbols of Han identity, vulnerable to rape and pillage by aggressive, ultramasculine warrior cultures.

A recognizable genre emerged in late Ming: the young heroine who is dedicated to Confucian virtues and undergoes horrific ordeals in their defense. Katherine Carlitz retells some of these stories in *Desire, Danger, and the Body: Stories of Women's Virtue in Late Ming China* (1994). In a fifteenth-century play called *Five Relationships Completed and Perfected* a concubine traveling to join her master is captured by an invader who demands her in marriage. Her mother exclaims that no Chinese can marry a barbarian; she bites her finger, writes a poem of fidelity in blood, then drowns herself. A late Ming wife, touched on the arm by a bandit, bites off and spits out the flesh of her arm. These motifs were not random themes; a Qing dynasty bibliography lists thirty-six thousand stories of virtuous women, one third of whom committed suicide or were murdered while resisting rape.

There were not just stories, but actually recorded increases in suicide among women. In 1405, a Confucian conduct book for women included detailed instructions on self-immolation. Thirty-eight concubines committed suicide at the death of the first Ming emperor. Resisting rape and resisting pressures to remarry were other idealized reasons for committing suicide. As Carlitz argues, "woman's body is a site or theater used by the imperium to constitute itself, asserting the impenetrability of its borders, undergirding the idealized Chinese pyramid of loyalties" (Carlitz 1994:104). Woman's body was "a site where the drama of resistance to invasion could be acted out."

But the most renowned stage for the enacting of culture on the woman's body in late imperial China was the foot. In western Hunan, little girls, like little boys, were presented with writing brushes. For the boy, it represented the beginning of his life as a reader, writer, scholar, speaker: the power of the word. For the girl, it signified the tiny points of her three-inch "lotus blossom" feet as they would look when finished at puberty: the power of her body when fully refashioned for her role in the Confucian household. Daughters, like sons, submitted to a Confucian world of obedience, self-discipline, and self-sacrifice for the larger group. A Confucian proverb encouraged mothers to oversee both protracted struggles: "If you care for your son, care not that he suffers in his studies. If you care for your daughter, care not that she suffers in her feet" (Blake 1994). But boys suffered to join in the authoring of the world; girls suffered to submit to it.

The custom of footbinding may have begun among dancers during Song dynasty. In one of the earliest references, eleventh-century writer Su Shih found a dancer's bound feet objects of wonder and wanted to hold them in his hand to get a better look. The foot was deformed to feed male erotic fancy; it took years of "painful, bloody, and terrifying labor [to make] the brute nature of her feet materialize into an object of beauty, mystery, and discipline" (Blake 1994:688). A man longed to touch the "golden lotus" of his lover; sexual play included kissing and nibbling on the curved toe; he might wash her feet or sip wine from her three-inch slipper. He rhapsodized over them as "bamboo shoots in winter."

The girl's ordeal finished about the time she reached puberty, and thus was a prelude to sexual maturation. It was thought to enhance fertility by concentrating blood in the upper legs and pelvis, working like pruning of trees to concentrate the sap for production of fruit. Soon she was ready for marriage in a family of good standing, and it was this essential goal of making a good match that impelled a woman to inflict such pain on her daughter. It was not overtly the eroticism of the bound foot, but the virtue of a disciplined daughter that neo-Confucianism valued. Women were so severely crippled by footbinding that they could barely walk; it served much the same function as parda in India, keeping women invisible inside the family compound and their virtue incontestable.

The practice that began as a trademark of dancers, something like the Western ballerina's painfully acquired grace on a single point, was by

7.7 Toes Like Dead Caterpillars

Born into an old-fashioned family at P'ing-hsi, I was inflicted with the pain of foot-binding when I was seven years old. . . Binding started in the second lunar month; mother consulted references in order to select an auspicious day for it. I wept and hid in a neighbor's home, but mother found me, scolded me, and dragged me home. She shut the bedroom door, boiled water, and from a box withdrew binding, shoes, knife, needle, and thread. . . . She washed and placed alum on my feet and cut the toenails. She then bent my toes toward the plantar with a binding cloth ten feet long and two inches wide, doing the right foot first and then the left. She finished binding and ordered me to walk, but when I did the pain proved unbearable.

That night, mother wouldn't let me remove the shoes. My feet felt on fire and I couldn't sleep; mother struck me for crying. On the following days, I tried to hide but was forced to walk on my feet. Mother hit me on my hands and feet for resisting. Beatings and curses were my lot for covertly loosening the wrappings. The feet were washed and rebound after three or four days, with alum added. After several months, all toes but the big one were pressed against the inner surface. Whenever I ate fish or freshly killed meat, my feet would swell, and the pus would drip. Mother criticized me for placing pressure on the heel in walking, saying that my feet would never assume a pretty shape. Mother would remove the bindings and wipe the blood and pus which dripped from my feet. She told me that only with removal of the flesh could my feet become slender. If I mistakenly punctured a sore, the blood gushed like a stream. My somewhat-fleshy big toes were bound with small pieces of cloth and forced upwards, to assume a new moon shape.

Every two weeks, I changed to new shoes. Each new pair was one- to two-tenths of an inch smaller than the previous one. The shoes were unyielding, and it took pressure to get into them. Though I wanted to sit passively by the *k'ang*, Mother forced me to move around. After changing more than ten pairs of shoes, my feet were reduced to a little over four inches. I had been binding for a month when my younger sister started; when no one was around, we would weep together. In summer, my feet smelled offensively because of pus and blood; in winter, my feet felt cold because of lack of circulation and hurt if they got too near the k'ang and were struck by warm air currents. Four of the toes were curled in like so many dead caterpillars; no outsider would ever have believed that they belonged to a human being. It took two years to achieve the three-inch model. My toenails pressed against the flesh like thin paper. The heavily-creased plantar couldn't be scratched when it itched or soothed when it ached. My shanks were thin, my feet became humped, ugly, and odoriferous; how I envied the natural-footed!

Quoted in Howard S. Levy, 1967, pp. 26–28.

In this early photograph, two Chinese women delicately reveal the tiny points of their "golden lotus" feet. A three-inch foot was achieved only with years of painful binding of the feet of young girls, which resulted in breaking the arch and the loss of several toes (see next photo). Beautiful hand-made slippers, often with tiny round "high heels" as seen here, were worn by women who could barely walk.

1900 practiced among all classes of Chinese, even spreading among farm families, where, although a woman's labor was needed, her feet were bound anyway as a sign of beauty and virtue, forcing her to a lifetime of painful hobbling as she swept her courtyard, carried rice and babies, spun, embroidered, and wove. In one study of 1,736 women in 515 families in a network of rural villages north of the Yellow River, 99.2 percent of women born before 1890 had bound feet. In southern China, on the other hand, footbinding was actively resisted by peasants as impractical and pretentious.

However, it would be misleading to focus so heavily on these customs that we miss other aspects of women's lives in traditional China. While it may be true that obedience, self-sacrifice, and purity were emphasized by neo-Confucians, and that submission to male authority was both idealized and demanded, recent scholars have looked beyond these restricting social structures to the accomplishments of women artists, poets, and writers within them. The Confucian literati was not guilty of ignoring women's contributions either, but praised them among them-

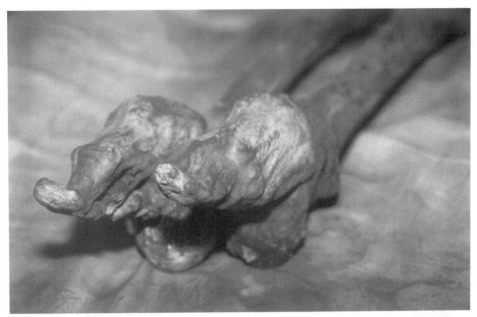

In the fourteenth or fifteenth century, a military officer died and was buried in his uniform. His concubine was strangled, her forehead was bashed in, and she was buried with him in the same coffin. He was in his sixties and she in her twen- ties. She had "golden lotuses," and this unusual photograph allows a view of the skeletal changes wrought by the binding of feet.

selves and included them in their many voluminous catalogs of poetry and art.

Members of the literati who served in the government or at least prepared for official careers often did educate their daughters, even though those young women were not eligible for the examinations and the government careers that were the aim of education for males. Chinese culture valued the private life spent in scholarly or artistic pursuit for both men and women; bureaucrats dreamed of retiring to become private men of letters, even while women were born to it. In the field of painting, the work of amateurs was considered superior to professional painting, which meant that women could become accomplished artists and gain fame by the same route as the scholar-official who painted, wrote poetry, or did calligraphy.

After the sixteenth century there were rising female literacy rates and women both wrote and enjoyed novels, poetry, and plays. Susan Mann documents a lengthy debate in the late eighteenth century on what women should learn, and why. Some women were writing poetry admired by men who were attracted to female sensuality. "Whether in the palace or in pleasure boats, whether at courier outposts or in the heart of the court, women's talents were mainly devoted to singing and dancing, all to please men," complained one critic (Mann 1994:31). But many other women poets were writing about their own lives as gentry women; the subject of death in childbirth, from illness, and by suicide recurs in women's writings in the eighteenth century. Mature women plumbed emotions born of empty marriages and cloistered lives. There was a "poetry of desire" that lifted women from their actual lives to imagined lives. Even very young women and girls earned fame as poets and lived writers' lives. The poet Jin Yi brought her inkstone and brushes into her marriage as part of her dowry and within a few days turned the bedroom into a study.

Women of literati households formed poetry and painting societies, such as the Banana Garden Poetry Society formed in early Qing in Hangzhou by Gu Yurui. They were painters as well as poets; Xu Can, one member, painted female figures, images of the goddess Guanyin, flowers, and plants. Ju Qing, member of a famous painting family in nineteenth-century Guangdong, captured a mood of tranquility and leisure in *Lady with Fan*.

8
JAPAN

Chronology of Japanese History

2000	**Jomon Period**	hunting and gathering 660–585 Legendary first emperor, Jinmu (?) 350 B.C. Introduction of wet-rice cultivation
250 B.C.	**Yayoi Period** (ca. 250 B.C.–A.D. 250)	Bronze bells
250 A.D.	**Old Tombs Period** **[Kofun]** (250–552)	Protohistoric period A.D. 183–248 Queen Himiko (297 Chinese text describes Queen Himiko) monumental tombs building of Ise Shrine
552	**Asuka Period** (552–645)	Yamato State 552 Arrival of Buddhism from Paekche (Korea) 574–622 Prince Shotoku 607 First embassy to China
647	**Nara Period** (645–794)	645 Taika Reform 645–710 "Era of Great Change" 710 Founding of Nara 712—*Kojiki* 720—*Nihon Shoku*
794	**Heian Period** (794–1185)	794 Founding of Kyoto Assimilation of Buddhism 837 End of embassies to China Murasaki Shikibu, *The Tale of Genji* 1180–1185 Gempei War
1185	**Kamakura Period** (1185–1333)	1185 Founding of Shogunate Eisai (1141–1215) brings Zen Buddhism to Japan
1333	**Nambokucho Period** (1333–1392)	
1392	**Muromachi Period** (1392–1573)	1467–1477 Onin War 1549 Francis Xavier Arrives in Japan 1568 Invasion of Kyoto by Oda Nobunaga
1573	**Momoyama Period** (1573–1615)	
1615	**Edo Period [Tokugawa]** (1615–1868)	Beginning of Early Modern Period 1853 Arrival of Admiral Perry 1868 End of shogunate 1877 Satsuma Rebellion
1868	**Modern Period** (1868–Present)	

A t first glance at a map of Japan, three thousand islands (but four main ones) strung along the 135th and 140th lines of east longitude and swinging westward toward Korea in the south, suggests a north-south axis, but the Japanese have always thought of their history unfolding east to west. The 35th parallel falls just south of Tokyo, cuts right through Kyoto, skims the lowest tip of Korea, and then cuts westward across China's ancient capitals: Kaifeng, Lo-yang, and Chang-an (Xian). (Beijing rides higher on the 40th latitude.) Latitude-wise, at least, ancient Japan and ancient China were on a par.

The drama of Japanese history was enacted on two main geographical stages, a western one with a Kyoto focus and an eastern one with a Tokyo focus. The western region is the most ancient, woven into the mythology of a Sun Goddess who sends her grandson to the southern island of Kyushu, carrying rice shoots; his grandson conquers northeast through the Inland Sea (the Seto Sea) to the coastal shores of Honshu at modern Osaka, and then inland to the Nara Basin. The Yamato River drains this region from eastern hills where sacred mountains rise, and gives its name to the highlands known as the Yamato Peninsula; beyond them toward the sunrise, at the eastern coast, is a sacred place called Ise. From Osaka Bay to Ise is the oldest heartland of Japanese culture. For many centuries, rice cultivation went no further north than modern Nagoya. But by the twelfth century, a new, vigorous provincial society had emerged in the west, where later extensions of rice cultivation had made the land valuable to people from court. Land had value in those days only to the extent there were peasants to make it produce; the fertile regions lying in a rough oval with modern Tokyo at the bottom, by the twelfth century supported an aristocratic rural elite, many of them descendants of junior lines of the imperial family with names like Taira and Minamoto. Kyoto in the west was culturally refined, spiritually rich with many sects of Buddhism and Shinto temples, but effete and without even a standing army. Tokyo did not yet exist, but there in the region known as the Kanto, powerful military leaders and a class of aristocratic warriors established a second center of power. Until 1867 a dual system of government and an increasingly complex culture fused into the modern society that, after the transformations of the Meiji Period, made Japan the richest and most powerful Asian nation of the twentieth century.

THE YAMATO STATE

At the time of the Qin Unification, 221 B.C., Japan's southern regions had had wet-rice agriculture less than a century and a half; the population growth that accompanies intensive agriculture was only beginning; the emergence of any social formation we would want to call a state was still several hundred years off. The Japanese could not yet write down the stories of their temperamental deities, Amaterasu, the Sun Goddess, or Susa no O, the god of storms, because no one had invented a script for their language.

During these centuries, the Chinese were diligently writing about all matter of practical things, as we have seen, among them the various barbarians on their borders. Among the eastern barbarians were the Wa people who occupied mountainous islands to the southeast of their Chinese commandery at Tai-feng (now Inchon in Korea). The Chinese got a closer look at Japan after the breakup of Han dynasty, when the brief Wei dynasty exchanged emissaries with the islands to the east; shortly after, China broke down into several centuries of disorder and the record goes dead. They knew about many "countries" in the islands, and in the book *Wei zhi*, composed by Chen Shou-you in A.D. 297, we get a fascinating account of the largest of these, a place called Yamatai ruled by a Queen Himiko. Her name meant "sun-shaman" or "shamaness of the sun" (*hi* = sun; *miko* = shaman), and she occupied herself with magic and sorcery, remained unmarried, and was served by a thousand female attendants. The only male allowed to come near her was her brother, who served her food and drink and assisted her in ruling the country. Her palace was surrounded by lookout towers and stockades manned by armed guards.

Queen Himiko was involved in disputes with rival rulers, and in this context she sent a delegation to Tai-feng to request an audience at the court of Lo-yang, the Wei capital. In 239, the Wei emperor Ming received her delegation and issued an edict in which he acknowledged her as a vassal state, bestowing on her the title of "Queen of Wa friendly to Wei" (see box 8.1). As signs of their sovereign-vassal relationship, they exchanged gifts of slaves, silk, swords, jade, gold, and bronze mirrors. A few years later Himiko made use of this relationship by asking for Chinese support in her dispute with the king of Kunu, whereupon China sent an officer to mediate, who stayed in Wa for a number of years. Himiko died in 248 and was buried in a mounded tomb 145 meters in diameter, accompanied in death by a hundred slaves. A man succeeded her, but could not maintain order, and so was replaced by a thirteen-year-old girl, a shamaness like Himiko, whose legitimacy was acknowledged by the Wei court with further exchange of gifts. With that, the Chinese record ends.

Queen Himiko lived at the end of the period defined by Japanese scholars as Yayoi (250 B.C.–A.D. 250) and just before Kofun, or the "Old

8.1   Edict to Queen Himiko from Emperor Ming A.D. 239

Herein we address Himiko, queen of Wa, whom we now officially call a friend of Wei. The governor of Tai-fang, Liu Hsia, has sent a messenger to accompany your vassal, Nanshomai, and his lieutenant, Toshi Gyuri. They have arrived here with your tribute, consisting of four male slaves and six female slaves, together with two pieces of patterned cloth, each twenty feet in length. You live very far away across the sea; yet you have sent an embassy with tribute. Your loyalty and filial piety we appreciate exceedingly. We confer upon you, therefore, the title of "queen of Wa friendly to Wei," together with the decoration of the gold seal with purple ribbon. The latter, properly encased, is to be sent to you through the governor. We expect you, O Queen, to rule your people in peace and to endeavor to be devoted and obedient.

Your ambassadors, Nanshomai and Gyuri, who have come from afar, must have had a long and fatiguing journey. We have, therefore, given to Nanshomai an appointment as commandant in the imperial guard. We also bestow upon them the decoration of the silver seal with blue ribbon. We have granted them audience in appreciation of their visit, before sending them home with gifts. The gifts are these: five pieces of crimson brocade with dragon designs, ten pieces of crimson tapestry with dappled pattern, fifty lengths of bluish red fabric, and fifty lengths of dark blue fabric. These are in return for what you sent as tribute. As a special gift, we bestow upon you three pieces of blue brocade with interwoven characters, five pieces of tapestry with delicate floral designs, fifty lengths of white silk, eight taels of gold, two swords five feet long, one hundred bronze mirrors, and fifty catties each of jade and of red beads. All these things are sealed in boxes and entrusted to Nanshomai and Gyuri. When they arrive and you acknowledge their receipt, you may exhibit them to your countrymen in order to demonstrate that our country thinks so much of you as to bestow such exquisite gifts upon you.

Okazaki Takashi, 1993, p. 288.

Tombs" Period (250–552). This was the crucial period of state formation, documented archaeologically and in Chinese texts, though there are no contemporary Japanese accounts. There are, however, two extraordinarily important Japanese chronicles written 170 years after the end of the period, the *Kojiki* (A.D. 712) and the *Nihon shoki* (A.D. 720), which describe events of this era in important detail but also link it to the origins of the cosmos, the gods, and the Japanese islands, making the accounts problematic for historians and archaeologists. Mysteriously, there is not a hint of a Queen Himiko. Could the *Nihon shoki*, a huge work in twenty-eight books that describes the reigns of each "emperor" from Jinmu in 660 B.C. to the sixth century A.D., have forgotten a powerful queen with ties to China who lived a mere five hundred years earlier? Or was something else going on? We will return to this question later.

Archaeologists studying the Japan of the Yayoi and Kofun periods find the largest polities on the island of Kyushu and the southern regions

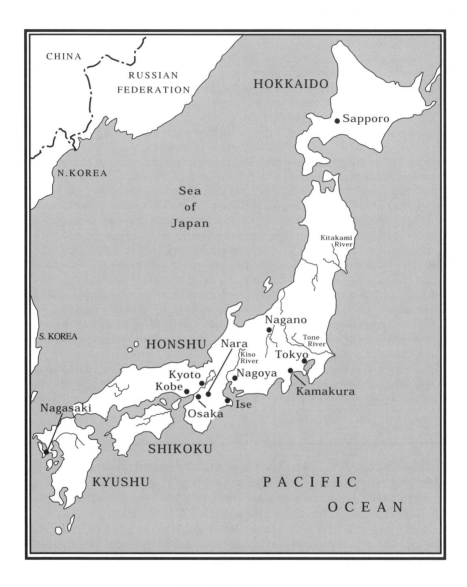

Map 8.1   Japan

of Honshu below the rough line demarcating the northern limit of rice cultivation (see map 8.1). This is not surprising, since rice cultivation, probably introduced from the Yangtze region of coastal China around 350 B.C., would have permitted population increase and thus the need for more complex forms of social organization. The diffusion of peoples and culture traits to the islands is a topic with little agreement and even political consequences today. We know that a very ancient people, the Ainu, were probably the islands' earliest settlers, though how and from where is unknown. Their remnants now are mostly located in the far northern island of Hokkaido. The people now known as the Japanese have close linguistic affinities with the Korean language, and the most logical route of settlement appears to have been through Korea to Kyushu, then a northward progression in claiming the entire chain. However, a look at the broad curve of China's coast and the islands just eastward suggest other possible sources of settlers in the distant past. Just as populations of southern China settled in Taiwan, taking rice cultivation with them, then moved south into the Philippines (at least on linguistic evidence; see chapter 3), there is reason to suppose that the Ryukyus, Okinawa, and Japan itself may also have received immigrants from the Chinese coast. Early ethnologists went further, pursuing similarities between certain Japanese cultural traits and similar ones in the Melanesian and Micronesian Islands and even among the Northwest Coast Indians, though such questions are long out of fashion.

It is possible that the rival domains evidenced by Queen Himiko's armed watchtowers and her petition to the court of Wei consisted of peoples of some ethnic diversity. Rival polities were thickest in the coasts and inland basins of the Inland Sea (Seto), the waterway separating Kyushu, Shikoku, and the southern peninsulas of Honshu. The archaeological record for the protohistorical period suggests the existence of two distinct cultural spheres, Western Seto (mostly Kyushu) and Eastern Seto (mostly lower Honshu). In Eastern Seto, cultural remains include hilltop settlements with large numbers of bronze bells; a kind of flat ax; and incised, comb-decorated pottery. In Western Seto the pottery style is not found, nor are hilltop settlements; the ax type is socketed, not flat, along with socketed bronze spearheads. The dead were buried with grave goods (though not in Eastern Seto), and there is jar and dolmen burial, also not found in Eastern Seto but common in Korea. Eventually it would be in Eastern Seto where the historic kingdom of Yamato would emerge in the Nara Basin (just inland from modern Osaka), but that was after several centuries of attacks and counterattacks between the two regions.

In the gap between Queen Himiko in the third century and the powerful Empress Suiko (r. 592–628) who reestablished relations with China in the early seventh century, the Yamato State flourished. Its center in the beginning was the Nara Basin, a region of 720 sq. km. from crest to crest of the fringing mountains. The Yamato River drains the basin into Osaka Bay directly to the west. Five peaks rise from the circle of hills; in the southeast are the "three peaks of Yamato," important in Fujiwara times, but the most important one, then and now, is Mt. Miwa. Early on, the Yamato kings established ritual ties with local deities, the *kami*, probably carrying on very ancient folk beliefs and practices but now investing them with political significance. The kami of Mt. Miwa spoke to kings through royal women, even as Himiko had had paranormal connections to the kami. The *Nihon shoki* tells of a love affair between the kami of Mt. Miwa and princess Yamato Totohi Momoso. And emperor Sujin received a revelation from a kami transmitted to him through a princess demanding worship to avoid future calamities. The *Kojiki* tells of a sacred marriage of the Miwa kami to a female relative of an early Yamato king from whom was born a son who founded the Miwa line of kings and worshipped the Mt. Miwa kami (Brown 1993:117–18). Shrine attendants later at Ise were called miko (shamaness) and were unmarried imperial princesses, like Himiko herself. Even today, young unmarried girls called miko dance for the kami at village shrines on festival occasions.

As the Yamato state became more vigorous, new institutions emerged that further strengthened it. One of these was the development of powerful clans, called *uji*, among the chieftains close to the king. Some of these uji took on specialized functions in relation to the king; for instance, the eldest son of Emperor Suinin founded the Mononobe clan, which became the military arm of the kingdom, while his younger brother became Emperor Keiko. This military arm made expeditions northward and carried out strikes against Korea over several centuries of successful expansion. They had their own kami cult at Isonokami, whose worship included weapons as the shrine's principal treasures. At the Isonokami storehouse today is a famous slightly rusted, gold-inlaid sword called the *shichishito,* or the "seven-pronged sword." A high priest at the Isonokami shrine in 1873 discovered it had inscriptions on it, which turned out to bear a date, A.D. 369, and a statement that it was forged in Paekche (Korea) for presentation to the king of Yamato. Unfortunately, seven of the characters were too rusty to read, the very ones which would clarify whether the gift was tribute to a superior state or a token of honor bestowed on an inferior state.

The uji were once thought to have been the original kinship grouping of the Japanese, but that view is now outmoded. Just as we saw in China, where large lineages only came into existence in certain kinds of economic and political contexts, so the uji came into existence after the fifth century among expansive elite families who were branching out to control ever larger and more distant areas. In the Nara Basin, each clan appears to have had its own territory. As clans acquired territory, the kami residing there and associated with the region came to be honored and claimed as the tutelary deities of the uji and were sometimes even claimed as ancestors. Thus, primitive Shinto was expanded and incorporated into the growing hierarchy of the Yamato state.

Men of the elite uji were granted honors according to the *kabane* system of titles, the highest being "great *omi.*" These titled families all had kinship ties to the Yamato king; families who gave daughters in marriage to the king would be grandfathers and cousins of the next king, their powers magnified. Beneath the elite uji, and supporting them, were occupational specialist groups, or guilds, known as *be*, who monopolized skills like ironworking, horse training, and weapons manufacture. These were the population units exploited for extraction of goods and services by the court. The term "be" is a Korean loanword first used for Korean artisans, such as a group of scribes who were the first to bring literacy to Japan. Even clan names sometimes came to possess the suffix -be, such as the high-ranking Mononobe, the military clan.

Shinto, Folk and Imperial

The woods, streams, mountains, and coasts of Japan are not only lovely but sacred, according to the most ancient spiritual ideas of Japanese tradition. In natural spaces beyond the household and village, there are powers and spirits both life-giving and dangerous, which live alongside and overlap the lives of humans. This is the realm of the kami:

> This other world is variously placed—across the sea, in the woods or hills or mountains—but in any case beyond the normal purview of civilized humanity. It is from the other world that fertility is introduced in the spring, and it is against the chaotic forces of this other world that various seasonal rites are invoked. It is, then, the prototypical locus of unrefined power according to the horizontal worldview of traditional Japan. The other world that I am referring to is the locus and source of extraordinary, unpredictable power, both constructive and destructive, and it is the regulation of intercourse with this other world that lies at the heart of all popular festival. (Gilday 1993:276)

Archaeology attests to ancient continuities with historic Shinto assumptions. Sacred sites are marked in the archaeological record by caches of bronze bells, which were ceremonial instruments in the Nara Basin in Yayoi and Kofun times. They are invariably found on hilltops overlooking plains and fertile agricultural land. The bells were ornamented with signs of prosperity: storehouses, grain pounding, and hunting of boar and deer (Barnes 1988:176). The distribution of the bells suggests they were the focus of community ritual activities, even as Shinto shrines today are centers of communal festivals, *matsuri*. But why are they located so far from human communities? What is their relation to human communities? The Chinese character for the word "shrine" (*mori*) includes the character for "woods" or "forest." Often there is no structure at all, for it is the space itself—e.g., Mt. Miwa—that is the kami. But there will invariably be the ubiquitous marker of a sacred space, a simple gate—or sometimes many of them, forming a tunnel up a hillside to a sacred spot—in the famous shape of the *torii* that has come to symbolize Japan itself in some ways (see box 8.2, "Encounter with a Kami").

An eighth-century provincial gazetteer, the *Hitachi Fudoki*, is among the oldest documentary sources on folk Shinto in early Japan. It tells of a legend associated with the first encroachment of human farmers into the wild lands of the kami. A cultivator named Matachi went to work clearing new land for rice fields. But this land was the home of terrible horned serpents, the *Yato no kami*, who attempted to halt this expansion of the human domain. So Matachi put on his armor and went to battle against them, driving them back to the surrounding hills. Then he dug a ditch at the foot of the hills and placed boundary stakes to mark the division, saying: "Above this line shall be the land of the kami; below it shall be the rice-fields of humans." But he built them a shrine and promised to serve them forever to prevent their curses, which, according to *Hitachi Fudoki*, his descendants were still faithfully doing (Gilday 1993).

Gilday describes a cycle of rituals in Hiroshima Prefecture in which the ancient patterns are still visible. It begins in the spring after the rice fields have stood silent and barren throughout the winter. The kami are invited from the hills to the sanctuary zone at the edge of the village, and then into the rice fields where essential exchanges between kami and humans can take place. In Shinto, rice itself is sacred; each rice grain has a soul and rice is alive in its hull. The soul of the rice grain is identified as a kami called *Uka no kami* (Ohnuki-Tierney 1993). Of all grains, rice alone requires ritual performances. Each planting season, the power of the kami must be lured into the rice fields and brought to fruition in the summer crop, which transfers the power (*nigimitama*) of the kami to the growing rice, and thus to humans who must eat rice to live. Therefore, essential interconnections of kami and humans have their most crucial intersection in rice cultivation. The festivals (matsuri) honoring the kami are human gifts to them; the kami give back life in the form of rice.

Come summer, the nigimitama of the kami has nourished the young rice shoots and has brought the monsoons, raising the humidity; life is swelling and bursting everywhere, including among insect populations that pester people and threaten the rice crops. The kami can overdo it, and in fact there is always danger as well as blessing in the presence of the kami. Throughout rural Japan there is a midsummer festival known as *musi-okuri*, the Bug Festival. There are local variations in how this festival is enacted, but their goal is to expel the pests that threaten the fields. The entire community and sometimes neighboring hamlets and even towns cooperate in the festivities. Certain elements of these Shinto festivals will be the same: an effigy of the kami is made and presented at the shrine where the kami—often a named figure such as Sanemori—resides, luring him out with splendid and noisy celebration with drums, flutes, and bells. The major actors are the Shinto priests and musician-dancers

8.2   Encounter with a Kami

On the outskirts of southern Kyoto lies the shrine of Fushimi Inari, where my intention as a first-time tourist to Japan was to climb to the top of a sacred mountain belonging to a spirit involved with rice and fire. As I passed through the grounds of the old shrine at the base of the mountain, it was obvious where the trail began—thousands upon thousands of vermilion-painted torii archways formed a shadowy tunnel twisting up the wooded side of the mountain. Though I knew next to nothing about the history of the place or even of the "religion" called Shinto, I was nevertheless astounded at the extravagance of religious devotion enabling the donation of so many archways.

After nearly thirty minutes of steady climbing, pausing here and there to watch a variety of worshippers make offerings of large smoky candles at wayside altars, I began to look forward to the coming glimpse of sky once the archways, less dense now than at the beginning of the trail, came to an end. I was not sure what I would find, but earlier climbs on other mountains associated with religious institutions had shown there was usually some small building housing or honoring the divinity, along with a sweeping view of the lowlands— a view which was, after all, my main purpose in making the ascent in the first place. The trail finally culminated with a huge stone torii nearly twenty feet high and I walked out under the open sky again, but the building I had expected was oddly absent. I felt disappointed because now I would lack a good photograph to distinguish this mountaintop from the others I had been to.

Even when I looked closely at the spot where other climbers had clustered— some of them in business suits, others in mountaineering knickers and hiking boots, and still others in skirts and high heels—I could not discern why they were drawn to what appeared to be a simple stone cairn. It was not until I was standing behind them that I finally saw atop the stones a round mirror tilted slightly toward the sky, reflecting the late-afternoon's silver-rimmed clouds as they rode a wind from the Inland Sea toward the blue mountains bordering Lake Biwa. Then suddenly it dawned on me—so *this* is what Shinto holds as divine! Not a text or dubious miracles or what someone maybe said or a particular structure but the *actual phenomena* of the world itself. If seen from a more level vantage point, the mirror of this open-air altar would show the climber's own face, as well as the path he or she had just traveled to enter the shrine (which was, as it turned out in this particular case, the *entire mountain*). My understanding was intellectual, of course, and not emotional in a way that might have led me to enact the same intense petitioning as the Japanese I watched bowing, chanting, and, in some instances, weeping before the mirror, but I felt I had some tiny grasp of what the Kami might signify and what part of the nebulous social and cultural reality called Shinto might be about.

John K. Nelson, 1996, pp. 25–27.

whose performance is to entertain the kami. They circle the temple precincts or parade through village streets and out into rice fields, carrying the effigy and waving banners and poles that purify the spaces they move through and dispatch the bugs. The procession may end at a stream, where the effigy is thrown in, or it may be transferred to the next village and then the next until it ends at the sea.

These antipestilence festivals are found as early as the Nara Period, when people suffered from a variety of things that have always plagued people: pests that ruin the crops, epidemics that bring disease and death, warfare and violence that cause untimely death. These various plagues were somehow equated in the popular mind, so that swarming insects and malevolent spirits bitter about their unexpected deaths all needed to be controlled by community ritual action enlisting the powers of the kami.

In the Nara Period, Shinto began to do another kind of work for the body politic. A variant form of Shinto was created by the Yamato court to provide a cosmological underpinning for the imperial line's authority to rule. In one of the great accomplishments in the history of the premodern state, myth, legend, and political ambition were pulled together into a single text that for fifteen hundred years was accepted as political doctrine and cosmological truth, and played a significant role in the astonishing continuity of the imperial family down to Emperor Akihito, the present 125th emperor of Japan. This text was the *Nihon shoki* ("Chronicles of Japan"). A Korean scholar named Wani had arrived from Paekche early in the fifth century, bringing eleven volumes of Chinese books, including *Analects* and the *Thousand-Character Sutra*; i.e., Confucian and Buddhist texts. Another of his books may have been the *Shi Ji* of Sima Qian. Then or later, the *Shi Ji* gave the Japanese court the idea of a dynastic history that tells the story of the past—as they want it told. They must have recognized the tremendous power that lies in the writing of history and the prestige that histories can give to kings, living and dead. But, if scholarly independence of mind is evident in Sima Qian's history, where some rulers were praised, others vilified, and all by a mere scholar who watched from the sidelines, inserting his own personality into the text, these flaws were not allowed to mar the *Nihon shoki*. It reveals nothing of its authors' personalities but is an official version of the past written by several imperial princes and a staff of ten, completed and presented to Empress Gensho in A.D. 720.

The following summarizes the basic mythology for an Imperial Shinto:

In the beginning the world was in a state of chaos, but gradually the light particles of matter rose to form heaven and the heavy particles settled to become the earth. Kami materialized and, after the passage of seven generations, the brother and sister gods Izanagi and Izanami were instructed to create a "drifting land." Izanagi thrust his spear into the ocean below, and as he withdrew it, brine dripping from the tip formed a small island. Izanagi and Izanami proceeded together by means of a heavenly bridge to the island and there begot the remainder of the islands of Japan and a vast number of other deities. In the process of giving birth to the fire deity, Izanami was badly burned and descended to the nether world. Izanagi went to fetch her but was so repelled by the appearance of Izanami's decaying and maggot-infested body that he hastily retreated. To purify himself, Izanagi went to a stream and, as he disrobed and cleansed his body, he produced a new flock of kami. Among these were the Sun Goddess, who sprang into being as Izanagi washed his left eye, and Susa no O, the god of storms, who appeared from his nose.

The Sun Goddess was appointed to rule over the plain of high heaven, and thus became the preeminent figure in the Shinto pantheon. Her brother Susa no O was given dominion over the sea. A fretful and ill-tempered creature, Susa no O insisted upon visiting the Sun Goddess in heaven to say good-bye before taking up his post. Upon arriving in heaven, he committed a series of offenses against his sister, such as breaking down her field-dividers, destroying her looms, and defecating in her palace. Outraged, the Sun Goddess, in a solar-eclipse, secluded herself in a cave and plunged the world into darkness. To lure her out, the other deities of heaven gathered in front of her cave with laughter and merrymaking. A shamaness deity danced semi-nude, causing uproarious laughter. They hung a mirror from a branch in front of her cave and shouted that there's a superior deity out front. Curious, she peeked out and saw her own reflection. As she emerged, another kami grabbed her and dragged her out, so the universe was again bright with sunlight.

This part of the myth is filled with identifiable elements of folk Shinto. There is the horror of death and the decaying body when Izanagi tries to rescue his sister, requiring purification in the nearest stream. There are the ritual offenses that outrage the greatest kami, the Sun Goddess who threatens survival of the world when she hides in a cave. The first matsuri is held to lure her out, filled with the same kind of riotous entertainment featured at modern kami festivals.

The Sun Goddess then dispatched her grandson, Ninigi, to the "land of luxuriant rice fields," commanding him to govern it. "Go! And may prosperity attend thy dynasty, and may it, like Heaven and Earth, endure forever." To seal her command, the Sun Goddess bestowed upon Ninigi a sacred regalia: a bronze mirror, a sword, and a curved jewel. Ninigi descended from heaven to a mountaintop in southeastern Kyushu, but did little to assert his rule. His grandson Jimmu conducted a campaign in the central provinces, destroyed aboriginal enemies, performed rites to his ancestress, the Sun Goddess, and became the first emperor of Japan.

Myths must be read in the context of the cultures in which they live, as that is how they are written. The myth of Izanagi and Izanami accounts for the origin of many essential features of Shinto and of the Japanese state, and in the process of explaining origins it gives a cosmic sanction to those beliefs and ideologies. How could you overthrow a dynasty descended from the Sun Goddess Amaterasu herself? There is a political genius at work in the myth—or "mythistory"—that we might wonder about from the political cynicism of our age. It is certain, of course, that the princes and scribes who produced the thirty books of the *Nihon shoki* drew on a large body of preexisting mythology, but it is unlikely that that mythology, coming down from earlier prestate societies, would have had such a political endpoint in mind; people do not put kings in their myths before kings have emerged in their society. And the compilers of *Nihon shoki* were almost certainly guarding against any appearance in Japan of China's concept of the Mandate of Heaven, whose political repercussions were so apparent in Sima Qian's history of the fall of dynasty after dynasty that grew corrupt and were replaced by new, righteous founder-emperors. And so they have Amaterasu say: "May prosperity attend thy dynasty, and may it, like Heaven and Earth, endure forever." We see why there is no mention of any Queen Himiko, so clearly documented in Chinese sources; she was not a part of the successful ruling line; thus, she has disappeared from Japanese historical memory. Clearly this was a construction intended to validate an existing power structure, and underwrite its authority forever, as Ebersole writes:

> The legitimation of the Temmu-Jito line of the imperial family was one of the primary intentions behind the commissioning of the *Kojiki*, the *Nihon shoki*, and the *Man yoshu*. In the process of the realization of the historiographic project of the imperial family, the editors of these texts had available for their use not only written documents and various clan histories but also oral histories, myths, legends, and a large corpus of poetry. We can assume that if their history was to be believable, they could not use a crude "cut-and-paste" method with complete abandon. Rather, certain narrative structures and paradigms were culturally available when these texts were committed to writing and given their final textual form. One such structure or paradigm was the ordeal at the time of the *niiname-sai* that proved the legitimacy or illegitimacy of an individual's claim to the throne. (1989:122)

It is an early example of the "invention of tradition" that wonderfully succeeded, for the divinity of the emperor, or *tenno*, himself a living kami, has been treated as truth itself until the postwar period when Emperor Hirohito renounced all claims to divinity in 1946.

Prior to the triumph of the Yamato line, other great families had similar myths of the kami origins of their ancestors. For instance, the Mononobe clan had an ancestral kami who descended from heaven in a stone boat, bringing ten treasures, including two mirrors, a sword, jewels with magical powers, and a scarf that repelled insects. He landed on Mt. Ikaruga in Kawachi Province. Archaeology supports the ritual ties of powerful uji to sacred spots in the hills where objects like those described in the myths (bronze mirrors, swords) have been found; and many of the hill locations are still sacred. However, it was the myth version and rituals of the Yamato line that won the day—and history.

The Yamato state's competition with Korea was very much a part of the picture at that time. Sun worship was important in the Korean courts, and founders of royal lines were often named "children of the sun." The Yamato uji thus abandoned their earlier tutelary kami, Takamimusubi, and turned to a little-known deity worshipped since ancient times by fishermen. Happily, this was to the east of Nara Basin—the direction of the rising sun—and there was a spot there where fishermen worshipped Amaterasu, the sun goddess. The *Nihon shoki*'s version of what happened goes like this: Amaterasu was first worshipped in the royal palace, but in the reign of Sujin her sacred mirror (her *shintai*) was enshrined in a humble village. In the next generation a more suitable place of worship was sought, so an imperial princess was sent around the country and finally reached Ise. The Sun Goddess said she wished to be worshiped here, and so the Grand Shrine of Ise was built. The structure built for her, probably in the sixth century (though said to be the first century in the *Nihon shoki*), was anomalous at the time, for structures were not part of kami worship until Buddhism arrived with its own distinctive architecture. What kind of building would be appropriate for a kami? They settled on something that looked like a Yayoi grain storage, a simple one-room raised structure of unpainted cypress, built among tall evergreens near the Isuzu River on a double compound. Every twenty years a new shrine is built on the adjacent empty compound and the old one is destroyed. The last rebuilding was in August 1993.

The myth of Amaterasu sanctions rites of succession that have been followed right down to the death of Emperor Hirohito, the Showa Emperor, on January 7, 1989, and the installation rites of Emperor Akihito in 1990. Over fifteen hundred years have elapsed since these rituals were initiated. At several critical junctures the dynasty itself was threatened with destruction, including most recently after the defeat of Japan in World War II. The Allied powers were determined to punish Japan not only by ending its military forces but by abolishing its imperial line. It was General MacArthur who successfully argued for maintaining Hirohito as the symbol of the Japanese nation around which society could be reconstructed. The new constitution created under General MacArthur's guidance severely redefined relations between the Japanese state and the Chrysanthemum throne, making the emperor a constitutional monarch much like Elizabeth II, and prohibited any support, control, or dissemination of Shinto by the government. According to Article I, "the Emperor shall be the symbol of the State and of the unity of the people, deriving his position from the will of the people with whom resides sovereign power." Sovereignty is now invested in the people, not in the divine descendant of the Sun Goddess.

Yet the death of an old emperor and the accession of a new one could be accomplished only by the known and ancient patterns of Shinto, which were simply declared to be a private matter of the imperial household, not acts of State, even though they were extensively covered by television and attended by heads of state from all over the world, including President Bush.

In rites followed since ancient times, the initiation of an emperor goes through three stages: *senso, sokui no rei,* and *daijosai.*

Senso are the rites of accession. Immediately after the death of an emperor, the new emperor is announced, not to the people but to the Sun Goddess. In the precincts of the imperial palace there are three shrines; one to the ancestors; one to the kami; and one, portable for reasons we shall see, containing a replica of the very bronze mirror said to have been given to Ninigi by Amaterasu herself when she sent him to earth to found the Japanese royal line. The original is perpetually housed in the inner shrine at Ise. The new emperor is announced at this portable shrine, and then he receives the sacred sword and the jewel also given by Amaterasu, which have been passed down from one emperor to another since the time of Jimmu, according to the *Nihon shoki,* in 660 B.C. Prior to the 1947 constitution, the emperor also received the State seal and the Imperial seal, signifying his position as head of state. Senso concludes with the first official audience with members of court and government. Meanwhile, the body of the dead emperor still lies in state.

The mortuary rites for a dead emperor usually went on for two years, and sometimes longer, although in the case of Hirohito, he was buried a mere forty-eight days later near the final resting place of his four immediate ancestors. In ancient Japan, secondary burial was practiced. The emperor's body reposed in a specially built mortuary house (the *mogari no miya*) where the empress and all consorts and concubines, all surviving sexual partners, were secluded with him for an unspecified period. It was their role to sing laments and attempt to hold the soul (*tama*) of the emperor, for death was not seen as immediately permanent or irreversible. At the end of the mourning period, the body received its second and final burial. This practice is also alluded to in the Izanami story when

Izanagi tries to retrieve her horribly decaying body. Izanami finally closes herself in the other world by rolling a stone into the entrance; Izanagi then goes to a stream to ritually purify himself. While the dead king lay waiting for the final burial, it was often the case that the court was filled with intrigue as various claimants to the throne attempted to advance themselves; one way, apparently, was to push one's way into the mogari no miya in an effort to take possession of one of the imperial concubines.

In January 1990, the Japanese government announced that installation rites for the new emperor would be the traditional ones; sokui no rei would be on November 12, 1990, and daijosai would be the night of November 22–23, 1990. Observers were taken by surprise, since the daijosai is so clearly Shinto and certainly seems to assert the emperor's kinship with Amaterasu. This was the first opportunity to perform this rite by a new emperor since Hirohito's renunciation of divinity and the new constitution of 1947 (Crump 1991).

The sokui no rei requires an imperial procession from Tokyo to Kyoto, the ancient capital, taking along the bronze mirror of the Sun Goddess in its portable shrine; i.e., the Sun Goddess is taken in procession to Kyoto. There are two main events. In the first, the emperor is seated in a temporary hall along with the portable shrine of Amaterasu, represented by her bronze mirror. Then the sacred sword and jewel are brought in, thus reuniting the three sacred objects with the person of the new emperor for the first and only time in each reign. He then worships the Sun Goddess.

In the afternoon of the same day there is a ceremony copied almost wholesale from China in a hall called *shishen*. In China, the shishen were the pole-star and the stars surrounding it, symbolizing the authority of the emperor. The emperor enters from the north and ascends the throne, facing south to receive congratulations from the court, the government, and the people, who give three shouts of "*banzai!*" Simultaneously, all over the nation, people shout "banzai!"

The ceremony that really counts is the daijosai. In the *Nihon shoki* records of reign after reign, especially those in dispute, the new emperor had to have everything in his control by the autumn rice harvest festival, the niiname matsuri, on November 23, for the emperor played a crucial role in it. The new emperor's first participation ended the liminal period of transition with his assumption of spiritual responsibility for rice production. The logic of the ceremony is that Amaterasu, who sent her grandson with rice for the people of Japan, continues to nurture rice growth and harvesting through her embodiment in her imperial descendants. Her role continues as the Sun Goddess who makes the crops grow; above all she must not become angry again and reenter the cave, which would bring destruction and death to the people of Japan.

Ten days after sokui no rei, Emperor Akihito performed daijosai in the ancient manner. A whole agricultural cycle is caught up in this ceremony. It begins in the preceding New Year, when a divination hut is built in the Imperial Precinct. A more ancient ceremony surviving into the twentieth century can hardly be imagined. Two ancient kami are summoned. The priest builds a fire, then performs a divination by holding a shell above the flames until cracks appear; they are interpreted and the interpretation is written down and put in a box. The information from the kami: names of two prefectures where the special rice for daijosai will be grown.

Every step of rice production in the two sacred fields is accompanied by ritual, until its ceremonial harvesting by virgins (now by rice farmers). During daijosai the emperor repeats the pattern of Amaterasu, who was herself performing daijosai before being interrupted by her brother and hiding in the cave. The emperor must be purified and protected against the wandering of his spirits; nine kami are summoned for his protection the night before daijosai. A priest claps while a priestess, waving bells and a vine-draped spear, performs a dance like the dance performed for Amaterasu outside her cave. Knots are tied in a silk rope to keep his soul from wandering; meanwhile an identical rope is put across Amaterasu's actual cave in Kyushu.

Then there is a totally private communal meal of rice between the emperor and the kami of rice. Black and white *sake* and boiled rice and millet are offered the kami and then eaten by the emperor. Only the occasional entry of a serving priest witnesses the event. These are the first-fruits of the year's harvest; they are offered to the kami and to the emperor in whose body now reposes the rice-souls that must be carried over to the next season; for every year during the winter, when the sun retreats, the rice dies, but must be safeguarded until spring when it will, with the help of the kami, grow again. This is the emperor's sacred office for the people of Japan.

THE CHINA CONNECTION: ASUKA, NARA, AND HEIAN PERIODS

Beyond a few stepping-stone islands and the Korean peninsula lay a civilization vastly superior to and different from Japan. By the end of the sixth century, the Asuka court (named for its new location) had become vastly more sophisticated. There were people at court who could read and speak Chinese (though most of them were Koreans or Chinese); Chinese books had been known for a century; and China itself was emerging from the disorder of the Six Dynasties Period. It was time to approach China directly. The first official Japanese mission was dispatched to China in 607, and it didn't start well. The letter from Prince Shotoku was addressed with elegant symmetry from "the emperor of the sunrise country" to the "emperor of the sunset country." The Sui emperor was not charmed; insulted to be addressed as an equal by the ruler of a small and uncultured barbarian state, he refused to accept the letter.

Between 607 and 837, nineteen formal missions were sent from Japan to China. These voyages were extremely hazardous, especially when they took the longer route to the mouth of the Yangtze; masts broke, ships went down, passengers were washed overboard, sometimes by the dozen. Many of these travelers stayed on in China for decades before returning home with deep knowledge of Buddhism, the Chinese classics, and the workings of the Chinese state. The period spanned two of China's most glorious epochs, the Sui (581–618) and the Tang (618–906). During Tang dynasty, China's borders reached westward as far as Persia, and if one wanted a metropolitan city in those days, Chang-an was the place to be: "Buddhist monks from India, envoys from Kashgar, Samarkand, Persia, Annam, Tonkin, Constantinople, chieftains of nomadic tribes from Siberian plains, officials and students from Korea and, in now increasing numbers, from Japan" (Sansom 1952:84).

Though Japan was awed by Chinese civilization, they refused to accept a tribute-state relation to the great empire in the direction of the setting sun. About the time of the first missions to China, they began calling their country Nihon, written with the Chinese character for "sun" and "source." (The name Japan is the Chinese pronunciation of Nihon, "Jihpen.")

The three eras—Asuka, Nara, and Heian—form what is called Japan's classical age, when shameless copying of Chinese culture and brilliant adaptations of it produced a court culture profoundly different from previous periods and also unlike transformations to come after 1185. We must call this "court culture" because the aristocratic structure of society combined with the new world of literacy, learning, and art set it apart as never before from the lives of ordinary people—about which very little is known for this period. But the new possibilities for preserving the lifestyle of the elite provided by the script borrowed from China (see chapter 3), along with graphic images in painting, sculpture, and bronze casting, also from China, preserve this life in astonishing detail. We see a society embracing a new religion rich in emotion and aesthetics while having to mollify the jealous and still-powerful kami; we see dangerous court politics of intrigue and assassination carried out by scheming great families, all the while filling their leisure moments with social exchanges in a refined cultural idiom of moonviewing, poetry writing, nuance, and sensuality; and a gendered world where men intrigue and carry on a Chinese philosophical discourse while women adapt the new script to their own lives of refined inactivity and intrigue of a romantic type.

Buddhism Comes to Japan

For several hundred years prior to the major embassies to China, Japan had been receiving predigested chunks of Chinese culture via the Korean states of Silla and Paekche. From the latter had come in 552 an image of Buddha, several volumes of sutras, and a recommendation that the Japanese ruler adopt Buddhism.

The Japanese could not read the sutras, but the Buddha image aroused intense interest and controversy. Here was a god whose form could be seen. No one had ever "seen" a kami or made an image of one; they were visible only as natural spaces of great imagined power or in mysterious symbols like the bronze mirror of Amaterasu, but here was a serene, human-like deity, a halo around his head, sitting cross-legged on a lotus blossom. This god's origin in a great civilization to the west (and another one even further west) added to his appeal, as did his association with sacred texts and beautiful works of art. The kami had no sacred texts and no art but nature. But—would the kami be angry?

The emperor was uncertain what to do about the Buddha image and the religion that came with it. He consulted his courtiers. The heads of the two most powerful clans, the Nakatomi and the Mononobe, were dead set against it. The Nakatomi were chief ritualists at court, and the military Mononobe were closely aligned with them. But they had a competing clan in the Soga, who administered the crown estates and had begun marrying their daughters to emperors. Looking for more opportunities to advance themselves, they seized on the new religion. The emperor presented the Buddha image to them, and they set it up in a shrine in their palace. But shortly after the enshrinement of the foreign god, there was a smallpox epidemic, and people had second thoughts about the stranger-god. The angry kami were getting their revenge. The image was thrown into a canal near modern Osaka.

But the Soga had now thrown their fortunes in with Buddhism. The next emperor, Yomei, brought in more holy relics from Korea, and with the political support of the Soga clan, temples and monasteries began to be built. The first worship of Buddha was mostly empty of actual spiritual or philosophical content. The Buddha was treated like a powerful foreign kami who could be petitioned for things. Sutras were recited like magical formulas, and the most lavish ceremonies were to heal sick kings or bring rain. Yakushi, the "King of Medicine," was the most popular bodhisattva in the beginning.

If Japan had its King Ashoka, it was probably Prince Shotoku. He was never emperor himself but was regent under his stepmother,

Empress Suiko, after Shotoku's father was murdered in 593. It was he who sent the first several embassies to China, beginning in 607, but long before that, he had been raised with Korean tutors who had taught him the Buddhist sutras and the Chinese classics in, of course, Chinese. He was among the first to truly grasp the depth of both Buddhist and Confucian thought, and the first to make serious efforts at restructuring Japanese society along Chinese lines. There still exists a commentary on the Lotus Sutra thought to be in the Prince's own handwriting with the introductory remark: "This is compiled by the Crown Prince of the country of Yamato. It is not a foreign book," and contains his own comments on the Chinese commentaries, like: "My own interpretation differs slightly," or "This view is no longer accepted" (Sansom 1952:119). He lectured on the scriptures, patronized Buddhist art, and sponsored the building of temples.

In the same year as his first embassy to China he had constructed the Horyuji Temple. This spectacular temple, parts of which still exist, was built by Chinese and Korean architects in the Chinese style, although Japanese adaptations can be seen in it already. It contrasts greatly to the simple, grain-storage style of the Grand Shrine at Ise. The portions that survived a fire in 670, the Golden Hall containing the Buddha images, is said to be the oldest wooden building in the world. The main image in Horyuji Temple is the "Shaka Trinity," figures of the historical Buddha, Gautama (known as Shaka in Japan), flanked by two bodhisattvas. It was cast in bronze by an artisan of Chinese descent and dedicated in 623 to Prince Shotoku, who had died the previous year. Like many things borrowed too directly from China in this early period, it hasn't the sensuousness of later Japanese adaptations, but a beautiful wooden sculpture of Miroku (Maitreya, the future bodhisattva) in a nearby nunnery is pensive and evocative, already showing signs of later directions of Japanese aesthetics.

The building of temples became a source of competition among the powerful clans and a great drain on national resources. By 640, forty-six temples had been built in Japan. In 741 each province was ordered by imperial edict to install a temple and a seven-story pagoda, with a monastery for twenty monks and a nunnery for ten nuns. Each temple was allotted economic support in the form of sixty acres of rice land and fifty households to work it.

The many provincial temples all required copies of the sutras, which were scarce and valuable in the beginning. The government established offices for copying the sutras in major temples around Nara and paid scribes to do the copying. Devout individuals would sponsor the copying of sutras in order to earn merit, and there are still in existence copies commissioned by Emperor Shomu, the Empress Komyo in 740 and again in 743, the daughter of Fujiwara Fusasaki in 740, and the Empress Shotoku in 769 (Tanabe 1988:32). Sutra copying as an industry and as an act of piety continued throughout the eighth and ninth centuries, as scrolls gradually became as much works of art as competent texts. Paper was dyed indigo and characters written in gold ink, with illustrated frontispieces attached to the beginning of the scroll. The entire five-thousand-volume canon was copied fifty-six times during the Heian period, and ceremonies of dedication were held at court with prayers, music, and dance. Sutra copying reached an extravagant extreme. A one-copy commission was no longer enough; when Emperor Shomu's beloved aunt died in 748, he had a thousand copies of the Lotus Sutra made to insure her happiness in the next world, and soon everyone who could afford it was doing the same. Then a custom called *gyakushu* developed: One could have one's funeral carried out ahead of time, in one's own lifetime, to be sure it was done right. These, of course, required forty-nine copies of the sutra for the forty-nine days of the ceremony. Finally, there were sutra burials. The doctrine of *mappo* held that a Buddhist Dark Age would descend fifteen hundred years after the life of the Buddha, when enlightenment would become impossible and dharma would go into oblivion until the coming of Maitreya. This period of mappo was thought to begin in the eleventh century. In 1007, Michinaga was the first to bury eight sutras to insure his return from Paradise to hear Maitreya's sermon, and this began a rush of sutra burials all over Japan.

It is clear from this and much else that Buddhism was becoming a state religion, but the conflict with the native religion, now needing a name to contrast it with Buddhism and so called "Shinto" (from the Chinese word shen for "spirits" and tao for "way," thus "the way of the kami"), had to be resolved. Shinto also was the state religion; remember that among the very first books written in Japan with the newly available script were the *Kojiki* (712) and *Nihon shoki* (720), and this in the very century that Buddhism was peaking in popularity. Revering the Buddha in no way reduced belief in the powers of the kami, and a way had to be found to integrate the two religions.

The ancient records describe a rapprochement between Amaterasu and Buddha. In 742, a monk named Gyogi carried a sacred relic of the Buddha to the shrine of the Sun Goddess at Ise to get her opinion about a great Buddha image that the emperor was planning to install in the capital. He prayed at her shrine for seven days and nights until finally she spoke to him. The Sun Goddess proclaimed (in classical Chinese verse and in Buddhist metaphors!) that "the sun of truth illumines the long night of life and death and the moon of reality disperses the clouds of sin and ignorance." And yes, she was delighted with the building of a great Buddha image in Nara. Shortly afterward she confirmed her approval by appearing to the emperor in a dream in the form of a radiant disc, proclaiming that she and the Buddha were one. In time, the high Shinto deities were redefined as avatars of bodhisattvas—Hachiman, the Shinto god of war, became a bodhisattva of high rank—and Buddhist monks began to participate in Shinto shrines.

The Buddha image that was the object of concern was the Daibutsu, the "Great Buddha" planned by Emperor Shomu for the new Todaiji Temple at Nara. It was an enormous undertaking, containing over a million pounds of copper, tin, and lead for an image fifty-three feet high. Gold was needed to gild the image, but, as a minister of state reported in the opening ceremonies: "In this land of Yamato, since the beginning of heaven and earth, gold, though it has been brought as an offering from other countries, was thought not to exist. But in the east of the land which we rule, gold has been found. Hearing this, we were astonished and rejoiced, feeling that this is a gift bestowed upon us by the love and blessing of Buddha." At the eye-opening ceremony for the Daibutsu, the eyes were painted by an Indian monk named Bodhisena, ten thousand monks were feasted, and Emperor Shomu declared himself a servant of the Three Jewels, abdicating in favor of his daughter to become a Buddhist monk. Buddhism had come a long way in the two hundred years since the first Buddha image had to be tossed into a canal.

The Failure of the Centralized State

It is easier to borrow a religion than a government, but the Japanese did make a brief, and ultimately ineffectual, effort to copy the Chinese system of government. It must be remembered how the centralized state first was introduced to China: by ruthless and revolutionary alterations carried out by Qin Shihuang after first conquering all the competing territories and lords. Qin had not been softened by Buddhist compassion nor rendered temperate by Confucian ethics. He made no claims of divine descent; he was a conqueror and a dictator, pure and simple. He had no equivalent in seventh-century Japan.

The first efforts at reform in Japan were attempted by Prince Shotoku. He is better compared, as we have already done, to Ashoka, not Qin. Like Ashoka, he attempted to reform the Yamato state, bringing personal ethics and civic responsibility to what had been, and unfortunately continued to be, rule by competing heads of great families motivated most by clan loyalties, competition for honors at court, and claims to semidivine status. However, unlike Ashoka, he did not attempt to reform the state on Buddhist values alone, for he also had access to the very sophisticated—by Sui and Tang times—Chinese model of the state, with its mix of practical bureaucratic centralization and Confucian ethics. He promulgated a "constitution" in seventeen articles that advocated such Buddhist values as reverence for the "Three Precious Things" (i.e., the Three Jewels: Buddha, Dharma, and Sangha) and avoidance of gluttony and covetousness, as well as Confucian ones like reciprocal duties between superior and inferior governed by "ceremony" (li), hard work by officials, reward of merit and punishment of faults, and filling positions by merit, not patronage. Most extraordinary of all, from a Japanese point of view, is a new theory of the centralized state expressed in the statement: "The sovereign is master of the people of the whole country; the officials to whom he gives charge are all his vassals."

Next, Shotoku attempted to regularize honors at court by a system of rank with corresponding visible signs in styles and colors of caps and robes as was practiced in China for scholar-officials. This got tinkered with over the next several decades, and is one reform that did survive.

The efforts to reform the state are tied up with the fortunes of the Soga clan. We have seen their rise with the coming of Buddhism in 552. They exercised powerful control from behind the scenes over seven emperors, except during the regency of Prince Shotoku from 593 to 621. After his death, the Sogas again showed their claws, making and deposing rulers and committing murder when they needed to. Meanwhile, the Nakatomi, pushed off center stage long before, had a brilliant son in Kamatari, who devoted his time to studying the political doctrines of the Chinese sages and eyeing the various imperial princes for an ally. He made friends with Prince Naka no Oye, and in 745 they moved against the Soga. Soga no Iruka was assassinated in the presence of the empress, a Soga nominee. Within days they killed the Soga leadership and burned their fortress, where all the state papers were being held. They made the empress abdicate and replaced her with someone they could control, making Naka no Oye heir apparent. Now it was Kamatari who was the supreme power, continuing a pattern of real power being exercised in the background, which already had several hundred years precedent and would continue for a millennium more.

Kamatari passed the Taika Reforms. These reformed land tenure, bringing everything under the ownership of the emperor, at least theoretically. Local magnates were deprived of their estates and serfs. Provinces were divided into districts and townships, with governors appointed from the local gentry. Townships consisted of fifty households under a headman who was responsible for crops, maintenance of order, and levying and collecting taxes. Population registers were to be drawn up and account books maintained so that more taxes could be collected, more reliably. Land was redistributed among the cultivators depending on the number of mouths in a family to be fed; the system was called literally the "mouth-share fields." The registers were necessary to insure that peasants didn't escape payment of taxes and that officials didn't embezzle any. All of these reforms were attempts to centralize the country under the control of the emperor, and raise revenues for the state, collected by appointed officials accountable to him; i.e., the Chinese system.

But it did not work in Japan for two principal reasons. First, the great aristocratic families were too powerful at court and too in control of their territories to be easily shoved out, so they were simply confirmed in their current possessions, though now, in theory, they held them as grants from the throne. Second, a great deal of riceland was made exempt from payment of taxes: land in possession of shrines and temples, and land granted to officials in lieu of salary, including large amounts to support great families. Over the next two centuries, the system slowly collapsed. At every level of the hierarchy from peasant to local official to regional lord to the central government, people managed to take shares from below without passing it up. The throne's share decreased, demands on peasants increased, and a larger and larger nonproductive, exploitive middle class prospered. "Despite all the efforts of the central authority to check the expansion of tax-free estates, there grew up once more a class of hereditary chieftains whose power rivaled that of the throne and in the course of some centuries finally overtopped it" (Sansom 1952:106). No scholar-official class like the Chinese shenshi ever emerged, for the hold of aristocratic territorial clans was never broken.

More successful, however, was the building of cities on the Chinese plan. Chang-an was the largest city in the world at this time, and its centrally planned, gridlike layout with the imperial palace in the north-central portion of the city was simply what a city should be, to the Japanese, who had none. Their administrative centers had been wherever the residence of a clan chief or a given Yamato ruler might be; the Shinto horror of death pollution required that residences be pulled down and destroyed at death, so no permanent court had emerged; rather their traces remain archaeologically all over the Nara basin.

So the eighth-century Japanese built themselves a city like Chang-an called Nara. This was a space to fill with the new culture coming from China, though Japan's total population of six million at that time could hardly sustain a major urban complex. Perhaps twenty thousand people lived there during its peak. Only the eastern half of the planned city was ever built, and this was filled with temples, monasteries, and mansions in Chinese architectural styles. It must have seemed a marvelous and foreign place to humble Japanese who came to see or work: Chinese was spoken here, there were new gods whose forms were visible, language was captured in the strange markings of the Chinese script, men of rank wore their rank visibly on Chinese-style robes.

But Nara remained the seat of government and learning a mere seventy-five years; the capital then moved twice, first to Nagaoka, then, more enduringly, to Kyoto. Some have supposed the move was decided because of the increasing power of the monastic establishment at Nara; or it may have been linked to some intrigue of the Fujiwaras. In any event, it was a hugely expensive undertaking. All the provinces were required to send all their taxes for the year to build the new city, plus all the materials needed for construction. Much of this income went to compensate the nobility, who also had to relocate to Nagaoka. Then, after only ten years, they picked up and moved again, to Kyoto, this time perhaps because of a series of inexplicable deaths of people of high rank, which were understood to be caused by angry spirits, of whom there continued to be tremendous, unalloyed fear. Kyoto was sited by Chinese geomancy, carefully announced to Amaterasu at Ise, and then, again, built on the Chang-an plan, with the imperial residence in north-center, a wall with fourteen gates, and a temple of Confucius. Here in Kyoto, the culturally splendid Heian or Fujiwara Period unfolded, and it remained the residence of the imperial line until the Meiji Restoration of 1868.

Romance at Court

We probably know more about the life of women at the Heian court than about any comparable class of women in any other premodern state. There are several remarkable things about this. The first is that women were allowed to learn to read and write at all. The second is that our view of their lives is not filtered through the imaginations of male authors writing about women; these women wrote about themselves and their times. And most remarkable of all, since there were no established indigenous genres to channel their self-expression, they had the liberty to make up their own.

We see women enjoying liberties that elite women of many later periods would envy, yet qualities of masculine and feminine were clearly drawn and their worlds finely demarcated. Learning, as it came to Japan, was Chinese learning, and only men were thought to be capable of the years of study required, first to master Chinese, then to master the script and the difficult literature that came from China. Men of standing attempted to speak Chinese, quoted Chinese sayings, and attempted to write philosophy and poetry in Chinese. The situation was much like the role played by Latin in European societies for many centuries. However, very early, perhaps through later acquaintance with Sanskritic syllabic scripts, Chinese characters were modified to produce a syllabic form, called *kana*. The fairly simple phonemic system of Japanese could be handled completely in kana, but by then the language had been so enriched with Chinese loanwords and the evocative quality of Chinese characters themselves, that written Japanese never did abandon *kanji* ("Chinese writing"). Kana, then, became a kind of private, vernacular script for writing about personal things, the emotions, the inner life, in the Japanese language. This simplified script was easy to learn and was eagerly adopted by women at court while not threatening status distinctions between men and women.

Women at court kept diaries and wrote about the life around them; in their writings we have the wonderful reversal of a male world portrayed through women's eyes. The best and deservedly most famous of these works is *The Tale of Genji* by Murasaki Shikibu. It was written about A.D. 1000 as a fifty-four-chapter novel and is thought to be the first novel ever written anywhere. The first English translation by Arthur Waley was published in six volumes; because of its length, most people know the work in various abridgments. Lady Murasaki was from a junior line of the great Fujiwara family whose father lamented that his brilliant daughter was not born a boy. He was not of high enough rank to give her a serious career at court, but she went into the service of Empress Akiko for several years, and then retired from court and wrote her novel.

The novel is a form of prose fiction that even the Chinese had not developed. Its emphasis is on characters more than plot. The main character of *The Tale of Genji* is "the shining Genji"; dazzlingly handsome, he is a romantic lover, poet, calligrapher, musician, and dancer: "A slight flush from too much drink made Genji even handsomer than usual. His skin glowed through his light summer robes." We trace the life of Genji through episode after intense episode, most of them romantic intrigues triggered by the sight of a silken sleeve and expressed in eloquent exchanges of poetic couplets under autumn moons. Beneath the refined surfaces of Heian life—layered silk in matching pastels, perfumed notes, the thirteen-stringed *koto*—were intense emotions: longing for past lovers, melancholy on briny shores, status jealousies, fear of exposure of indiscretions, laments for the dead. Good breeding made itself visible in exquisite taste and polished manners. You could tell a person of third rank from a person of first rank by their conduct, and did, but never rudely.

In this world, there were careers for ladies at court. But ladies, as well as men, needed good family connections to really have a chance. Genji's mother was beloved of the emperor, but being the emperor's favorite, without important kinship connections, only subjected her to jealous torment from others until she retired from court and died. Even being the emperor's favorite son, as Genji was, was not enough without powerful maternal relatives; princes were regularly reduced to commoner status to minimize the number of royals competing politically with the Fujiwara regents and needed support, and a popular surname for them to take (the imperial family has no surname) was Genji, a Chinese form of Minamoto. Women's careers, however, were never official posts in government; no Minister of the Left or of the Right or other positions were available to them. A royal princess was always appointed as High Priestess at Ise, and women could retire to become Buddhist nuns and read the sutras. Lady Murasaki, however, was largely interested in that other career, the life of romantic intrigue. These court women had the freedom to write love let-

Among the most-beloved of themes for illustrated scrolls were scenes from the Tale of Genji. The aesthetics of the Heian court are expressed in the diagonal composition of paintings; emotional barriers are represented in screens and low walls that separate people, and passionate intensity is suggested in moments like this one, where observers from the balcony witness the sorrowful presentation of a mourning robe in a wintry setting.

ters, welcome men into their boudoirs, and initiate affairs, and they often gave birth to babies with dangerous resemblances to men at court. These intrigues, however, bear little resemblance to the silly frivolities of aristocratic Europe in the eighteenth century, for every flirtation is a sincere one and even lapsed affairs retain a melancholy emotional integrity. The love affair now over is like the fallen blossom, beautiful, transient, sorrowfully and irretrievably lost.

A major subplot is the love of Genji for Fujitsubo, his father's favorite consort, who later was promoted to empress. His one-night tryst with her results in a young prince with all of Genji's charms, who is thought by the emperor to be his own son; he is made Crown Prince and eventually becomes the Reizei emperor, thinking all along that Genji is his half-brother rather than his father. Throughout the book, Fujitsubo is terrified the truth will come out, which would threaten her son's prospects and bring her shame. Their occasional later meetings (see box 8.3) are filled with the romantic tension known later in Japan as *iki*. In another episode, Genji's wife has a child by another man, and, when rumor circulates, rather than demonstrating anger at her infidelity, Genji himself, touched and sympathetic to her intense sense of shame, seeks a way to ease her unhappiness.

8.3   Genji's Exile to Suma

For Genji life had become an unbroken succession of reverses and afflictions. He must consider what to do next. If he went on pretending that nothing was amiss, then even worse things might lie ahead. He thought of the Suma coast. People of worth had once lived there, he was told, but now it was deserted save for the huts of fishermen, and even they were few. The alternative was worse, to go on living this public life, so to speak, with people streaming in and out of his house. Yet he would hate to leave, and affairs at court would continue to be much on his mind if he did leave. This irresolution was making life difficult for his people.

Fujitsubo, though always worried about rumors, wrote frequently. It struck him as bitterly ironical that she had not returned his affection earlier, but he told himself that a fate which they had shared from other lives must require that they know the full range of sorrows. . . .

On the night before his departure he visited his father's grave in the northern hills. Since the moon would be coming up shortly before dawn, he went first to take leave of Fujitsubo. Receiving him in person, she spoke of her worries for the crown prince. It cannot have been, so complicated were matters between them, a less than deeply felt interview. Her dignity and beauty were as always. He would have liked to hint at old resentments; but why, at this late date, invite further unpleasantness, and risk adding to his own agitation?

He only said, and it was reasonable enough: "I can think of a single offense for which I must undergo this strange, sad punishment, and because of it I tremble before the heavens. Though I would not care in the least if my own unworthy self were to vanish away, I only hope that the crown prince's reign is without unhappy event."

She knew too well what he meant, and was unable to reply. He was almost too handsome as at last he succumbed to tears. "I am going to pay my respects at His Majesty's grave. Do You have a message?"

She was silent for a time, seeking to control herself.

"The one whom I served is gone, the other must go.
Farewell to the world was no farewell to its sorrows."

But for both of them the sorrow was beyond words. He replied:

"The worst of grief for him should long have passed.
And now I must leave the world where dwells the child."

Her face was with him the whole of the journey. In great sorrow he boarded the boat that would take him to Suma. It was a long spring day and there was a tall wind, and by late afternoon he had reached the strand where he was to live. He had never before been on such a journey, however short. All the sad, exotic things along the way were new to him. The Oe station was in ruins, with only a grove of pines to show where it had stood.

"More remote, I fear, my place of exile
Than storied ones in lands beyond the seas."

The surf came in and went out again. "I envy the waves," he whispered to himself. It was a familiar poem, but it seemed new to those who heard him, and sad as never before. Looking back toward the city, he saw that the mountains were enshrouded in mist. It was as though he had indeed come "three thousand leagues." The spray from the oars brought thoughts scarcely to be borne.

"Mountain mists cut off that ancient village.
Is the sky I see the sky that shelters it?"

This is what he wrote to Fujitsubo:

"Briny our sleeves on the Suma strand; and yours
In the fisher cots of thatch at Matsushima?
My eyes are dark as I think of what is gone and what is to come, and 'the waters rise.'"

Murasaki Shikibu, 1986, trans. Edward G. Seidensticker.

The Tale of Genji, as Varley writes, illustrates the value of *mono no aware*—"sensitivity to things," or "capacity to be moved by things," a distinctively Japanese aesthetic value. "The Japanese are . . . essentially an emotional people . . . who have always assigned high value to sincerity as the ethic of the emotions" (Varley 1984:57–64). This sensitivity is tinged with sadness because much of what is lovely and moving is also transient, such as the perishable beauties of nature. Genji, in exile from court at a remote seaside village in the Suma chapter, hears the call of geese winging overhead and says in one of the many couplets that ornament the prose: "Might they be companions of those I long for? Their cries ring sadly through the sky of their journey."

The great novel was frequently illustrated by Japanese artists. One popular medium was the handscroll, which contained both text in beautiful pure-kana calligraphy and illustrations and which was read by unrolling it across a table. Often, members of the aristocracy worked on these scrolls themselves. One of the earliest and best of the Genji handscrolls was done in 1120–1130 and survives in fragments that are now in the Tokugawa and Goto Museums. The artists sought to portray the most emotionally intense moments—the moment the Reizei Emperor confronts Genji, having just learned Genji is his father, or the moment Genji's wife is prostrate on the *tatami*, unable to tell her father, the retired emperor, the truth of her child by Kashiwagi or to face her husband Genji. We view these intense scenes from a surprising angle, looking down into rooms with their roofs removed, always with strong diagonal lines representing the architecture of interiors and people separated by walls and screens. Emotional turbulence is expressed by ribbons hanging in disarray, and by the sharp tilt of the composition itself (Baker 1984).

WARRIOR CULTURE IN FEUDAL JAPAN

Attention must turn to the provinces in order to understand Japan from the twelfth century onward. This was the realm of the Japanese peasant and a landed class of elite families, many of them provincial branches of great court families. The Taiko Reforms imposed on this old system a new system of provincial governors (*zuryo*) whose job it was to raise income for the imperial government. They fulfilled this responsibility, in many cases, so rapaciously, and were themselves so greedy to acquire land however they could, that there was a saying, "When a zuryo falls down, he comes up holding dirt." Everyone, peasants and aristocrats, hated the zuryo and the system that they administered, and worked to find ways to undercut it in self-protection. Peasant men who were forced into military service for indefinite periods simply disappeared. From the official point of view, a whole class of missing persons had appeared—real people but without registered identities—who came to be called *ronin*. The new system that had been imposed from the center was apparently experienced by people in the provinces as an early version of odious "Big Brother" centralized control. Every household, once blissfully autonomous, was registered by the state, their land was allotted by the state, taxes due were determined and rigorously collected, and, theoretically, every six years all the land could be redistributed. Never had the state been so intrusive.

The system was equally despised by local elites, who developed their own brand of evasion. Some of them—the old court families who had been too powerful to be dispossessed—had been allowed to keep their lands tax-free. Many of the aristocratic families in the provinces were descendants of emperors who were victims of "dynastic shedding"; they had, like Genji, lost their princely titles and been given surnames (Minamoto, Taira, Tachibana, Ariwara) and estates in the provinces, where they were free to make their fortunes. These estates were called *shoen*. Buddhist monasteries and Shinto temples also had shoen, often extensive tracts of land that came with cultivators to work them. The rest were at the mercy of the despised zuryo. To protect themselves, they began "commending" their lands to local shoen, religious or aristocratic, attaching themselves in vassal-like relationships to the shoen overlord, the *daimyo* ("great name," a term applied to any lord who controlled lands producing more than fifty thousand bushels of rice a year). This practice was so widespread that it drastically altered the nature of Japanese society and its power structure in a couple of centuries. By the twelfth century, nearly all the rice lands of the country had been gathered into huge private estates, and the capital was close to bankruptcy from loss of revenue. Further, because the court had no standing army, all the military muscle was in the provincial estates where overlords were able, with the growing wealth of their estates, to raise their own armies. Since the conscription of peasants had proved a failure, warriors were recruited from the rural elite, and this gradually turned into a permanent class of mounted warriors known as the *samurai*. The word means "to serve"; its earliest use was for domestic servants at court, and later came to be used for the imperial guardsmen; but with the growth of feudal society, the samurai became an elite class that formed its own code of honor based on courage, loyalty, and martial skills. The "Way" *(-do)* of the warrior *(bushi)* was not originally codified, but its ideals were enshrined in sung and acted war tales. Only later, as the samurai class began to sense its own decline, were works such as the *Code of the Samurai* by Daidoji Yuzan written down. Thus, greatly simplified in the telling, arose the feudal society of Japan's middle period.

The Shogunate

Three great families emerged and competed in the Heian Period: the Fujiwara, the Taira, and the Minamoto; the latter two, and especially the Minamoto, which branched into regional groupings, dominated Japan until the nineteenth century. In the beginning, the Fujiwara were vastly more powerful, exercising regency over a succession of emperors who were never allowed to govern, were often forced to abdicate, and invariably were married to Fujiwara daughters. Their zenith was the eleventh century, when the funeral of Fujiwara Michinaga was as splendid as for an emperor: Ten thousand priests prayed for his recovery, a general amnesty was declared, and back taxes were forgiven throughout the country (Sansom 1952:265). But elsewhere things were falling apart. The Fujiwara strategy was to control emperors and parcel out honors at court, which in the good old days mattered more than anything else. They did not bother with warriors. But out in the chaotic provinces, armed might mattered, and symbols of prestige other than titles and the color of caps and robes came to be valued. The Taira and Minamoto were chief rivals in bloody battles fought between 1156 and 1160. In 1160, Taira Kiyomori moved in on the Fujiwara to settle an imperial succession dispute; then, following the usual strategy, he married his daughter to the emperor, and twenty years later put his grandson on the throne. It looked for two decades as if the Taira had won; two young Minamoto boys barely escaped with their lives, but the young and brilliant Yoritomo put together an alliance of warriors and military leaders, moved on Kyoto in 1185, drove out the Tairas, and put an end to the Fujiwaras.

> This terrific struggle to the death between rival houses established beyond question the dominance of the military families and created a definite warrior class which, under the stress of danger and conflict, developed a special code of behavior, a special morality. The events of those years have left deep marks upon the imagination of the Japa-

nese, and the rise and fall of the two clans is perhaps their true epic. Its history abounds in heroic legends of loyalty and courage and sacrifice, which have inspired their art and their literature and shaped their sentiment. This was the period of the formation of the *samurai* caste, cultivating as supreme virtues fidelity and contempt of death. (Sansom 1952:269–70)

Yoritomo then set up his headquarters three hundred miles to the east of Kyoto, at Kamakura, to be near his estates and vassals; he was going to need the support of these people, and armed and ambitious as they were, they were more dangerous to his control than the establishment in Kyoto. He does not seem to have considered overthrowing the imperial dynasty; rather, he continued to use the monarchy as the source and authority for honors and titles, beginning with himself: He had the emperor grant him an old defunct title, *shogun,* formerly used by generals fighting the northern barbarians; it meant supreme commander of all military forces. The government he founded at Kamakura had the flavor of a field encampment; it was called the *bakufu,* or "tent government." All over Japan, holders of shoen transferred their allegiance to him.

This was the system of government until 1867: under the title shogun, control was exercised by a military government from Kamakura and later Edo (Tokyo), while the emperors carried on with their refined court culture, their Shinto state rituals, and their Buddhist retirements in Kyoto. From Kamakura, warrior clans dominated the next 400 years; then when a branch of Minamotos, the Tokugawas, came to power in 1600, there were another 250 years of a warrior regime until the Meiji Restoration.

The Samurai Class

The samurai class came into existence, flowered, and disappeared in six hundred years, marking the imagination and character of modern Japanese and, it must also be said, of the world. The code of honor of the samurai warrior, which came to be known as *bushido*—a blend of Confucian, Zen Buddhist, and martial values—dignified militarism in the first half of the twentieth century, leaving traces in modern popular culture (*The Karate Kid,* Ninja Turtles) and, it is sometimes speculated, in the psyches of the salarymen and executives of corporate Japan.

If there is a "key scenario" of samurai culture, it is captured in a true event of 1701 that was preserved and reenacted (and embellished) in play and story: the tale of the Forty-Seven Loyal Ronin. In 1701, Lord Asano, daimyo of the Ako domain, was assigned to perform ceremonial duties at the shogun's court in Edo. Because he was unfamiliar with court practices, he offended an official named Kira, who insulted him in return. A rough-and-ready daimyo from the provinces, Lord Asano drew his sword to avenge his honor with an attack on Kira. But this was a violation of a strict law at the shogun's court, forbidding the drawing of weapons, and he was ordered to commit suicide. He promptly complied. When word of his death reached his domain at Ako, forty-seven of his vassals, rendered masterless by the death of their master and confiscation of his lands, formed a secret covenant to avenge him. Knowing that Kira would be expecting such an attack, they plotted to behave like lawless and dissolute ronin, wandering, drinking, and gambling until the moment of revenge. On a snowy morning in 1703, they attacked and killed Kira at his residence in Edo and carried his head to the temple where their lord had been buried. But they had broken Tokugawa law against vengeance killings and were condemned to die. They did so by committing suicide in the honorable manner.

By the time of the forty-seven loyal ronin, the samurai class had begun their transformation into a cultivated, urbane, and bureaucratic elite, who still carried the best swords ever made at their waists but hardly ever drew them, being put to work instead by the Tokugawa shogunate, running a unified and—at last—peaceful Japan. Tokugawa Ieyasu moved to Edo in 1590 as the daimyo of the eight Kanto provinces. After the Battle of Sekigahara (1600), he unified the country and was appointed shogun, and from this time Edo has been the capital of Japan. (Its name was changed to Tokyo, the "Kyoto of the East," during the Meiji Era). The contrasts with Kyoto were great; whereas Kyoto was laid out like a Chinese city on a north-south axis and grid plan, Edo had a concentric circle plan, with Edo Castle high on a plateau at the center. Edo had no resident divine monarch, but was instead a fortress, surrounded by a wall and a moat, to protect the shogun. Its central plateau was carved by ravines that left five terraces splayed like fingers on a hand. On these terraces the three great allies of the Tokugawa—the daimyos of Kii, Owari, and Ii—built their residences to protect the shogun, and over the next half-century, Edo came to resemble a miniature version of the country as a whole, as all the daimyos in the land, including Lord Asano, were required to build mansions in the city on land designated by the shogun. They were required to leave their wives and children in permanent residence in Tokyo and spend alternate years there themselves; the second year they could spend watching over their affairs back in their domains (Nishiyama Matsunosuke 1997:23–40). Besides the direct vassals and guardsmen of the bakufu, the great daimyo households brought with them their retainers and families. By the eighteenth century, Edo was a city of a million people, half of them warriors.

It was in Edo that samurai culture shifted from a martial culture to a martial arts culture, quite a significant shift; to know the samurai at their most dramatic and idealized, one must back up to rougher times; say, the twelfth through fourteenth centuries.

Warfare was a highly ritualized affair in the beginning of the samurai period. As seen in war tales like the *Konjaku Monogatari, Heike Monogatari*, and the *Taiheiki*, armies would first arrange a time and date of battle; they would then exchange envoys as the armies faced each other in the field and fire "humming arrows" to announce the commencement of fighting. As the armies moved together, they exchanged volleys of arrows, and warriors finally paired off sword-to-sword for the climax of the fighting. Rank counted even in battle, for you had to find someone of your own rank, as evidenced by insignia on armor, to slug it out with. Often one shouted one's own name and genealogy to attract an opponent of suitable rank, but there were other reasons for shouting your name. You might need to establish witnesses for later claims to reward, or to promote the fame of yourself and your family.

The victorious shouting of one's name (*kachi-nanori*) was a ritual formula that included one's genealogy. Varley records the following exchange between a Taira and a Minamoto, whose parties encounter each other at the entry to the capital:

> "[I am] the police lieutenant of Aki, Motomori; descended in the twelfth generation from Emperor Kammu; a distant relative in the eighth generation of the Taira general [shogun] Masakado; grandson of the minister of punishments, Tadamori; and second son of the governor of Aki, Kiyomori." Not to be outdone, Chikaharu then recites his lineage: "I am the resident of Yamato province Uno no Shichiro Chikaharu; descended in the tenth generation from Emperor Seiwa; a distant relative of the Sixth Grandson Prince; five generations removed from the governor of Yamato, Yorichika, the younger brother of the governor of Settsu, Raiko; grandson of the vice-minister of central affairs, Yoriharu; and oldest son of the governor of Shimotsuke, Chikahiro." (Varley 1994:60)

In the *Hogen*, a nineteen-year-old warrior is initiated into battle during the attack on Shirakawa Palace. He wrestles with two brothers who are famous for their strength and stabs them to death. Taking their heads and remounting his horse, he shouts:

> I, Kaneko no Juro Ietada, a resident of Musashi province, have come forth, before the renowned Tametomo of Tsukushi, and with my own hands have taken the heads of two noted warriors (samurai). Observe this, both enemy and ally! A feat rarely achieved either in ancient times or the present! . . . I am the Ietada who wishes to bequeath his name (na) to generations to come. If there are warriors among Tametomo's band who feel they are my match, let them come and grapple with me! (Varley 1994:61)

At the end of the battle, a few hours or a day later, enemy heads were cut off and carried to Kyoto or Kamakura for display. This was bloody and defiling work; usually retainers did the actual decapitation, and the head was carried by sticking one's sword into the victim's topknot. Part of the system of honor of the samurai was to prevent comrades' heads from falling to the enemy. In *Heiji* there is a story of a commander in flight from Kyoto along with his injured son. Seeing that his son cannot continue traveling, he kills him and takes his head to keep it from falling into enemy hands (Varley 1994:27).

Vassal loyalty is the principal theme of the war tales. Warriors from the eastern Kanto area were exemplars of *kenshin*, the absolute self-sacrificing loyalty of a warrior for his lord. The forty-seven loyal ronin exhibited this kind of ultimate loyalty, and also another trait: the vendetta (*katakiuchi*), or blood revenge. Intent on following their lord into death, they could not do so until they had rendered him the final service: avenging his death. Samurai justified the vendetta by quoting Confucius:

> Tzu-hsia asked Confucius, saying, "How should [a son] conduct himself with reference to the man who has killed his father or mother?" The Master said, "He should sleep on straw, with his shield for a pillow; he should not take office; he must be determined not to live with the slayer under the same heaven. If he meet with him in the marketplace or court, he should not have to go back for his weapon, but [instantly] fight with him. (Varley 1994:33)

Loyalty meant to the death. Daidoji Yuzan's *Code of the Samurai* begins with the famous words: "One who is a samurai must before all things keep constantly in mind, by day and by night . . . the fact that he has to die." This point was not just a theoretical one in the pre-Tokugawa era. Hostilities frequently interrupted the unstable peace of the first four centuries of shogun rule, and one entire century, known as the Era of Warring States (1467–1568), was given over to chaotic and largely pointless violence, what Berry calls the "culture of lawlessness" (Berry 1994). The era is known in part through the diaries of persons who lived through, and tried to make meaning of, the destruction of Kyoto as sometimes hundreds of thousands of warriors fought in its streets and savaged its neighborhoods, reducing the city to isolated, fortified pockets of townspeople, with a northern and a southern zone, and the imperial compound to a weedy wasteland. In romanticizing samurai culture, we must remember all its modes.

Berry opens an account of this century with the diary entries of a Kyoto aristocrat:

> Yakushiji Yoichi Motoichi, the deputy governor of the province of Settsu, who is a retainer of Hosokawa Ukyo Daibu Minamoto Masamoto Ason, has rebelled against Masamoto and turned enemy. He is marching toward Yodo in our province. All of Kyoto is in an up-

roar over these events; the exodus of residents carrying their valuables is shocking, people say.

Seventeen days later, the day-by-day descriptions of the havoc wreaked by this adventurer end with the following:

> The castle at Yodo fell at daybreak. The principal in this affair, Yakushiji Yoichi, whose formal name is Motoichi, has been captured; the leader of the Shinomiya house and his son have cut their bellies. They say one hundred fourteen heads collected during this incident have been brought back to Kyoto. The unexpectedly swift victory is miraculous.

And finally:

> I hear that the prisoner [Yakushiji] Motoichi, age twenty-nine, cut his belly at dawn. (Berry 1994:2)

Samurai culture required of loyalty the willingness to follow one's lord into death, as we saw in the tale of the forty-seven ronin; in the face of defeat, pride in name required a death made heroic by the ritual of suicide. Lord Asano, the forty-seven ronin, the Shinomiya lord, and finally Yakushiji Motoichi "cut their bellies."

Often, as in the cases described above, *seppuku* or *hara kiri* (the latter term is considered vulgar; both mean disembowelment or "cutting the belly") was a spontaneous act of the autonomous samurai. In Tokugawa times it also became an elite mode of execution for a member of the samurai class to spare him the humiliation of a common public beheading. In the nineteenth century, there were occasional European witnesses, such as the execution described by A. B. Mitford in Kobe in 1868. The condemned man had purified himself and dressed in white, the color of death, and then was ushered into a sand-covered room in a Buddhist temple. He knelt before a tray containing a sharp, twelve-inch knife, and his *kaishaku* (second) knelt beside him with a sword. The charges were read by an official, and the samurai said: "I, and I alone, unwarrantedly gave the order to fire on the foreigners at Kobe, and again as they tried to escape. For this crime I disembowel myself, and I beg of you who are present to do me the honor of witnessing this act." Then:

> Bowing once more, the speaker allowed his upper garment to slip down to his girdle, and remained naked to the waist. Carefully . . . he tucked his sleeves under his knees to prevent himself from falling backward; for a noble Japanese gentleman [samurai] should die falling forward.

> Deliberately, with a steady hand he took the dirk that lay before him; he looked at it wistfully, almost affectionately; for a moment he seemed to collect his thoughts for a last time, and then stabbing himself deeply below the waist on the left hand side, he drew the dirk

slowly across to the right side, and turning it in the wound, gave it a slight cut upward. Through this sickeningly painful operation he never moved a muscle of his face. Then he drew out the dirk, leaned forward and stretched out his neck [for the swordsman to strike]; an expression of pain for the first time crossed his face, but he uttered no sound. At that moment, the kaishaku, who, still crouching at his side, had been keenly watching his every movement, sprang to his feet, poised his sword for a second in the air; there was a flash, a heavy, ugly thud, a crashing fall; with one blow the head had been severed from the body. (King 1993:152)

Seppuku continues in the twentieth century to be a rare, shocking, yet still heroic act carried out by individuals. When Emperor Meiji died in 1912, on the final day of his funeral ceremonies, just as the cortege was preparing to leave the palace, hero of the Russo-Japanese War General Nogi Maresuke and his wife, Shizuko, seated themselves in front of the emperor's portrait and committed suicide, he by disemboweling himself and she by stabbing herself in the heart. The act shocked the Japanese nation; it aroused tremendous controversy, and it was said of the event: "Nothing has so stirred up the sentiments of the nation since the vendetta of the forty-seven ronin in 1703" (Gluck 1985:221).

Under the Tokugawas, as I have already pointed out, samurai culture began to change, and the warrior culture of the previous four centuries began to shift to resemble in some ways their equivalent elite class in China, the shenshi. Until the Edo period, no two elite cultures could have been more divergent than that of the Chinese scholar-official class and the Japanese samurai. Remarkably, both were based in Confucian values, which goes to show how structures of power and historically embedded social actors can utilize philosophies in tremendously diverse ways. Neo-Confucianism and samurai culture were developing over roughly the same centuries but took very different courses. However, the gap began to close in the seventeenth century, as the Tokugawa regime needed to turn warriors into administrators, and samurai lifestyles were increasingly urban and cultured along lines that would be recognized in, and were again influenced by, China.

The Confucian influence is strong in the ethical injunctions for warriors in Daidoji Yuzan's *Code of the Samurai*, written in the late eighteenth century. He was a member of the Taira family; his father was a vassal of Tokugawa Ieyasu's son, and Yuzan became an orthodox Confucian scholar and expert on military affairs. He wrote this text (see box 8.4, "Excerpts from the *Code of the Samurai*") for young samurai at a time when the samurai class was seen as falling away from the austerity and simplicity of the old days, but it was also a time when Confucian values borrowed in the eighth century were getting reinforcements from the neo-Confucianism of the seventeenth and eighteenth centuries. We see the

8.4   Excerpts from *The Code of the Samurai*

On what should a samurai focus his mind?

"One who is a samurai must before all things keep constantly in mind, by day and by night, from the morning when he takes up his chopsticks to eat his New Year's breakfast to Old Year's night when he pays his yearly bills, the fact that he has to die. That is his chief business. If he is always mindful of this, he will be able to live in accordance with the paths of Loyalty and Filial Duty. . . .

"One who is a samurai should base his conduct on a strong sense of filial duty. And however capable and clever and eloquent and handsome one may be born, if he is unfilial he is of no use at all. For Bushido, the Way of the Warrior, requires a man's conduct to be correct in all points."

It is most important that one who is a samurai should never neglect the offensive spirit at any time and in all matters. For our country is different from other lands in that even the least of the people, farmers, merchants, and artisans, should all cherish some rusty blade, wherein is revealed the warrior spirit of this Empire of Nippon. . . . Much more must the higher samurai. . . . "When you leave your gate, act as though an enemy was in sight." So since he is a samurai and wears a sword in his girdle he must never forget this spirit of the offensive. And when this is so, the mind is firmly fixed on death.

What is jin [ren] for the samurai?

For Bushido the three qualities of Loyalty, Right Conduct, and Bravery are essential. We speak of the loyal warrior, the righteous warrior, and the valiant warrior, and it is he who is endowed with all these three virtues who is a warrior of the highest class.

How do you show respect for your lord?

In Bushido, however loyal and filial a man may be in his heart, if he is lacking in the correct etiquette and manners by which respect is shown to lord or parent, he cannot be regarded as living in proper conformity with it. . . . Wherever he may be lying down or sleeping, his feet must never for an instant be pointing in the direction of his lord's presence. If he sets up a straw bale for archery practice anywhere, the arrows must never fall toward the place where his lord is.

How does a samurai treat his wife?

One who is a samurai should, if he finds in his wife matters that do not please him, admonish her to agree with him by reasonable argument, though in trifles it is well that he be indulgent and patient with her. But if her disposition is consistently bad and he considers she will be of no further use, he may divorce her and send her home to her parents under exceptional circumstances. But should he not do this but keep her as his wife so that people address her by the respectful titles of **okusama** *and* **[o]kamisama***, and then shout at her and revile her with all sorts of abusive expressions he is behaving in a way that may be suitable to hirelings and coolies who live in the back streets of the business quarter but is certainly not proper for a samurai. Much less is it fitting for such a one to lay his hand on his sword or menace his wife with his clenched fist, an outrageous thing that only a*

cowardly samurai would think of doing. For a girl born in a warrior house and of age to be married would never, if she were a man, for a moment tolerate being threatened by the fist of anyone. It is only because she is unfortunately born a woman that she has to shed tears and put up with it.
How does a samurai face death?
The samurai has to set before all other things the consideration of how to meet his inevitable end. However clever or capable he may have been, if he is upset and wanting in composure and so makes a poor showing when he comes to face it all, his previous good deeds will be like water and all decent people will despise him so that he will be covered with shame. For when a samurai goes out to battle and does valiant and splendid exploits and makes a great name, it is only because he made up his mind to die. And if unfortunately he gets the worst of it and he and his head have to part company, when his opponent asks for his name he must declare it at once loudly and clearly and yield up his head with a smile on his lips and without the slightest sign of fear.

Daidoji Yuzan, 1941, trans. A. L. Sadler.

ethics of filial piety, though the recipient is the lord, not the parents; on correct conduct and "etiquette" (li); on *jin/ren*. But there is another dimension to bushido as enunciated by Daidoji Yuzan, a single-minded concentration on death. We will need to return to Buddhism for clarification.

Zen Buddhism and Samurai Culture

There was a saying during the Kamakura period: "Tendai is for the imperial court, Shingon for the nobility, Zen for the warrior class, and Pure Land for the masses." The saying reflects high consciousness of a class structure and of a multistranded Buddhism, diverse enough to provide disciplines and doctrines suited to the very different social locations of its devotees.

Tendai was founded by the monk Saicho (767–822), who traveled to China and returned to open a monastery at Mt. Hiei. He attempted to synthesize all the sects of Buddhism that perplexed the court with their various claims, teaching a form of universal salvation with the notion that Buddhahood is found in all sentient beings. This is the teaching of the Lotus Sutra, which, as we have seen, so captured the imagination of the court.

Shingon was founded by the brilliant monk, Kukai (775–835), whose monastery on Mt. Koya may still be the most flourishing monastery in Japan. Shingon means "True Word"; its focus is the bodhisattva Vairocana, known in Japan as Dainichi, the supreme Buddha from whom emanates all the others. Shingon took the lead in assimilating the major Shinto deities by equating Dainichi with Amaterasu. Shingon was influenced more than the other sects by the mysteries of Tantra; believers are helped toward enlightenment with a rich array of talismans, mantras, rites, and symbolism.

Pure Land has a simple message, which accounts in part for the spread of Buddhism, which had been a faith of the elite, to the peasants and townspeople of Japan. In the degenerate post-1052 age of mappo, only the saving grace of Amida Buddha can bring salvation and rebirth in the Pure Land (*jodo*). Salvation required the simple initiative of calling on the name of Buddha by chanting the *nembutsu*.

Zen, however, was the Buddhism of the samurai. This presents something of a puzzle, most famously posed by the great popularizer of Zen in the West, D. T. Suzuki: Buddhism is a religion of compassion, of love and peace, which has never been engaged in warlike activities. How is it that Zen came to activate the fighting spirit of the Japanese warrior (Suzuki 1959)?

It was pure historical coincidence that when the monk Eisai returned from his studies with Chinese masters of Chan Buddhism in 1191, a new political order had emerged in Japan. The government was now divided between Kyoto and Kamakura, and finding Kyoto uninterested in his new ideas, he pushed on to Kamakura. There, Minamoto Yoritomo had just died, but his widow took a deep interest in the new ideas. She built Eisai a temple and brought attention to his teachings, which became the Rinzai school of Zen. The next important convert was the fourth Hojo regent, Hojo Tokiyori, who was certified by a Chinese master as having attained enlightenment. Soon samurai were going to Zen monasteries for training and discipline to make them better warriors. Half a century later, another monk, Dogen (1200–1253) went to China and came back to found a competing branch, Soto Zen. Soto and Rinzai became and remained the two principal forms of Zen Buddhism.

Because of Zen's stress on self-discipline and control, it appealed to the warriors of the samurai class. It emphasized religious values that harmonized with the spartan warrior values of simplicity, asceticism, discipline in the martial arts, single-minded devotion to one's lord, and willingness to risk all, to die for him. Takeda Shingen (1521–1573), one of the great warlords, admonished his followers to practice Zen by quoting an old saying: "The practice of Zen has no secret except standing on the verge of life and death." There was a kind of salvation in dying for one's lord. "He who dies for the sake of his lord does not live in vain, whether he goes to the sea and his corpse is left in a watery grave, or whether he goes to the mountain and the only shroud for his lifeless body is the mountain grass" (Bellah 1957:93).

But samurai could not become full Zen monks except, as they often did, in retirement. One might suppose there was insuperable conflict between the life devoted to meditation and the activism of the warrior's life, and indeed Yoshida Kenko wrote critically of the monk Shinkai that "he was wont to sit all day long pondering on his latter end; this is no doubt a very suitable attitude for a recluse but by no means so for a warrior. For so he would have to neglect his military duties and the way of loyalty and filial piety, and he must on the contrary be constantly busy with his affairs both public and private. But whenever he has a little spare time to himself and can be quiet he should not fail to revert to this question of death and reflect carefully on it" (Bellah 1957:92).

Something that can be identified as "zen culture" emerged from these spartan, martial, and Buddhist values. It included a valuation of death; a romanticization of the withered, the cold, the lonely; the tea ceremony for its simplicity; *sumi-e* painting for its monochromatic abstraction and austerity; the severe zen landscape of rocks, gravel, and natural arrangements; and the self-abnegation of the zen monkhood. All this is far from the hedonism and desire for plunder usually associated with warrior cultures; the samurai warrior, like the Buddhist monk, lived a life of selfless devotion to his ideals.

The focus on death in bushido is not immediately apparent in the views and practices of Zen; we shall have to return to this question.

The Practice of Zen

Zen rejected the popular Buddhist views that salvation can come from faith in a savior (Amida Buddha) or a magical book (the Lotus Sutra) or recitation of mantras like the nembutsu, and returned to an older Buddhist view that enlightenment can only happen through the focused, committed effort of the seeker. Two concepts from very early Indian Buddhism became central features of Zen. From the writings of Nagarjuna (ca. 150–250) the doctrine of śunyatā, or emptiness, urges recognition that nothing has origination, dissipation, permanence—nothing has existence in and of itself. This is true as well for fundamental Buddhist doctrines, which, to use modern language, Nagarjuna deconstructed: karma, self (atma), the fully enlightened one, and nirvana. This view was wedded to a second ancient tradition, the practice of rigorous meditation (*dhyāna*, from which derive the Chinese *chan* and Japanese *zen*). On what does one meditate? Not on the image of Buddha, not on the Lotus Sutra, not on the nembutsu, but on emptiness itself. The goal remains attainment of Buddhahood, but what Buddhahood might be is, of course, the problem. According to the seventeenth-century *Warrior of Zen: Diamond-hard Wisdom of Mind of Suzuki Shosan,* "What we call Buddhahood is the fact that all things are originally empty. Fundamentally, there is no me, no you, no dharma, no Buddha. Buddhahood is complete separation from everything, letting go and being free" (Braverman 1994:29).

The doctrine of emptiness swept aside almost all other doctrines (paradoxically, it was itself a doctrine); it removed the need for texts and creeds. Texts, creeds, doctrines, and relics were, in fact, part of the illusory nonreality of the world. They took special aim at the intellectual world of ideas, categories, logic, reason. The "wisdom of the belly" (*hara*) was superior to any wisdom of study, preaching, reciting, or rites. This wisdom was gained by "sitting in oblivion," i.e., by meditation on emptiness. The Zen form of enlightenment is known as *satori*. For Zen masters, it was the intellect, more than the body (which perplexed Hindu mystics), which stood in the way of enlightenment. Zen masters were keenly aware that breaking the hold of the structured world of ideas and concepts, of reason itself, to get to the state of emptiness that is satori was extraordinarily difficult. Thought keeps creeping back in. If reason was the problem, then perhaps deliberate, befuddling un-reason was the way to break its hold. So, at the early stages of movement toward satori, when emptiness is still a distant goal, Zen novices are given intellectual puzzles called *koan* to meditate on. These are very far from the kinds of mantras and sutras used in meditation in other forms of Buddhism. The term once meant an authoritative public document, but koan now tend to be anecdotes about some ancient master or a dialogue between a master and his disciple. They tend to be obscure, illogical little stories presented as puzzles to solve or interpret. "The sound of one hand clapping." D. T. Suzuki provides some examples; one is an exploration of the nature of Self:

Ki of Unryu-in monastery:

Q: "What is my Self?"

A: "It is like you and me."

Q: "In this case there is no duality."

A: "Eighteen thousand miles off!" (Suzuki 1959)

The goal is not to solve the koan-puzzle in the way one would solve a mathematical formula or a logical puzzle; the goal is to break through thought barriers to the direct existential insight of satori itself.

The nature of satori has always been a mystery, perhaps the key mystery of Zen. It is a postulated reality that hardly anyone ever successfully attains or maintains. By definition it is indescribable—anything capturable in words cannot be the wordless experience of Zen. (The influence of Taoism is evident here; "The Tao that can be spoken is not the eternal Tao" could also be said of the illusive experience of satori.) Nevertheless, there are some descriptive accounts to inspire seekers:

> It was beyond description and altogether incommunicable, for there was nothing in the world to which it could be compared. . . . As I looked round and up and down, the whole universe with its multitudinous sense-objects now appeared quite different; what was loath-

some before, together with ignorance and passions, was seen as nothing else but the outflow of my own inmost nature, which itself remained bright, true, and transparent. (Ross 1960:42)

Another account is given by Shosan:

> Kensho (seeing into one's own nature), too, is something I have experienced. From the twenty-seventh to the twenty-eighth day of the eighth month of my sixty-first year, I felt completely detached from life and death and in touch with my true nature. I danced with gratitude, feeling that nothing existed. At that time, you could have threatened to cut off my head and it wouldn't have meant a thing. Yet after thirty days like this, I decided it didn't suit me. It was nothing more than a realization based on a particular state of mind. So I discarded it and returned to my previous state. I filled my heart with death and practiced uncompromisingly. As I might have known, it had all been a big delusion. And here I am now, treasuring this bag of manure called Shosan. (Braverman 1994:36)

An attempt is sometimes made to capture the state of satori in a curious English term: "is-ness." That is, pure being; "a direct pointing to the soul of man"—but not soul in any Western or Hindu sense, only seeing into one's nature, that pure, empty, inner core. The emphasis in the statement should be on "direct," unmediated by concepts, words, symbols, or images.

One of the most beloved attempts to visually rather than verbally express the nature of Zen enlightenment is the *Oxherd Tale*. This is a sequence of ten drawings, first conceived in China during Sung dynasty, and there have been many versions, including new drawings made in 1994 (Braverman 1994) though with little variation in the content of the ten figures. An oxherd boy searches for his lost ox. The ox, a simple and common farmer's companion, symbolizes his own nature. In the first six images, the boy holds the rope and looks for his ox, spots footprints, catches sight of his ox, gets the rope around its neck, and finally masters it. This much represents the seeker's effort through self-discipline and meditation to grasp his true nature. In the seventh scene, the ox is now forgotten; "you are a man of no-Mind." The eighth is an empty circle; the boy and ox have both disappeared. The ninth is a scene of pure nature; trees, streams, hills, with neither boy nor ox. Finally, in the last scene, he returns to the world, and we see him in a marketplace as an old man carrying his few belongings on a pole, indistinguishable in appearance from other persons still fully embedded in their lives, far from encounters with satori. As Shosan comments on the tenth picture: "'Entering the Marketplace with Giving Hands' depicts a selfless person with outstretched hands. For him, delusion and enlightenment, the ignorant and the saintly, are all the same. Whatever he does, nothing obstructs him. Evil becomes good. Liquor stores and fish markets become places of conversion to Buddhahood" (Braverman 1994:97).

Reality has now been grasped fully and it seems the boy is back to the beginning, but not exactly. The Japanese term *kono-mama* means "this-ness"; *sono-mama*, "that-ness." *Mama* means something like "as-it-is-ness." Or, we might use a somewhat better English term for "is-ness," "immediacy." There is nothing beyond—and one directly connects to—the immediate reality of trees, streams, fish markets, and other people.

Zen Buddhism's Institutions

Somehow one doesn't expect Zen's anti-intellectual, antistructural, antirationality to be embedded in a rigid hierarchy of monasteries, a specific lineage of patriarchs, and highly regimented monastic culture. Yet that is another of Zen's strange contradictions: the contradiction between direct unmediated experience and a high degree of institutionalization. During the period of the formation of Zen as a warrior's religion, the four large Kyoto temples and five large Kamakura temples were given first-rank status. A second-level class of sixty temples was then established, and there were two hundred additional temples scattered elsewhere. Monks and warriors who had achieved enlightenment were given written certificates in proof of their status!

The Zen monastery is a severe place one does not easily gain admission to, and its discipline bears traces of the warrior culture it was once linked to. In *The Training of the Zen Buddhist Monk*, Suzuki describes what it is like with another series of parablelike illustrations. The would-be monk arrives and begs to be let in, but is told to go away. He spreads out his cloth near the door to meditate and wait. Some time later, maybe in the middle of the night, they let him into the lodging room. He spends the night inside in meditation. The rejection and humiliation may go on for days. Finally he will be given a place in the *zendo* and given initiation into the brotherhood. But he has still to meet the master (*roshi*). Finally, he is taken to meet the roshi, and allowed to join the other monks in evening *zazen* (seated meditation). Meditation may be overseen by a monk with a whip to give a warning lash to the novice whose back slumps in sleep. The real beginning of his Zen life is when the master gives him his first koan. But the relation between him and the master may be filled with tension, for the master's task is to monitor the breakdown, sometimes compared to a psychological breakdown, of the false structures of the mind. The time not spent in meditation is devoted to simple, menial, real-life tasks like sweeping, carrying water, chopping wood, and gardening.

Zen Culture: Zen and the Arts

The interwoven culture of bushido and zen produced corresponding expressions in the arts for the aristocratic samurai class. If the soul is identified with the entire universe, then one has or should develop a close affinity to a hummingbird hovering at a spring blossom, a length of bamboo under a new fall of snow. Looking closely at the small, the insignificant, the fleeting brings you closer to yourself and your own impermanence, linking your death to the myriad small deaths of all beings and all moments, and gives you tranquility in its contemplation. Zen painters aimed to capture such moments in spontaneous ink on silk paintings known as sumi-e.

The Zen garden is not like any other garden style in the world. Forget the luxurious density of flowers in an English country garden; forget even Japan's own glorious landscapes of coast and hillside. A Zen garden may be three carefully arranged stones in the middle of a bed of raked gravel. The most famous Zen garden is one created at Ryoanji in Kyoto in 1499 for monks to view while meditating. It consists of fifteen rocks of immense value (huge sums can be paid for the perfect aesthetically shaped rock) arranged in five groups in a sea of perfectly raked white sand.

An aesthetic value came to the fore during the feudal period that gives conceptual unity to the various cultural strands coming down to the present: the austere lifestyle of the warrior, the severity of Zen Buddhism, the starkness of the Zen garden, the typical themes of *haiku* and sumi-e:

> The concept of *wabi* has loomed large in Japanese cultural history because it both identified a remarkable taste in things and provoked a substantial discourse on the philosophy and aesthetics guiding that taste. A term of classical origin with numerous medieval associates as well, wabi came to the center of tea discourse from the end of the sixteenth century. It was linked to various traditions—classical and medieval poetry, noh drama, Zen Buddhism, eremetic practices. It was glossed by a rich, not specifically artistic, vocabulary—by words like *chill, withered, rustic, lonely, pure, austere, lowly,* and *imperfect.* Descriptive of peculiar objects (crudely lacquered caddies, celadons with yellow-brown glazes, storage or water jars of rough workmanship), it also evoked a mentality. (Berry 1994:277)

Perhaps the tea ceremony best came to embody wabi, though as Berry has said, the value permeates Japanese culture. Tea was brought to Japan by the monk Eisai in 1191 in the form of seeds, which he planted on the hillside outside Kyoto. Tea drinking began in temples and quickly spread in all social directions, first among the elite at the shogun's court and soon to the urban merchant class. Tea's practical function is captured in a legend of its origin. Bodhidarma (Daruma), the first Zen patriarch, spent nine straight years meditating before a blank wall, struggling constantly against falling asleep. Finally, in exasperation he ripped off his eyelids and threw them on the ground. Where they fell, the first glossy-leaved tea plants grew. Later, when his disciples also had trouble staying awake in meditation, they began making a drink of the leaves of the tea plant. This kept them awake.

In the chaotic sixteenth century, Berry writes, elite Japanese in Kyoto and Kamakura began keeping tea diaries to record details of the parties they attended, the names of the hosts and guests, details about objects in the rooms (generally works of art from China), and menus of the food served afterward. Tea drinking became a social passion that more resembled a modern gallery opening than our image of the Japanese tea ceremony. People milled around, served tea by servants, and admired the art. The best known of such parties were those given by military men of highest rank, including the shogun.

But a social transformation occurred in the sixteenth century as tea was appropriated by commoners and a group of experts who eventually founded schools of tea practice and lineages of tea masters who carried specific tea traditions forward in time. Under these experts, tea was transformed from a vehicle for elite communication and a respite from war to a ritual in which a host himself humbly prepares the tea in the presence of his guests and serves them. Special rooms or buildings were created just for the serving of tea in a standard four-and-a-half-mat room. Tea parties became more intimate and became less a show of one's Chinese paintings than a place to value a few simple, perhaps even rustic, functional items: a rude kettle, a bamboo whisk, a roughly glazed cup. Thus, the simple act of drinking a cup of plain tea was raised to an art form, a ritual, and an embodiment of a unique Japanese aesthetic.

THE COLONIAL PERIOD

Chronology of Colonial Asia

1400	
	1453—Fall of Constantinople to Turks, European access to Asia closed
	1494—Treaty of Tordesilla divides world between Portugal and Spain
	1498—Vasco de Gama sails around Cape of Good Hope to India
1500	
	1510—Portuguese found Goa in India
	1511—Portuguese capture Malacca
	1549—Francis Xavier arrives in Japan
1600	1601—Matteo Ricci permitted residence in Beijing
	1635—Japanese close to foreign trade by shogunal edict
1700	
	1725—China bans Christianity
	1767—Destruction of Ayutthaya by Burma
1800	1819—Raffles acquires Singapore
	1840—First Opium War
	1842—Treaty of Nanjing; Britain acquires Hong Kong
	1853—Commodore Perry arrives in Japan
1900	
	1937—Nanjing Massacre

A t midnight, June 30, 1997, at a carefully selected gathering at the brand-new Hong Kong Exhibition Centre in Hong Kong, Prince Charles gave a brief speech and the Union Jack was drawn down. The red flag of the Peoples' Republic of China was hoisted and Jiang Zemin gave an equally brief speech, and the ceremony was over. Prince Charles, ex-governor Chris Patten, and his wife and daughters boarded the royal yacht and sailed out of Victoria Harbor. The British empire and the period of European colonialism were truly over. Looking back from the vantage point of the 1990s, it is hard to imagine that colonialism could ever have happened at all.

One of the great mysteries of the colonial era is how a small group of traders, adventurers, soldiers, and missionaries from a handful of small European nations ten thousand miles away could have come to dominate nearly every Asian nation. There is a perception about the beginning of the colonial period that when the first galleons and schooners full of energetic merchants from Europe's advanced societies appeared in harbors and deltas, they encountered Asian nations economically adrift under sluggish skies, limited by subsistence economies and weak trade only in luxury goods. Having "discovered" the East—places with names like the Spice Islands, Hindoostan, and Cathay—the European nations soon transformed it, first with trade, later with direct colonial intervention, which, whatever its evils, at least served to provide modern infrastructures for transportation, communication, education, and medicine. In this telling of the story, the initiatives, the dynamism, the innovations, and the perspective are all European. If it could truly be said that colonialism set in place infrastructures that would promote economic growth and competitive advantage in the world system, then the economic dynamos of the present period should be Jakarta, Calcutta, Saigon, and Rangoon. That it's Tokyo, Taipei, Seoul, Singapore, Hong Kong, and increasingly Guangdong and Shanghai makes even the silver lining of colonialism look implausible.

This final chapter attempts to summarize the nature of the colonial impact on the regions we have been examining. What was the state of trade and international relations prior to the European intervention? Why did the Europeans come at all? Could the British have acquired their empire in a "fit of absentmindedness," as they sometimes like to put it, or if not, how and why? Which nations came under external control? Which nations escaped? Why? And finally, how were things left when the last colonial administrators packed their bags and went home to retirements in England, France, and Holland? (The Americans didn't go home to quite the same degree.)

These are far too many questions for the space remaining, and in
any case, no definitive answers could be provided, even with enough
space and time. For now, in the historical period known as postcolonialism, all the old issues undergoing the process of reexamination. "Postcolonialism" refers, first of all, simply to a historical period on the order of
Ming dynasty or the Mughal Era. Colonial powers have fallen; something
else is now going on. Of course, such historical periodizing is the product
of intellectual labor; otherwise history is just "one damn thing after
another." A second sense of "postcolonialism" is the continuing cultural
impact of the colonial period. Colonialism left its impact everywhere it
went in Asia, in the dominance of alien languages over others now in
decline; in radically altered systems of production; in restructured class
systems and the disappearance of whole classes; in electoral politics and
political cultures honed first in Europe, then in nationalist resistance
movements; in tastes for material goods. There is a postcolonial literature; a postcolonial feminism.

The third sense of postcolonialism is the drive to deconstruct its
remnants. This is being done politically in the once-colonized nations as
they attempt to reconstruct their identities and evaluate how much of the
old colonial culture they wish to keep and what to change, if and where
they can. This is also being done intellectually, by the scholarly project of
deconstructing colonial knowledge. Colonialism's intellectual underpinnings were the Enlightenment confidence about progress and the dedication to science to bring it about. Science meant both the technological discoveries that fueled the emerging world economic system and also the sci-
ences of cartography, geography, botany, and anthropology. The Enlightenment was about understanding the world; that is, building knowledge
about the world. One of its myths is that science somehow stands free of
the social and political order, and that "knowledge" and "truth" are independent of context. Enlightenment thinkers believed that it was irrelevant that this vast new knowledge base was built within the framework
of colonial domination of the world. This scientific project could not have
been the sheer, neutral, objective truth that was its fundamental goal and
declared methodology. This search for "truth" and "objective knowledge"
could not have failed to be colored by the social location of the scientists,
who were almost all European-American. Now, in the postcolonial era, we
are heirs to this vast structure of knowledge, and we must look at it with
suspicion. Perhaps not the pure technology that sends spaceships to Mars
(though the goal might be questioned), but certainly the part that tries to
account for human nature and human diversity; that posits a historical
direction and a value called progress; and that tries to theorize the correct
relation between political systems and economic ones.

Edward Said, a Palestinian professor of English and Comparative
Literature at Columbia University, published *Orientalism* in 1978, which

radically altered how we viewed the knowledge of non-Western societies that has accumulated over more than two centuries. By "Orient" he did not mean the actual societies of Asia and the Middle East as known to the people who were born into them; he meant instead the knowledge compiled in the West *about* these societies. He argued that "ideas, cultures, and histories cannot seriously be understood or studied without their force, or more precisely their configurations of power, also being studied. . . . The relationship between Occident and Orient is a relationship of power, of domination, of varying degrees of a complex hegemony" (Said 1978:5).

Orientalism as an intellectual project and growing knowledge base began during the early centuries of colonialism. In the case of Britain, it began with the generation of Sir William Jones, sometimes then called "Oriental Jones," who studied Sanskrit and began the process of trying to understand Indian languages and ideas (chapter 3). The process went on throughout the decades and centuries of British, French, and Dutch colonial administration. As they put institutions into place, codified law, established schools and hospitals, supported some classes and undermined others, they were informed by their own knowledge base, so that all those institutions, so thoroughly embedded into the colonized nations by the end, bear the marks of Orientalist knowledge. Even the heirs of the modern, postcolonial nations of Asia today are shaped by Orientalist knowledge. That includes the leadership of independence movements who were recipients of "handovers" stretching from 1947 (India) to 1997 (Hong Kong) as well as the classes created, then educated, under colonialism. As Said put it, "Orientalism, therefore, is not an airy European fantasy about the Orient, but a created body of theory and practice in which, for many generations, there has been a considerable material investment" (Said 1978:6).

I raise this issue as a caveat for what follows. I will attempt to avoid "Orientalist" pitfalls, but reevaluation of the period is a major scholarly enterprise these days, in which researchers from Asian nations are playing a prominent role. New understandings of the past are constantly emerging in this postcolonial period of world history.

TRADE IN THE PRECOLONIAL PERIOD

It could not have been predicted, in the fourteenth century, that among the several international trade networks then existing, the one up in the far western corner of the Eurasian landmass would come to dominate almost the entire world. It was far from the richest one at the time. In the fourteenth century, there were several major trade networks.

China during Ming dynasty was the central power of a far-flung trade-tribute system. They had developed excellent ocean-going junks, some as long as 180 feet, benefiting from the Chinese invention of the magnetic compass (carried by Arab traders to the west), the sextant that could chart courses at sea by fixing on the big dipper, watertight compartments, dry docks, paddle-wheel ships, and weather forecasting. During the period from 1405 to 1480, China became a maritime power that might have come to dominate the Pacific and Indian oceans as Europeans later did. In 1405, a Muslim eunuch from Yunnan named Zheng He commanded a fleet of over three hundred ships and twenty thousand men, which sailed as far as India, Hormuz, and the east coast of Africa. This armada set out not to conquer but to trade. They were specially concerned with the strategic city of Melaka (Malacca) on the strait between Malaysia and Sumatra, which controlled the waters connecting the Indian and Pacific oceans. But by 1480, bureaucrats at the capital began to worry about the costs of these maritime excursions, and perhaps worried about the growing wealth and power of merchants in the eastern coastal cities. They turned down new requests for funds, burned records of Zheng He's accomplishments, and turned inward, leaving the seas to others.

The Straits of Malacca that were of such interest to China during its brief period as a maritime power were a center of maritime trade from a very early period. Whoever controlled the straits and nearby islands and peninsula reaped the benefits of a continuous sea-based trade, the southern trade route of Eurasia. The first to do so was the Srivijayan Empire, a contemporary of the very different, land- and agriculture-based state of Angkor. Srivijaya thrived on a trade that linked the treasures of China—porcelain, silk, lacquers—with India, the Middle East, and ultimately Europe. This trade link was based on a model of international trade very different from the one Europeans were to bring in a later period—the theoretical notion, at least, of free trade among equal nations, this idea that dominates even today. For Srivijaya to be able to play the middleman role between China, on the one hand, and a host of Indian and Arab traders on the other, the empire had to submit to the Chinese model of international trade. For China, there could only be exchanges between the Middle Kingdom and its tributary states. There was no question of equal trade between equal nations. No nation was the equal of China, and the emperor was the Son of Heaven; nominally, at least, he claimed to be the emperor of the entire world. The Chinese knew of the existence of nations beyond their control and made no particular assertions about them, but any nation wanting to engage in trade with China had to formally acknowledge China's suzerainty by arriving with "tribute" and performing the three kneelings and nine prostrations before a symbol of the emperor. In return, they were lavished with gifts of greater value than they had brought, plus an imperial letter of patent, a seal of rank, and the

Chinese calendar. They then had the legal right to trade and could get on with business. This vassal status may have seemed like a small humiliation for Srivijaya, since it did not involve them in any effort by China to dominate them politically, and it gave them access to the wealth of Chinese goods so desired in the rest of the world.

A third center of trade was a network linking Indian and Arab merchants in the Indian Ocean. Imagine the Indian Ocean as an enormous version of the Mediterranean Sea; small, coast-hugging trading ships could make stops along a vast semicircle from Zanzibar to Arabia to the two coasts of India to Burma to Indonesia. Calicut on the Malabar coast was a rich trade city where merchants who worked these waters exchanged gold, jewels, ivory, silk, and spices.

In the early 1500s, when the first Portuguese ships began going directly to the Spice Islands, they described encountering enormous ships plying Southeast Asian waters, larger than their own largest ships. All were over two hundred tons, and some were as large as one thousand tons and carried one thousand men. They were called *jong* in Malay and Javanese, which the Portuguese called *junco.* (The English learned this term, "junk," and applied it to Chinese ships.) The main builders of these ships, heirs to two thousand years of shipbuilding, were all along the north coast of Java, southern Borneo, and Pegu, close to the teak forests. The Srivijayan empire was long gone, and these were local sultans and merchants engaged in the lucrative long-distance, high-seas shipping, traveling to southern China, Melaka, the Coromandel coast of India, Aden, the Red Sea, and Madagascar.

A fourth center of trade was the land-based northern Eurasian route, the stretch of central Asia crossed by the ancient Silk Road. Throughout its history, this venerable trade link between the Far East and the Mediterranean opened and closed depending on the local political climate, but from 1240 to 1340 it was again open, protected by Mongol outposts. During that "window of opportunity" thousands of European merchants poured eastward, including Marco Polo (though revisionist history now questions whether he actually got to China; he may have written his famous book on the basis of accounts of his father and uncles).

Finally, there was the trade center of the eastern Mediterranean, where merchants from the Italian city-states, Byzantium, and North Africa were in a lucrative transnational trade system.

Each of these networks was a "world system," in the phrase made famous by Immanuel Wallerstein (1976). This term contrasts with the term "empire." Both an empire and a world system are transnational bonds among polities of various size and type, but an empire is a system of political domination whereas a world system is an economic system. There may indeed be inequities in such systems—Wallerstein's analysis of the capitalist world system is an analysis of economic dominance—but they are not based on direct political dominance. Of course, it can happen, and did, that a world system produces empires, and that is the topic we turn to next. But the capitalist world system was always larger than, and different from, the empires that thrived on it.

EUROPEAN EMPIRES IN ASIA

Portuguese Port Cities and Priests

The European period in Asia opens with the Portuguese. Prince Henry of Portugal, "The Navigator," in one of the earliest partnerships of science and commerce, sponsored exploration by Vasco da Gama in search of a new route to the Indian Ocean that avoided the unfriendly Turkish-controlled Red Sea. Could you get there via the Cape of Good Hope? As it turned out, you could; and soon, Portuguese trading ships were going all the way to Southeast Asia. When Vasco da Gama arrived home at the end of the fifteenth century with a cargo of cinnamon mixed with clay—for which he had paid double its market value in Calicut, then sold it for sixty times the total cost of his two-year expedition—the European rush to Asia was on.

Four years before this fortuitous voyage, the Pope had sought to contain Portuguese and Spanish rivalry by dividing the world between them in the Treaty of Tordesilla (1494). Spain got the New World and Portugal got Asia. This meant that during the sixteenth century, Portugal had no competition from Spain except for Spain's backdoor entry to the Philippines via the Pacific late in the century.

The first viceroy of Portugal in the East was Dom Affonso d'Albuquerque (1509–1515) whose vision of an Asian empire was fired by a loathing of Muslims. This made the Islamic Mughal Empire in India, then in its prime, a particular challenge. Albuquerque's strategy was to establish a series of fortresses along the major coasts of the Indian Ocean. Unlike Arab and Indian trading vessels, his ships were armed. His first conquest was at Goa on the Malabar Coast, a city that still retains its Portuguese flavor and was the very last spot in India to be relinquished 450 years later. From here the Portuguese controlled the pilgrim route to Mecca and could interfere with the spice trade from Southeast Asia. In 1511, Albuquerque captured the crucial city of Melaka, and Macao was founded after Portuguese traders were expelled from Guangzhou. With coastal trade fortresses in India, Ceylon, Southeast Asia, and China, Prince Henry was soon one of the richest princes in Europe, enhanced by another source of wealth: pirating Arab ships in lonely waters.

At mid-century, three sailors who had taken passage in a Chinese junk were stranded by a typhoon off the coast of Japan. The Japanese welcomed them with curiosity and friendliness. The Japanese were particularly interested in the weapons of the Portuguese castaways; very soon there were Japanese copies of them, which would transform the war culture of the samurai. Before long, both traders and missionaries were making their way to Japan.

Francis Xavier and two other members of the Order of Jesus, known as the Jesuits, having just left Goa, landed in 1549 in early Tokugawa Japan, and immediately began making converts. At first, Christianity seemed to the Japanese to be another form of Buddhism; Christ was a saving bodhisattva, as loving and merciful as Amida or Kannon. The daimyo were given to understand that the price of lucrative trade was allowing the Jesuits to preach, a deal they were willing to make. But the intolerance of a form of Christianity that then was gearing up for the Inquisition back in Europe made enemies among the Buddhist monks, especially Xavier's insistence that anyone who died without being a Christian would burn in hell forever. For people who revered their ancestors and had never really believed in hell, despite all the Buddhist iconography of hell, this was a shocking doctrine.

Jesuits were received by Nobunaga in 1568 with a courtesy that astonished people who knew him; he had them to private suppers and listened to their religious views even while remaining a Tendai Buddhist. The samurai admired the Jesuits because they shared values of asceticism, loyalty, learning, and a certain aristocratic arrogance. And the Jesuits introduced material items the Japanese came to desire: tobacco, clocks, globes, maps, musical instruments, bread (still called by its Portuguese name, *pan*), rosaries, and European clothes. Perhaps most significant of all were the castle-fortifications that the daimyo began to build in the Portuguese style. Hideyoshi's castle at Osaka is the most beautiful example.

But when Spanish Franciscans arrived, the two orders began to intrigue against one another. Dutch and English arrived next, and gave Ieyasu a Protestant view of Rome. These foreigners described the ambitions of European monarchs, and Spanish armadas arriving in the Philippines vividly illustrated the dangers. There were a great many Christian converts, perhaps as many as three hundred thousand at the peak, along with a number of daimyo, and these, it was feared, might align themselves with a foreign power against the shogun. Acting on his growing suspicions, Hideyoshi executed six Franciscans, three Jesuits, and seventeen Japanese converts in 1597, thus beginning four decades of persecution. In 1638, thirty-seven thousand Christians led by five samurai took refuge in an old feudal castle in Shimabara. They held out for two months, but were finally overtaken and all but 105 were killed. This was virtually the end of Christianity in Japan. After 1640, no foreigners remained except a handful of Dutch who were practically imprisoned at

Nagasaki, Japan's sole source of knowledge about the outside world (this knowledge thus was called "Dutch Learning") until Perry arrived in 1853.

The Spanish were, of course, cheating on the Treaty of Tordesilla when they established a presence in Manila, but politics back home—uniting the crowns of Portugal and Spain—made all that moot. They named the Philippines after Philip II of Spain, and made themselves welcome in Asia by sending shiploads of Mexican silver across the "Spanish lake," the Pacific. By the end of the sixteenth century, seventy-two metric tons of silver were arriving every year from the New World on the famous "Manila galleons," and Mexican dollars became the de facto standard currency in international trade, the role of the US dollar in the twentieth century. In the Philippines, no strong state had emerged on the order of China or Japan, and the many small-scale tribal societies were unable to fend off the Spanish. Thus, the Philippines became the first Asian region, aside from the small Portuguese coast towns, to succumb to colonial dominance.

Half a century after Japan's ill-fated encounter with Europeans, the Italian Jesuit Matteo Ricci was granted residence in Beijing, and for 125 years, until they were banned from China in 1725, the Jesuits were a conduit for knowledge of China in Europe and of European learning in China. Europe was having its own form of Enlightenment (not the Buddhist one), and the learned Jesuits were the right monastic order to bring this new learning to China. Jesuits translated Euclid's geometry, over a hundred treatises on Western science and technology, and many Christian works into Chinese. The Chinese emperor Kangxi (1661–1722), a man of tremendous energy and curiosity, was particularly favorable to the Jesuits, especially to Ferdinand Verbiest, with whom he endlessly discussed science and religion (Spence 1974). The Jesuits wrote back to Europe that China was ruled by "philosopher-kings" (they meant the Confucian scholar-official class), provoking great admiration for China among Europe's intellectuals. "Chinoiserie" came into vogue, with Chinese-style furniture, fabrics, and ceramics ornamenting mansions, and pagodas rising from lavish gardens. But the Catholic mission to China self-destructed in much the same way it did in Japan, and in 1724, Christianity was banned from the Middle Kingdom.

During the sixteenth century, Portuguese were also stopping along Vietnam's long coastline to buy raw silk, and soon they were followed by Jesuits. Again, Jesuits had great success in converting the people. The Vietnam elite, the Nguyen dynasty, had begun its conquest of Vietnam from their central capital at Hue, gradually taking over the Mekong delta and establishing a Confucian state on the Chinese model. They organized an examination system for selecting officials on the basis of scholarship in the Confucian classics, and created a script for their language derived from Chinese characters. The Jesuits had little success with this sinicized elite, but by the nineteenth century, there were more Christians in Vietnam than in all of China. The Jesuits created a romanized script for Vietnamese, which eventually beat out the Chinese script. The Christianization of Vietnam continued for the next two hundred years; persecution of Christians did not begin until the nineteenth century, when it provided a pretext for French invasion.

English and Dutch Merchant Companies

When the Spanish and Portuguese were powerful enough to divide the world between them, they didn't leave any little spaces for other nations, and consequently they largely owned the sixteenth century, reducing people like Sir Francis Drake to risky adventures and piracy. But when the English defeated the Spanish armada in 1588, the seas were less dangerous for English and Dutch sailors, who wanted their share of discovery and trade. The Dutch were a bit ahead of the English, with an excellent center of cartography in Antwerp, ambitious merchant houses, and nationalist loathing of the Spanish tyrants they had only recently escaped. In the 1590s, they sent no less than ninety-one ships to run the Spanish blockade to the Spice Islands. English ships were having less success, although Ralph Fitch had visited Mughal emperor Akbar's two capital cities in 1585 and reported that each was twice the size of London. At that point, England's only ambition was a share of the Indonesian spice trade.

At the beginning of the seventeenth century, two unique and crucial organizations were founded. On the last day of 1600, Queen Elizabeth I signed a charter creating the East India Company; in 1602, the Dutch East India Company was chartered (the VOC, for Vereenigde Oostindische Compagnie). Both were joint-stock companies, early forms of the financial corporation. No English or Dutch merchant could afford the huge costs and risks of outfitting a ship and supporting it for a two-year voyage to Southeast Asia; one ship, the *Red Dragon*, cost thirty-seven hundred pounds and took four years to complete a round trip. But 217 London merchants each contributed a few hundred pounds, thus forming the first great trading company. The Dutch raised ten times more capital than the British, and thus were able to send thirty-eight ships to the Indian Ocean, where they defeated the Portuguese fleet and seized Amboina. The English were only able to send out four ships on their first venture, but their risk was handsomely repaid by an average profit of 170 percent on the first seven voyages.

The crowns of both countries granted their corporation a monopoly on trade for a specified number of years and the right to conclude treaties with native princes, maintain armed forces, build forts, and found "factories," which then meant only warehouses and trade establishments in foreign places. Both companies began as trade enterprises but became deeply involved in local politics, joined Asian princes in warfare, and ended up territorial empires. Merchants became colonial administrators, factories grew to huge cities, and investment expanded from trade alone to production by means of another social invention of colonial times, the plantation system.

Better funded, the Dutch became the foremost naval and commercial nation in the first half of the seventeenth century. They captured the Javanese city of Jacatra, renaming it Batavia (it's now Jakarta), and from here the first company governor-general, Jan Coen, ruthlessly extended Dutch control, both maritime and inland. In order to monopolize local trade in spices, they used their armies to destroy independent producers and traders. Cloves could only be grown in the Dutch-controlled region around Amboina; so sixty-five thousand clove trees were destroyed in the Moluccas. When nutmeg growers on Banda Island resisted Dutch control, twenty-five hundred inhabitants were massacred and eight hundred taken to Batavia. This process reduced whole island populations, once prosperous with spice production and trade, to poverty.

The Dutch also killed whole sectors of long-distance trade that once enriched Asian communities from Southeast Asia to India. For instance, Indonesian and Indian merchants had traded island spices for Indian cloth; cloth imported to Southeast Asia between 1620 and 1650 had been worth sixty tons of silver a year. The Dutch killed this trade by importing their own cloth; and then, by ruining the indigenous Southeast Asian trade system, caused the buying power of the people to plummet so that even the Dutch textile trade was permanently depressed.

The British East India Company also had ambitions in the Spice Islands, but the Dutch were intent on monopolizing this trade. There was an ugly incident in 1623 when the Dutch captured seventeen British traders whom they tortured and decapitated. This was the turning point; the British turned to India as second best.

Britain's Indian Empire

Neither China nor India ever imagined maritime empires, though both countries have lengthy coastlines with vigorous trading communities, which, for centuries, were engaged in rich long-distance international trade. Their capitals were never coastal, but always deep inland. The enemies they worried about were even further inland, across passes and corridors from which aggressive, mounted warriors periodically emerged. Wealth and glory could be had by conquering territories and putting populations to work. The seas, by contrast, seemed merely empty; they were the borders you didn't have to worry about. Who could imagine a maritime empire?

Thus, when the East India Company turned from the Spice Islands to India, looking for trade, it found the Mughal Empire at its peak, which had a mighty army but no fleet. England first sent high-ranking ambassadors to court to ask for trade treaties; here, too, there were Jesuits speaking against them, and there was also the problem that England didn't really produce anything that India needed or wanted. They had their own thriving cloth industry; anyway, in the Indian climate, who needed English woolens? But they were happy to sell Indian products for silver or gold. Emperor Jahangir finally granted permission to trade and build a factory, but refused to give them the monopoly they desired.

The first factory of the East India Company in India was in the Mughal capital at Agra. But Agra was not convenient for maritime trade; they needed a factory on the Ganges delta, which would turn the entire Ganges system into a vast trade network. They were given permission to build a factory at Hooghly near a Kali shrine and a *ghat*, from which came the name Calcutta (*Kali-ghat*). Down on the southeast coast, the company bought some land from a minor *raja* near the village of Mandraz to build a fort they called St. George in 1639. The city that grew there came to be called Madras, after the village. And finally, on the west coast, there was a small island that King Charles II got in his dowry when he married the Infanta of Portugal. He rented it to the East India Company for a loan at low interest and ten pounds a year; this became Bombay. These three posts, now India's three largest cities, gave England a triangulation on India; convenient at first for shipping, they became toeholds, then the founding territories, and finally the three "Presidencies" from which Britain moved inland as the Mughals went into decline after 1707.

India became the place where ambitious young men went to seek their fortunes. Salaries were low, but the expectation was you would use your entrepreneurial ingenuity to engage in business on the side, where fabulous fortunes were to be made. The greatest of the early adventuring Company men was Robert Clive, a hothead who regularly got into trouble until his father sent him to India to straighten him out. He went to Fort St. George as a clerk, but this work bored and depressed him so severely that he once tried to blow out his brains. It turned out there were better adventures ahead for Robert Clive.

The French had also established a post near Madras, and they got good at the game everyone (the English, the Dutch in Indonesia) learned: Use your troops to support weak contenders for local thrones, put them in power, then use them as puppets. They repay you in currency, treasure, and trade; you get rich. Clive was only twenty-three when he made his fame in India. There was one throne in nearby Arcot and two claimants; the French backed one, the English backed the other. The local prince (*nawab*), backed by the French, took all his troops from the capital to lay siege to the British candidate in Trichinopoly. Clive hatched the plan of taking Arcot while the nawab was away. A million spectators watched as he marched in with two hundred British soldiers and three hundred Indian sepoys (from *sipahi*, "soldier"). It was so bold and brilliant that Clive's fame immediately spread throughout India. The outcome was that the British-backed contender was declared king; the French-backed contender was executed; the French general, Dupleix, was humiliated and went back to France; and Clive was said to be invincible.

Not long afterward there was an incident in Calcutta that again began as competition between the English and French but embroiled them with local rulers. The young prince, Siraj-ud-Daula, became suspicious when the English began to fortify Fort William against the French, and he moved an army to put a stop to it. The British official in charge took fright and fled down river, leaving a small army behind, which was captured and imprisoned by Siraj in a small cell used to lock up three or four drunks at a time. As many as 145 men and one woman were forced inside to spend the night in the heat of May; only 23 survived until morning. This incident, known as the "Black Hole of Calcutta," provoked outrage in England, and Clive was sent to Bengal to take vengeance. There was a round of intrigue and duplicity, leading to British victory in the Battle of Plassey in 1757, which resulted in another Clive puppet being put on a throne. Siraj-ud-Daula, who was only twenty years old, was captured, cut into pieces, and his remains paraded through the streets on an elephant. Clive was rewarded with the Mughal title of *mansabdar*, an administrative position that carried the right to a certain number of cavalrymen and an estate. His rank as mansabdar included a cavalry of six thousand, for which he was responsible, equivalent to that of a Mughal prince; this rank came with an estate of 880 square miles from which the expenses of the cavalry and his own personal fortune were to be raised. Overnight, "Clive of India" became the richest man in England.

By the end of Clive's career, the East India Company was the most important power in North India. In 1765, the Mughal emperor, Shah Alam, proclaimed the East India Company his *diwan* or governor for the provinces of Bihar, Bengal, and Orissa. The Company was now to rule the millions of people in this region and collect the millions of rupees of revenue it generated. In return, they owed loyalty and support—plus 260,000 pounds annually—to the emperor in Allahabad. The East India Company was no longer just a trading company; it had become the government of a vast territory of India.

As the official government with responsibility for the welfare of millions of Indians, it was felt that the East India Company ought to behave more responsibly than it had up to now. This was brought home when nearly a third of Bengali peasants starved to death in the famine of 1770. The famine was caused in large measure by British exploitation and was worsened when grain stores were sold at vast profit to the starving peasants who had produced them in the first place. Back in London, there was a growing sense that the Crown must take greater responsibility for what was happening out in India. Pitt's India Act of 1784 attempted to force responsible government on the Company by establishing a supervisory Board of Governors made up of British ministers, and required the Company to begin training and adequately paying officials who would work diligently and honorably in India. It also called for regularizing the land-holdings of Indians from whom revenues were collected. This resulted in a vast undertaking, in which the holdings and claims of every small and large *zamindar* were investigated, and then British concepts of private property ownership were imposed on what had been a vastly more fluid system of land use. The Permanent Settlement of 1793 thus made possible the displacement of the old Mughal princes of Bengal by newly rich Indian commercial families who could afford to buy them out when they fell on hard times.

Meanwhile, during the first half of the nineteenth century, economic philosophy was undergoing a shift. The philosophy under which the East India Company had first been chartered held that the purpose of trade was both to profit the merchants and to bring glory to the nation. The East India Company was given a monopoly on trade, which insured it would become rich and powerful and simultaneously maintain and strengthen British power in competition with other sovereign nations. Business—international trade, at least—was to serve national interests. This philosophy was known as mercantilism.

But new ideas were in the wind, ideas associated with the growing middle class and with Britain's emerging manufacturing base. This was the idea of "free trade," destined to dominate the nineteenth and twentieth centuries. From the point of view of Manchester textile barons, the East India Company monopoly on trade meant flooding Britain with cheap Indian cloth just when English factories were becoming so productive that they needed constantly expanding markets to absorb all they could now produce. The monopoly on trade was abolished, but just to be on the safe side, tariffs were raised against Indian cloth entering Britain to protect the English textile industry. Thus, economic policy under the name of free trade was shaped to insure England's continued economic advantage. The result was the destruction of the Indian hand-loom industry.

A second new idea began to emerge: the linking of the British and Indian economies in a new way. Where before India had primary industries (grain, raw materials) *and* secondary industries (hand-loom cloth manufactures), India would now specialize in primary production while Britain specialized in secondary production, using its new industrial technology to add value to India's raw goods. A permanent relationship and a single, pan-imperial economy would result. Rather than importing industrial technology to India, a new technology for raw goods production was invented: the plantation system. Tea, cotton, opium, sugar, and indigo all were grown on vast estates owned by English planters employing Indians on a wage basis. Now instead of cultivating for themselves on small plots of land that could be passed down from father to son, the Indian peasant had no land, worked for wages kept artificially low in order to keep wages high and prices low in England, and had to buy food with these low wages. In this way, colonial economies were distorted by the growing imperial system, artificially simplified to the production of primary products only.

Meanwhile, piece by piece, throughout the eighteenth and nineteenth centuries, Britain gobbled up India. One means was the "doctrine of lapse." According to Hindu law, when a raja was about to die without an heir, he could adopt a son, who would be treated like a firstborn natural son. But in 1849, the British declared that "heirs and successors" in all treaties applied only to natural sons. Otherwise, the princely state reverted to the Company. In this way, state after state reverted to the Company—and many dispossessed heirs were skulking around, biding their time.

A crisis was brewing, and it exploded in 1857. The Company's private army had grown to forty thousand troops—supplemented by three hundred thousand Indian sepoys. The sepoys tended to be men of the upper castes, and were well trained by the British and overall intensely loyal, even though their commanders were almost always British and the handful of Indian officers were never put in command over Indian troops. There had been a series of unpopular regulations, such as requiring sepoys to accept service in Burma, "across the Black Waters," which caused pollution and outcasting. The triggering event, however, was a new Enfield rifle that fired a bullet greased, it was believed, by a mixture of cow and pig fat. The end of the cartridge had to be torn open with the teeth, which meant both Hindu and Muslim soldiers were polluted by using the new rifle.

The rebellion began in the garrison town of Meerut on May 10, 1857, when sepoys turned on their officers, killed some of them, then headed for Delhi. There they gathered under the window of Emperor Bahadur Shah in the Red Fort, fired a twenty-one-gun salute and declared him emperor of all Hindustan. Europeans in Delhi were hunted down and killed. Between Meerut and Oudh, most garrisons joined the rebellion, murdering English military and civilian men, women, and children. The war raged throughout the hot summer, as the sepoys, at first spontaneous and disorganized, were joined and led by Indian princes like Nana Sahib of Oudh and the Rani of Jhansi. However, the rebellion was limited to the central Ganges basin. Bengal and Bihar stayed loyal; so did the Panjab, central India, and Madras. The telegraph system had just been completed, so communication was reduced to minutes rather than days or weeks in calling for reinforcements. Troops were summoned from Persia, Madras, Ceylon, Rangoon, and even an expedition to China was intercepted at Singapore and called back. By spring of 1958 all the territory had been reclaimed and often brutal vengeance inflicted. Emperor Bahadur Shah was exiled to Burma where he soon died, and the last twenty-one princes of the blood were hanged, thus extinguishing the Mughal dynasty.

After these events, Britain passed the Government of India Act, transferring all rights and responsibilities of the East India Company to the Crown, and in 1877 Victoria was proclaimed Empress of India. Her representative in India was the Viceroy, who began to invent imperial rituals that were extraordinary amalgams of Mughal, British, and brand-new extravaganzas. The lesson of 1857 had been, in part, that the Indian elite—heads of princely states of all sizes and called by an assortment of titles (raja, *maharaja*, nawab, *rana*, etc.)—had to be drawn into bonds of loyalty and mutual self-interest with Britain. What couldn't be done before with the Company might better be done with the Crown. Relations with Indian princes were improved by ending the doctrine of lapse, honoring all treaties made with them, and incorporating them in a new "symbolic-cultural constitution" of titles, honors, "imperial assemblages," and *darbars* (see box 9.1). The result was not to lessen but to strengthen British control by interfering less with religious custom, binding the Indian elite more closely in ties of mutual interest, and continuing policies of economic interdependence.

China: Opium Wars and the Treaty Century

For a thousand years, India exported religious ideas and learned masters to China; then for half a dozen centuries there was little to send from India to a China who had everything and wished for nothing except possibly acknowledgment of the superiority of the Celestial Empire over every other nation on earth. Then in the eighteenth century, a new product in the form of hard, brown resinous balls wrapped in poppy petals and packed forty to the crate in Banares and Patna began arriving in Canton. From the beginning, Beijing did not like this import and tried to prohibit it as early as 1729, when opium was already reaching China in very small quantities. But the edict prohibiting the importing of opium passed almost without notice, and the trade continued to grow throughout the century. By the 1820s, India was sending over five thousand chests a year.

Although opium was contraband in China, opium cultivation was perfectly legal in India. Of course, it had extremely important medical uses in the nineteenth century, some of which continue today. Morphine and codeine are made from *Papaver somniferum*, the opium poppy. In the

9.1   Victoria, *Kaiser-i-Hind*

After the Rebellion of 1857, the Crown replaced the Company as ruler of India. The British were to be the New Mughals, and Victoria the new Empress; so a grand ceremonial was devised to which all India's many princes would come to personally express fealty to Victoria.

The main ritual of the Mughal darbar (public audience) was a rite of incorporation, a highly formalized exchange between the Mughal and the person to be honored. The ruler sat on cushions on a low throne on a raised platform; everyone else stood in vertical rows from left to right down the audience hall. On entering, each person prostrated himself and touched his head in a sign that the seat of the senses was given to the emperor as a gift. Then the person would step forward and give a gift of *nazar* (gold coins with the image of the ruler stamped on them) and *peshkash* (valuables such as elephants, horses, jewels, and precious objects). The nazar, which meant "vow" in Persian, acknowledged that the ruler was the source of wealth and well-being; and the peshkash was a gift acknowledging the superiority of the Mughal. In return, the Mughal presented *khelat*, a specified set of clothing depending on rank which included cloak, turban, shawls, ornaments for turbans, a necklace and other jewels, arms and shields, horses and elephants. The king stood for a system of rule of which he was the incarnation; and when he gave khelat, he incorporated into himself the body of the person being honored, so that now he, too, in a narrower domain, embodied that rule. He then took the khelat back to his territory to be put on display and worn on significant occasions.

The British never really understood this system, but referred to it as "bribe" and "tribute" and assumed they were paying for favors or buying rights. When early British officials entered into this Mughal system on the same terms, this was defined as "corruption."

However, now that Victoria was to replace the Mughal emperor, a way had to be found for the Crown to do as the emperor had done: give titles, establish precedents, determine the number of gun salutes princes of various states should receive. The Viceroy was now the locus of authority in India, and a new social order was created from remains of the old one. The princes were grouped by region, and the order of precedence for each region was worked out on the basis of the size of their state, the amount of their revenue, the date at which they had become allies of the East India Company, their family histories, and their standing in relation to the Mughal empire. When the Viceroy or regional governor held darbars, it was specified in detail what clothes the princes were to wear, the weapons they could carry, the number of retainers that could accompany them, the number of gun salutes, whether the viceroy would rise and come forward to greet them, how much nazar they could give, whether they were entitled to a return visit from the viceroy, and forms of salutation and closing in letters. The Star of India Order was invented for creating Indian knights.

The Imperial Assemblage of 1877 was planned by Lord Robert Lytton, a handsome, dreamy man who had published five books of poetry. The site was Delhi, associated with Mughal power for centuries, not at the Red Fort but at a site near Delhi Ridge, a tragic and heroic location from the Rebellion of 1857.

The central imperial camp stretched one and a half miles on the site of the old pre-mutiny English cantonment. An enormous Darbar tent was erected where the viceroy held court seated on a throne behind which hung the portrait of the Queen. Scattered over one to five miles were the Indian camps, organized regionally. In each region, the most powerful, highest-ranking king was given the site closest to the Imperial Camp. Lytton had had a coat of arms created for each prince, which was then embroidered by the ladies at Simla and fixed on a large silken standard in the fashion of feudal Europe. A prince would appear at the appointed time accompanied by some of his retinue. He would be greeted according to his rights in the established code, and then Lytton would bestow on him his coat of arms. Thus Indian princes became feudal knights of Victoria, owing her fealty. It wasn't clear to the princes what to do with the banners. They were awkward because of the brass poles; some tried to fix them to the houdahs of their elephants.

The Queen needed an appropriate title to add to her others. A professor of Oriental Languages suggested "Kaiser-i-Hind." The word was well known in India, having been used by Muslim writers to refer to the Roman Caesar; it neatly combined Roman "Caesar," German "Kaiser," and Russian "Czar" in connotation. It wouldn't be mispronounced, it would avoid over-used titles like "Shah," and it wasn't identifiably either Hindu or Muslim.

Based on Bernard Cohn, 1983.

---

nineteenth century, opium was the source of the most important drugs, without which a physician could hardly practice medicine. Prior to the invention of the hypodermic needle, opium was mixed with water or alcohol in drugs like laudanum that were essential to treatment of dysentery, diarrhea, asthma, diabetes, cholera, rheumatism, fevers, malaria, bronchitis, and any kind of pain. There was hardly any other drug available to physicians. Opium cultivation for these uses produced no moral dilemmas.

Indians chewed opium, as did most peoples in the world before the nineteenth century. Smoking the drug appears to have been invented in southern China, where first it was mixed with tobacco—a New World import that Beijing had also tried to block—then gradually the tobacco was omitted and opium was smoked by itself in little clay pipes. The pipe containing a small ball of opium is held over a flame until the opium bubbles and evaporates. The heavy white smoke drawn into the lungs produces the effect described by the American traveler Bayard Taylor at Canton: after his sixth pipe he began to see brilliant colors that floated before his eyes "in a confused and cloudy way, sometimes converging into spots like the eyes in a peacock's tail, but often melting into and through each other, like the hues of changeable silk" (Fay 1975). The opium smoker withdraws into his own world, something of a vegetative state

(Cocteau said, "Opium is the only vegetable substance that communicates the vegetable state to us"). After years of addiction, he becomes emaciated, dull-eyed, lethargic, and lives for nothing but the next pipe of opium.

In the late nineteenth century, four hundred thousand acres of poppy were processed in Ghazipur and sold in Banares; in Bihar, half a million acres were devoted to poppy, which was processed at Patna. Somewhat later, a third major area opened near Malwa in central India. These three regions produced about six thousand tons a year, almost all bound for China. Opium production had been legal under the Mughals, for whom it was an important source of revenue. As the British took control from the crumbling Mughal Empire, the East India Company took over a monopoly in opium production. Opium was sown in November; came into bloom in January; was lanced and collected in April and May. During the intense dry heat of May, the moisture content was reduced to 30 percent; then the opium was formed into three-pound balls or cakes, wrapped in sheets made from the poppy petals, and dried. In October and November they were packed in mango-wood crates, forty cakes in two layers, about 120 pounds total. These crates were loaded into boats and shipped down the Ganges to Calcutta.

In Calcutta, opium was the property of the Government of India's Board of Customs, Salt, and Opium. No one else could deal in opium in India. The Government of India (still at that time the East India Company) auctioned off the opium to private merchants who carried it to China. The profit, after paying costs of production and transport, went to the Government of India, but the East India Company, by selling to private shippers at Calcutta, wiped its hands of the delicate problem that all opium entering China was illegal.

In China, as we have already seen, there was only one way to trade; that was to come as a tributary nation, perform the nine prostrations before the emperor (the "kowtow"), and present tribute. Only then, as an act of benevolent good will, would the emperor grant the barbarian the right to engage in a little trade. Most nations were willing to play this game for the sake of the treasures that China produced; Siamese, Nepalese, Inner Asians, Russians, Portuguese, and Dutch would all kowtow to trade. But not the English. When Macartney arrived in Beijing in 1792, he was determined to be received as an emissary from an equal, sovereign nation. He would drop to one knee to honor another great monarch, but would kowtow to the Son of Heaven only if some mandarin would kowtow to a picture of George III. The Chinese refused this sign of equality, but allowed trade anyway, enrolling England as a tributary state whether they wanted it or not, after having received Macartney's ship with an honor barge carrying inscriptions reading "envoy bearing tribute."

In Canton, the barbarians could engage in trade only under extremely controlled conditions. The Chinese government assigned Chinese merchant houses, called *hongs*, to handle all foreign trade. These were organized into a guild called the *cohong*. The chief official was known by the foreigners as the *Hoppo*, the superintendent of customs whose job was to determine import duties and who performed these duties by exacting as much as he possibly could from the foreigners. Fifteen acres of riverbank were assigned to all western nations for their factories, which were long, narrow buildings that served as warehouses, living quarters, servants' rooms, and cookhouses. Foreign merchants were not allowed to leave these fifteen acres to go into the city, still less to take an outing in the countryside. They might do a little rowing on the river just off their quarters, but that was all. Anything they needed from the China beyond their fifteen acres had to be managed by the hong. They hired Chinese "compradors" to manage their day-to-day operations. Every year, from April to October, the entire European establishment moved down to the Portuguese city of Macao for the summer. In Macao, they had rather ordinary freedoms, but in Canton they were entirely dependent on the hongs.

Hong merchants were far from ordinary shopkeepers; their appointment by the government entitled them to scholar-official status, though mostly of the lowest (ninth) rank; a few had somewhat higher status, as indicated by a blue button at the top of their hats. Relations between the "foreign devils" and the hong merchants were surprisingly good, and the Canton trade was famous for being an honest place where, aside from the exactions of the Hoppo and the predictable squeeze paid to smaller clerks and officials, you could at least trust the quality of the merchandise and expect not to be cheated. Of course, they were all complicit in the illegal drug trade, but even that was viewed as the "safest trade in China" by people like William Jardine and James Matheson. They did not consider themselves smugglers. The Chinese were smugglers. Foreigners arrived in Canton waters with ships of perfectly legal opium from India. Getting it into China was the illegal part. After buying the opium in certificates of trade or pure silver, hong merchants sent small boats out to take the crates of opium from the merchant vessels anchored in the river.

Selling opium in China was essential to get the products of Chinese industry: silks, sugar, porcelain, lacquerware, wallpaper, and above all, tea. The problem was finding something the Chinese wanted in return. The self-sufficiency which enabled China to cut itself off from international trade in the twentieth century until the reforms of Deng Xiaoping in the 1980s had a very long history. In the early nineteenth century, there was very little produced in Europe that anyone in China would pay for. But by the late 1820s, England was drinking thirty million pounds of tea a year, and the only place it could be bought was China; not till later would tea production begin in India and Ceylon. The duty levied on tea in

Britain provided three million pounds annually to the government. In order to keep the tea flowing, opium had to go the other way; otherwise the trade imbalance would drain Britain of silver, which was the only product the Chinese government really wanted.

But in the 1830s, the silver flow began to reverse. China was now buying more opium than it was selling tea. Silver was now flowing out of the Celestial Empire. Moreover, the addiction problem was out of control. An effort by the imperial government to discover the extent of addiction turned up frightening news. From the imperial household to regional governments and to workers in urban areas, everywhere but the countryside, people were lying with their pipes in opium dreams.

The Qing emperor invoked his Manchu ancestors, who would hold him responsible for the damage done the empire by the foreign drug. He solicited opinions from his highest-placed officials about how to solve the problem. These proposals were not so different from those heard today with respect to our current drug problem. Some urged legalizing it. Others urged cracking down on foreign suppliers. But the unpleasant reality was that the foreigners arrived in armed merchant ships that China's weak coastal boats could not stand up to. It was easier to concentrate on the Chinese end of the problem and go after the Chinese smugglers and traders. One official the emperor listened to closely was Lin Zexu, who wrote a lengthy analysis of the situation, complete with a concrete strategy for dealing with it. Lin Zexu was appointed the emperor's drug czar and sent to Canton.

There were early signs that trouble was ahead for the opium business. A crowd of soldiers arrived outside the European factories one day with a captured Chinese smuggler in a basket. In minutes the prisoner was hoisted and strangled before the horrified eyes of the watching foreigners. The body was left to hang as a sign of the government's new resolve. Then, one morning in 1939, shortly after Commissioner Lin's arrival, workmen arrived and began bricking up the entrances to Hog Lane, New China Street, and the various alleys by which servants entered the fifteen-acre area of European factories. Servants disappeared. Travel to Macao was forbidden. Next the foreigners were ordered to turn over all their crates of opium. They balked at first, then realized they had no choice but to give in. Twenty thousand chests of opium were delivered to Commissioner Lin, who systematically destroyed it all before allowing the foreigners to finally escape downriver to Macao (see box 9.2).

The perfectly reasonable—in retrospect—actions of Commissioner Lin provoked war with Britain. The reasoning of the British government might at first be hard to grasp. They did not go to war directly to defend the opium trade, although there was as much blind-sighted defense of it as one now hears from the tobacco industry. One British official in India wrote: "During the nearly nine years I was attached to the Banares

9.2 Twenty Thousand Chests of Opium

In June, the twenty thousand chests were destroyed. Five or six miles above Chuenpi, at a point where a creek flows into the river from the east, the high commissioner had three shallow basins dug, each roughly fifty yards by twenty-five, with timbered sides and flagstoned bottoms. Fresh water was let into the basins. Across each ran wooden platforms; to these coolies brought the balls and cakes, broke them there by stamping upon them, and pushed the fragments into the water with their feet. Lime and salt were scattered on the surface, other coolies waded in and stirred vigorously with hoes and shovels, and at last the watery mess, stinking horribly, was allowed to run into the creek and out to sea with the tide.

The work began on June 3 and proceeded without interruption for three weeks. Part way through King and Bridgman went up to Chuenpi on the *Morrison* and obtained permission to see for themselves how swiftly and efficiently it was being carried on. Sixteen hundred chests were destroyed the day of their visit. Officers were everywhere, making certain that not a cake escaped. After a time the high commissioner invited the two Americans to an interview in a pavilion overlooking the basin. Picking their way to him through piles of broken chests and torn coverings, many with the East India Company's mark upon them, bowing low (for they had made sure in advance that the kowtow would not be required), they attempted through the official interpreters to present two petitions. One urged fundamental changes in the way China met the West. The other requested compensation for the losses Olyphant and Company had sustained through the interruption of trade. (King's hands, after all, were clean, *he* had never dabbled in opium!) Lin would not touch either petition; they were not, he pointed out, in Chinese; instead he plied King and Bridgman with questions of his own. Why were the English all leaving the river? How could he best communicate with England's queen?

The two Americans did not allow themselves to be put out by the *ch'in-ch'ai*'s refusal to meet them on their own ground. They had just seen the deliberate destruction of property worth millions, by officers deemed corrupt beyond redemption, and they were impressed. "Have we anywhere on record a finer rebuke administered by Pagan integrity to Christian degeneracy?"

Peter Ward Fay, 1975, pp. 160–61.

Agency, I never knew one solitary instance of impaired health amongst natives resulting from use of the drug, not even in the factories, where people passed twelve hours a day in an opium atmosphere and ate as much as they could consume" (Fay 1975:185). The opium merchants pressed England to reimburse the two million pounds' value of the opium as Elliot, the British official in Canton, had promised the government would do. Where to get the money? Times were hard in England,

and no better in India where the future of opium was in doubt; why not make China pay?

But that was not the main rationale of Britain. Rather it was the interruption of international trade that would have such far-reaching consequences. Further, it was the refusal of the Chinese government to enter into the *culture* of the emerging nineteenth-century world system. The pretense that the emperor was the highest monarch of earth, the Son of Heaven for all, was absurd. This pretense of the Chinese was worse than a mere legitimating device to shore up authority at home; for refusing to communicate with other nations on equal terms or to permit envoys to negotiate with Beijing directly, China had to receive a harsh challenge from abroad.

So it was that five warships blockaded Canton while a large force headed up the coast and initiated half a dozen engagements. It soon ended with humiliation for the Qing government and their forced acceptance of the Treaty of Nanjing in 1842. This treaty began the saga of Hong Kong.

The treaty provided that foreign nationals would be subject to their own laws under their own resident consuls, a principle known as extraterritoriality. China agreed to pay an indemnity for the value of the confiscated opium and the cost of the British operation against them. Fair tariffs and the right to deal directly with customs collectors and freedom to trade at designated "treaty ports" were guaranteed. The island of Hong Kong was granted to Britain in perpetuity as its main East Asian base.

The First Opium War and the Treaty of Nanjing thus began what is often called the Treaty Century, a period from 1842 to 1949 when China had its most continuous and pervasive encounter with other nations, which ended with the reclosing of all those doors after the Communist revolution. Two more opium wars as well as treaties with France, the United States, and Russia were forced on China. The first five treaty ports were eventually expanded to more than eighty, all located along China's eastern seaboard where large enclaves of foreigners lived under their own laws and introduced their own churches, arts, and lifestyles. Free trade was a form of imperialism benefiting these nations, since Chinese industries were kept infantile against the new products of the Western industrial revolution by the simple device of forcing agreement to low tariffs in the treaties. Opium continued to flow from India until 1917.

From the Treaty of Nanjing in 1842 to the Nanjing Massacre in which one hundred thousand Chinese were slaughtered by Japanese invaders in 1937, China's Treaty Century of "openness," "free trade," and interaction with the outside world left China helpless, humiliated, bitter, and extremely cautious about giving it all another try. The reforms of the 1980s and 1990s should be viewed not just against the backdrop of the

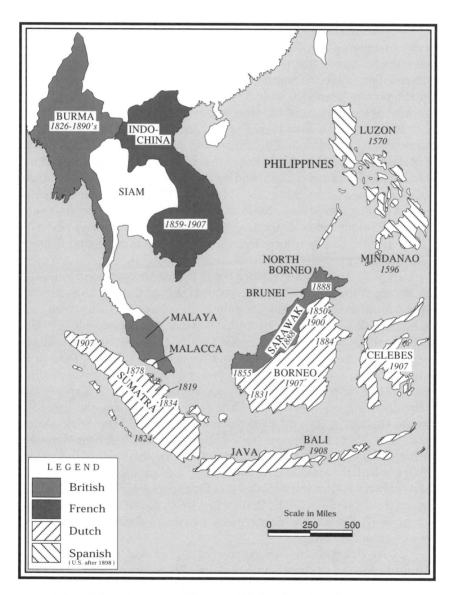

Map 9.1   European Powers Divide Up Southeast Asia

Communist experiments of the Great Leap Forward and the Cultural Revolution, but also of China's experiences during its Treaty Century.

"Below the Winds"—Colonizing the Islands

On the Malay Peninsula and in the islands of Southeast Asia, Malay-speakers identified their region as "below the winds," that is, below the monsoons that picked up moisture from the southern seas and dumped it on India, the Southeast Asian mainland, and southern China. Outsiders from "above the winds" rode these winds into Malay territories to trade: Arabs, Gujaratis, Chinese, Japanese, and Europeans.

Muslim traders from India had brought a new faith to peoples below the winds as Hinduism and Buddhism had come earlier. A Hindu prince of Melaka named Parameshvara converted to Islam and changed his name to Megot Iskander Shah, and because of the strategic and commercial importance of the Sultanate of Melaka (1403–1511), Islam rapidly spread among the Malay chiefs of the region. As the Thai had once embraced Buddhism to distinguish themselves from the more powerful Khmer Hindus, Malay princes fighting off Thai ambitions found the new religious identity useful.

Thus, as British trading ships began to pass through the Straits and the waters of the South China Sea on their way to Canton, they encountered a number of Malay-Muslim sultans in control of coasts where they thought it would be convenient to have one or two dependable (British) ports of call. In 1785, Captain Francis Lightfoot rendered a little military assistance to the Sultan of Kedah and received the island of Penang in return. In 1819, Stamford Raffles took advantage of a little conflict between two other Malay chiefs to acquire the island of Singapore. The Dutch had long since booted the Portuguese from Melaka, but turned it over to Britain in 1824 when the two nations signed the Anglo-Dutch treaty identifying separate spheres of interest to keep them out of trouble with each other. The Dutch would keep to the lower islands of Indonesia, while the British would keep to the Malay Peninsula. This gave England three key cities—Penang, Melaka, and Singapore—which merged as the Straits Settlements in 1826. At first they were governed from Calcutta, but in 1867, the Straits Settlements became a Crown Colony ruled directly from London.

These changes, and others, created a good deal of turmoil on the peninsula in the early nineteenth century. Chinese were moving south in large numbers, fleeing the Taiping Rebellion (1851); this migration, part of a southward migration that had been going on for several centuries, left a legacy of expatriate Chinese communities in many Southeast Asian towns and cities. On the peninsula, many worked inland at opening up tin mines for commercial profit (40 percent of the world's tin comes from

Malaysia). In coastal towns they established trading communities and served British firms as compradors, as they had in China. The composition of towns averaged 70 percent Chinese.

When the East India Company monopoly was abolished, private merchants and planters flocked to the region. Rubber became commercially important for shoes and clothes in the late nineteenth century, then hugely important after the beginning of the automobile industry in the twentieth century. But rubber was not native to Malaya. Early efforts to transport rubber seeds from the Amazon had failed. Trying again, a trader in rubber in Brazil and a botanist from Kew Gardens outside London gathered seventy thousand seeds and hired an empty steamer to rush them to England before they deteriorated. In England they were sped by a special freight train to Kew, where greenhouses were cleared to make room for them. As soon as they germinated, 1,919 rubber seedlings were rushed to Ceylon for planting, and from there—at a more leisurely pace—they were carried to Malaya (Hepper 1982). Eventually half the world's natural rubber was produced there.

The rubber plantations and tin mines required cheap labor; the Malay population filled some of this need, but were more inclined to keep to their traditional adaptations of rice agriculture, and so Chinese and Indian laborers were imported to work the plantations. Between 1891 and 1901, over fifty-eight thousand Indians came to Malaya; the Chinese population grew to almost three hundred thousand. This growing ethnic complexity, along with the economic and political transformations, created social turmoil that concerned the Malay sultans, who were frequently at war among themselves, as much as it did Chinese and European traders who could only benefit from a government that would keep order without interfering or taxing too much. Britain was urged to intervene.

The sultans of the Malay states of Perak, Pahang, Selangor, and Negri Sembilan were persuaded to form a federation in 1896, with its central administration in Kuala Lumpur, then just a small Chinese tin-mining town. The sultans of the Federated Malay States (FMS) retained their titles and their authority over *adat*, Malay custom, while practical administrative control was in the hands of a British official known by the unalarming term "Resident." Things got off to a bad start when the first Resident, a "tactless and impatient Victorian," was deservedly hated and eventually murdered, but his successor, Hugh Low, was a good administrator who operated in the black, kept the peace, and made prosperity possible. For all the growing prosperity, however, the loss of real power by the sultans of the federation and the control of Britain was a warning to the sultans who remained outside of the FMS. Five of these unfederated states became known as the Unfederated Malay States, each operating independently unless some crisis required joint action. Each of them had an appointed British official, not a Resident but merely an Advisor. The Straits Settlements, the Federated Malay States, and the Unfederated Malay States maintained their separate identities until the Japanese invasion.

Meanwhile, a curious form of colonialism rose on the north coast of Borneo. In 1838, a rich Englishman named James Brooke sailed his private armed yacht to Sarawak on a scientific exploration. There he found the Sultan of Brunei backed against the wall by Malays and Dayaks who were rebelling against his rule. In the seventeenth century, these sultans had ruled all of Borneo and also the Sulu archipelago of the Southern Philippines, but were now reduced to Sarawak. The Sultan got Brooke to help him out against the rebels, and after they were crushed, Brooke was made Rajah of Sarawak in 1841. This was the prototypical White Rajah of many a grade B film and novel. He and his successors—his nephew "Rajah Charles" and Charles' son, Rajah Vyner—ruled as the Brooke dynasty for a century, stamping out piracy, expanding at the expense of the Sultan of Brunei, and protecting the tribal peoples of their territories from exploitation by outsiders.

Burma and Thailand

The nineteenth century was not Burma's century. Rather, it was a century of humiliation and dismemberment at the hand of—not even a proper king—the crowd of merchants who called themselves the Government of India. Burma's century was the eighteenth century. At mid-century, a chief from the central Burma town of Swebo proclaimed himself king of all Burma, took the name Alaungpaya, "The Great Lord Who Shall Become the Buddha," and began moving against the ethnic Mons, Shan, Siamese, and other competing polities, establishing the Third Burmese Empire. From the capitals of Shwebo and later Ava, both near modern Mandalay, this militant state was in arm's reach of a number of significant powers. To the northeast was China's Yunnan Province; Burma was historically one of China's tributary neighbors. To the southeast was the kingdom of Chiangmai, now Thailand's second largest city, but then a small independent kingdom; south of Chiangmai was Ayutthaya, where Siamese culture had reached a glittering peak. To the west were Indian territories of Assam and Manipur under the control of the East India Company. Closer in were any number of tiny states and chiefdoms belonging to Mon, Shan, Karen, Chin, and Kachin groups.

During the second half of the eighteenth century, Burma moved against all these neighbors in an expansive effort to restore the lost glory of previous eras. There is little evidence that these wars were about the things states were to fight about later—trade, land, or self-defense, though insults to national pride were high on the agenda. Twice they captured Chiangmai, then moved on to Laos and to Yunnan Province to demonstrate their control over the whole region. The great goal, however, was Ayutthaya. The Burmese king Hsinbyushin sent his army down the Mekong from Laos, conscripting additional soldiers along the way, and arrived at the gates of Ayutthaya in January 1766. The Siamese Army, with full confidence in their strength, burst out the gates and were promptly defeated. Those who could, retreated inside, and then settled in for a lengthy siege that did not end until 1767. When the monsoons came, the Burmese had bricked in their canons and kept firing; Burmese soldiers built rafts and cruised the flooded fields, keeping the Siamese cut off from the world. When the monsoons were over, they dug tunnels beneath the foundations of the city and set fire to the walls, making an opening for their army. They captured the king and entire court and marched the entire surviving populace off to Burma. The city was stripped of all its valuables and burned. The walls were leveled and the moats filled in. The capture of artists and artisans, monks and poets, and the entire treasury of Siam left a ghostly ruin at Ayutthaya but created a cultural renaissance in Burma.

The Ayutthaya that was destroyed in 1767 had been built on wealth gained largely through international trade during the previous two centuries. The Siamese kings made Ayutthaya a leading entrepôt for ships coming up and going down the Chao Phrya River to the Gulf of Siam. There was nothing introverted about Ayutthaya. The Siamese kings, who had a monopoly on all trade in their realm, welcomed traders from all over the world to their court, so long as they respected the royal monopoly (Dhiravat na Pombejra 1993). They exchanged embassies with other Asian and European nations, and hundreds of Europeans lived in Ayutthaya and served in the court. One of these was a Greek named Phaulkon who became a high minister of state. Most of the king's revenues came from foreign trade and were spent on magnificent architecture, meritmaking on a grand scale, and support of an enormous royal establishment. The royal monopoly allowed setting high prices on goods leaving the kingdom, like lead, tin, copper, gunpowder, areca, precious woods, deerskins, elephants, ivory, and rhinoceros horn. Dutch records viewed the Siamese king as a key rival. The Siamese sent junks to China, Japan, India, and the Philippines, conducting their own trade, and these countries also sent regular ships. Troubles occurred, however, with the East India Company and the VOC (Dutch East India Company), who wanted their own monopolies on trade with Ayutthaya. The events of 1767, however, put a halt to this internationalism while the Siamese rebuilt their state under the brilliant general Taksin in Bangkok.

Burma ran into trouble on their western frontier when they captured the border region of Arakan in 1784 and carted off the great gold-covered Mahamuni Buddha that was the pride of the Arakanese people.

This put them up against the British in India. Arakan dissidents fled to the Indian town of Chittagong and unfriendly exchanges across this frontier became common. In 1819, the Arakanese rebelled, and Burma pursued the rebels across the border, occupied Assam, attacked Manipur and Chohar, and threatened Chittagong. This led to the First Anglo-Burmese War in 1824. British and Indian forces captured Rangoon and camped in the Golden Pagoda. Burma was forced to accept a humiliating treaty. They ceded Tesasserim, Arakan, Manipur, and Assam to Britain; accepted a British Resident and a commercial treaty, agreed not to attack Siam again, and paid an indemnity of ten million rupees.

In 1840, the Burmese king repudiated this treaty and broke off diplomatic relations. Britain was then involved in the Opium War and since Burma was a tributary state to China, in name at least, it seemed to the Burmese like a good time to make a try at getting out from under the British. But in 1852, there came the Second Anglo-Burmese War, which ended with Burma losing the rest of her coastline and the fertile heartland of lower Burma, including the whole Irrawadi delta. The Bay of Bengal was now a British lake, and Burma was incorporated into the Indian Empire. The Third Anglo-Burmese War occurred in 1885 when British troops went by steamship up the Irrawadi. This time, the Burmese monarchy was abolished even though, in the rest of the Indian empire, relations with India's princes had never been better and their security was virtually guaranteed.

Vietnam

While most of Southeast Asia was being Indianized during the first few hundred years of the Christian Era, Vietnam was coming under the influence of China. In 214 B.C., China established a military post just north of the Tonkin delta, and by 111 B.C. controlled most of the north. For about a thousand years the Vietnamese of the northern region were considered to be China's southernmost province, which they called Giao Chi.

During the first millennium, this province was strongly influenced by Chinese culture. They used Chinese irrigation and terracing methods. The Vietnamese elite became Confucianists and also Mahayana Buddhists, and there were important Buddhist centers in the region, but, as in China, Buddhism never became the dominant religion. Confucianism was always more significant. The peasants continued to worship numerous spirits and deities of indigenous origin.

All this did not mean they liked the Chinese or thought of themselves as Chinese. In fact, they were highly ambivalent toward the Chinese. Like the Japanese at the same time, the Vietnamese greatly admired China as the center of civilization. But unlike Japan, China was close enough to exert real control, and as a result, there were many uprisings against the Chinese rulers, until in 939, one of these was successful and the Vietnamese gained their independence.

By the thirteenth century, there were three main regions, peoples, and dynasties in the area now known as Vietnam: (1) In the north, the Tran dynasty (1225–1407); (2) In the central region, the Chams, Indianized speakers of Austronesian languages, whose kingdom was known as Champa; and (3) In the south, the Khmer, whose kingdom stretched from Cambodia to the Mekong delta. The cultural and political distinctions between north and south were so great that once, in the 1630s, a Nguyen ruler built two great walls across the narrow waist of the country near Dong Hoi, to keep the northerners out.

Vietnam did not overcome these regional and ethnic differences and begin the formation of the modern sense of national identity until the late eighteenth century. French Catholic missionaries played a role in this development. Because Vietnam's long, long coastline had many places for Western ships to put in, Portuguese began to come in the sixteenth century to buy raw Vietnamese silk. They were followed soon by Jesuits, who had much success in converting the Vietnamese. By the eighteenth century, there had been two centuries of Christian proselytizing; there were more Christians in Vietnam than in all of China, and Christianity was fully integrated into rural culture and political life. The priests romanized the language, a much simpler system that won out over the Chinese script, which is why Vietnamese today is written with roman letters.

Politically, there were small, mutually hostile states in Hanoi under the Trinh dynasty and at Hue under the Nguyen. A third force in the form of a peasant rebellion led by three brothers from Tay Son caused major disturbances, and massacres of both families in 1777. One young Nguyen prince escaped with the help of a French priest, Bishop Pigneau, who then spent several years seeking assistance from any powers that might help him take back his country. The Thai provided aid, as did, eventually, the French, even though the French had troubles enough of their own as the French Revolution broke out in 1789. During the very summer of the outbreak of the French Revolution, Nguyen Anh reoccupied Saigon; recaptured the southern provinces; and moved north, defeating his rivals, capturing Hue and Hanoi, and unifying the whole country. He reestablished his Nguyen dynasty at Hue and was crowned emperor under the title of Gia Long.

Gia Long continued to protect Catholic Vietnamese and was on good terms with the French, who had assisted his return to power. Bishop Pigneau became foreign minister, and French advisors assisted in modernization of the army and administration, which nevertheless retained its Confucian characteristics and remained in the control of the mandarin class. Gia Long's successors, however, became more xenophobic as the nineteenth century wore on, and conversions to Catholicism continued. In

1825, the emperor declared Christianity a "perverse religion which corrupts men's hearts"; in the next decade seven French missionaries were executed; and in 1847, when Tu Duc came to the throne, concerted attacks on French missionaries began. By 1860, they had killed twenty-five European priests, three hundred Vietnamese priests, and thirty thousand Vietnamese Christians.

In the meantime, French explorers had been roaming up the Mekong into Cambodia and "discovered" Angkor and other fabulous ruins, which excited the imagination of French people back home, who began to dream of an Indo-Chinese empire. The French were trying hard to keep up with British successes, and so, perhaps, cared more deeply about the fate of French missionaries than the increasingly secular French, after the Revolution, might otherwise have done. In 1859 they seized Saigon. Emperor Tu Duc at Hue was forced to sign a treaty ceding three provinces to France. In 1882, they attacked Tonkin and took Hanoi, then turned on Hue. The emperor had just died, and during the inevitable confusion of the transition, the Vietnamese were forced to negotiate away their independence. The central area of Vietnam, called Annam, became a protectorate of France, as did the northern region of Tonkin. But "Cochin China"—the southern provinces around the Mekong delta—was governed directly by France.

Cambodia

After the French successfully took over Annam in 1859, they claimed to be successors to every territory Annam had ever claimed. That included Cambodia. But Siam also claimed overlordship of Cambodia. The current Kmer ruler, King Norodom, was thus in a dangerous position, but on balance he felt that Siam, being a more ancient enemy, represented the greater danger. In fact, the first initiatives toward a French protectorate over Cambodia appear to have come from King Norodom's father before his death. Cambodia and France agreed that a French "resident" would be established in the Cambodian court but that no other countries could have consuls there unless the French agreed. French citizens could settle in Cambodia, and Cambodians could settle anywhere throughout the French Empire. France would protect Cambodia from attack from the outside and would maintain order within Cambodia. French goods could move freely into the territory. French citizens would be ruled under their own laws by the principle of extraterritoriality used in other European colonies and in China.

The king of Siam threatened war if this treaty was signed. Siam viewed Cambodia as their protectorate; only a few years before, King Ang Duong had fled to Bangkok during a rebellion, taking with him the crown, the sacred sword, and the seal that were the symbols of Cambodian monarchy. Siam provided the troops that enabled Norodom to take back his own throne—while retaining possession of the royal regalia that symbolized the legitimacy of the Cambodian state. While the French were getting signatures to the treaty with Cambodia in Paris, Cambodia worked at retrieving the royal regalia from Siam; they signed a secret treaty that acknowledged Siamese suzerainty and ceded several provinces that were under Siamese control in any case. But when the French found out about this, they put pressure on Siam and got back the crown, so that King Norodom could be crowned in 1864. This was the beginning of French rule in Cambodia.

France continued to press inland against the Siamese in a series of diplomatic and military moves. In 1893, they sent a gunboat and an ultimatum to Bangkok; the British urged the Siamese to negotiate with France. Under this pressure, Siam ceded to France Laos and the whole east bank of the Mekong; they even evacuated the areas around Angkor. And thus, French Indochina was complete.

Throughout the nineteenth century, the Siamese watched what was going on to the east and west of them with dismay. The great King Mongkut (Rama IV), a devout Buddhist and shrewd ruler who was determined to preserve the independence of Siam, was in a better position than Burmese, Vietnamese, or Cambodian rulers, each of whom had only a single, determined European power bearing down on them. Mongkut had the English on the west, the French on the east. Their mutual jealousies and frequent clashes could be manipulated in the interests of Siamese independence. He set about making treaties of friendship and commerce with all the European trading nations, giving them what they had always wanted: trade opportunities. By and large, this strategy worked; they were forced to cede Laos to the French, and also some Cambodian territories; and several small areas to the British in Burma. But their strategy worked, and they were the single Southeast Asian nation to escape direct colonial control.

Mongkut's son, Chulalongkorn, was brought up to be king in a world increasingly dominated by Europeans. He traveled widely in his youth, and by the time he came to the throne in 1868, he had a better understanding of European culture and character than most Asians of his age. As Rama V, he instituted important reforms, modernizing his country without needing colonial powers to do it for him (contrary to the self-serving ideology of colonialism). He created a modern army; he built railroads, which opened up the interior to commercial development and assisted in extending the capital's control over outlying provinces; and he reformed education and modernized the revenue system.

THE MEIJI ERA

Late on a summer day in 1853, twenty thousand troops belonging to the shogun looked helplessly out over Tokyo bay as four American ships dropped anchor. For 250 years, Japan had closed itself to foreign nations and dealt harshly with the occasional shipwrecked sailor or tentative call paid by a hopeful merchant ship. But these American ships, two of them steamers, all of them heavily armed, could not be resisted by the soldiers on the hillside. They could mow down the wooden residences and warehouses edging the bay. The Japanese would have to deal with the barbarians.

Japan had kept so successfully closed that Admiral Perry did not understand the power structure of the society he sought to visit. The ruler at Edo was the shogun, but Perry thought this was the emperor. With his keen sense of the ceremonial, Perry had himself welcomed ashore with his own Marine band in full dress; as a sign of the technological delights to be had through trade with Americans, he presented a working model of a railroad. Like the British in China, what he sought was a treaty of trade between his country and Japan. He was not allowed to see the shogun, so he left letters and gifts, stoked up the steam engines, and said he'd be back the following spring.

The commotion that followed was not entirely Perry's doing, but his visit did usher in a fifteen-year period known as the *bakumatsu*, or "end of the shogun's rule" (1853–1868). The Tokugawa dynasty was long past its prime, indecisive, rigid, and on the verge of bankruptcy. The energy of the samurai class of earlier time had dissipated as samurai were turned into urbanized bureaucrats whose swords had become merely precious ornaments and heirlooms, and their warrior lifestyle replaced by the martial arts. When Perry returned with eight ships, and then negotiations stretched to four years, the weakness of the shogunate was on public view. Unable to make the decision himself, the shogun took the extraordinary step of circulating the draft of the treaty among the daimyo and asking for their opinions. They offered a mixed set of responses. Some saw potential good from limited and controlled trade with the West; others foresaw a dangerous future in which barbarian commercial values would infect and corrupt samurai ones. In the end, the shogun signed a treaty much like those forced on China: certain port cities were designated treaty ports, customs duties were kept low, and resident Americans were governed under their own laws by the principle of extraterritoriality.

For many reflective Japanese—most of them from the privileged samurai class—the next decade was one of painful reevaluation of their own heritage. Most remained full of respect for the classical samurai idea, but did not see those ideals much in evidence around them. The shogun's ineffectualness embarrassed and angered them. Some began to turn to the emperor at Kyoto as still representing a spirit mostly lost in Edo. Many felt there were gains to be made by taking advantage of some of what the West represented—technological advance, surely, and especially in military technology—though they were ashamed at the weakness of the shogun in dealing with the foreigners. To the astonishment of many, the imperial court took the rare step of refusing to ratify the treaty and ordering the shogun to drive out the barbarians immediately. Although they soon backed away from this posture, and the treaty was approved, the court's action was a sign of the growing disaffection.

Some of the more belligerent domains mobilized against the shogun, led by Satsuma and Choshu in the south. And in less than a decade from Perry's first arrival, two major overseas missions had taken Japanese to America, Europe, and China. Mid-century Europe and America had already been transformed by the industrial revolution. Japanese were shocked by what they saw. They were equally shocked by China, which had always been "Greece and Rome rolled into one," as Frank Gibney puts it, incomparably behind the developments in the West, corrupt in late-Qing times, and overrun with Europeans who had turned the major coastal towns into European outposts.

On January 3, 1868, a successful coup brought an end to the shogunate and restored the emperor as head of state, thus ending the system of dual government that had begun in 1185. The emperor, whose name was Mutsuhito, was only sixteen years old. It was not his coup, and he was not destined actually to rule, but the transformation of Japanese society would be carried out in his name. Accompanied by thousands of his Japanese subjects, Mutsuhito was carried to Edo and given the name Meiji, meaning "Enlightened Rule." Edo was renamed Tokyo, the "Kyoto of the East."

The small cadre of elite samurai now set about to dismantle the social system of feudal Japan and create a modern nation-state. At that time, there were about 260 domains, which were largely self-governing so long as they acknowledged the ultimate overlordship of the shogun. These domains were competitive and quarrelsome. People in the domains identified themselves first and foremost as people of Choshu or Tosa, not as Japanese; and their daimyo were powerful competitors without any potential central power. A Japanese state had to be built that was strongly centralized before the technological reforms that were also needed could be brought about.

Pressure was put on sympathetic daimyo to turn their lands over to the emperor, giving them high government posts as inducements. Other daimyo were declared to be governors acting under appointment by Tokyo; two years later, their domains were turned into prefectures and the governors were replaced by administrators with new staffs. Care was taken to recruit men of talent from the former Tokugawa regime or from the old daimyo or samurai class, wherever good men could be found. The upper echelon of the samurai were pensioned off if they proved unadaptive and unassimilable into the new order.

Thus the daimyo were disinherited and the samurai class destroyed. Though there *was* resistance, most violently in the Satsuma Rebellion of 1877, the most remarkable feature of the era was how radically society could be altered and with relatively little loss of life. It was in part because the commoner class of Japan, or *chonin* ("city dwellers"), had already achieved a degree of autonomy in the many castle towns that had sprung up in Tokugawa times. The disruptions of the early Meiji Era thus affected them far less than they did the privileged classes they had worked free of. The urban economy had already moved forward into a market economy, which would soon expand exponentially to their advantage. The new language of "freedom" and "people's rights" rang true to them. When the Meiji Constitution was adopted in 1889—modeled not on the American or the French but on the German constitution of Bismarck—it was the first in Asia. In this, as in other ways, Japan led the way into the twentieth century.

REFERENCES

Abu'l Fazl 'Allami. 1927. *The A'in Akbari*, trans. H. Blochmann. Calcutta: Oriental Books Corp.

Alley, Kelly. 1994. Ganga and Gandagi: Interpretation of Pollution and Waste in Banaras. *Ethnology* 33(2): 127–44.

Andaya, Leonard Y. 1992. Interactions with the Outside World and Adaptation in Southeast Asian Society, 1500–1800. In *The Cambridge History of Southeast Asia*, ed. Nicholas Tarling. Pp. 346–402. Cambridge: Cambridge University Press.

Atkinson, Jane Monnig, and Shelly Errington, eds. 1990. *Power and Difference: Gender in Island Southeast Asia*. Stanford, CA: Stanford University Press.

Attali, Jacques. 1997. Asia's Ahead, Europe's Behind. *Far Eastern Economic Review*, 9 January, 26.

Baker, Joan Stanley. 1984. *Japanese Art*. London: Thames and Hudson.

Barnes, Gina L. 1988. *Protohistoric Yamato: Archaeology of the First Japanese State*. Ann Arbor: The University of Michigan Center for Japanese Studies.

Barnes, R. H., Andrew Gray, and Benedict Kingsbury, eds. 1995. Indigenous Peoples of Asia. Association for Asian Studies Monograph and Occasional Paper Series, No. 48.

Barrett, T. H. 1990. Religious Traditions in Chinese Civilization: Buddhism and Taoism. In *Heritage of China: Contemporary Perspectives on Chinese Civilization*, ed. Paul S. Ropp. Pp. 138–63. Berkeley: University of California Press.

Bechert, Heinz, and Richard Gombrich. 1984. *The World of Buddhism: Buddhist Monks and Nuns in Society and Culture*. London: Thames and Hudson.

Becker, A. L. 1995. Biography of a Sentence. In *Beyond Translation: Essays Toward a Modern Philology*. Ann Arbor: University of Michigan Press.

Bellah, Robert. 1957. *Tokugawa Religion: The Values of Pre-Industrial Japan*. Boston: Beacon Press.

Bellwood, Peter. 1980. The Peopling of the Pacific. *Scientific American* 243(5): 174–84.

_____. 1991. The Austronesian Dispersal and the Origin of Languages. *Scientific American* 265(1): 88–93.

_____. 1992. Southeast Asia Before History. In *The Cambridge History of Southeast Asia*, ed. Nicholas Tarling. Pp. 55–136. Cambridge: Cambridge University Press.

Benedict, Paul. 1972. *Sino-Tibetan, A Conspectus*. Cambridge: Cambridge University Press.

Berry, Mary Elizabeth. 1994. *The Culture of Civil War in Kyoto*. Berkeley: University of California Press.

Berthon, Simon, and Andrew Robinson. 1991. *The Shape of the World: The Mapping and Discovering of the Earth*. Chicago: Rand McNally.

Blake, C. Fred. 1994. Footbinding in Neo-Confucian China and the Appropriation of Female Labor. *Signs* 19(3): 677–712.

Blakney, R. B., trans. 1983. *The Way of Life: Lao Tzu*. New York: New American Library.

Blusse, Leonard. 1989. Chinese Commercial Networks and State Formation in Southeast Asia. Paper presented to the Conference on Southeast Asia from the Fifteenth to the Eighteenth Centuries, Lisbon, December. P. 3.

Bofman, Theodora Helene. 1984. *The Poetics of the Ramakian*. DeKalb: Northern Illinois University.

Brandauer, Frederick P. 1977. Women in the *ching-Hua Yuan*: Emancipation Toward a Confucian Ideal. *Journal of Asian Studies* 37(4): 647–60.

Braverman, Arthur, trans. 1994. *Warrior of Zen: The Diamond-Hard Wisdom Mind of Suzuki Shosan*. New York: Kodansha International.

Brown, Carolyn Henning. 1997. Contested Meanings: Tantra and the Poetics of Mithila Art. *American Ethnologist* 23(4): 717–37.

Brown, Delmer M., ed. 1993. *Ancient Japan*. Vol. 1 of *The Cambridge History of Japan*. Cambridge: Cambridge University Press.

Brown, MacAlister. 1986. *Apprentice Revolutionaries: The Communist Movement in Laos 1930–1985*. Stanford, CA: Hoover Institution Press.

Buhler, George, trans. 1886. Occupations of the Castes, *The Laws of Manu*. Oxford: Oxford University Press.

Burger, Julian. 1987. *Report from the Frontier: The State of the World's Indigenous Peoples*. London: Zed Books.

Carlitz, Katherine. 1994. Desire, Danger, and the Body: Stories of Women's Virtue in Late Ming China. In *Engendering China: Women, Culture, and the State*, ed. Christina K. Gilmartin, Gail Hershatter, Lisa Rofel, and Tyrene White. Pp. 101–24. Cambridge: Harvard University Press.

Castke, Timothy N. 1993. *At War in the Shadow of Vietnam. U.S. Military Aid to the Royal Lao Government, 1955–1975*. New York: Columbia University Press.

Chan Sucheng. 1994. *Life in Laos and America*. Philadelphia: Temple University Press.

Chan, Wing-tsit. 1987. Neo-Confucianism. In *The Encyclopedia of Religion*, Vol. 4, ed. Mircea Eliade. Pp. 24–35. New York: Macmillan.

Chandarsi, Nusit. 1976. *The Religion of the Hmong Njua*. Bangkok: The Siam Society.

Chandler, David. 1992. *A History of Cambodia*. Boulder: Westview Press.

Chang, Chung-li. 1955. *The Chinese Gentry: Studies on Their Role in Nineteenth-Century Chinese Society*. Seattle: University of Washington Press.

Chang, K. C. 1977. Chinese Archaeology Since 1949. *Journal of Asian Studies* 36(4): 623–46.

Chiang Yee. 1973. *Chinese Calligraphy: An Introduction to Its Aesthetic and Technique*. Cambridge: Harvard University Press.

Chou, Hung-hsiang. 1979. Chinese Oracle Bones. *Scientific American* 240(4): 135–49.

Chow, Kai-wing. 1994. *The Rise of Confucian Ritualism in Late Imperial China: Ethics, Classics, and Lineage Discourse.* Stanford: Stanford University Press.

Ch'u T'ung-tsu. 1972. *Han Social Structure*, ed. Jack L. Dull. Seattle: University of Washington Press.

Cohn, Bernard. 1983. "Representing Authority in Victorian India." In *The Invention of Tradition*, ed. E. Hobsbawm and T. Ranger. Cambridge: Cambridge University Press.

Conze, Edward. 1988. *A Short History of Buddhism.* London: George Allen and Unwin.

Cranston, Edwin A. 1993. Asuka and Nara Culture: Literacy, Literature, and Music. In *The Cambridge History of Japan*, Vol. 1, *Ancient Japan*, ed. Delmer M. Brown. Pp. 453–503. Cambridge: Cambridge University Press.

Crump, Thomas. 1991. *The Death of an Emperor: Japan at the Crossroads.* New York: Oxford University Press.

Cultural Survival. 1987. *Southeast Asian Tribal Groups and Ethnic Minorities.* Cambridge, MA: Cultural Survival, Inc.

Daiyun, Yue, and Carolyn Wakeman. 1983. Women in Recent Chinese Fiction—a Review Article. *Journal of Asian Studies* 52(4): 879–88.

Dawson, Raymond. 1981. *Confucius.* Oxford: Oxford University Press.

Day, Tony. 1996. Ties That (un)Bind: Families and States in Premodern Southeast Asia. *Journal of Asian Studies* 55(2): 384–409.

De Bary, Wm. Theodore. 1991. *The Trouble with Confucianism.* Cambridge: Harvard University Press.

———, ed. 1958. *Sources of Indian Tradition*, Vol. 1. New York: Columbia University Press.

Dersin, Denise, and Charles J. Hagner. 1993. *China's Buried Kingdoms.* Alexandria, VA: Time-Life.

Dhiravat na Pombejra. 1993. Ayutthaya at the End of the Seventeenth Century: Was There a Shift to Isolation? In *Southeast Asia in the Early Modern Era: Trade, Power, and Belief*, ed. Anthony Reid. Pp. 250–72. Cornell: Cornell University Press.

Diamond, Norma. 1995. Defining the Miao: Ming, Qing, and Contemporary Views. In *Cultural Encounters on China's Ethnic Frontiers*, ed. Stevan Harrell. Pp. 92–116. Seattle: University of Washington Press.

Dirks, Nicholas. 1989a. *The Hollow Crown: Ethnohistory of an Indian Kingdom.* Cambridge: Cambridge University Press.

———. 1989b. The Original Caste: Power, History and Hierarchy in South Asia. *Contributions to Indian Sociology* 23(1): 59–77.

Dirks, Nicholas B., Geoff Eley, and Sherry B. Ortner, eds. 1994. *Culture / Power / History: A Reader in Contemporary Social Theory.* Princeton: Princeton University Press.

Dull, Jack L. 1990. The Evolution of Government in China. In *Heritage of China: Contemporary Perspectives on Chinese Civilization*, ed. Paul S. Ropp. Pp. 55–85. Berkeley: University of California Press.

Ebersole, Gary L. 1989. *Ritual Poetry and the Politics of Death in Early Japan.* Princeton: Princeton University Press.

Ebrey, Patricia. 1978. *The Aristocratic Families of Early Imperial China: A Case Study of the Po-Ling Ts'Ui Family.* Cambridge: Cambridge University Press.

_____. 1990. Women, Marriage, and the Family in Chinese History. In *Heritage of China: Contemporary Perspectives on Chinese Civilization*, ed. Paul S. Ropp. Pp. 197–223. Berkeley: University of California Press.

_____. 1991a. The Chinese Family and the Spread of Confucian Values. In *The East Asian Region: Confucian Heritage and Its Modern Adaptation*, ed. Gilbert Rozman. Pp. 45–83. Princeton: Princeton University Press.

_____. 1991b. *Chu Hsi's Family Rituals: A Twelfth-Century Chinese Manual for the Performance of Cappings, Weddings, Funerals, and Ancestral Rites*. Princeton: Princeton University Press.

Egami Namio. 1967. *Kiba Minzoku Kokka*. Tokyo: Chuokoronsha.

Ember, Carol. 1983. The Relative Decline in Women's Contribution to Agriculture with Intensification. *American Anthropologist* 85:285–304.

Errington, Shelly. 1990. Recasting Sex, Gender, and Power: A Theoretical and Regional Overview. In *Power and Difference: Gender in Island Southeast Asia*, ed. Jane Monnig Atkinson and Shelly Errington. Pp. 1–58. Stanford: Stanford University Press.

Evans, Grant. 1990. *Lao Peasants Under Socialism*. New Haven: Yale University Press.

_____, ed. 1993. *Asia's Cultural Mosaic: An Anthropological Introduction*. New York: Prentice-Hall.

Fairbank, John King. 1992. *China, A New History*. Cambridge: Harvard University Press.

Fairservis, Walter A., Jr. 1975. *The Roots of Ancient India: The Archaeology of Early Indian Civilization*. Chicago: University of Chicago Press.

Faure, David, and Helen F. Siu. 1995. *Down to Earth: The Territorial Bond in South China*. Stanford: Stanford University Press.

Fay, Peter Ward. 1975. *The Opium War, 1840–1842*. Chapel Hill: University of North Carolina Press.

Feng, Gia-fu, and Jane English, trans. 1972. *Tao Te Ching*. New York: Vintage Books.

Francis, Peter, and Stephen Self. 1983. The Eruption of Krakatau. *Scientific American* 249(5): 172–87.

Freedman, Maurice. 1958. *Lineage Organization in Southeastern China*. London: Athlone Press.

Freeman, Michael, and Roger Warner. 1990. *Angkor: The Hidden Glories*. Boston: Houghton Mifflin.

Fruzzetti, Lina, Alfred Guzzetti, Ned Johnston, and Akos Ostor. 1994. *Seed and Earth*. Middletown, CT: Department of Anthropology, Wesleyan University.

Gamble, Sidney D. 1968. *Ting Hsien: A North China Rural Community*. Stanford: Stanford University Press.

Geddes, William R. 1976. *Migrants of the Mountains: The Cultural Ecology of the Blue Miah (Hmong Njua) of Thailand*. Oxford: Clarendon Press.

Geertz, Clifford. 1960. *The Religion of Java*. New York: The Free Press.

_____. 1968. *Islam Observed: Religious Development in Morocco and Indonesia*. Chicago: University of Chicago Press.

_____. 1971. *Agricultural Involution: The Process of Ecological Change in Indonesia*. Berkeley: University of California Press.

———. 1980. *Negara: The Theatre State in Nineteenth-Century Bali*. Princeton: Princeton University Press.

Gilday, Edmund T. 1993. Dancing with Spirit(s): Another View of the Other World in Japan. *History of Religions* 18:273–300.

Gilmartin, Christina K., Gail Hershatter, Lisa Rofel, and Tyrene White, eds. 1994. *Engendering China: Women, Culture, and the State*. Cambridge: Harvard University Press.

Gluck, Carol. 1978. The People in History: Recent Trends in Japanese Historiography. *Journal of Asian Studies* 38(1): 25–50.

———. 1985. *Japan's Modern Myths: Ideology in the Late Meiji Period*. Princeton: Princeton University Press.

Gombrich, Richard. 1984. Introduction: The Buddhist Way. In *The World of Buddhism: Buddhist Monks and Nuns in Society and Culture*, ed. Heinz Bechert and Richard Gombrich. Pp. 9–14. London: Thames and Hudson.

Greenblatt, Stephen. 1994. The Circulation of Social Energy. In *Culture / Power / History*, ed. Nicholas B. Dirks, Geoff Eley, and Sherry B. Ortner. Pp. 504–19. Princeton: Princeton University Press.

Greenough, Paul R. 1982. Comments from a South Asian Perspective: Food, Famine, and the Chinese State. *Journal of Asian Studies* 41(4): 789–97.

Hamilton-Merritt, Jane. 1993. *Tragic Mountains*. Bloomington: Indiana University Press.

Hannay, S. F. 1837. Abstract of the Journal of a Route Travelled by Captain S. F. Hannay in 1835–36. *Transactions of the Asiatic Society of Bengal* 6.

Harrell, Stevan. 1979. The Concept of Soul in Chinese Folk Religion. *Journal of Asian Studies* 38(3): 519–28.

———. 1993. Geography, Demography, and Family Composition in Three Southwestern Villages. In *Chinese Families in the Post-Mao Era*, ed. Deborah Davis and Stevan Harrell. Pp. 77–102. Berkeley: University of California Press.

———. 1995. Civilizing Projects and the Reaction to Them. In *Cultural Encounters on China's Ethnic Frontiers*, ed. Stevan Harrell. Pp. 83–88. Seattle: University of Washington Press.

Harrell, Stevan, and Deborah Davis. 1993. *Chinese Families in the Post-Mao Era*. Berkeley: University of California Press.

Hawley, John Stratton. 1994. *Sati: The Blessing and the Curse: The Burning of Wives in India*. New York: Oxford University Press.

Hepper, F. Nigel. 1982. *Kew Gardens for Science and Pleasure*. London: Her Majesty's Stationery Office.

Higham, Charles. 1984. Prehistoric Rice Cultivation in Southeast Asia. *Scientific American* 250(4): 138–46.

———. 1989. *The Archaeology of Mainland Southeast Asia*. Cambridge: Cambridge University Press.

Hitchcock, John T. 1959. The Idea of the Martial Rajput. In *Traditional India: Structure and Change*, ed. Milton Singer. Pp. 10–17. Philadelphia: American Folklore Society.

Hoffmann, Steven A. 1981. Faction Behavior and Cultural Codes: India and Japan. *Journal of Asian Studies* 40(2): 231–54.

Hopkirk, Peter. 1980. *Foreign Devils on the Silk Road: The Search for the Lost Cities and Treasures of Chinese Central Asia*. Oxford: Oxford University Press.

Horton, H. Mark. 1992. Japanese Spirit and Chinese Learning: Scribes and Storytellers in Pre-Modern Japan. In *The Ethnography of Reading*, ed. Jonathan Boyarin. Pp. 156–79. Berkeley: University of California Press.

Hsu Cho-yun. 1979. Early Chinese History: The State of the Field. *Journal of Asian Studies* 38(3): 453–75.

Hutterer, Karl L. 1982. Early Southeast Asia: Old Wine in New Skins? A Review Article. *Journal of Asian Studies* 41(3): 559–70.

Johnson, David. 1981. Epic and History in Early China: The Matter of Wu Tzu-Hsu. *Journal of Asian Studies* 40(2): 255–71.

Johnson, David G. 1977. *The Medieval Chinese Oligarchy*. Boulder: Westview Press.

Johnson, Graham E. 1993. Family Strategies and Economic Transformation in Rural China: Some Evidence from the Pearl River Delta. In *Chinese Families in the Post-Mao Era*, ed. Deborah Davis and Stevan Harrell. Pp. 103–38. Berkeley: University of California Press.

Keay, John. 1988. *India Discovered*. London: Collins.

Keightley, David N. 1982. Shang China Is Coming of Age—A Review Article. *Journal of Asian Studies* 41(3): 549–57.

———. 1990. Early Civilization in China: Reflections on How It Became Chinese. In *Heritage of China: Contemporary Perspectives on Chinese Civilization*, ed. Paul S. Ropp. Pp. 15–54. Berkeley: University of California Press.

Keyes, Charles F. 1977. *The Golden Peninsula: Culture and Adaptation in Mainland Southeast Asia*. New York: Macmillan.

———. 1983. Economic Action and Buddhist Morality in a Thai Village. *Journal of Asian Studies* 42(4): 851–68.

———. 1995. Who Are the Tai? Reflections on the Invention of Identities. In *Ethnic Identity: Creation, Conflict, and Accommodation*, ed. Lola Romanucci-Ross and George DeVos. Pp. 136–60. Walnut Creek, CA: Altamira Press.

King, Winston L. 1993. *Zen and the Way of the Sword: Arming the Samurai Psyche*. New York: Oxford University Press.

Kingsbury, Benedict. 1995. "Indigenous Peoples" as an International Legal Concept. In *Indigenous Peoples of Asia*, ed. R. H. Barnes, Andrew Gray and Benedict Kinsbury. Pp. 35–58. Ann Arbor, MI: Association for Asian Studies.

Kirsch, A. Thomas. 1996. Buddhism, Sex-Roles and the Thai Economy. In *Women in Southeast Asia*, ed. Penny Van Esterik. Pp. 13–32. DeKalb: Northern Illinois University.

Kopf, David. 1977. Review of A New History of India by Stanley Wolpert. *Journal of Asian Studies* 37(1): 569–70.

Lach, D. 1965. *Asia on the Eve of Europe's Expansion*. Englewood Cliffs, NJ: Prentice-Hall.

Langlois, John D., Jr. 1978. Yu Chi and His Mongol Sovereign: The Scholar as Apologist. *Journal of Asian Studies* 38(1): 99–116.

Lansing, J. Stephen. 1983. The "Indianization" of Bali. *Journal of Southeast Asian Studies* 14(2): 410–21.

———. 1991. *Priests and Programmers: Technologies of Power in the Engineered Landscape of Bali*. Princeton: Princeton University Press.

Lapidus, Ira M. 1988. *A History of Islamic Societies*. London: Cambridge University Press.

Lau, D. C., trans. 1963. *Lao Tzu: Tao Te Ching.* New York: Penguin.

Leach, Edmund R. 1964. *Political Systems of Highland Burma: A Study of Kachin Social Structure.* London: Athlone Press.

Lee, James. 1982. Food Supply and Population Growth in Southwest China, 1250–1850. *Journal of Asian Studies* 41(4): 711–46.

Lee, Thomas H., 1977. Life in the Schools of Sung China. *Journal of Asian Studies* 37(1): 45–60.

Legge, James, trans. 1885. The Li Chi. Vol. 27. In *The Sacred Books of the East.* P. 229. Oxford: Clarendon Press.

_____. 1886. *A Record of Buddhistic Kingdoms: Being an Account by the Chinese Monk Fa-Hien of His Travels in India and Ceylon (A.D. 399–414) in Search of the Buddhist Books of Discipline.* New York: Dover Publications.

Levine, Norman. 1977. The Myth of the Asiatic Restoration. *Journal of Asian Studies* 37(1): 73–85.

Levy, Howard S. 1967. *Chinese Footbinding: The History of a Curious Erotic Custom.* New York: Walton Rawls.

Lewis, Mark Edward. 1990. *Sanctioned Violence in Early China.* New York: State University of New York Press.

Leys, Simon, trans. 1997. *The Analects of Confucius.* New York: W. W. Norton.

Li, Lillian M. 1982. Introduction: Food, Famine, and the Chinese State. *Journal of Asian Studies* 41(4): 687–707.

Liu, Zhiwei. 1995. Lineage on the Sands. In *Down to Earth: The Territorial Bond in South China*, ed. David Faure and Helen F. Siu. Pp. 21–43. Stanford: Stanford University Press.

Luther, Norman Y., Griffith Feeny, and Weiman Zhang. 1990. One Child Family or Baby Boom? Evidence from China's 1987 One-Per-Hundred Survey. *Population Studies* 44:341–57.

Mabbett, Ian, and David Chandler. 1995. *The Khmers.* Cambridge, MA: Blackwell.

Madsen, Richard. 1984. *Morality and Power in a Chinese Village.* Berkeley: University of California Press.

Mair, Victor. 1983. *Tun-Huang Popular Narratives.* London: Cambridge University Press.

_____. 1988. *Painting and Performance: Chinese Picture Recitation and Its Indian Genesis.* Honolulu: University of Hawaii Press.

Maloney, Clarence. 1974. *Peoples of South Asia.* New York: Holt, Rinehart and Winston.

Malony, William K. 1987. Hindu Dharma. In *The Encyclopedia of Religion*, ed. Mircea Eliade. Pp. 329–32. New York: Macmillan.

Mann, Susan. 1994. Learned Women in the Eighteenth Century. In *Engendering China: Women, Culture, and the State*, ed. Christina K. Gilmartin, Gail Hershatter, Lisa Rofel, and Tyrene White. Pp. 27–46. Cambridge: Harvard University Press.

Mao Zedong. 1965. In Memory of Norman Bethune. In *Selected Works of Mao Tse-Tung.* 4 vols. P. 337. Beijing: Foreign Languages Press.

Marriott, McKim, and Ronald Inden. 1977. Towards an Ethnosociology of North Indian Caste Systems. In *The New Wind: Changing Identities in South Asia*, ed. Kenneth David. Pp. 227–38. The Hague: Mouton.

Matisoff, James. 1983. Linguistic Diversity and Language Contact. In *Highlanders of Thailand*, ed. John McKinnon and Wanat Bhruksasri. Pp. 56–86. Oxford: Oxford University Press.

———. 1991. Sino-Tibetan Linguistics. *Annual Reviews in Anthropology* 20:469–504.

McCoy, Alfred. 1972. *The Politics of Heroin in Southeast Asia*. Singapore: Harper and Row.

McRae, John R. 1995. Buddhism. *Journal of Asian Studies* 54(2): 354–70.

Metcalf, Richard, and Peter Huntington. 1991. *Celebrations of Death: The Anthropology of Mortuary Ritual*. 2d ed. Cambridge: Cambridge University Press.

Miller, Barbara Stoler, trans. 1986. *The Bhagavad-Gita: Krishna's Counsel in Time of War*. New York: Bantam.

Mirsky, Jeannette, ed. 1964. *The Great Chinese Travelers*. Chicago: University of Chicago Press.

Mitchell, Stephen, trans. 1988. *Tao Te Ching*. New York: HarperPerennial.

Molnar, Peter, and Paul Tapponnier. 1977. The Collision Between India and Eurasia. *Scientific American* 237:30–41.

Morris, Ivan, trans. and ed. 1991. *The Pillow Book of Sei Shonagon*. New York: Columbia University Press.

Murasaki Shikibu. 1985. *The Tale of Genji*, trans. Edward G. Seidensticker. New York: Random House.

Murray, Julia K. 1996. The Temple of Confucius and Pictorial Biographies of the Sage. *Journal of Asian Studies* 55(2): 269–300.

Nelson, John K. 1996. *A Year in the Life of a Shinto Shrine*. Seattle: University of Washington Press.

Nishiyama Matsunosuke. 1997. *Edo Culture: Daily Life and Diversions in Urban Japan, 1600–1868*. Honolulu: University of Honolulu Press.

Norman, Jerry. 1988. *Chinese*. Cambridge: Cambridge University Press.

O'Flaherty, Wendy Doniger. 1988. *Textual Sources for the Study of Hinduism*. Manchester: Manchester University Press.

Ohnuki-Tierney, Emiko. 1993. *Rice As Self: Japanese Identities Through Time*. Princeton: Princeton University Press.

Oldenburg, Veena. 1994. The Roop Kanwar Case: Feminist Responses. In *Sati: The Blessing and the Curse: The Burning of Wives in India*, ed. John Stratton Hawley. New York: Oxford University Press.

Ortner, Sherry B. 1996. The Virgin and the State. *Making Gender: The Politics and Erotics of Culture*. Pp. 43–58. Boston, Beacon Press.

Overmyer, Daniel L. 1994. World Linguistic Diversity. *Scientific American* 270(1): 116–23.

Owen, Stephen. 1997. Master and Man. *The New Republic*, May 5, 36–39.

Pollock, Sheldon. 1986. The Ramayana of Valmiki, an Epic of Ancient India. In Vol. 2 of *Ayodhyakanda*. Princeton: Princeton University Press.

———. 1993. Ramayana and Political Imagination in India. *Journal of Asian Studies* 52(2): 261–37.

Raheja, Gloria Goodwin. 1988. *The Poison in the Gift: Ritual, Presentation, and the Dominant Caste in a North Indian Village*. Chicago: University of Chicago Press.

Raheja, Gloria Goodwin, and Ann Gold. 1994. *Listen to the Heron's Words: Reimagining Gender in North India*. Berkeley: University of California Press.

Ramsey, S. Robert. 1987. *The Languages of China*. Princeton: Princeton University Press.

Rankin, Mary Backus. 1982. "Public Opinion" and Political Power: *qingyi* in Late Nineteenth Century China. *Journal of Asian Studies* 41(3): 453–84.

Renfrew, Colin. 1987. *Archaeology and Language: The Puzzle of Indo-European Origins*. Cambridge: Cambridge University Press.

_____. 1989. The Origins of Indo-European Languages. *Scientific American* 261(4): 106–14.

_____. 1994. World Linguistic Diversity. *Scientific American* 270(1): 116–23.

Reynolds, Frank. 1991. *Ramayana, Rama Jataka*, and *Ramakien*: A Comparative Study of Hindu and Buddhist Traditions. In *Many Ramayanas: The Diversity of a Narrative Tradition in South Asia*, ed. Paula Richman. Pp. 50–63. Berkeley: University of California Press.

Richman, Paula, ed. 1991. *Many Ramayanas: The Diversity of a Narrative Tradition in South Asia*. Berkeley: University of California Press.

Risso, Patricia. 1995. *Merchants and Faith: Muslim Commerce and Culture in the Indian Ocean*. Boulder: Westview Press.

Ropp, Paul S., ed. 1990. *Heritage of China: Contemporary Perspectives on Chinese Civilization*. Berkeley: University of California Press.

Ross, Nancy Wilson. 1960. *The World of Zen: An East-West Anthology*. New York: Random House.

Rozman, Gilbert. 1991. The East Asian Region in Comparative Perspective. In *The East Asian Region: Confucian Heritage and Its Modern Adaptation*. Pp. 3–44. Princeton: Princeton University Press.

Sahlins, Marshall. 1968. *Tribesmen*. Englewood Cliffs, NJ: Prentice-Hall.

Said, Edward W. 1978. *Orientalism*. New York: Vintage Books.

Sampson, Geoffrey. 1985. *Writing Systems*. London: Hutchinson.

Sansom, G. B. 1952. *Japan: A Short Cultural History*. Stanford: Stanford University Press.

Scalapino, Robert A. 1982. The Evolution of a Young Revolutionary: Mao Zedong in 1919–1921. *Journal of Asian Studies* 42(1): 29–59.

Schechner, Richard. 1993. *The Future of Ritual: Writings on Culture and Performance*. London: Routledge.

Schwartz, Benjamin. 1985. *The World of Thought in Ancient China*. Cambridge: Harvard University Press.

Seidensticker, Edward G. 1985. Introduction. In *The Tale of Genji*. New York: Random House.

Shenon, Philip. 1995. King Knows His Rights: He'll Speak His Mind. *New York Times*, 9 November, A4.

Shikibu, Murasaki. 1986. *The Tale of Genji*, trans. Edward G. Seidensticker. New York: Random House.

Shosan, Suzuki. 1994. *Warrior of Zen: The Diamond-Hard Wisdom Mind of Suzuki Shosan*, trans. Arthur Braverman. New York: Kodansha International.

Shulman, David. 1979. Divine Order and Divine Evil in the Tamil Tale of Rama. *Journal of Asian Studies* 38(4): 651–69.

Skilton, Andrew. 1994. *A Concise History of Buddhism*. Birmingham: Windhorse Publications.

Smith, Martin. 1995. A State of Strife: The Indigenous Peoples of Burma. In *Indigenous Peoples of Asia*, ed. R. H. Barnes, Andrew Gray, and Benedict Kinsbury. Pp. 221–45. Ann Arbor, MI: Association for Asian Studies.

Smith, Richard J. 1994. *China's Cultural Heritage: The Qing Dynasty, 1644–1912*. Boulder: Westview Press.

Somers, Robert M. 1978. The Society of Early Imperial China: Three Recent Studies. *Journal of Asian Studies* 38(1): 127–42.

Spence, Jonathan D. 1974. *Emperor of China: Self Portrait of K'Ang-Hsi*. London: Pimlico.

Stein, Aurel. 1912. *Ruins of Ancient Cathay*. London: Macmillan.

Stevenson-Moore, C. J. 1901. *Final Report on the Survey and Settlement Operations in the Muzaffarpur District, 1892–1899*. Calcutta: Bengal Secretariat.

Stoesz, Willis. 1992. The Universal Attitude of Shinto as Expressed in the Shinto Sect Kurozumikyo. *Journal of Ecumenical Studies* 29(2): 215–29.

Stover, Leon, and Takeko Kawai Stover. 1976. *China: An Anthropological Perspective*. Pacific Palisades, CA: Goodyear Publishing Company.

Strong, John S. 1983. *The Legend of King Ashoka*. Princeton: Princeton University Press.

Suzuki, D. T. 1959. *Zen and Japanese Culture*. Princeton: Princeton University Press.

Swaminathan, M. S. 1984. Rice. *Scientific American* 250(1): 80–93.

Swearer, Donald K. 1995. *The Buddhist World of Southeast Asia*. New York: State University of New York Press.

Takashi, Okazaki. 1993. Japan and the Continent. In *The Cambridge History of Japan*, Vol. 1, *Ancient Japan*, trans. Janet Goodwin. Cambridge: Cambridge University Press.

Tambiah, S. J. 1970. *Buddhism and the Spirit Cults in North-East Thailand*. Cambridge: Cambridge University Press.

———. 1976. *World Conqueror and World Renouncer: A Study of Buddhism and Polity in Thailand Against a Historical Background*. Cambridge: Cambridge University Press.

Tanabe, Willa J. 1988. *Paintings of the Lotus Sutra*. Weatherhill Press.

Tapp, Nicholas. 1989. *Sovereignty and Rebellion: The White Hmong of Northern Thailand*. Singapore: Oxford University Press.

Tarling, Nicholas, ed. 1992. *The Cambridge History of Southeast Asia*. Vol. 1. Cambridge: Cambridge University Press.

Taylor, Jay. 1987. *The Dragon and the Wild Goose: China and India*. Westport, CT: Greenwood Press.

Taylor, Rodney L., and Gary Arbucle. 1995. Confucianism. *Journal of Asian Studies* 54(2): 347–53.

Teiser, Stephen F. 1995. Popular Religion. *Journal of Asian Studies* 54(2): 378–96.

Totman, Conrad. 1979. English-Language Studies of Medieval Japan: An Assessment. *Journal of Asian Studies* 38(3): 541–51.

Turner, Victor. 1967. *Forest of Symbols: Aspects of Ndembu Ritual.* Ithaca: Cornell University Press.

Van Esterik, Penny. 1996. Laywomen in Theravada Buddhism. In *Women in Southeast Asia,* ed. Penny Van Esterik. Pp. 42–61. DeKalb: Northern Illinois University.

Van Schendel, Willen. 1995. The Invention of the "Jummas": State Formation and Ethnicity in Southeastern Bangladesh. In *Indigenous Peoples of Asia,* ed. R. H. Barnes, Andrew Gray, and Benedict Kingsbury. Pp. 121–44. Ann Arbor, MI: Association for Asian Studies.

Van Slyke, Lyman P. 1988. *Yangtze: Nature, History, and the River.* Menlo Park, CA: Addison-Wesley.

Varley, H. Paul. 1980. *A Chronicle of Gods and Sovereigns: Jinno Shotoki of Kitabatake Chikafusa.* New York: Columbia University Press.

_____. 1984. *Japanese Culture.* Honolulu: University of Hawaii Press.

_____. 1994. *Warriors of Japan as Portrayed in the War Tales.* Honolulu: University of Hawaii Press.

Verellen, Franciscus. 1995. Taoism. *Journal of Asian Studies* 54(2): 322–46.

Wallerstein, Immanuel. 1976. *The Modern World-System: Capitalist Agriculture and the Origins of the European World-Economy in the Sixteenth Century.* New York: Academic Press.

Watson, Burton. 1958. *Ssu-Ma Ch'ien, Grand Historian of China.* New York: Columbia University Press.

Watson, James L. 1984. Chinese Kinship: Anthropological Perspectives on Historical Research. *China Quarterly* 92.

Watson, Rubie S. 1986. The Named and the Nameless: Gender and Person in Chinese Society. *American Ethnologist* 13(4): 619–31.

Webster, Peter. 1981. Monsoons. *Scientific American* 250(4): 138–46.

Weidner, Marsha, Ellen Johnston Laing, Irving Yucheng Lo, Christina Chu, and James Robinson. 1988. *Views from Jade Terrace: Chinese Women Artists 1300–1912.* Indianapolis: Indianapolis Museum of Art.

Welch, Stuart Carey. 1978. *Imperial Mughal Painting.* New York: George Braziller.

Wills, John E., Jr. 1994. Empress Wu. In *Mountain of Fame: Portraits in Chinese History.* Pp. 127–48. Princeton: Princeton University Press.

Wolcott, Leonard T. 1978. Hanuman: The Power-Dispensing Monkey in North Indian Folk Religion. *Journal of Asian Studies* 37(4): 653–1.

Wolpert, Stanley. 1993. *A New History of India.* New York: Oxford University Press.

Wu Lien-teh. 1959. *Plague Fighter: The Autobiography of a Modern Chinese Physician.* Cambridge: Heffer Press.

Wu Rukang, and Lin Shenglong. 1983. Peking Man. *Scientific American* 248(6): 86–94.

Yamazaki, Masakazu. 1996. Asia, a Civilization in the Making. *Foreign Affairs,* July/August, 106–18.

Ye Xian'en. 1995. Notes on the Territorial Connections of the Dan. In *Down to Earth: The Territorial Bond in South China,* ed. David Faure and Helen F. Siu. Pp. 83–88. Palo Alto: Stanford University Press.

Yearley, Lee H. 1980. Hsun Tzu on the Mind: His Attempted Synthesis of Confucianism and Taoism. *Journal of Asian Studies* 39(3): 465–80.

Yee, Chiang. 1973. *Chinese Calligraphy: An Introduction to Its Aesthetic and Technique*. Cambridge: Harvard University Press.

Yue, Daiyun, and Carolyn Wakeman. 1983. Women in Recent Chinese Fiction—a Review Article. *Journal of Asian Studies* 42(4): 879–88.

Yuzan, Daidoji. 1941. *The Code of the Samurai*, trans. A. L. Sadler. Rutland, VT: Charles E. Tuttle Co.

Zasloff, Joseph J., and Leonard Unger. 1991. *Beyond the Revolution*. New York: St. Martin's Press.

Zurcher, Erik. 1984. Beyond the Jade Gate: Buddhism in China, Vietnam, and Korea. In *The World of Buddhism*, ed. Heinz Bechert and Richard Gombrich. Pp. 193–211. London: Thames and Hudson.

_____. 1987. Buddhism in China. In *The Encyclopedia of Religion*, Vol. 2, ed. Mircea Eliade. Pp. 414–21. New York: Macmillan.

Zurndorfer, Harriet T. 1984. Local Lineages and Local Development: A Case Study of the Fan Lineage, Hsiu-Ning *hsien*, Hui-Chou 800–1500. *T'Oung Pao* 70(1–3): 18-59.

INDEX